W9-AFK-178

FORMING AND
REFORMING IDENTITY

GENDERS 21

FORMING AND REFORMING IDENTITY

Edited by Carol Siegel
and Ann Kibbey

NEW YORK UNIVERSITY PRESS
NEW YORK AND LONDON

NEW YORK UNIVERSITY PRESS
New York and London

ISBN 0-8147-8006-7 (cloth) — ISBN 0-8147-8007-5 (pbk.)

New York University Press books are printed on acid-free paper,
and their binding materials are chosen for strength and durability.

Manufactured in the United States of America

10   9   8   7   6   5   4   3   2   1

ftw
AGC4059

Contents

PART ONE

Remolding Woman

ONE

Maidenform(ed): Images of American Women in the 1950s

Barbara J. Coleman

In New York, I was over saturated with the too "polished" look of American women. Super sophistication is the enemy lurking behind most American women.
— Christian Dior

A young woman floats through a surreal sketch of a grocery store filled with fancifully drawn canned goods, salad dressings, vegetables, and a shopping bag (Fig. 1.1). In a world of postwar abundance, it seems only natural that cheese, bread, eggs, and potatoes should fall freely like leaves from exotic trees. The model, whose bare feet hover above an invisible ground line, twirls imaginary link sausage, a shopping bag, and a purse. She wears a large flared skirt — an extravagant fashion statement made popular by Christian Dior in 1947 — and a wide striped cummerbund. Except for one rather striking element, this neatly coifed and tastefully bejeweled model appears ready to embark on a serious shopping extravaganza. As she arches her back forward, however, she exposes her bare midriff and reveals the Maidenform "Alloette" brassiere. The viewer is witnessing the reverie of a woman who mutters:

Asleep . . . but it all seemed so real. Leafing through lettuce, browsing through broccoli . . . all eyes gave my figure a big "aye." . . . And all because of my Maidenform brassiere. No figure can ever get out of line with Maidenform at the controls.[1]

"I dreamed I went shopping in my Maidenform bra," a slogan adapted in October 1949 by Maidenform, Inc., was the first of many such adver-

Fig. 1.1. I dreamed I went shopping . . . *Woman's Home Companion*, October 1949. Reprinted courtesy of Maidenform, Inc.

tisements destined to become the company's trademark throughout the 1950s and 1960s. The theme of shopping was a logical one for a culture infatuated with the abundance of material goods flooding consumer markets after World War II. However, the real shock of the ad was its daring presentation of a woman going grocery shopping with her chest, and Maidenform brassiere, displayed for public view.

Its suggestive format made Maidenform's advertising strategy one of the best-known campaigns of the 1950s. The provocative layout revealed the postwar American need to enhance and control the female body visually through elasticized undergarments. But the ads also disregarded or parodied women's unrealistic occupational aspirations. In a climate of strict gender roles and domesticity, women were encouraged to stay home and raise children. At first glance, Maidenform's ad suggested liberation from the confines of the house, but its condescending portrayal of a woman in a grocery store wearing only her brassiere implied the opposite.

Like a *Playboy* centerfold, the Maidenform model exposes her body to the observer's private gaze. *Playboy* began publishing in 1953, ushering in a new era of mass media attention to the scantily clad female. But Maidenform's "I Dream . . ." ad contained more than simple cheesecake. It implied the tantalizing world of popular psychology: a Freudian fantasy revealing secret dreams and suppressed sexual desires. But whose sexual fantasy is represented? Is it the woman who wakes from a dream to find herself half-clothed in a public place, or the viewer who sneaks a peek at her embarrassing predicament? From the point of view of Maidenform, the ad was quite successful. In Freudian terms, the purpose of a tendentious joke was to persuade a third party to side with the teller without too much reflection. Both male and female viewers find themselves complicit with Maidenform and laughing at a woman wearing only her underwear at the grocery store.[2] By making its model the brunt of a sexual joke and an object for a prurient gaze, Maidenform's ads denied women their autonomy as productive and professional beings within the public sphere.[3]

But the history of the Maidenform company began long before the advent of the "I Dream . . ." campaign. Ida Rosenthal, the founder of Maidenform, Inc., and treasurer of the company at the inception of the "I Dream . . ." ads, came to the United States in 1905 from Minsk. In 1906, at the age of nineteen, she opened her first dress shop in Hoboken. By 1922, she had met an Englishwoman named Enid Bissett and together they started a dress boutique on 57th Street in New York City. According to *Fortune* magazine, Rosenthal and her partner never liked the "flapper" style of 1920s women's fashion, the cummerbund look in which dresses tended to bind the breasts to the body. In Rosenthal's judgment, this silhouette was "unfeminine" and she "did not like the fit of her dresses on flat-chested women."[4] To counteract this style, Rosenthal and Bissett put small strips of tucked cloth into their dresses. To their amazement, these "mock brassieres" were more in demand than the dresses themselves. As a result of their success, the women entered into the undergarment business full time. They incorporated in 1923 and, by 1929, had actually placed the first small space advertising for bras in a national newspaper.[5]

Although Rosenthal and Bissett were pioneers in the undergarment industry, the modern brassiere had been invented in 1913 by Mary Phelps Jacob. Fashion historian Elizabeth Ewing asserts that Jacob was tired of uncomfortable corsets and their whalebone supports. Using handkerchiefs and ribbons, she constructed a short brassiere that was free of boning, leaving the midriff bare. The garment's main function was to provide a clear, natural separation of the breasts. It was not until the mid-twenties when curves returned to women's fashions, however, that the bra developed a reputation as a shaping mechanism. It was commonly used throughout the 1930s and 1940s, but it was not until the beginning of Dior's "New Look," which emphasized the bosom, that women started to see the bra as an essential element of fashion and style.[6] Although there were many other brassiere companies in the 1950s — including Munsingwear, Playtex, Peter Pan, Formfit, Warner's, and Exquisite Form — it was Maidenform that capitalized on the New Look with its "I Dream . . ." ads.

The Dream ads were really begun under the direction of Rosenthal's son-in-law, Dr. Joseph Coleman, an ear, nose, and throat specialist who gave up his medical career after World War II to become vice-president in charge of Maidenform's advertising and promotion. The William H. Weintraub Advertising Agency, formed in 1941 with the money Weintraub received for selling his interest in *Esquire* magazine, submitted the first Dream ad campaign to Coleman in 1948. Mary Fillius, a copywriter at Weintraub and actual creator of the "I Dream . . ." motif, wanted Maidenform to adapt strong trademark themes in its advertising. She urged the corporation to concentrate on moving its promotional copy forward from the back pages of women's magazines. Her splashy, albeit controversial, "I Dream . . ." advertisements would accomplish this feat.[7]

Mrs. Rosenthal was initially skeptical of the theme, but the ads were an instant hit when they ran. From 1949 to 1969, Maidenform released over 100 thematic Dream ads in which elaborately costumed women fantasized about adventures while wearing their Maidenform bras. Many times the ads also suggested, in the words of the Maidenform company, "tasteful" double entendres such as the "pistol-toting public enemy" who "dreams [she] was wanted in [her] Maidenform bra," or the dress designer who labels herself a "designing woman" (Fig. 1.2).[8]

Throughout the 1950s, the Dream themes were determined in Dream meetings held twice a year with the top officials. By 1961, those officials included Joseph Coleman, president; Beatrice Coleman, Mrs Rosenthal's daughter and vice-president in charge of design; and the advertising firm of Norman, Craig and Kummel, successors to the Weintraub agency.

According to *Advertising Age*, the Dream executives looked for ads that drew "attention . . . by putting a bra in an unusual, unexpected situation" to create a shock value.[9] In a decade often described as the age of consensus, it is not surprising that the planners arrived at these themes through mutual agreement, closely matching the product and the dream to what they hoped would be an appropriate target market. The company credited the "I Dream . . ." ads with making Maidenform one of the largest bra manufacturers in the United States. Gross sales increased from 14 million in 1949 to over 43 million by 1963. The company had modest beginnings in 1923, but, by 1963, it employed more than four thousand workers and controlled over 20 percent of the brassiere market.[10]

Three principles were considered vital to any given ad. These elements were determined by the subjective analysis of the Dream committee, and included shock value, good taste, and the opportunity to exhibit the product. In conjunction with the rules for each campaign, every model was also required to meet certain strict standards. She was to be "healthy, unmarried, twenty-six and more fulsome than a 34B cup," which was the average size of the Maidenform customer in 1961.[11] Throughout the 1950s, the company's elaborate advertising settings varied from the sur-real pencil sketches of the supermarket ad to more "realistic" photographs by mid-decade, when spreads grew larger as a result of the successful Norman, Craig, and Kummel campaign. The basic structure of the ad always remained constant, however: women exposed their torsos while dreaming of exotic adventures in their Maidenform bras.

The sexually titillating aspect of the ad was not its only appeal. The popularity of the Maidenform ad in the United States during the 1950s

Fig. 1.2. I dreamed I was wanted ... *Ladies' Home Journal*, 1960. Reprinted courtesy of Maidenform, Inc.

also reflected the country's obsession with large breasts. Film historian Marjorie Rosen refers to the 1950s as a time of "Mammary Madness," whereas fashion historian Doreen Caldwell suggests that the postwar period was "the age of the cultivation of the mammary gland."[12] Various theories have attempted to account for this obsession. Some argue that breasts were symbols of abundant nourishment after the Great Depression; others insist they were signs of female fecundity in a time of booming postwar reproduction. Popular culture critics Jane and Michael Stern see the inherent fixation as an outgrowth of a "fascination with so many things grown abnormally huge, from superwide CinemaScope movies and giant mutant monsters to bloated cadillacs."[13] Hollywood stars such as Jayne Mansfield, Marilyn Monroe, Diana Dors, and Mamie Van Doren attested to the culture's fascination with blonde, big-breasted women. Breasts and sex were openly touted in movies, advertisements, and novels. According to Caldwell, the brassiere and the breast became synonymous; thus it comes as no surprise that the bra was the most advertised underwear item of the decade.

And who could blame Maidenform for capitalizing on the spirit of the times? Thanks to a booming war economy, millions of women had entered the workplace during World War II. To the surprise and consternation of the servicemen, women on the homefront were making larger salaries than their husbands or boyfriends had ever made. Despite the fact that women had been encouraged to join the war effort and work in the munitions factories, many of the returning soldiers viewed women riveters and other assembly-line workers as alien invaders of sacred male institutions. As *Fortune* noted, the returning American soldier was "worried sick about postwar joblessness."[14] After what the G.I. viewed as his patriotic sacrifice, he felt justified in demanding his old job back. Although women expressed a desire to continue working after the war, massive government and popular culture propaganda urged women to return to the home. Considering this pervasive media attention, it is a small wonder that an advertisement that made women look vulnerable in a public space should catch the eye of the American public. After all, women in the 1950s belonged at home.[15]

But it was not only women's professional aspirations that were being controlled. Their bodies were also being controlled by constricting rubberized undergarments. Much of this interest in underwear is credited to Christian Dior's "New Look" in fashion, introduced in Paris on 2 February 1947. The New Look stressed curved shoulders, an hourglass silhouette, high rounded breasts, and tiny waists. Dior sculpted bosoms and corsetted curves in the Victorian tradition. He also favored the look of a fully flared skirt, a textile extravagance previously prohibited during the austere period of World War II. Dior states, "We came from an epoch of war and uniform, with women like soldiers with boxer's shoulders. I designed flower women, soft shoulders, full busts, waists as narrow as liana and skirts as cordlas."[16] Although this style was introduced in 1947, it dominated fashions well into the fifties. The broad shoulders, narrow waists, and slender hips of the prewar years were replaced by an hourglass shape and its accompanying "functional internal structure . . . of bra, girdle, falsies and hip padding."[17] In a society based on strict gender roles, women needed to look like women. They could not resemble Norman Rockwell's *Rosie the Riveter* (1943). Rockwell's *Rosie*, a successfully employed and independent woman of the war years, had the arms of a weight lifter and the grin of a woman secure in her autonomy. When a woman needed to be home raising children and cooking her husband's dinner, Rosie — as a strong, self-directed female — was everything the decade deplored. Even the oversized power tool on her lap implied that Rosie did not require a man for *anything*.

In the scramble to reshape the feminine form, women, in their large Dior skirts, began to resemble the nose cone of a rocket. The fashionably short poodle hair cut, coupled with a blooming skirt and a cinched waist, created a conical body shape. The female head became the apex of a large triangle with the skirt providing its vast base. According to *Vogue*, "The silhouette was the important thing, the proportions of the body beneath quite irrelevant so long as it could be squeezed, padded out and elastic-coated into an acceptable shape."[18] The breasts, as well as other parts of the body, became sculpted objects subject to the confines of elasticized rubber, wire stays, and clever stitching. In the fashion world, breasts became decorative, sexual, and symbolic — not functional. It seems to be no coincidence that during the 1950s, breast feeding of infants dropped from 60% before 1950 to only 38% by 1961. In the 1950s, breasts connoted sex appeal, not maternity.[19]

Women's breasts, like the rest of their bodies, were also molded into conical, nose-cone shapes. The "conical bust cups [had] pointed tips [which] seemed almost to penetrate the tight sweaters in vogue." Doreen Caldwell notes that sharp-edged "bosoms were in. While the French aimed for the soft, apple shape, Americans turned breasts into warheads."[20]

The cups came to aggressively sharp points. Many had spiral stitching that enhanced their belligerent size and shape. These conical cups paralleled the popular aesthetic of the acute angle, which, according to

Thomas Hine, suggested the high-speed design of the rocket during the 1950s. The acute angle implied the aggressive speed of a fighter plane built for battle or shattering the sound barrier. It embodied modernity and technical superiority. With the conical bra, breasts were actually sculpted to resemble the nose cone of a Douglas F-4D Skyray or perhaps the taillight of a 1955 Dodge.[21] This symbol of military power and penetration was worn prominently by women of the period. This was hardly the first time that women's bodies were associated with war power. As Elaine Tyler May notes, after World War II, sexy women were called bombshells, and bikinis were actually named for the explosive power of the atomic bomb dropped on the Bikini Islands.[22]

The Chansonette line designed by Ernest Silvani in 1949 was Maidenform's bestselling bra. Originally designed for the younger figure for wear under clinging fabrics and sweaters, Chansonette's conical shape and prominent concentric circles exhibited a tornado-like design that prophetically symbolized society's confusion about breasts in postwar America.[23]

The breast connoted danger, too. Film historian Peter Biskind jokes that the plethora of Hollywood's big-breasted floozies "appeared too dim to hurt a fly, unless you bumped into them in the dark and put an eye out."[24] Despite Biskind's dismissal of the blonde bombshell, breasts were serious business for men and women in the 1950s. They symbolized the potency of female sexuality, a problem for a society concerned for the state of masculinity. As historian Beth Bailey illustrates, many American men were afraid of losing their masculinity in the age of domesticity. Despite society's efforts to codify them, men and women's gender roles were in flux and the culture worried about the effects of these changes on the masculine psyche. Emasculating women were often sighted as the cause of men's demise. As *Esquire* stated in 1962, the "crisis of masculinity be damned, the problem is the crisis of femininity."[25] Unless restrained and kept in her proper sphere of influence, a woman was dangerous to a man's very soul.[26]

Given the emphasis on the aggressive contour of the brassiere, its design was seen as an engineering problem and an aesthetic battle. The brassiere ads of this period are filled with phrases like "uplift," "cantilevered comfort," and "suspension." Ida Rosenthal was quoted in *Fortune* magazine as saying her brassieres were a matter of design as well as of engineering. Even in popular fiction like Harold Robbins's *The Carpetbaggers*, for example, a fashion designer quits in despair when she must construct a brassiere for a new starlet. She screams in frustration that she is a designer, not a structural engineer. The director recognizes the mechanical design principles inherent in this ticklish predicament. Just as Howard Hughes prided himself on inventing Jane Russell's uplift bra for *The Outlaw* (1943), the director commissions a male engineer to calculate with calipers the depth and points of stress of the starlet's breasts. To everyone's relief, the engineer designs "a bra on the suspension principle in a little less than an hour."[27] Engineering technology and Cold War preoccupation with high-speed military aesthetics combined to sculpt the breast into a miracle of space-age rocketry and modern engineering know-how.

Despite wearing these prominent badges of modernity, women were marginalized from whatever power was associated with all of this speed and science. In *The Carpetbaggers*, it is a female dress designer who cannot construct a brassiere for the starlet. A male engineer is able to solve the problem. Although women reflected the dangerous aesthetic of the warhead, they seldom participated in its construction. Women's nose-cone brassieres suggested phallic power. As Laura Mulvey notes, women are often "requisitioned, to be recreated in the image of man."[28] They are formed in the shape of male power "still tied to [their] place as bearer of meaning not maker of meaning."[29] The wire-stayed brassiere was a constant reminder that women had no aesthetic power of their own. They were not naturally virile, only artificially uplifted to reflect male potency and to reaffirm masculine power.

Not coincidentally, the underwear industry was inextricably connected to the military establishment during World War II. Because the industry was already equipped to work with large quantities of fabric, many companies, including Maidenform, were conscripted to make war supplies such as camouflage nets and parachutes. In fact, from 1941 to 1945, Maidenform's Bayonne, New Jersey, plant was partially converted to make head nets, mosquito bars, mattress covers, and pigeon vests with little cup-shaped pieces of cloth designed to carry courier pigeons. Maidenform was also given priority during the war to make brassieres, because the government believed that women working in the war industry would experience less fatigue if they were "supported." As William Chafe reports, advertising executives concluded that women workers in the defense plants who wore uplift were less tired "during those hectic days of added responsibility."[30]

Spurred by increased research and development in the war years, Maidenform was well equipped to reenter the brassiere market in full force. And like other underwear companies, Maidenform capitalized on the synthetic materials now available for mass consumption. Nylon and elasticized rubber, for example, were being produced more efficiently as a result of the war effort. These form-fitting, resilient materials, combined with the laborsaving circular rib machine — a sewing machine that could create conical brassieres in a wide range of sizes and shapes — allowed for the more efficient production of massive amounts of body-sculpting underwear. Such goods could be manufactured cheaply, efficiently, and in mass quantity. The bra went totally democratic; almost any woman could now afford to mold herself to the New Look.[31]

Considering Maidenform's military connections, it is not surprising that the company's strongest markets during the 1950s included female members of the armed services and female dependents of military men. Many of the countless parodies of the brassiere ads also originated with the military. At Selfridge Air Force Base in Michigan, for example, "pilots cut out the cups [of the brassieres] and put them in the ear sections of their helmets to reduce noise," and an airplane mechanic, recalling the aesthetics of the conical rocket, called the leading edge of one type of plane a "Maidenform." A serviceman writing for the *Stars and Stripes* showed a "frontline soldier storming enemy breastworks in a 'fadin-form' bra." The Maidenform image even joined the ranks of Cold War propaganda when a Fidel Castro lookalike dreamed he ruled Cuba in his Maidenform bra.[32] Although the company did not create these parodies, it clearly benefited from millions of dollars of free publicity.

Maidenform ads did more than just reflect the popular military aesthetic and concern for technological advancements of the times. They also mirrored the decade's interest in popular psychology and Freudian symbolism. "Dreaming" played an important part in the 1950s. Whether it was a dream house, Dream Whip, dream kitchen, dream cake, or a "Dream Lover," the opulence and technology of the decade optimistically suggested that many of these dreams could come true. But dreams had a darker side, too. They suggested the uncontrollable subconscious world of hidden desires and unleashed libidos, things that were clearly exciting and yet unacceptable in an age of Cold War vigilance and anxiety.

At this time, the media abounded in images of dreaming, psychology, and Freudian phallic symbols. Bal de Tete, a French fragrance, which literally translated means "head dance," featured a Rorschach-like design over the phrase "psychologically speaking." Postwar America's fascination with French culture, coupled with titillating psychological references, suggested the fragrance's overwhelming influence in the realm of intimate romance. In a more provocative vein, Jockey underwear depicts a young boy about to hide a cap pistol in his briefs. Although she is out of focus and relegated to a secondary position next to her washing machine, his mother smiles proudly at her son's underwear and proclaims that Jockey shorts "never droop, never sag."

The public was well aware of the psychoanalyst's couch, the Rorschach ink blot test, and the Freudian phallic symbol. According to Sigmund Freud, any elongated objects — such as sticks, tree trunks, umbrellas, and sharp weapons — were considered symbols of the phallus. Freud stated that even "articles of dress [such as] a woman's hat [could] often be interpreted with certainty as the male genitalia."[33] Although many of these assertions have been refuted over the intervening decades, the postwar public enthusiastically followed popular interpretations of Freud's theories. As a result, the phallic symbolism in the Jockey underwear ad would probably not have gone unnoticed by a 1950s audience. Maidenform's depiction of the editor's aggressively pointed hat, skirt, and umbrella, or the outlaw's breasts, gun, and Stetson also carried obvious psychological references (Fig. 1.3). Once again, but this time in the subconscious world of Freudian analysis, women's clothing style and secondary sexual characteristics took on the aggressive suggestion of male penetration.

In 1955, Norman B. Norman, president of Norman, Craig and Kummel, commented openly on the "Freudian" appeal of the ad, fearing that the "sight of these active dreams might not be good for teenage girls . . . even 50 year olds might get ideas."[34] Dr. Coleman, an exuberant supporter of the "I Dream . . ." campaign, also expressed anxiety over the possibility that these unleashed fantasies might get out of control: "we don't let the girls dream in their girdles."[35] Presumably, girdles were a bit too close to the center of action to be in "good taste." After all, as the 1958 marketing manual *What Makes Women Buy* suggested, women were "easily excited to feeling, prone to fantasy and imagination and stimulated by pictures."[36] Whereas the appeal to women's fantasy might stimulate purchasing, it could also unleash dangerous subconscious desires. In a decade of early marriage and domestic frenzy, a woman who dreamed she

Fig. 1.3. I dreamed I was a lady editor . . . *New York Times*, 25 February 1951. Reprinted courtesy of Maidenform, Inc.

was an unmarried twenty-six-year-old with a successful career might have been too threatening for society to tolerate.[37]

At this time, underwear advertising and its accompanying editorial copy abounded with archetypal dream imagery of movement and suspension, even though the girdle and the bra were specifically designed to mold the body into rigid, preconceived shapes. In the Maidenform ads, for example, the 1949 model glides through grocery stores, her feet hovering over nonexistent ground lines. In other ads, women drift in hot air balloons, are propelled in roller coasters, and float over the crowds at the opera. Playtex and Permalift also stressed freedom of movement. Their models frolic effortlessly in the company's underwear. Permalift's "Magic Oval Crotch Panty," does not seem to hamper the acrobatic antics of its model and, best of all, the company assured its customers that the girdle would not "ride-up, ever." In a 1959 issue of the *New Yorker*, Vassarette, a division of Munsingwear, promised a form of emancipation unparalleled since the Nineteenth Amendment: "Proclaiming The Most Revolutionary New Freedom For American Women Since They Won The Right To Vote In The Dramatic Introduction Of A Complete STAY THERE Family Of Bras And Girdles."[38]

Advertising copy of this sort seems to suggest that corsetted women actually achieved freedom through confinement. In other words, the irony of the Cold War period, which film historian Brandon French refers to as "schizoid doublethink," permeated society right down to its underwear.[39] Although brassieres and girdles were clearly designed to "hold you in," the advertisers ironically suggested a liberty that defied the laws of gravity.

Many women who wore the longline bra and girdle had different recollections of this supposed "freedom." Novelist Marge Piercy recalls:

Longline brassieres underneath staved in the ribs, shoved the stomach up into the esophagus, raised the rigid breasts till their padded peaks brushed the chin: . . . Girdles: My mother bought me one when I turned twelve, saying to me now I was a woman. I weighed ninety-two pounds and cast no shadows standing side-ways. Rubber coffins. . . . Who could eat with pleasure in a girdle? I remember pain at restaurant tables, the squirming, the itching, the overt tweaking and plucking. Who could dance? Run or bend over or climb a ladder? Fuck? Scratch? No, in a girdle you stand and stand. You sit rigidly and nothing jiggles, nothing bounces.[40]

Despite the bra's constricting nature, the breast actually displayed its feminine power through this artificial structure. Underwear of the period accentuated the female form and emphasized women's sexual allure. But unrestrained sexual attraction could be a problem in the 1950s. Unaban-doned sex was a direct route to a Communist takeover. According to Elaine May's description of domestic containment, unleashed sexuality led to moral laxity, which led to a lack of vigilance, which inevitably led to Communist domination:

From the Senate to the FBI, from the anticommunists in Hollywood to Mickey Spillane, moral weakness was associated with sexual degeneracy, which allegedly led to Communism. To avoid dire consequences, men as well as women had to control their sexuality in marriage. . . . In the domestic version of containment, the sphere of influence was the home. Within its walls, potentially dangerous social forces of the new age might be tamed, where they could contribute to the secure and fulfilling life to which postwar women and men aspired.[41]

Control of sexuality, therefore, was essential to safeguarding freedom. In a time of Cold War anxiety, Doreen Caldwell notes, "America in the 1950s was an age of corsetry in which [the] miracle of scientifically constructed elastic and nylon removed the necessity of muscular control and control was good."[42] Whether it was nuclear power or libidinous sexuality, potentially dangerous forces had to be controlled lest the world fall to totalitarian domination.

Maidenform did its patriotic duty and promoted a "24 Hour A Day Control" campaign.

At 10 a.m., a woman tidies up in Chansonette. At noon, she lunches with the girls and then goes shopping in Concertina girdle and Day Dreams Bra. At 6 p.m., she enjoys cocktails in her most daring low-backed dress and Pre-lude bra. From 9 p.m. until midnight, she dances in an Underline full length strapless bra. Then in her Sweet Dreams ensemble — bra, panties and cap — she goes off blissfully to sleep.[43]

Like the public service television announcement that proclaimed, "Sleep well tonight, your National Guard is awake," Maidenform's "24 Hour A Day Control" protected American society from women's sexuality, even in the dead of night! Squeezed into a modern space-age aesthetic, women's breasts reflected this compelling need to stay ever vigilant.

Breasts and body shapes, however, were not the only things that had to be contained. As sociologist Wini Breines remembers in *Young, White and Miserable*, there was

a fixation on grooming, cleanliness, on controlling the body. . . . Hair had to be fair and light, short for males, contained and curly for women. Unruly hair, too much hair, hair in the wrong place was asking for trouble. . . . Controlling the body was about controlling sex. . . . Hair, too, had to stay in place.[44]

In the 1950s, control and vigilance were the watchwords.

Besides these contradictory images of physical freedom and control, Maidenform ads also implied that women had a freedom to make stimulating occupational choices. In 1951, for example, Maidenform's model could be an editor or an artist. Despite the "stay-at-home mom" image so popular on television shows like *Leave It to Beaver*, more women than ever before were working outside of the home. According to William Chafe, by 1952, "10.4 million wives held jobs — 2 million more than at the peak of World War II."[45]

At first glance, Maidenform's ads appear to respond to this influx of women in the work force. But, after a closer look, they are curious in their depictions of the career women. In the editor's office, for example, telephones dangle from their hooks as the model frantically tries to keep ahead of her incoming calls. Although she wears aggressively sharp clothing and has facial features to match, her office is a disaster area. Is it lunch time or five minutes to midnight? The clock ominously reminds the viewer of the pressurecooker world of big city newspaper deadlines. Planning is obviously not her strong suit either: She has six uncontrolled telephones, two umbrellas, one extra shoe, and no blouse. The woman in the ad appears agitated and incompetent, and her job as editor hardly reflected the occupational reality of the typical female worker of the time. Although movies frequently portrayed women as high-powered editors, most of the jobs held by females throughout the decade were low-paying clerical and manufacturing positions. Whereas more women than ever before were working outside of the home, the proportion of women entering the professions had declined steadily since the 1930s.[46] Because of blatant sexual discrimination, most women simply could not realistically entertain the "dream" of becoming an editor, artist, conductor, or firefighter. In fact, despite Maidenform's protestations that their ads "fed women's hunger for excitement, for personal achievement and for independent power," these images simply did not depict women as competent members of a managerial team.[47] The editor's copy states that it is "nice work . . . if you can get it," which was blunt but mercifully more truthful.

In 1951, Maidenform's model holds a palette and brush and proclaims herself a painter (Fig. 1.4). On closer scrutiny, however, the viewer notes that she is behind a transparent canvas; she is not an active artist but the object of the canvas itself. The ad says she "dabbles in dreams." By comparison, it seems unlikely that art critic Harold Rosenberg would have described Jackson Pollock as "dabbling" in the Jungian collective unconscious; art, after all, was a serious business for Abstract Expressionists. But in Maidenform's 1951 ad, art critics are clearly more interested in the artist's hourglass shape than in what she might actually create. And

Fig. 1.4. I dreamed I was an artist . . . *New York Times*, 9 September
1951. Reprinted courtesy of Maidenform, Inc.

I dreamed I was a Work of Art in my *maidenform bra*

Fig. 1.5. I dreamed I was a work of art ... *Vogue*, 1 September 1956.
Reprinted courtesy of Maidenform, Inc.

by 1956, although the sketchy backdrop has been replaced by Rococo props, the model freely admits what the observer probably knew back in 1951: she was never really an artist at all, but merely an elaborate, objectified work of art (Fig. 1.5). There are no specific references to any historical figures, but the model's hair, elaborate costume, and haughty glance have a decidedly "let them eat cake" appearance. Lest the viewer forget, Marie Antoinette had extravagant fantasies too. There are consequences for dreams that get out of hand.

Art was not to be in her future, so the Maidenform model tried another activity: she went back to school (Fig. 1.6). Her books include a prominent copy of *Vogue* magazine. Sitting atop a desk and flashing her torso, her best subjects will be fashion and romance. At age twenty-six,

Fig. 1.6. I dreamed I went back to school . . . *Harper's Bazaar*, August 1955. Reprinted courtesy of Maidenform, Inc.

her notebook — where $2 + 2 = 5$ — clearly reveals that mathematics will not be in her future either.

By 1960, devoid of all setting, she is once again an object. But this time she is a fugitive on the post office wall. Although her breasts thrust forward with aggressive power, she is made doubly impotent as an image within an image: thankfully, twice removed from the viewer's real-life experience.

For women of the period, Maidenform rather cruelly represented the dream world of employment opportunity. Firefighters, cowboys, railroad engineers, boxers, police officers: these were all romantic male occupations in the 1950s. Except for dress designing, most women were not accepted into Maidenform's world of newspaper editing, art, detective work, or bull fighting.

Whether hanging precariously from a hot air balloon, riding a roller coaster, standing in front of a speeding train, or swinging from a crane atop the city, Maidenform's models scream with delight despite their dare-devil antics. Move one frame forward, however, and they would all be doomed to bloody deaths. As her cart flies from the tracks, the amusement park model cackles with laughter, seemingly unaware of her obvious fate (Fig. 1.7). Unfortunately, it also looks grim for the hot air balloonist (Fig. 1.8); she does not seem to understand that sitting on the edge of the basket could pitch her to a grisly death. She has another half second to grasp the laws of physics or, she too, will experience the early demise typical of the Maidenform "I Dream . . ." woman. Independence is exhilarating but, as Thelma and Louise discovered while flying off the lip of the Grand Canyon, a woman pays a high price in the world of male privilege (*Thelma and Louise*, 1991).

Elaborately photographed or simply sketched, Maidenform's "I Dream . . ." ads reflected America's postwar interest in rocket technology, speed, and domestic containment as well as sex, psychology, and French fashion. They mirrored the need to confine and reshape power within the parameters of a controlled aesthetic. By making women the object of a joke, the audience tacitly agreed with the advertisers; women looked ridiculous in public spaces. Shaped to imitate the male phallus, the ads also reminded the public that women were not naturally powerful but artificially constructed to reflect male potency. It is no coincidence that women in the late sixties chose to discard their bras in symbolic protest. The brassiere was a symbol of sexual containment and an uncomfortable daily reminder

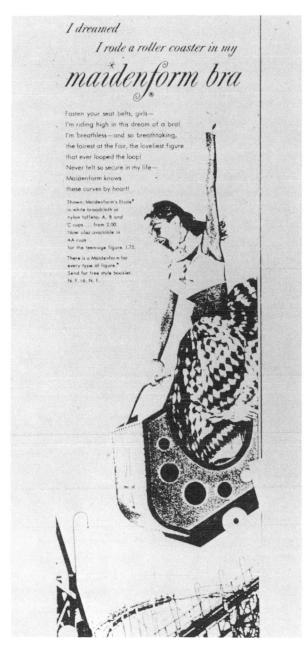

Fig. 1.7. I dreamed I rode a roller coaster ... *New York Times*, 13 September 1953. Reprinted courtesy of Maidenform, Inc.

Fig. 1.8. I dreamed I went up in a balloon ... *Life*, 20 June 1955. Reprinted courtesy of Maidenform, Inc.

of constricted gender roles. Raised and educated in an entrepreneurial culture, women no longer wanted to "dream" of being a railroad engineer. They wanted to be one.

NOTES

I am deeply grateful to Erika Doss, Karal Ann Marling, and Tamara Stoner for their encouragement and support.

1. The fashionable French skirt, a reference to the song "Alloette," and the Picasso-esque sketch of the grocery store also suggest a link between the risque world of dreams and French culture. American advertisers and consumers were fascinated with the Parisian mystique in the 1950s. Such notable new arrivals as Christian Dior, Hubert de Givenchy, Pierre Cardin, and Yves Saint Laurent greatly influenced American fashion during this period.
2. For a complete discussion of the tendentious joke in psychoanalysis, see Sigmund Freud, *Jokes and Their Relations to the Unconscious*, trans. and ed. James Strachey (New York: W. W. Norton and Company, Inc., 1960).
3. Women were, however, "productive" in other ways. The postwar baby boom was in full swing. By 1960, the percentage of people nineteen and under constituted almost 40 percent of the total American population. U.S. Department of Commerce: Bureau of the Census, *Statistical Abstract of the United States, 1961* (Washington, D.C.: Government Printing Office, 1961), 6, 7, and 28.
4. "Maidenform's Mrs. R.," *Fortune* (July 1950): 75. When tube-like profiles were in fashion, Rosenthal, who was herself quite full-figured, was perhaps more sympathetic to the hourglass shape.
5. "Papers Can Dream of Maidenform Ads," *Editor and Publisher* (18 August 1962): 17.
6. Elizabeth Ewing, *Dress and Undress: A History of Women's Underwear* (New York: Drama Book Specialists, 1978), 115–32.
7. "Kummel Leaves Norman, Craig, Joins Interpublic," *Advertising Age* (14 September 1964): 8; "Maidenform Dreams Big . . . ," *Sales Management* (5 April 1963): 38; "Papers Can Dream of Maidenform Ads," 17; and Susan Bain, Publicity and Public Relations Coordinator of Maidenform, Inc., letter to the author, 26 May 1992.
8. "Maidenform Dreams Big . . . ," 118.
9. "Maidenform Dreams Up New Product–Swimsuit; Augments Media Line-Up," *Advertising Age* (20 March 1961): 108.
10. "Maidenform Dreams Big . . . ," 36.
11. "Maidenform Dreams Big . . . ," 118; and "Maidenform Dreams Up New Product," 108. During the decade of the 1950s, the mean age for a woman's first marriage consistently remained at approximately twenty years of age.

12. Marjorie Rosen, *The Popcorn Venus* (New York: Avon Publishing, 1973), 282–99; and Doreen Caldwell, *And All Was Revealed: Ladies' Underwear 1907–1980* (New York: St. Martin's Press, 1981), 88.

13. Jane Stern and Michael Stern, *The Encyclopedia of Bad Taste* (New York: Harpers, 1990), 57.

14. *Fortune* quote from Elaine Tyler May, *Homeward Bound: American Families in the Cold War* (New York: Basic Books, 1988), 77.

15. For more information on domesticity in the 1950s, see ibid. For more statistics on women in the workplace, see William Chafe, *The American Woman: Her Changing Social, Economic and Political Roles, 1920–1970* (New York: Oxford University Press, 1972).

16. Diana de Marly, *Christian Dior* (London: B. T. Batsford Ltd., 1990), 19.

17. Christina Probert, *Lingerie in Vogue since 1910* (New York: Abbeville Press, 1981), 54.

18. Ibid., 55.

19. U.S. Department of Health, Education, and Welfare, *Trends in Breast Feeding among American Mothers* (Washington, D.C.: Government Printing Office, 1979). For a fictional discussion of breast feeding in the 1950s, see Mary McCarthy, *The Group* (New York: Harcourt, Brace and World, Inc., 1954).

20. Caldwell, *And All Was Revealed*, 83.

21. Thomas Hine, *Populuxe* (New York: Alfred A. Knopf, 1986), 88; and May, *Homeward Bound*, 110–11.

22. May, *Homeward Bound*, 110–11.

23. "Maidenform's Mrs. R.," 76.

24. Peter Biskind, *Seeing Is Believing: How Hollywood Taught Us to Stop Worrying and Love the Fifties* (New York: Pantheon Books, 1983), 272.

25. George Frazier, "The Entrenchment of the American Witch," *Esquire* (February 1962): 100.

26. Beth Bailey, *From Front Porch to Back Seat: Courtship in Twentieth Century America* (Baltimore: Johns Hopkins University Press, 1988), 104–8. For more information on the crisis of masculinity and the *Playboy* mystique, see Barbara Ehrenreich, *The Hearts of Men: American Dreams and the Flight from Commitment* (Garden City, N.J.: Anchor Books, 1983).

27. Ewing, *Dress and Undress*, 162; Harold Robbins, *The Carpetbaggers* (New York: Pocket Books, 1961); and "Maidenform's Mrs. R.," 75.

28. Laura Mulvey, "You Don't Know What Is Happening, Do You, Mr. Jones?," in *Framing Feminism: Art and the Woman's Movement, 1970–85*, ed. Rozsika Parker and Griselda Pollock (London: Pandora, 1987), 128.

29. Laura Mulvey, "Visual Pleasure and Narrative Cinema," *Screen* 16 (autumn 1975): 7.

30. William Chafe, *The Unfinished Journey: America since World War II* (New York: Oxford University Press, 1988), 10; "Maidenform's Mrs. R.," 76.

31. "Circular-Rib Machines Versatile for Women's Underwear," *Textile World* (August 1948): 118. Before the advent of the circular rib machine, Rosenthal

reported in *Fortune* that each brassiere consisted of twenty separate pieces, some no bigger than the size of a quarter. Seventy-five percent of labor time was spent folding, tucking, and manipulating cloth; 25 percent was spent sewing. After the circular rib machine, the ratios were reversed allowing for increased production.

32. "Maidenform Dreams Big . . . ," 39.
33. Sigmund Freud, *The Interpretation of Dreams*, trans. A. A. Brill (New York: Modern Library, 1950), 242, 247.
34. "Maidenform Dreams Big . . . ," 38. By 1964, Norman, Craig and Kummel (N, C & K) was the 23rd largest advertising agency in the United States. From its inception in 1955, N, C & K went from an annual income of 17,500,000 to over 77,550,000 by 1964.
35. "Maidenform Dreams Big . . . ," 117.
36. Janet L. Wolff, *What Makes Women Buy? A Guide to Understanding and Influencing the New Woman Today* (New York: McGraw-Hill, Inc., 1958), 253.
37. See May, *Homeward Bound*, for statistics on marriage age and rate.
38. *New Yorker* (20 February 1959): 3.
39. Brandon French, *On The Verge of Revolt: Women in American Films of the Fifties* (New York: Frederick Unger Publishing, 1978), 18.
40. Marge Piercy. *Parti-Colored Blocks for a Quilt* (Ann Arbor: University of Michigan Press, 1982), 121.
41. May, *Homeward Bound*, 99.
42. Caldwell, *And All Was Revealed*, 66.
43. "Maidenform Dreams Big . . . ," 124.
44. Wini Breines, *Young, White and Miserable: Growing Up Female in the Fifties* (Boston: Beacon Press, 1992), 149.
45. May, *Homeward Bound*, 167, and Chafe, *American Woman*, 182.
46. Chafe, *American Woman*, 183.
47. Bain, letter of 26 May 1992.

REFERENCES

Bailey, Beth. *From Front Porch to Back Seat: Courtship in Twentieth Century America.* Baltimore: Johns Hopkins University Press, 1988.
Bain, Susan. Publicity and Public Relations Coordinator for Maidenform, Inc. Telephone interview by author and letter of 26 May 1992.
Biskind, Peter. *Seeing Is Believing: How Hollywood Taught Us to Stop Worrying and Love the Fifties.* New York: Pantheon Books, 1983.
Breines, Wini. *Young, White and Miserable: Growing Up Female in the Fifties.* Boston: Beacon Press, 1992.
Caldwell, Doreen. *And All Was Revealed, Ladies' Underwear, 1907–1980.* New York: St. Martin's Press, 1981.
Chafe, William. *The American Woman: Her Changing Social, Economic and Political Roles, 1920–1970.* New York: Oxford University Press, 1972.

————. *The Unfinished Journey: America since World War II*. New York: Oxford University Press, 1991.

"Circular-Rib Machines Versatile for Women's Underwear." *Textile World* (August 1948): 118–19.

De Marly, Diana. *Christian Dior*. London: B. T. Batsford Ltd., 1990.

Ehrenreich, Barbara. *The Hearts of Men: American Dreams and the Flight from Commitment*. Garden City, N.J.: Anchor Books, 1983.

Ewing, Elizabeth. *Dress and Undress: A History of Women's Underwear*. New York: Drama Book Specialists, 1978.

Frazier, George. "The Entrenchment of the American Witch." *Esquire* (February 1962): 100–103, 138.

French, Brandon. *On the Verge of Revolt: Women in American Film of the Fifties*. New York: Frederick Unger Publishing Co., 1978.

Freud, Sigmund. *The Interpretation of Dreams*. Translated by A. A. Brill. New York: Modern Library, 1950.

————. *Jokes and Their Relation to the Unconscious*. Translated and Edited by James Strachey. New York: W. W. Norton and Company, Inc., 1960.

Hine, Thomas. *Populuxe*. New York: Alfred A. Knopf, 1986.

"Kummel Leaves Norman, Craig, Joins Interpublic." *Advertising Age* (14 September 1964): 1.

"Maidenform Dreams Big. . . ." *Sales Management* (5 April 1963): 35–39.

"Maidenform Dreams Up New Product–Swimsuit: Augments Media Line-Up." *Advertising Age* (20 March 1961): 3.

"Maidenform Drops Dream Motif in Russian Ad Effort." *Advertising Age* (25 March 1963): 3.

"Maidenform's Mrs. R." *Fortune* (July 1950): 75–76, 130, 132.

May, Elaine Tyler. *Homeward Bound: American Families in the Cold War*. New York: Basic Books, 1988.

McCarthy, Mary. *The Group*. New York: Harcourt, Brace and World, Inc., 1954.

Mulvey, Laura. "Visual Pleasure and the Narrative Cinema." *Screen* 16 (autumn 1975): 6–18.

————. "You Don't Know What Is Happening, Do You Mr. Jones?" In *Feminism: Art and the Woman's Movement, 1978–85*, ed. Rozsika Parker and Griselda Pollock. London: Pandora, 1987.

"Papers Can Dream of Maidenform Ads." *Editor and Publisher* (18 August 1962): 17.

Piercy, Marge. *Parti-Colored Blocks for a Quilt*. Ann Arbor: University of Michigan Press, 1983.

Probert, Christina. *Lingerie in Vogue since 1910*. New York: Abbeville Press, 1981.

Robbins, Harold. *The Carpetbaggers*. New York: Pocket Books, 1961.

Rosen, Marjorie. *Popcorn Venus*. New York: Avon Publishing, 1973.

Stern, Jane, and Stern, Michael. *The Encyclopedia of Bad Taste*. New York: Harpers, 1990.

U.S. Department of Commerce: Bureau of the Census. *Statistical Abstract of the United States, 1961*. Washington D.C.: Government Printing Office, 1961.

U.S. Department of Health, Education, and Welfare. *Trends in Breast Feeding among American Mothers.* Washington, D.C.: Government Printing Office, 1979.

Wolff, Janet L. *What Makes Women Buy? A Guide to Understanding and Influencing the New Woman Today.* New York: McGraw-Hill, 1958.

Nationalism and Respectable Sexuality in India

Mrinalini Sinha

In December 1987, two Indian policewomen, Lila Namdeo and Urmila Srivastava, were married in a Hindu temple in a small town in Madhya Pradesh. When news of the marriage became public, the two female police constables were promptly dismissed from service without a show-cause notice. They were also subjected to a humiliating medical examination, on the basis of which the state's Director-General of Police claimed that no medical evidence of "lesbian tendencies" was found in the two women.[1] The authors of *Less than Gay: A Citizen's Report on the Status of Homosexuality in India* point out that whereas the mixture of hostility and denial in the bureaucratic response to this lesbian marriage was not in itself surprising, what was amazing was the stunning silence of social and political activists in India as regards the violation of the two women's human rights. Although the popular press — in keeping with its recent "discovery" of the existence of a supposedly new homosexual subculture in India — offered sensationalized accounts of this public lesbian marriage, there was little in the way of a public critique of the discourse of "respectable" Indian sexuality that followed.

Indeed, political activists in India, including various women's rights groups, have been slow in mobilizing around issues of sexuality.[2] Notions of what constitutes "respectable" Indian sexuality thus remain hegemonic: challenges to it continue to be viewed as an embarrassing "new phenomenon," associated primarily with an elite and Westernized class and therefore of little relevance in a poor country like India. Neither of these women, however, was either elite or (in terms of this hegemonic discourse) "Westernized."

The contemporary implications of a discourse on same-sex relations — whether or not self-consciously gay — for the politics of Indian nationalism today remain beyond the scope of this chapter. Nevertheless, the history of representations of sexual relations and sexual identities in the formation of new nationalist subjectivities and the modern community of the Indian nation in colonial India provides a useful starting point for politically enabling critiques of a nationalist sexual politics.[3]

The history of colonial debates on the restructuring of (hetero)sexual family norms in India provides a context for locating the politics of nationalisms and sexualities in terms of the historically particular forms that became available for the reconstitution of political, economic, and ideological relations of domination in a world system fashioned by imperialism. Under the conditions of colonialism and anti-colonial nationalism in India, the politics of nationalism and "respectable" sexuality served to retain older social hierarchies in a new guise. By grounding the politics of nationalisms and sexualities in the context of the reconstitution of various relations of power, whether in imperial or in imperialized social formations, it becomes possible not only to demonstrate the parochial or "provincial"[4] nature of a Western politics of sexuality, but also to bring the politics of sexuality in imperial and imperialized social formations within the same field of debate. Indeed, any project that aims at acknowledging the relevance of a critique of sexual politics for emancipatory political projects in India cannot afford to ignore how the intersection of nationalisms and sexualities has historically served to reconstitute and realign earlier social hierarchies with new social arrangements.

The "globalizing"[5] context of the imperial social formation complicates the current debates in historiography and literary theory on the role of the discourses of nationalisms and sexualities in constituting new social arrangements. The most systematic examination of the historical dynamics between national and sexual identities is found in *Nationalisms and Sexualities*.[6] Of all the authors associated with this project, Doris Sommers has most explicitly sought to bring Benedict Anderson's *Imagined Communities: The Rise and Spread of Nationalism* and Michel Foucault's *History of Sexuality* in dialogue with one another.[7] Sommers seeks to extend Foucault, who connects the rise of a new discourse of sex in the late eighteenth century to the self-definition of the European bourgeoisie, by further linking the emergence of this discourse to the contemporaneous rise of nation-states. Sommers reminds us that this new discourse of sex was not only engaged in the production of "abnormal" sexualities but also in the obsessive elaboration of "normal" sexuality, embodied in the norms of bourgeois respectability and reproductive sexuality. The new discourse of sex, she argues, was crucial in serving as the model for the popular representation of the nation as a modern community. Yet if the historical interplay between nationalisms and sexualities enabled the emergence of new social arrangements, then it also made possible the reconstitution of earlier social arrangements. For whereas — according to Foucault's analysis of Western culture — the "deployment of sexuality" gradually replaced the "deployment of alliance" or kinship ties as an "especially dense transfer point for the relations of power" during the nineteenth century, in India the constitution of new nationalist subjectivities and new relations of power did not, under the conditions of territorial imperialism, require the same change: that is, the displacement of the negative repression associated with the "deployment of alliance" that maintained and reproduced preexisting hierarchies of power with the productive nature of regulations associated with the "deployment of sexuality."[8]

At the same time, a globalized history of the imperial social formation also complicates evolutionary models of the politics of nationalisms and sexualities in the capitalist "first world" and the formerly colonized "third world." It is such an evolutionary model that ultimately limits Frederic Jameson's otherwise perceptive insight about the different investment in the "private/libidinal" and the "public/national" in first- and third-world cultural productions in his now infamous essay on third-world literature.[9] Jameson's argument purports that whereas in the literary texts of the West even political or public commitments get expressed mainly in private or psychological terms, in the third world psychological, or specifically libidinal investments, appear primarily in political and social terms. Hence he claims that "all third world literatures — even those that are seemingly private and invested with a properly libidinal dynamic — necessarily project a political dimension in the form of national allegory."

Jameson's critics have rightly challenged his model of world literature, in which even contemporary third-world texts continue to reflect some preindustrial unity of the public and the private spheres.[10] What is needed, as Madhava Prasad suggests, is precisely an analysis that situates the hypervisibility of the nationalist framework in the third world and, by comparison, its relative invisibility in the West in the context of the global history of the "uneven and combined development of capitalism."[11] For if elite national culture in India has a different investment in the domains of the public/national and private/libidinal, it is not because, as Jameson seems to suggest, the dominant classes in India did not fully experience the public-private split that characterizes capitalist modernization. Rather, this difference results precisely from the nature of the spread of capitalist modernization and the consolidation of an indigenous national-ist elite in India under conditions of territorial imperialism.

Although scholars of colonial India have been scrupulously attentive to the contradictions of capitalist modernization introduced via colonial rule in India, their emphasis on the uniquely colonial contradictions has tended to obscure the larger picture: the contradiction involved in the realignment of earlier social hierarchies with new relations of power that has historically accompanied the modernization project itself.[12] These contradictions are manifested in different forms in imperial and imperi-alized social formations.

The contradictions of colonialism in the reconstitution of social ar-rangements in India, however, provide a useful starting point for recon-textualizing the politics of nationalisms and sexualities. Partha Chatterjee, who more than any other contemporary theorist of nationalism has brought European nationalisms and the "official" nationalisms in the colonies of Europe within the same field of debate, offers an insightful critique of Anderson's Eurocentric model of nationalism by demonstra-ting that imperialism made different domains available for the elaboration of national culture in European and Indian nationalisms. While in the West the rise of a bourgeois public sphere provided the site in which the homogenized forms of national culture were forged through the medium of "print capitalism," in India the public institutions of colonial civil society, which denied the rights of citizens to all colonial subjects, could not become the primary arena for the elaboration of an elite national culture.[13] Official Indian nationalism, therefore, was confronted with a contradiction. On the one hand, there was the desire for modernizing indigenous society to keep pace with the West, and, on the other, there was the need to avow a unique and distinctive cultural identity for the nation on the basis of which the political claim to nationhood could be made. Official Indian nationalism consequently elaborated the spiritual and material domains of culture as distinctive and autonomous domains and located "its own subjectivity in the spiritual domain of culture, where it considered itself superior to the West and hence undominated and sovereign."[14]

For Chatterjee, however, it was the "derivative" nature of official Indian nationalism that accounted for the nationalist construction of the private sphere as an uncolonized space, off-limits to colonial intervention. But through her analysis of the arguments on "Hindu" conjugality and domesticity in late nineteenth-century nationalist politics, Tanika Sarkar demonstrates the vitality of orthodox and traditional social forces reactivated under colonialism.[15] Sarkar's analysis of the role of orthodox and traditional social forces in the nationalist restructuring of domestic sexual relations begins to suggest that the historically particular form for the politics of nationalism and "respectable" sexuality in colonial India had at least as much to do with the reconstitution of earlier social hierarchies under conditions of colonialism as with the "derivative" project of official Indian nationalism.

This framework — the accommodation of preexisting hierarchies of caste, class, and gender in new social arrangements — situates the following debates on the Age of Consent Act (1891) and the Child Marriage Restraint Act (1929), both in terms of the particular history of colonialism in India and in terms of the more general history of the politics of nationalisms and sexualities in an imperial world system. The colonial debates around the consequences of early sexual intercourse, enforced widowhood, and child-marriage intensely politicized the restructuring of (hetero)sexual family norms in both colonialist and official nationalist rhetoric in India. These debates also marked important turning points in the history of elite nationalist struggle in India: whereas the strength of the nationalist opposition to the Consent Bill rejuvenated elite nationalist critiques of colonial rule, the relatively greater nationalist support for the passage of the Child Marriage Restraint Act preceded one of the more dramatic elite nationalist initiatives of mass mobilization in the Salt *Satyagraha* (the Gandhian Civil Disobedience Movement of 1930).

Although nationalist opinion had remained divided in both these debates, the difference in the relative strength of the reformist position was the product of a shift in historical conditions that made possible the accommodation of preexisting hierarchies in the formation of new nationalist subjectivities and the political community of the nation. The historical conditions of these debates were shaped both by the internal contradictions of elite nationalist culture and by the tension between elite nationalism and the "popular" nationalisms of peasant struggles that not only preceded elite nationalism but continued long after it to offer an alternative arena for challenging colonial rule.[16] Indeed, insofar as the debates over the Age of Consent Act and the Child Marriage Restraint Act reveal the ways in which political, economic, and ideological relations of domination were reconstituted under conditions of colonialism, they also recontextualize the politics of nationalisms and sexualities from the broader perspective of the realignment of older social hierarchies in new social arrangements in an imperial world system.

THE AGE OF CONSENT ACT

On 19 March 1891, the Viceroy of India signed the Age of Consent Act, amending the Indian Penal Code of Criminal Procedure.[17] The age of consent referred to the age at which the law recognized that an individual was eligible to give consent to sexual intercourse. Nineteenth-century consent regulations, however, were designed primarily for the protection of young women, illustrating the Victorian bourgeois consensus that young girls, more than young boys, needed protection from premature sexual intercourse. Feminists and purity crusaders had campaigned for the passage of consent regulations in Britain in 1885, following the sensationalized accounts of child prostitution and "white slavery" brought to light by the British tabloids.[18]

In India, consent regulations were prompted by the incidence of premature consummation of child marriage, believed to be especially common in the province of Bengal. Whereas the Indian Penal Code of 1860 specified that the age of consent for married and unmarried Indian women was ten years, the 1891 Act raised it to twelve years; henceforth intercourse with married or unmarried women below age twelve was classified as rape and punishable by ten years imprisonment or transportation for life.

The consent controversy in India inaugurated one of the first efforts at mass mobilization under elite leadership against a government-sponsored social legislation. Historians of the consent controversy, therefore, have typically focused on the strength of the revivalist-nationalist opposition to the Bill.[19] Yet equally significant for contextualizing the politics of nationalisms and sexualities were the ambiguities that surrounded even male nationalist support for the Bill. Although supporters of the Consent Bill made available startling statistics of the sexual abuse of child wives, the gendered critique of child marriage that Padma Anagol-McGinn identifies in Indian women's public participation in the consent controversy in Bombay was typically absent from much of the male nationalist support for the Bill.[20] The center of the consent controversy was located in the colonial province of Bengal and to a lesser extent in Bombay, both regions that were the hotbed of political radicalism against colonial rule. Even though the Indian National Congress, the most important all-India middle-class political organization, refrained from issuing an official position on the Consent Bill, nationalist preoccupations set the terms of the debate for reformists and revivalists alike. Despite the obvious difference in the dominant reformist and revivalist responses to the Consent Bill, the points of agreement between the two are significant for what they indicate about the historical position of the indigenous elites in the late nineteenth century: the historical circumstances were not yet ripe for absorbing the reform of indigenous social hierarchies within an elite nationalist agenda.

The limited nature of the Consent Bill was not meant to interfere directly with the institution of child marriage, which was originally an upper-caste Hindu custom that became fairly widespread among different caste/class and religious groups in India. The Bill aimed only at modifying the premature consummation of child marriage, which was believed to be most common in the province of Bengal. The colonial initiative was limited in nature both out of consideration for political expediency and out of a new-found respect for orthodox patriarchal practices in India in the face of an antifeminist backlash in Britain. By the late nineteenth century, therefore, the institution of child marriage in India had acquired several powerful defenders in Britain.

Child marriage was praised as an "organization of protection," or, as in the words of a special correspondent of *The Times*, a "system which endeavoured to give maximum security to Hindoo women as a whole, and which deliberately acted on the principle that their general safety must be insured, even at the cost of hardships to individuals among them."[21] Even the rather limited interference in the institution of child marriage posed by the Consent Act was criticized in such papers as the *St. James Gazette* in London, which had previously led the attack against the feminist campaign for the British Consent Act or the Criminal Amendment Act of 1885.[22] Added to this underlying ambivalence toward child marriage, of course, was the fact that the colonial authorities in the period after 1857 had commited themselves to a policy that abdicated responsibility for reforming social legislation in India for fear of provoking orthodox opposition to colonial rule. The colonial initiative in introducing the Consent Bill, therefore, came only after the highly publicized case of a husband's murder through brutal sexual intercourse of a child-wife in Bengal and after equally well-publicized efforts of one Indian reformer in London for exerting the pressure of British public opinion on the government.

The Bombay politician Bal Gangadhar Tilak, one of the more prominent nationalist champions of orthodox Hindu practices against social reform legislations at the turn of the century, set the tone of the dominant nationalist response to the Consent Bill: he challenged the right of an alien government and an unrepresentative legislature to legislate the social and cultural practices of the nation. Even male nationalist supporters of the Consent Bill had to be impressed by the power of this rhetoric. The nationalist suspicion of colonial interference and the shared project of "nationalizing" the middle-class Indian home, however, considerably weakened nationalist support for the Bill. Hence the General Secretary of the Congress noted that although four fifths of its membership supported the Bill in private, the organization had refused to take a public position on the Bill.[23]

For middle-class Bengali reformers, for whom reform of the Indian home was impelled not only by colonial criticisms of Indian domestic practices, but also, as Sumanta Bannerji reminds us, by their own class consolidation against lower caste/class groups in India, the consent controversy had posed a particular dilemma.[24] Surendranath Banerjea of the Indian Association in Calcutta, for example, was unwilling either to leave the Indian home in the hands of orthodox revivalists or to relinquish Indian initiative for the reform of the Indian home to the colonial government. Banerjea and other like-minded nationalists therefore qualified their support for the Consent Bill with criticism not only of particular aspects of the Bill, but also of its failure to go far enough in legislating against child marriage: "I entirely sympathize with the object it has in view, viz. to afford protection to child wives, but I should have preferred a measure which more directly dealt with one of the worst evils of child marriage, vis. premature consummation by declaring marriage void under a certain age."[25]

Manmohun Ghose, a former supporter of reforms for women in Bengal, was even more equivocal in his opposition to the Consent Bill. He criticized various anomalies in the government proposal that undermined real protection for the child-bride and recommended that the government enact a civil law declaring that no marriage should be valid if either of the contracting parties at the time of their marriage were below a certain age. He further argued that orthodox opposition to his proposal would be no more than that already provoked by the Consent Bill.[26] Whether these suggestions were "red herrings" in the path of reform or genuine efforts for a more comprehensive reform, it is remarkable that in Bengal (apart from the radical reformers of the *Sadharan Brahmo Samaj* and a group of about 150 women petitioners led by Kadambini Ganguly, who recorded their unqualified approval of the Bill) reservations about the Bill were also expressed on one point or another by the majority of the Bill's supporters.[27]

The points of agreement between the dominant reformist and revivalist positions on the Consent Bill in Bengal reveal not only the weakness of the pro-reform camp, but also the limited nature of the goals for restructuring heterosexual family relations among the dominant nationalist elites. One premise shared by many of the reformists and revivalists alike suggested that colonial social legislation was valid to the extent that it conformed with indigenous religious or social practices. Even though the colonial authorities had initiated consent regulations with the express purpose of avoiding interference in orthodox religious practices, the opponents had interpreted the Consent Bill as an example of colonial interference in Indian religious practices.

Whether in recognition of the strength of orthodox arguments about religious interference or in general sympathy with the nationalist agenda for claiming Indian autonomy in the private sphere, male nationalist supporters of the Consent Bill were just as anxious to demonstrate that the Bill did not interfere with the religious practices of the Hindus.[28] Yet by conceding validity to arguments about colonial interference and the inviolability of Hindu social and religious practices, the reformists could scarcely hope to compete with the rhetoric of the Bill's opponents. For although reformists cited the *sastras* (Hindu scriptures) in support of the consent legislation, the opponents not only took refuge in alternative interpretations of the *sastras,* but pointed to the weight of local customs to develop a powerful rhetoric around colonial interference.

In an argument that could be characterized as disingenuous at best, the opponents appealed for a sympathetic consideration of the special hardship imposed by the Bill on poor low-caste men, who, having to cohabit with their child-wives in one-room hovels, would not be turned into "saints" by the passage of the Consent Bill.[29] The rhetoric of the opponents of the Bill served to ally orthodox landed magnates with the rural literati and other groups marginalized by the more cosmopolitan and Westernized gentry associated with the Congress and the Indian Association in Calcutta. In the context of the specious maneuvering of different factions within the elites, all equally cut off from a popular base of mass support, the indictment of the Bengali reformers by the Maharanee Surnomoyee, the powerful female *zamindar* (landlord) of Cossimbazar, struck a responsive chord. They were, she claimed, an elite out of touch with the real India who, having visited England, had returned to their mother-country with new-fangled ideas.[30] The anomaly in the social position of the nationalist elites that gave rise to the shared premise on colonial social legislations ultimately served to marginalize the reformist interpretations of the upper-caste religious and social prescriptions offered by the Bill's supporters.

Between the dominant reformists and the orthodox revivalists there was another shared premise on the definition of female consent. Whereas many male reformers, the majority of the "lady doctors" consulted on the Bill, and the Indian women who petitioned in support of the Bill favoured a broader interpretation of female consent, the majority view defined female consent on the basis of the reproductive function of women. In other words, it was the age at which women could be considered physically mature to bear healthy children without injury to themselves or to the health of the race. In raising the age of consent to twelve, the colonial authorities had cited medical opinion stating that twelve was the "natural" age at which Indian women reached puberty, as determined by the onset of menstruation. Evidence of menstruation before twelve was seen as proof of the degraded sexual atmosphere of Hindu society, which encouraged premature menstruation by the "artificial stimulation" of young women through the excitation of their sexual instincts.[31]

Even though orthodox Hindu priests agreed that neither the *sastras* nor custom enjoined intercourse with a girl before she reached puberty, they produced evidence to establish a lower menearchial age for Indian women. The opponents thus claimed that arbitrarily fixing the age of puberty for Indian women at twelve interfered with the observance of various Hindu religious customs and practices. Because neither side conceived of female sexuality as independent of the primary reproductive function of women, many reformists wavered in their support for a chronological criterion to determine female consent. Those arguing for substituting puberty as the criterion for determining female consent, for example, found some adherents even among the Calcutta Committee (which supported the Consent Bill) formed in February 1891.[32]

Both supporters and opponents also expressed common reservations about the marital rape clause in the Exception to Section 375 of the Indian Penal Code on female consent. Although in 1837 the Law Commission under Lord Macaulay had decided to follow the law in Britain as regards the legal exclusion of marital rape in female consent regulations, when the Indian Penal Code was adopted in 1860, a husband's sexual intercourse with a wife who was not ten years of age was included as rape.[33]

The departure in the Indian Penal Code from the law in Britain was a response to the reformist initiatives in India that urged governmental action on the abuses of child marriage. Bengali reformers like Pandit Ishwarchandra Vidyasagar had campaigned vigorously for the acceptance of the provisions of the 1860 Penal Code. The Bengali opposition to the Consent Bill of 1891, however, brought up the marital rape clause as an argument against the Bill. Manmohum Ghose, for example, ingenuously situated his reservations against the marital rape clause in the Indian Consent Bill in the context of the deliberate exclusion of such a clause from the Criminal Amendment Act of 1885 in Britain. He thus portrayed the Indian Consent Bill as a deliberate infringement on the rights of the Indian husband when the laws of most "civilized" nations had guaranteed the husband certain patriarchal privileges over his wife. Ghose argued that whereas the law in Britain had consistently refused to recognize rape within marriage on the grounds that by virtue of the marital contract the wife was supposed to have automatically surrendered sexual consent to her husband, the colonial British government was refusing to accord the Indian husband the same privilege.[34] He urged the colonial government, without much success, to substitute some other offence for rape in the case of the under-age sexual intercourse between husband and wife.

Opponents of the Bill claimed to be at a "loss to understand from what standpoint — rational, moral or legal — the lustful seducer of a guileless and yielding virgin, and the passionate husband of a loving wife are to be placed under the same category and alike to be branded as a criminal of the blackest dye."[35] The argument against treating the Indian husband in the same category as any other ordinary rapist persuaded even many of the more committed supporters of the Bill to urge the government to substitute "criminal assault" for rape in the provisions affecting the sexual intercourse between a husband and his wife. In fact, the *Bengalee*, which was edited by Banerjea, concluded that "the strongest supporters of the Bill, as well as its strongest opponents, are all at one in pressing upon the Government the desirability of introducing at least this one modification" (i.e., the removal of the marital rape clause).[36] The emotionally charged issue of marital rape thus brought out shared reservations about a discourse of female sexuality that was independent of the control of the husband.

The context of child prostitution in the British consent debate had allowed British feminists to mobilize the language of purity to define their own image of female sexuality, which, however limited and contradictory, offered a challenge to male sexual double standards.[37] But the context of marital sexual relations in the Indian Consent debate was less conducive to the deployment of a language of purity for redefining the regulation of female sexuality. The consent controversy in Bengal, as Dagmar Engels argues, essentially involved two contrasting views on the control of female sexuality: the orthodox Bengali male control over female sexuality was pitted against the control over female sexuality in a Victorian British gender ideology.[38] Whereas British feminists and purity crusaders mobilized the notion of female "passionlessness"[39] to bolster their campaign for the protection of women from the sexual immorality of men in the British consent controversy, orthodox Hindus in Bengal argued that women had a strong and powerful sexual drive that had to be contained safely within the bounds of marriage to argue against the Indian Consent Bill. Hence the *Bangabasi*, the vernacular Bengali language paper that led the opposition against the Bill in Bengal, predicted the terrible scenario of "females in groups hurrying from door to door begging males to gratify their lust" if the Consent Act were passed.[40]

For Sir R. C. Mitter, the Bengali member in the Viceroy's Legislative Council, the reformers were being excessively "puritanical" and unsympathetic to the sexual passion that naturally resulted from the cohabitation of a young boy and his bride. He urged the government, therefore, to show leniency in the case of the mutually desired sexual intercourse of a young couple that did not result in any injury to the young bride. Mitter's views were roundly criticized by the British press in India. The *Pioneer*, the semi-official British newspaper in India, condemned Mitter's views as the "selfish gratification of voluptuous men," and declared that "truly civilized men" could not condone the lack of manly self-control that Mitter was so willing to excuse.[41]

Moreover, even when the language of purity was deployed by male reformers in the context of marital sexual relations, as in the Indian Consent debate, it was seldom an argument to remove the control of female sexuality from the orthodox institution of child marriage. For P. C. Majoomdar, for example, a Consent Bill was to be preferred over a Bill that directly affected the institution of child marriage precisely because the former could ensure the "purity" of the Indian household by delaying sexual intercourse for young boys and young girls without relaxing the familial control over sexual morality that, he believed, resulted from the institution of adult marriages.[42]

The terms of the Consent controversy had to do with the modification, and not the radical transformation, of the familial regulation of sexual relations. The central question even for reformers, as the author of "Child Marriage and Enforced Widowhood in India" acknowledged in *The Times*, was "how to secure for wives and daughters the old safety of dependence [provided by child marriage] with a larger measure of the freedom of modern independence."[43] Under the conditions of colonialism and anti-colonial nationalism, the answer to this question had to wait until the greater institutional strength and ideological maturity of elite nationalist culture in the first half of the twentieth century. For following the consent controversy, the colonial government not only issued an executive order that made the implementation of the Bill virtually impossible, but it also refrained from undertaking any major piece of social reform legislation from 1891 until the passage of the Child Marriage Restraint Act in 1929.[44]

THE CHILD MARRIAGE RESTRAINT ACT

In 1929, the colonial government finally passed the Child Marriage Restraint Act raising the age of marriage for women to fourteen and for men to eighteen.[45] The Bill, the first one of its kind since the storm over the 1891 Consent Act, was passed at the initiative of an Indian legislator, Har Bilas Sarda. Indeed, ever since the political changes instituted by the Reform Acts of 1909 and 1919, which associated greater numbers of Indians with the legislative bodies of the colonial administration, "modernizing"[46] Indian legislators had been at the forefront of the call for consent and child marriage legislations. It was the colonial officials who now dragged their feet over reform legislations that might alienate the support of orthodox sections of Indian society from the government at a time when nationalist opposition to colonial rule appeared at its peak.

The stalemate over marriage reforms, however, was finally broken as both the colonial government and Indian popular opinion were aroused out of their apathy by the controversy following the 1927 publication of the infamous *Mother India*.[47] Its American author, Katherine Mayo, claimed that her purpose in writing the book was simply to reveal the horrible plight of the Hindu child-bride and child-mother. Yet, as both the argument of the book and Mayo's collaboration with the official British propaganda machine reveals, her primary agenda was to indict the predominantly Hindu upper-caste- and middle-class-led nationalist movement in India. Her book was meant to convince the world in general, and American public opinion in particular, that Indians were not yet ready for political self-determination and needed the continuing "civilizing" presence of British colonial rule.[48]

Mayo's shocking revelations of the abuses of child-marriage, however, did embarrass the colonial authorities out of their inaction. As yet, the Viceroy had been willing only to commission an Age of Consent Committee to study public opinion and determine the incidence of premature sexuality in India. The Committee, comprising both British and Indians (including a single Indian woman, Rameshwari Nehru), conducted a nationwide survey on the matter. The report of the Committee concluded that there was urgent need for child-marriage reform.

It was in this context that the Government agreed to take up Sarda's Bill on child marriage, which had been awaiting action by the legislative assembly for some time. Women activists of the newly formed All India

Women's Conference lobbied both Indian and British legislators and their wives to ensure passage of the Bill. Around three hundred women from the fledgling all-India women's organization attended the debate over the Bill in the Legislative Assembly.[49] Despite vigorous orthodox Hindu and Muslim opposition to the Bill, it was finally passed in the Legislative Assembly by a vote of seventy-seven in favor and fourteen against.

Although Mayo herself and many of her admirers saw the passage of the Sarda Bill as the outcome of Mayo's exposé, the Indian women activists, as well as generations of nationalist historians, give Mayo little credit for this important piece of social reform legislation.[50] The notoriety that Mayo's book had achieved in India, Britain, and the United States, and the proliferation of nationalist responses to Mayo's diatribe on India, however, serves as a useful background for understanding the changes that led to the passage of the Child Marriage Restraint Act.

In her efforts to discredit middle-class Indian nationalists, Mayo had chosen to focus specifically on sexuality and the sexual organization of Hindu society. Mayo believed that all of India's political, economic, and social woes were the result of the sexual organization of Hindu society: Hindus, she argued, were oversexed because they indulge their sexual passions from an early age until their death. This not only accounted for the gross sexual abuse of Hindu women through early marriage and premature sexuality, but also for the physical and mental degeneracy of the Hindu male resulting from the debilitating effects of excessive sexual indulgence. As proof of the overly sexual nature of the Hindus, Mayo cited alarming — but grossly exaggerated — statistics of the spread of venereal diseases in India.

To further substantiate her sexual thesis, Mayo cited dubious information of men having sex with young boys and of mothers obtaining sexual satisfaction from their infants as examples of the sexual degeneracy of Indian society. By arguing that "depraved" sexual practices were either enjoined or condoned within Hinduism itself, Mayo was hoping to discredit nationalist claims about Hinduism's higher spirituality and morality, popular among the so-called India-lovers in the West. More crucially, however, she was also making an argument about the very nature of India's political agitation against colonial rule. According to Mayo, Indian nationalism was an outcome of the peculiar sexual pathology of Hindu society. Hence she writes that Bengal was the "seat of bitterest political unrest — the producer of India's main crop of anarchists, bomb-throwers and assassins" because it was also "among the most sexually exaggerated regions of India." She saw a close link between "sexual exaggerat[ion]" and the "queer criminal minds" that were behind Indian nationalism.[51]

Over a dozen books, pamphlets, letters, and newspaper articles written in response to *Mother India* took up Mayo's challenge by arguing that "sexual deviance" was more common in materialist Western societies than in the spiritually superior Eastern societies. Most famous of these responses was K. L. Gauba's *Uncle Sham: Being the Strange Tale of a Civilization Run Amok*.[52] Gauba's book, which had almost as enduring an impact on Indian perceptions of American society as Mayo's *Mother India* has had on American perceptions of Indian society, detailed various examples of sexual excesses in American society. Another noteworthy example was written in Hindi by an Indian woman, Chandravati Lakhanpal, and entitled *Mother India Ka Jawab* (The Reply to Mother India).[53] Lakhanpal's book dwelt on the homosexual practices, to which elite British males were exposed in English public schools, and quoted at length from Havelock Ellis and other famous authorities on sex to argue that "sexual perversion" was more common in Britain than in India. These popular responses, however, elicited little serious attention; they were then, and continue now, to be dismissed simply as *tu quoque* responses.

Yet the alleged dichotomy that these authors noted between Western sexual degeneracy and Eastern sexual propriety is important in one crucial respect: it reflected the coming of age of a new nationalist perspective on Indian domestic and sexual norms. Although the language of purity had little resonance during the consent controversy of 1891, the discourse of the higher spirituality of the Indian home and the virtue of the Indian woman served not only to turn Mayo's critical lens back on the West and Western-style reforms, but also to underwrite the effort to secure a higher age of marriage for girls. Thus the male author of *Sister India*, a book written in response to *Mother India*, could argue that whereas the materialist West had fallen prey to sexual permissiveness and sexual perversion, India could combine freedom from oppressive sexual practices with an inherently superior Indian spiritual and sexual morality. The author supported the reform of Indian marriage practices, but was careful to warn readers that "we frankly consider that it would be an evil day for India if Indian women indiscriminately copy and imitate Western women."[54] The radical difference between a Western and an Indian moral and sexual code allowed the reformist nationalist elite, as Dipesh Chakraborty would argue, to "indigenize" and domesticate the norms of bourgeois domesticity in a manner that would enable the nationalist elite to address the West or Britain as "Indian."[55] At the same time, however, the reluctance of a male-dominated nationalist elite to ensure the proper implementation of the Sarda Act and to transform the basis of marital practices was evidence of a continued investment in keeping the control of sexual relations in orthodox social arrangements.

The moral authority of M. K. Gandhi, who emerged as the leader of the nationalist movement from the 1920s onward, played an important part in the reorientation of elite nationalist culture. For although Gandhi had his own unique blueprint for the societal changes necessary to rejuvenate Indian culture, his contributions to the official nationalist movement in India brought a new ideological maturity to elite nationalist culture.[56] Mayo, who later wrote several articles critical of Gandhi, was forced to acknowledge grudgingly in *Mother India* that Gandhi had both spoken and written extensively about the evils of child marriage and premature sexuality. Gandhi had responded with a scathing review of Mayo's book, in which he referred to it as a "Drain Inspector's Report." Although Gandhi accused Mayo of being an unabashed Anglophile and an Indophobe, he also urged Indians to take stock of existing domestic and sexual arrangements in Indian society.[57] During the debate over the Sarda Bill in the Indian Legislative Assembly, for example, Gandhi leant the weight of his moral authority to Indian legislators to support the passage of the Bill.

If Gandhi, despite his heterodox discourse of sexuality, was able to facilitate a fuller incorporation of a reformist agenda in the official nationalist platform, his success was partly enabled by the significance of his contribution to the nationalist movement: the incorporation of the majority of Indians (the peasantry) within a predominantly male, upper-caste/class-dominated nationalist movement. Gandhi's highly problematic views on sexuality, and female sexuality in particular, have been the subject of recent articles by Madhu Kishwar, Sujata Patel, and Ketu Katrak.[58] These authors point out that Gandhi, more than any other contemporary nationalist, was responsible for mobilizing women in the anti-colonial struggle and for creating a more positive attitude toward women generally, but his revolutionary impact was also recuperated by his rigid notions of "respectable" female sexuality. Katrak focuses on this aspect of Gandhi's impact: Gandhi provided women with an option other than that of the typical heterosexual marriage by encouraging young women and widows to give up marriage and remain single to serve the nation. But because Gandhi believed female sexuality was valid only within the traditional bounds of marriage, his goal was not to encourage women to explore their own definitions of female sexuality, but rather to encourage them — through sexual abstinence — to gain greater autonomy within marriage or to become sexless workers for the cause of the nation.[59] Hence, despite his radical departure from the normative prescription of heterosexual marriage, the implications of the Gandhian language of female purity dovetailed nicely with the overall elite nationalist project that retained the control of female sexuality, as the work of Janaki Nair suggests, in familial and caste networks.[60]

Here, then, was the making of a new nationalist consensus on the norms of Indian sexual respectability. This "politics of respectability,"[61] as Geraldine Forbes so aptly calls it, not only shaped Indian women's participation in the nationalist movement, but also served as the ground for the early success of Indian women's campaign for domestic and sexual reform. On the one hand, the emerging consensus on the higher spirituality and virtue of the Indian woman enabled the interventionary practices of Indian women themselves. One of the most famous women in the nationalist and women's movement of the time, Sarojini Naidu, asserted in 1928 in the wake of the controversy over *Mother India* that

the women of India should answer all those who come in the guise of friendship to interpret India to the world and exploit their weakness and expose the secrets of the home, with the words "whether we are oppressed, treated as goods and chattels and forced on the funeral pyres of our husbands, our redemption is in our hands. We shall break through the walls that imprison us and tear the veils that stifle. We shall do these by the miracle of our womanhood. We do not ask any friend or foe in the guise of a friend, to come merely to exploit us while they pretend to interpret, succour and solace our womanhood."[62]

The upper-caste- and middle class-dominated all-India women's organizations could legitmately claim the passage of the Child Marriage Restraint Act as the first major triumph of their nationwide campaigns for women's reform. On the other hand, however, the very conditions that enabled the early success of the organized Indian women's movement in the campaign for marriage reforms also disabled, as essentially "un-Indian" or "Westernized," their further criticism of the reconstituted nationalist patriarchy. As many Indian feminists discovered after the passage of the Sarda Act, their efforts to secure real changes in marriage practices not only remained an uphill battle, but met with new resistance from both within and without the women's movement. Rameshwari Nehru, a Gandhian-socialist and a leading women activist in the campaign against child marriage, went on to declare that "I do not think that the home should be made a forum for women's battles." Her views reflected the price that accompanied the visibility of Indian feminist demands within the nationalist movement.[63]

In this context, the relative strength of the reformist rhetoric in the debate over the Child Marriage Restraint Act in 1929 (compared to the debate over the Age of Consent Act in 1891) did not reflect a new commitment to the displacement of orthodox and feudal patriarchal control of sexual relations. Rather, it reflected the greater institutional strength and ideological maturity of an elite nationalist culture that could now accommodate more successfully the preexisting hierarchies of gender, caste, and class in the restructuring of sexual relations for the constitution of new nationalist subjectivities and the modern community of the nation.

Two points emerge from the debates over the Age of Consent Act and the Child Marriage Restraint Act in India: first, the link between nationalisms and sexualities has served historically not only to displace earlier attachments and forge new relations of power, but also to realign and reconstitute earlier social relations; and, second, the imperial social formation has provided the context for the historically particular forms in which preexisting social hierarchies have been accommodated in the rhetoric of nationalisms and sexualities. Under conditions of colonialism and anti-colonial nationalism in India, therefore, the reconstitution of new nationalist subjectivities not only retained the negative repression of female sexuality in the "deployment of alliance," but also reactivated competing conceptions of community based on religious and caste affiliations in the process of constituting the modern community of the nation. For insofar as the defense of a "Hindu" way of life and upper-caste prescriptions were part of the political imagination of the nation, even the more secular conceptions of the political community existed in an uneasy relationship with other rival religious and caste-based "imagined communities."

The interplay between official Indian nationalism and sexuality in colonial India reveals an accommodation with preexisting hierarchies of caste/class and gender that are secured by and, in turn, themselves secure the history of capitalist modernization in imperialized social formations. Similarly, the politics of nationalisms and sexualities in imperial formations in the West reveal contradictions in the development of capitalist modernity. For although the representation of sexual relations in the nationalist rhetoric in colonial India more directly reflected an accommodation with feudal and pre-capitalist social relations, the "deployment of sexuality" for the formation of new subjectivities in the West was no less an accommodation with the older system of kinship ties and family alliances. One dimension of this accommodation, as Rosemary Hennessy suggests, was the interdependence of the apparatus of alliance and the new discourse of sex in the institution of heterosexuality and its accompanying patriarchal gender hierarchy. This hierarchy is constituted by the assumption that sex differences are binary opposites and the further equation of this binary sex difference with gender.[64] Whereas Foucault only dimly acknowledges the interdependence between the old apparatus of alliance and the new discourse of sexuality in the nineteeenth-century West, Hennessy's materialist-feminist analysis suggests that insofar as the discourse of sexuality reproduces this patriarchal gender system, it ties the emergence of the ideology of the modern individual to the interests that were upheld by the deployment of alliance.

A parallel argument that sees the "nation" as emblematic of the inner contradictions of "modernity" has been made by such scholars as Slavoj Zizek, who suggests that the nation is a "pre-modern leftover which functions as an inner condition of modernity," and Chatterjee, who finds in the nation a "suppressed narrative of community" that remains unacknowledged in the global narrative of capital.[65] The nation seeks to replace "organic" pre-modern communities with a new form of social organization; the constituents of the modern nation-state, unlike those of pre-modern communities, are "citizens" — people as abstract individuals, not as members of a particular estate, family, or religious group. Yet insofar as the global narrative of capital cannot do without the reconstituted community of the "nation" and must also naturalize it as the only legitimate form of community in modern societies, the nation becomes the site at which the public domain of civil society — made up of supposedly "free" individuals/citizens — sits uneasily with the private domain that reproduces sexualized, racialized, and class subjects as the constituents of the new national community.

The modern community of the nation thus reconstructs, without supplanting, the particularism of traditional "organic" ties reproduced in premodern communities; for, as Chatterjee argues, the fundamental contradiction of capitalist modernization is that the community "continues to lead a subterranean, potentially subversive life within [the narrative of capitalism] because it refuses to go away."[66] The different forms in which these contradictions become manifest in the politics of nationalisms and sexualities in different regions in the world is at least in part the product of the historical experience of imperialism.

Although the imperial social formation as the basis for recontextualizing the politics of nationalisms and sexualities suggests, on the one hand, that the nineteenth-century "deployment of sexuality" was the product of a historically particular political, economic, and ideological conjuncture in the imperial West, it also suggests, on the other hand, the continuities between the mobilizations of the politics of nationalisms and sexualities in imperial and imperialized formations. For even though the interconnection between the public/national and the private/libidinal was most apparent in the counternationalisms of the colonies, it has never been very far beneath the surface in the nationalist discourses in the primary areas of capitalist accummulation in the West, where it has resurfaced dramatically in specific historical moments. In recent years, this has been made apparent in the United States, for example, in the talk about "American" family values following the last Republican National Convention and in the ongoing debate over gays in the military.

Although the nature of a historical critique cautions against reading the colonial debates on the restructuring of heterosexual relations into the contemporary dynamics of nationalist and sexual politics in India, understanding that history does provide the critical tools for developing a politics of sexuality that goes beyond sterile debates over "Indian" and "un-Indian" sexualities and focuses instead on the political, economic, and ideological interests that produced and continue to be served by such a dichotomy. This mode of analysis, moreover, has implications for facilitating a more politically enabling discussion of sexualities in India. For self-consciously gay groups, which have been around at lcast since the 1970s in India, raising the issue of gay sexuality has often been a prescription for self-marginalization.[67] Critiques of nationalist sexual politics have been typically recuperated by labelling them as "un-Indian" or "Westernized." If gay political activists in India, however, are to expand the terms of the debate on sexuality, then they cannot afford only to revive — its strategic value notwithstanding — the more positive or neutral attitude toward same-sex behavior in classical or pre-colonial times or simply to duplicate the more individualist language of the politics of sexuality in the West.[68] In order for a gay sexual politics to have relevance as an emancipatory politics in India, it must unpack the ways in which sexualities have been produced by, and helped to sustain, specific political and socioeconomic agendas.

The fact that sexual norms have often served as the nodal point for the reproduction of various forms of gendered political, economic, and ideological domination should also caution various women's rights and other political activists in India from too quickly dismissing a politics of sexuality as simply an elite or "bourgeois" concern. In this context, it is useful to note, as Gail Omvedt does, that the lead in raising "women's rights not only to property and to political power, but also to reproduction and sexuality" have often been taken by the rural mass movements in India.[69] Omvedt provides the example of the Shetkari Sanghatana, a mass-based rural peasant/farmer organization. This group did not hesitate to take up the question of redefining female sexuality at its November 1986 women's conference, held at Chandwad, a small village in Maharashtra, and that involved some thirty thousand women and even greater numbers of men. According to Omvedt, *Shidori*, the Marathi booklet prepared for the meeting, treated lesbianism not as an "unnatural deviation" but as a method of "living independently of men."[70] What the recontextualizing of the politics of nationalisms and sexualities does is to uncover its imbrication in various political, economic, and ideological relations of domination so as to begin to challenge the consensus that has so far treated a politics of sexuality as either "un-Indian" or as totally irrelevant to the apparently more urgent social and economic disabilities confronting the majority of Indians.

NOTES

1. See *Less than Gay: A Citizen's Report on the Status of Homosexuality in India* (New Delhi: AIDS Bhedbhav Virodhi Andolan, 1991), 67–68. Also see Anu and Yiti, "Inverting Tradition: The Marriage of Lila and Urmilla," in *A Lotus of Another Color: An Unfolding of the South Asian Gay and Lesbian Experience*, ed. Raresh Ratti (Boston: Alyson Publishers, 1993), 81–84.

2. See Gabriele Dietrich, *Reflections on the Women's Movement in India: Religion, Ecology, Development* (New Delhi: Horizon India Books, 1992), 35–51. See also Yiti Thadani, "No Lesbians Please — We Are Indians," *Trikone* 9, no. 2 (April 1994): 5–6. Although homosexuality is not criminalized in India, Section 377 of the Indian Penal Code retains criminal sanctions against sodomy (lesbianism does not come under this sanction). The AIDS Bhedbhav Virodhi Andolan (ABVA) is at the forefront in calling for the repeal of Section 377; see Anuja Yupta, "Sodomy Law Challenged," *Trikone* 9, no. 3 (July 1994): 9.

3. I remain aware of the dangers of collapsing too easily colonial and postcolonial histories. This issue has been discussed in Ania Loomba, "Over-worlding the 'Third World,'" *Oxford Literary Review* 3, nos. 1–2 (1991): 164–92.

4. I take the notion of "provincializing" the West from Dipesh Chakrabarty, "Provincializing Europe: Postcoloniality and the Critique of History," *Cultural Studies* 6, no. 3 (Oct. 1992): 337–57.

5. I borrow the term from Rosemary Hennessy, who defines a global social analytic in two crucial ways: first, it is truly global rather than a regionalism (history of one region) masquerading as the global; second, it is global in its understanding of the social as the product of interconnecting political, economic, and ideological levels. See R. Hennessy, *Materialist Feminism and the Politics of Discourse* (New York: Routledge and Kegan Paul, 1993).

6. Andrew Parker et al., eds., *Nationalisms and Sexualities* (New York: Routledge, 1992). For a survey of some scholarship on sexuality in India, see Dagmar Engels, "History and Sexuality in India: Discursive Trends," *Trends in History* 4, no. 4 (1990): 15–42.

7. Benedict Anderson, *Imagined Communities* (London: Verso, 1983); and Michel Foucault, *The History of Sexuality: An Introduction*, trans. Robert Hurley (New York: Vintage Books, 1980). The argument is developed in Doris Sommers, "Love and Country in Latin America: An Allegorical Speculation," *Cultural Critique* 16 (fall 1990): 109–28.

8. Foucault, *History of Sexuality*, 105–11. I am grateful to Janaki Nair's comments on an earlier draft of this chapter for helping me to clarify this point. Nair has developed this argument in her unpublished manuscript, "Law, Modernity and Patriarchy, Mysore, 1890–1940, Part 2, Prohibited Marriage: State Protection and the Child Wife."

9. Frederic Jameson, "Third World Literature in the Era of Multinational Criticism," *Social Text*, no. 15 (fall 1986): 65–88.

10. See Aijaz Ahmed, "Jameson's Rhetoric of Otherness and the National Allegory," *Social Text*, no. 17 (fall 1987): 3–27; Henry Schwartz, "Provocations toward a Theory of Third World Literature," *Mississippi Review* 17 (1989): 177–201.

11. See Madhava Prasad's critical reading of both Jameson's essay and Ahmad's response, "On the Question of a Theory of (Third World) Literature," *Social Text*, no. 31–32 (1992): 57–83.

12. Ranajit Guha, "Dominance without Hegemony and Its Historiography," in *Subaltern Studies 6: Writings on South Asian History and Society*, ed. R. Guha (Delhi: Oxford University Press, 1989), 210–309; and his "Discipline and Mobilize," in *Subaltern Studies 7: Writings on South Asian History and Society*, ed. P. Chatterjee and G. Pandey (Delhi: Oxford University Press, 1993).
13. See Partha Chatterjee, "A Response to Taylor's 'Modes of Civil Society,' " *Public Culture* 13, no. 1 (fall 1990): 119–32. For a fuller development of this argument, see his *Nationalist Thought and the Colonial World: A Derivative Discourse?* (London: Zed Books, 1986); and, more recently, *The Nation and Its Fragments* (Princeton, NJ: Princeton University Press, 1994).
14. See P. Chatterjee, "The Nationalist Resolution of the Women's Question," in *Recasting Women: Essays in Indian Colonial History*, ed. Kumkum Sangari and Sudesh Vaid (New Brunswick, NJ: Rutgers University Press, 1990), 233–53; and "Colonialism, Nationalism and Colonized Women: The Contest in India," *American Ethnologist* 16, no. 4 (Nov. 1989): 662–83.
15. Tanika Sarkar, "The Hindu Wife and the Hindu Nation: Domesticity and Nationalism in Nineteenth Century Bengal," *Studies in History* 8, no. 2 (1992): 213–35; and "Rhetoric against Age of Consent: Resisting Colonial Reason and Death of a Child Wife," *Economic and Political Weekly* 28, no. 36 (4 Sept. 1993): 1869–78.
16. The contribution of the Subaltern Studies series on Indian history has been highlighting this domain of colonial Indian history; see R. Guha, "On Some Aspects of the Historiography of Colonial India," in *Subaltern Studies 1: Writings on South Asian History*, ed. R. Guha (Delhi: Oxford University Press, 1982), 1–8. Also see Guha's review of B. Anderson's *Imagined Community*, "Nationalism Reduced to 'Official Nationalism,' " *Asian Studies Association of Australia* 9, no. 1 (July 1985): 103–8.
17. Mrinalini Sinha, "The Age of Consent Act: The Ideal of Masculinity and Colonial Ideology in Late Nineteenth Century Bengal," in *Shaping Bengali Worlds: Public and Private*, ed. Tony Stewart (East Lansing, MI: Asian Studies Center, 1989), 99–111.
18. See Deborah Gorham, "The 'Maiden Tribute of Modern Babylon' Reexamined: Child Prostitution and the Idea of Childhood in Late Victorian England," *Victorian Studies* 21, no. 3 (spring 1978): 353–79. For the Consent Act in Britain, see also Michael Pearson, *The Age of Consent: Victorian Prostitution and Its Enemies* (London: Newton, Abbot, Dawia and Charles, 1972); and Judith Walkowitz, *City of Dreadful Delight: Narratives of Sexual Danger in Late Victorian London* (Chicago: University of Chicago Press, 1992), chs. 3–4.
19. See Charles Heimsath, "The Origin and Enactment of the Indian Age of Consent Bill, 1891," *Journal of Asian Studies* 21, no. 4 (Aug. 1962): 491–504; Amiya Sen, "Hindu Revivalism in Action — the Age of Consent Bill Agitation in Bengal," *Indian Historical Review* 7, nos. 1–2 (July 1980–Jan. 1981): 160–84; Dagmar Engels, "The Age of Consent Act: Colonial Ideology in Bengal," *South Asia Research* 13, no. 2 (Nov. 1983): 107–32; Meera Kosambi, "Girl

Brides and Socio-Legal Change: Age of Consent Bill (1891) Controversy," *Economic and Political Weekly* 26, nos. 31–32 (3–10 Aug. 1991): 1857–68; and Sarkar, "Rhetoric against Age of Consent."

20. See Padma Anagol-McGinn, "The Age of Consent Act (1891) Reconsidered: Women's Perspectives and Participation in Child Marriage Controversy in India," *South Asia Research* 12, no. 2 (Nov. 1992): 100–18.

21. *The Times* (London) 13 Sept. 1890, 8. Some famous defenders of the institution of child marriage in India included Prof. Max Mueller; Sir George Birdwood; and Frederic Pincott, whose article on the "Hindu Marriage Agitation" in the *National Review* became one of the most oft-cited by Indian opponents of the Bill.

22. *St. James Gazette* (London) 20 Jan. 1891, 4; and 2 March 1891, 4. I am grateful to Prof. Judith Walkowitz for first pointing out to me the connection between the *St. James Gazette*'s stand on the British and Indian Consent Acts.

23. Cited in Sinha, "The Age of Consent Act," 104.

24. Sumanta Banerjee, "Marginalization of Women's Popular Culture in Nineteenth Century Bengal," in *Recasting Women*, 127–79; and *The Parlour and the Streets: Elite and Popular Culture in Nineteenth Century Calcutta* (Calcutta: Seagull Books, 1989).

25. Quoted in Sinha, "The Age of Consent Act," 101.

26. Ibid.

27. Ibid., 104.

28. See the tract by the pro-reform R. G. Bhandarkar, *A Note on the Age of Marriage and Its Consequences According to Hindu Religious Law* (Poona, 1891), 1–53; and the reply by the anti-reform B. G. Tilak, *Express Texts of the Shastras against the Age of Consent Bill* (Poona, 1893), 1–13, in *India Office Records Tracts*, vol. 711, India Office Library and Records (London). Also see the support for consent on religious grounds in N. G. Chandavarkar, *The British Government and Hindu Religious Customs — a Plea for Consent* (Bombay, 1891), Tract no. 10; and Ram Nath Tarkaratna and Nilmani Mukherjee (on behalf of the Calcutta Committee in support of the Bill), *The "Garbhadhan Vyavastha"; Opinions on the Question in Hindu Religion Arising Out of Consent*, Tract no. 12, in *Tracts on Indian Marriage Customs 1887–1891*, British Museum Library (London).

29. See T. N. Mukharji, *The Sisters of Phulmani or the Child Wives of India* (Calcutta, 1890).

30. For the Maharanee Surnomoyee's opposition to the Bill, see *Statesman* (Calcutta), 24 Jan. 1891, 4.

31. See Sinha, "The Age of Consent Act," 101–2.

32. For the Calcutta Committee, see *Reis and Reyyet* (Calcutta), 28 March 1891, 152; and *Indian Mirror* (Calcutta) 20 Feb. 1891, 2.

33. For a fuller discussion of the marital rape clause, see Mrinalini Sinha, *Colonial Masculinity: The "Manly Englishman" and the "Effeminate Bengali," 1883–1891* (Manchester, U.K.: Manchester University Press, forthcoming), chapter 4.

34. According to the law in England, "the husband cannot be guilty of rape committed by himself upon his lawful wife, for by their mutual matrimonial contract the wife hath given up herself in this kind unto her husband." Although the legal age of marriage in Britain was twelve, the Criminal Amendment Act of 1885 had made only "unlawful carnal intercourse" with a woman below thirteen criminally liable. See, Sinha, "The Age of Consent Act," 103.
35. Letter from Ramottam Ghosh, *Statesman*, 17 Jan. 1891, 1.
36. *Bengalee* (Calcutta), 14 March 1891, 125.
37. See Frank Mort, *Dangerous Sexualities: Medico-Moral Politics in England since 1830* (London: Routledge and Kegan Paul, 1987), 101–50; Walkowitz, *City of Dreadful Delight*.
38. Engels, "The Age of Consent Act."
39. The concept is from Nancy E. Cott, "Passionlessness: An Interpretation of Victorian Sexual Ideology 1790–1850," *Signs* 4 (1978).
40. Quoted in Sinha, "The Age of Consent," 102.
41. *Pioneer* (Allahabad), 26 March 1891, 396.
42. Cited in *Pioneer*, 19 March 1891, 359.
43. *The Times*, 13 Sept. 1890, 8.
44. Charles Heimsath, *Indian Nationalism and Social Reform* (Princeton, NJ: Princeton University Press, 1964).
45. For a history of child marriage reform, see Geraldine Forbes, "Women and Modernity: The Issue of Child Marriage in India," *Women's Studies International Quarterly* 2 (1979): 407–19.
46. Kumkum Sangari and Sudesh Vaid make a distinction between the "modernizing" of gender relations in the social reform and the nationalist movements and the "democratizing" of gender relations in peasant movements; see the introduction to *Recasting Women*.
47. Katherine Mayo, *Mother India* (New York: Harcourt Brace and Company, 1927).
48. For a detailed examination of Mayo's role in the propaganda for the British, see Manoranjan Jha, *Katherine Mayo and India* (New Delhi: People's Publishing House, 1971).
49. See Aparna Basu and Bharati Ray, *Women's Struggle: A History of the All India Women's Conference 1927–1990* (New Delhi: Manohar, 1990).
50. Nationalist scholars dismiss Mayo's contribution to the child marriage reform, see R. K. Sharma, *Nationalism, Social Reform and Indian Women* (Patna: Janaki Prakashan, 1981), 198–212. Others have given it too much importance; William W. Emilsen, for example, has tried to resurrect Mayo's reputation by highlighting her contribution to the cause of social reform (ignoring her imperialist objectives as well as the contribution of Indian feminists); see his "Gandhi and Mayo's 'Mother India,' " *South Asia* 10, no. 1 (1987): 69–82. The radical feminist scholar Mary Dayly had earlier offered a similar defense of Mayo in *Gyn/Ecology* (Boston: Beacon Press, 1979), 119. For a critical reading of the Mayo controversy from the perspective of the "woman ques-

tion" in India, see Mrinalini Sinha, "Reading 'Mother India': Empire, Nation, and the Female Voice," *Journal of Women's History* 6, no. 2 (summer 1994): 6–44; and "Gender in the Critiques of Colonialism and Nationalism: Locating the 'Indian Woman,' " in *Feminists ReVision History*, ed. A. L. Shapiro (New Brunswick, NJ: Rutgers University Press 1994), 246–75.

51. Mayo, *Mother India*, 122.
52. (Ludhiana: The Times of India Corp. Ltd., 1929).
53. (Dehradun: Gurukula Press, 1928), cited in Sinha, "Reading 'Mother India,' " 14.
54. World Citizen [S. G. Warty], *Sister India: A Critical Examination of and Reasoned Reply to Miss Katherine Mayo's* Mother India (Bombay: Sister India Office, 1928), quoted in Sinha, "Reading 'Mother India,' " 14–15. For a discussion of a nationalist reversal of the sexual degeneracy of Mayo's *Mother India* in the different context of the Hindi film of the 1950s by that name, see Rosie Thomas, "Sanctity and Scandal: The Mythologization of Mother India," *Quarterly Review of Film and Video* 11 (1989): 11–30.
55. Dipesh Chakraborty, "Postcoloniality and the Artifice of History: Who Speaks for 'Indian' Pasts?" *Representations* 37 (winter 1992).
56. Gandhi's anti-modern views are best expressed in his pamphlet *Hind Swaraj or Indian Home Rule* (Ahmedabad: Navajivan Trust, 1938). For a useful discussion of the implications of Gandhi's views, see Partha Chatterjee, "Gandhi and the Critique of Civil Society," in *Subaltern Studies 3: Writings on South Asian History*, ed. R. Guha (Delhi: Oxford University Press, 1984), 153–95.
57. For Gandhi's views on *Mother India*, see Emilsen, "Gandhi and Mayo's 'Mother India.' "
58. Madhu Kishwar, "Gandhi on Women," *Economic and Political Weekly* 20, no. 40 (5 Oct. 1985): 1691–1701 and no. 41 (12 Oct. 1985): 1753–57; Sujata Patel, "Construction and Reconstruction of Women in Gandhi," *Economic and Political Weekly* (20 Feb. 1988): 377–87; and Ketu Katrak, "Indian Nationalism, Gandhian 'Satyagraha,' and Representations of Female Sexuality," in *Nationalisms and Sexualities*, 395–406.
59. Katrak, "Indian Nationalism."
60. Nair, "Law, Modernity and Patriarchy."
61. Geraldine Forbes, "The Politics of Respectability: Indian Women and the Indian National Congress," in *The Indian National Congress: Centenary Hindsights*, ed. D. A. Low (Delhi: Oxford University Press, 1988).
62. Quoted in Sinha, "Reading 'Mother India,' " 21–22.
63. Rameshwari Nehru, *Gandhi Is My Star: Speeches and Writings of Smt. Rameshwari Nehru* (Patna: Pulakbandhan, 1950), 2.
64. Hennessy, *Materialist Feminism*, 87–91.
65. See Slavoj Zizek, *For They Know Not What They Do: Enjoyment as a Political Factor* (London: Verso, 1991), esp. 20: " 'nation' designates at one and the same time the instance by means of reference to which traditional 'organic' links are dissolved and the 'remainder of the pre-modern in modernity.' . . . It is precisely the new 'suture' effected by the Nation which renders possible

the 'desuturing,' the disengagement from traditional organic ties. 'Nation' is a pre-modern leftover which functions as an inner condition of modernity itself, as an inherent impetus of its progress." Also P. Chatterjee, "A Response to Taylor's 'Modes of Civil Society.' "

66. For a fuller development of this contradiction, see P. Chatterjee, "A Response to Taylor's 'Modes of Civil Society.' "

67. This problem has been addressed by the authors of *Less than Gay*. The first national gay and lesbian conference in India was held in December 1993; see Lawrence Cohen, "Reclaiming Our Heritage: India's First Seminar on Alternative Sexualities," *Trikone* 9, no. 2 (April 1994): 1–2.

68. Current scholarship does provide sufficient evidence to support such a view, see Michael J. Sweet and Leonard Zwilling, "The First Medicalization: The Taxonomy and Etiology of Queerness in Classical Indian Medicine," *Journal of the History of Sexuality* 3, no. 4 (1993): 590–607; and Shivananda Khan, "Yili Thadani: Sexuality and Gender in Ancient India," *Shakti Khabar* 15 (Aug.–Sept. 1991): 2. For transgender identities, see Serena Nanda, *Neither Man nor Woman: The Hijras of India* (Belmont, CA: Wadsworth, 1990).

69. Gail Omvedt, "India: Rural Women Take the Lead," *Committee on South Asian Women Bulletin* 6, nos. 3–4 (1988): 1–5.

70. Cited in Gail Omvedt, "The Farmer's Movement in Maharashtra," in *A Space Within the Struggle: Women's Participation in People's Movements*, ed. Ilina Sen (New Delhi: Kali for Women, 1990), 238–39.

THREE

Re-Shooting World War II: Women, Narrative Authority, and Hollywood Cinema

Karen Schneider

Despite, or perhaps because of, American culture's compulsive efforts to exorcise its collective angst regarding the Vietnam War, World War II has once again become a compelling site for representation and negotiation of America's political and ideological concerns. Indeed, a post-Vietnam, "post-feminist" resurgence of World War II films invites scrutiny of the various ways in which the "Good War" is being appropriated, revised, and recuperated for complex and often paradoxical ideological manipulation.[1] For, like their Vietnam counterparts, World War II films are "looking backward [in order to] serve contemporary political ideological agendas."[2] To varying degrees, these films undoubtedly signal the continued mythologization of the war — a nostalgic revival of an era of (apparent) national unity and ideological stability. Indeed, some, like *Memphis Belle* (1990), seem nothing more than intentionally amnesic reenactments of an idealized past. Other recent World War II films, however, ostensibly have revisionist, and specifically feminist, agendas.

In particular, I would like to examine three pictures that not only lay claim to women's cinematic narrative authority, but also attempt to redefine or to interrogate woman's "place" in war and, less directly, in classical Hollywood cinema. *Women of Valor* (1986), *Shining Through* (1992), and *For the Boys* (1992), all depict women's self-consciously rebellious confrontations with the symbolic order and its correlative master narratives. More specifically, these films are concerned with the subject status of women in heterosexual romance as it intersects with militarism and war, perhaps the quintessential "form of masculine romance."[3] In fact, albeit from widely divergent "feminist" positions, all three protest the crude and cruel logic of the gendered dichotomy that in time of war relegates women to weeping and men to mayhem. Finally, all three pictures have female first-person narrators, women who apparently testify to their positions as speaking subjects both within and in opposition to phallic discourse. It would seem, then, that these re-presentations of World War II explicitly challenge both the forms of gendered subjectivity conventionally codified by war and the axiom that in classical Hollywood cinema the female subject "has been excluded from positions of discursive authority."[4]

I would argue, however, that all three films demonstrate that contemporary culture's inevitable representations of women's symbolic and material plight has prompted a reactionary (though not necessarily conscious) recontainment of popular culture's accommodation of "feminism"; it is an accommodation that, as represented in these films, is rendered paradoxical in the extreme. As we shall see, this recontainment is accomplished by various means, including conventional treatment of the female voice-over (or, more accurately, voice-off) and other classical cinematic devices. The most inclusive means by which these films defuse the discursive challenge, however, is alignment of the "feminist" discourses with seductive forms of institutionalized phallic authority — in particular, the military and the patriarchal family.

Women of Valor turns to World War II to address a currently controversial topic on which Vietnam films have remained stubbornly silent: American women in combat situations.[5] Of the three films discussed here, this one is unique because it is a made-for-television movie and a remake of *So Proudly We Hail* (1943), a fictionalized account of the experience of Army nurses interned by the Japanese on Bataan. The recent film's revision clearly constitutes a liberal feminist statement that women are quite capable of serving their country with distinction and should be duly recognized as the equals of their male comrades in arms. By locating its argument in World War II, however, *Women of Valor* tactfully deflects the timely, increasingly imminent issue of the reassessment of women's suitability for combat. Moreover, (and in keeping with the original) it decidedly dispels any interrogation of female complicity with militarism as an institutionalized form of patriarchalism that (re)generates women's status as objectified Other. Quite the contrary, the film celebrates the pre-Vietnam virtue of patriotic sacrifice and claims female participation in militarism as an appropriate and laudatory means of achieving a "post-feminist" shift toward gender equality.

The two movies' very different narrative frames, like their titles, signal a definitive ideological shift toward redefining female subjectivity. As *So Proudly* opens, the lead character (Lieutenant Davidson, or Davie), in a grief-induced catatonia, is literally speechless.[6] A man, a military doctor, organizes Davie's story, which finally ends with her decision to return to civilian life in keeping with the wishes of her dead husband, whose voice-over from the beyond revives her and motivates her tale. In sharp contrast, *Women of Valor* opens and closes with a military commission hearing, at which Col. Margaret Jessup is testifying to the courage of military women who are still denied medals explicitly designated for valor in combat. Jessup, a career officer, narrates her own story, a point on which her intermittent voice-off insists.

Jessup's tale begins with a wedding shower on the eve of Pearl Harbor — seemingly, a conventional indication that peace and "normal" romantic relations are about to be violently, but temporarily, disrupted. However, in contrast to the 1943 rendition, in which the women are and remain fundamentally defined by their place in the heterosexual romance, in the revised version women become subjects in their own right. As Koppes and Black point out in *Hollywood Goes to War* (1990), *So Proudly*'s "seriousness was severely undercut by its lapses into stereotypical conventions of a woman's place. . . . What motivates them [the nurses] is not their work — or even the war — but men."[7] In *Women of Valor*, the men's roles are severely curtailed. Marriage, ultimately, represents but one choice among several that are available to the characters. Indeed, in most cases, survival and self-determination are contingent on eschewing familiar but debilitating identities and the gender-encoded representations that guarantee them.

At first two of the nurses are identified as being strongly attached to markers of femininity as the embodiment of male desire, a negligee and lipstick. The two eventually abandon these items and the debilitation they effect. Helen, the newlywed who prizes the negligee, recovers from a rape and her husband's death, eventually escaping with her baby. She thus carries the film's conventional "women's" issues, but she contrasts sharply with the character in *So Proudly* whose fiance dies. Preferring death to rape and life without her man, the original character commits sacrificial suicide with a grenade hidden in her bosom. Helen chooses self-rescue over self-immolation. Moreover, she gives birth to a *girl*; notably, and unlike typical war-era narratives, this baby is not a replacement for her husband, but a renewal of herself.[8] The other male-identified character, Gail, at first complies so completely with her own subjugation that she will not be seen without makeup and, in prison, will not eat. She too finally rejects her oppressed status, defiantly withstanding a beating rather than give up the camp radio. Afterward, Jessup confirms the worth of Gail's new self-assertion, telling her, "You look great without makeup." By contrast, in *So Proudly* we see the rescued women relearning to walk in high heels, that is, carefully reconstructing their femininity. This scene was omitted from the remake; instead we see Colonel Jessup challenging military policy in full uniform.

Another captive, not a nurse, is so thoroughly androgynous that she is mistaken for a boy. Known only by her last name, Nolan is tough enough to disabuse other women of their illusions of imminent rescue, but compassionate enough to lie to a wounded soldier about the same thing. Either directly or through clever manipulation, she kills several Japanese before she is shot. Nolan represents yet another twist on the *So Proudly* character who kills several Japanese with the grenade in her blouse. Significantly, however, Nolan does not sacrifice herself and she is not eroticized. Rather, she is always the resistance fighter, never the victim; she even manages to shoot the sadistic jailer with his own gun. These portrayals, revisions of the original script, reflect some of the additional, more flexible modes of female subjectivity that have become increasingly visible, largely due to the Woman's Movement.

As the Allies converge on the prison camp, the commander, whose respect Jessup has earned, gives her his family's Samurai sword. Taken aback, Jessup exclaims, "But I'm a woman." "And a Samurai, like my mother," he responds. Thus honored even by the enemy, the young Lieutenant Jessup signals the American military's wrong-headed refusal to acknowledge women's capacity to be warriors. Implicitly criticizing them for refusing to honor women as they do men, the older Colonel Jessup reminds them of their failure to acknowledge the new realities of American militarism. As the many uniformed women at the hearing attest, women have become a crucial, integral part of the Armed Forces. Unlike Lieutenant Davie, Colonel Jessup will not be silenced and she will not go away. Unlike the women in *So Proudly We Hail*, whose "source of moral and emotional sustenance is ultimately male," the *Women of Valor* not only draw on the strength and durability in themselves, but are models of self-determination and *restraint* for the male characters.[9] At one point, Jessup must admonish the camp commander not to be ruled by his emotions.[10] When Jessup's husband is dying, she risks all to stay with him, but (again unlike Davie and the nurse who kills herself) she is not disabled by his death. She is, in fact, *freed* to pursue her career.

Whereas many women like Margaret Jessup undoubtedly served with distinction during World War II, it is significant that the vehicle for the narrator's very contemporary plea for equality is the war Americans feel good about, rather than the one in which women's military service, more timely and to the point, has been minimized. The post-Vietnam military's need to reestablish its virility and its authority during the Reagan years made a fifty-year-old war the more politic choice. Although *Women of Valor* provides demonstrable proof of women's courage and endurance, it also strongly appeals to patriotic feeling. At the same time, "looking backward [in order] to serve [a] contemporary political and ideological agenda," it tactfully avoids invoking a negative emotional response to the unresolved gender dislocations of its time.[11]

Choosing to recast an old story rather than script a new one, to locate this plea for women's "equality" in World War II, exacts a substantial price. *Women of Valor* was televised the same year that *Platoon* was released, a Vietnam film that Susan Jeffords has argued is centrally about "reproducing" masculinity via the warrior role, on the one hand, and about violently controlling women, "whose entrance into combat and the masculine collective demands death and silence," on the other.[12] To be sure, *Women of Valor* not only deconstructs conventional notions of femininity, it posits women's "entrance into combat" as a given, thus challenging the male/female, strong/weak dichotomy that structures gender and militarism alike. Nevertheless, the film conspicuously softens women's penetration (as it were) of the "masculine collective" by misrepresenting, by contemporary standards, such women as reassuringly contained, not by any inherent lack of stamina or courage, but by confinement to the traditionally feminine activity of nursing — a care-taking, as opposed to a deadly, endeavor. Despite women's incursion into militarism, then, in this most fundamental sense they remain the feminized, marginalized Other. The only character who is not a military nurse, the androgynous Nolan, is also the only woman who *kills* and, significantly, *is killed.* In this way, the film sets limits on just how much blurring of gender distinctions will be tolerated. Men and women remain different but equal, the film implies, thus positing an essentialist form of feminism despite itself, and minimizing the radical destabilization of gendered interests that women's entrance into combat potentially represents.[13] At the same time, it represents the militarization of women as an unproblematic route to "equality."

As in *Women of Valor*, the female narrator of *Shining Through* (1992) is "testifying" — in this case as part of the "Women in the War" segment of a BBC series on Hitler's Germany. Although this film is not itself a remake, a significant portion of its plot concerns the narrator/protagonist's attempt to revise class and gender master narratives and to adapt to her own ends the World War II spy thrillers that have captured her imagination. The film calls particular attention to an anti-Nazi melodrama entitled *The Mortal Storm* (1940), whose climactic escape sequence we view through Linda's eyes. In her BBC interview, Linda recounts how, inspired and educated by movies, she became a spy, infiltrated Nazi Germany, obtained plans for Peenemünde, killed a German double agent, and was finally rescued by Ed Leland, her employer and lover.

Shining Through emphatically calls attention to Linda's subjugated status as both woman and Jew by foregrounding her active resistance to it. Her partial success reflects both the possibility and the limitation of contestation from within the symbolic order that constitutes that status. Linda gets her job as secretary/translator for Ed Leland (an undercover OSS agent) because she "knows another language," a "secret language" — German. As her father's language *and* that of the Nazi fatherland, German signifies both her immersion in a patriarchal symbolic order and the related but more immediate threat to her life as a Jew. Paradoxically, however, the language that oppresses is also her passport to self-determination. Linda's linguistic situation is, then, paradigmatic of women's more or less vexed relation to language (and cinema) in general. Her knowledge of German enables her to ferret out counterspies, and her ear for code uncovers Ed's secret identity. In fact, her linguistic expertise makes her "a better spy" than Ed Leland, who "has a tin ear for languages."

Linda is similarly and equally skilled at deciphering and manipulating the heavily encoded sex-gender system as well, at times interpolating it against itself. During her interview, she declines to stand up and turn around for what she assumes is a physical inspection. Although assured it is merely a test of her powers of observation, she obviates this conflation of objectifying male gaze and assessment of her "skills." Defiantly maintaining eye contact, she calls attention to objects in the room that signify the class and gender differences ("pictures of sailboats and polo ponies, fancy books and diplomas") that presumably guarantee Ed's power, privilege, and authority.[14] I see through your little game, with its thicket of signs, she seems to say, and I will not be daunted. The final object of her dis-ordering gaze is "a couple of guys from Harvard who are surprised that a girl who needs a job won't be treated like a slave." Linda is able to undermine both the fascist and the patriarchal enterprise because she is wise to and adept at manipulating the sign systems that structure human relations.

As Linda's voice-off admits, however, "it was only a matter of time" until she and Ed become lovers — until, that is, the wartime romance plot threatens to subvert her self-conscious self-determinism. Nonetheless, for the bulk of the film, whenever Linda's life seems doomed to conform to romantic conventions, she succeeds in defying them. For example, flying off to war, Ed *does* initially abandon Linda, who then helplessly joins the "anonymous" ranks of homefront women waiting fearfully for their men's return. The secrecy that attends Ed's role as spy gives him complete control. When sometime later they coincidentally turn up at the same nightclub, she understands that he has no intention of resuming their romance. Ed remains oblivious of Linda until she compels his attention by the force of her relentless gaze (emphasized by a series of point-of-view and reverse shots). Realizing she had fallen into a subordinate role, an arrangement Ed apparently would prefer, Linda confronts him and denies his right to define her or their relationship unilaterally. Her subjectivity here is once again reinforced by her possession of "the power of the look," which, atypically in Hollywood film, in Linda's case goes unpunished.[15] As Byars has pointed out, "control of the gaze" is crucial, for it seems to confirm "control of the narrative."[16]

This scene ends abruptly with a disorienting cut to a seemingly unrelated scene, in which several men sit around a conference table discussing a murdered spy's failure to obtain plans for Germany's rocket production. For the time being, resolution of Linda and Ed's confrontation is suspended. As the men discuss their options, Linda appears carrying a tray of coffee things. This leads one to conclude that her role is now exactly that which Ed proposed, that of a "good secretary," which is perhaps the price she paid for being "allowed" to accompany him. But at once and to good effect she belies this assumption by sitting at the table, forcefully criticizing their plan, and logically explaining why *she* should be the new spy. This jarring deviation from expectations encourages viewers to acknowledge the unconscious ease with which one closes off meaning by filling in gaps with predetermined significance derived from already familiar stories. The unpunished power of Linda's "look," the omission of Ed's interiority, and the self-conscious deviation from the conventions of romance insistently identify Linda — her desire, her consciousness, her self-definition — as the Subject of the narrative.

Despite Ed's insistence that she is "not suited" for the demanding task at hand, Linda once again determines the course of action, ironically demonstrating her suitability by redefining domestic skills (cooking) as a resource for espionage. Claiming that "it's more my war than yours," *Linda* now privileges self-determination over romance: "This is not about you and me," she informs Ed. "I want to do something important with my life." And that something has nothing to do with her relation to a man or duty to her country; it has everything to do with subverting patterns of dominance while giving others (her Jewish relatives hiding in Berlin) hope that they may do the same.

Typically, on several other occasions, Linda refuses to follow the script outlined by Ed and the Office of Strategic Services (OSS). In fact, she obtains the information she seeks *only because* she acts independently, ignoring any authority except her own moral authority, which drives the plot — until, that is, a gunshot wound renders her helpless. Betrayed by a woman aligned with the Nazis, a German counterspy with "no use for Jews," Linda must ultimately be rescued by a man. At this point, by necessity, she loses control of the narrative, but this scripted helplessness has profound implications. Literally unconscious for almost all the remaining action, Linda becomes a damsel in distress, thus enabling Ed, whose role has been relatively "weak," to metamorphose into a spectacular war hero. He carries Linda across enemy lines, guns blazing, in the film's only combat scene. While Linda has been felled by her wound, Ed superhumanly stays on his feet to complete the rescue despite two gunshot wounds. This incredible conclusion suggests that Linda's claim, "I may be a better spy than you are," though true, is utterly unacceptable.

It also brings to mind Susan Jeffords's argument that "combat sequences are produced by and relieve moments of crisis in the construction of the masculine subject."[17] Up to this point, the whole picture represents such a crisis. In general, this combat sequence is produced by Ed's failure to control Linda's behavior, by her assumption of agency, and by her refusal to define herself as a lack, as Other. More specifically, the scene is motivated by his inability to speak German. Thus lacking authority, linguistic and otherwise, Ed proves his manly worth by demonstrating extraordinary physical prowess. Linda, on the other hand, falls silent and is hopelessly disabled. Thus, Ed finally does not have to be as skilled at interpreting the symbolic order as Linda because, however paradoxically, that order seems to have indelibly written masculine (phallic) primacy into the script.

Significantly, this conclusion closely resembles the sequence the film samples from *The Mortal Storm* (1940), the anti-Nazi thriller to which Linda overtly compares her own experience. Linda's use of popular film, one of *Shining Through*'s more interesting features, underscores reception's crucial role in the meaning-making process. Not only do World War II movies inspire Linda to act, they have educated her in the art of reading and manipulating sign systems — the art of survival — as she repeatedly attests. And, although she is unable to help her German-Jewish family, she otherwise realizes her dream to accomplish something vital, to be self-defined, a resistance fighter. From watching cinematic representations of characters who are not what they appear to be, she has learned, literally and figuratively, to recognize secret codes, to see through false identities, to avoid detection by constructing misleading clues, and to secrete vital information. Equally important is what Linda has seemingly *not* learned: to accept a fixed gendered identity.

Linda's insistence on the central role of movie-viewing in her success renders *Shining Through* a metafictional comment on popular film's relation to social formations, which remains slippery at best. In particular, the film raises questions about female spectators' ability to escape the logic of masculine desire (which may be subtle indeed) by assuming, through fantasy, appealing "identificatory positions" regardless of their gender associations, thus "transform[ing]" the text "at the level of reception."[18] The pleasure and utility Linda derives from viewing wartime thrillers seemingly do not arise, in the main, from masochistically identifying against herself, as some film theorists have argued female spectators must.[19] Her position as spectator is more ambiguous than that, more flexible and more tenuous. Janice Radway, John Fiske, and other critics of popular culture have demonstrated that women can and often do read texts against the phallocentric grain, extracting meanings that support female agency and resistance.[20] When Linda informs Ed that she knows he's a spy and then proceeds to unravel his fabrications, he attempts to discredit her insight by telling her, "You've seen too many movies." From his perspective, he is right, because that is precisely what enables her to unmask him and to redefine herself.

Yet, at the crucial moment, Linda's self-assertive appropriation of Hollywood narrative gives way to its passive reproduction. In the end, the script requires that defiance doubly gives over to compliance, self-conscious control to unconscious inevitability. When Linda meets Ed, he reminds her of Jimmy Stewart, the anti-fascist hero of *The Mortal Storm* who saves the fatally wounded Margaret Sullavan from the Nazis by carrying her over the German border (on skis!). Thus, in her role as spectator, Linda identifies with both the hero and the "love interest" when her story is set in motion. She thus challenges the ontological divide that usually constitutes these two roles as essentially different. Moreover, when forced to choose between them, she privileges the more active and linguistically potent position. Ultimately, however, the film's resolution almost exactly replicates the conventionally gender-encoded model it had up to that point refashioned.[21] *Shining Through* goes to some lengths to suggest not only that women can be speaking subjects in classical cinema, but that fictional representations can empower real women. Less emphatically, it at the same time suggests that women's ability to disregard or to disrupt the symbolic order is ultimately futile and perhaps illusory. Thus, in this context the notions of self-determinacy and discursive authority for women seem but a placating fiction, fully recuperated for the "normalization" of structures of gender, cinema, and war.

The wartime sequences conclude like a chivalric romance or a fairy tale, which in fact carries over into the narrative frame's closure and concretizes Linda's re-feminized position. We learn that, indeed, Linda and Ed married and lived happily ever after, having produced two male heirs. As Linda's interview concludes, she seems to have maintained narrative control throughout. Her ability to revise "master narratives" is here again belied, however, by the new knowledge that the structure of her life since the war, here figured by the classical family tableau, has fundamentally conformed to the sexual order that mandated her rescue.[22] Indeed, Linda's confrontation with the male-identified enemy (the Nazi counterspy), her consequent wounding and lapse into *unconsciousness*, her rescue/journey across the border, and her eventual marriage represent yet another manifestation of "Freud's story of femininity," here described by Teresa de Lauretis: "After an 'uneven battle with penis envy,' the female child remains forever scarred by a narcissistic wound, forever bleeding. . . . Bereft of weapon or magical gift . . . her transformation into woman will take place; but only if she successfully negotiates the crossing . . . into passivity. If she survives, her reward is motherhood."[23] "Normal" gendered social formations, especially the patriarchal (Oedipal) family, in jeopardy during World War II have been restored; the threat has been contained in every dimension.[24] Linda's wartime insurgency may be viewed as an aberration, a temporary dis-order. Moreover, the film's closing shot suggests that Linda's war story is her life story in miniature: despite her exceptional and self-conscious challenge to the given order, Linda must contend with psychosexual, social, and narrative mechanisms over which, finally, she has only local and temporary influence.

Thus, on the one hand, in the matters of spectatorship, narrative control, and subjectivity, *Shining Through* explicitly asserts that women can defy the notion that classic Hollywood film allows them no position that is not innately inimical. In depicting the resolve, resourcefulness, and heroism of a Jewish woman who resists subjugation by patriarchy and fascism alike, the film's ostensibly feminist agenda is nevertheless undermined by its reversion to the ideological order it purports to critique, as represented by the filmic narrative it ultimately failed to revise. On the one hand, the narrator repeatedly breaks free of the trajectory of both conventional femininity and wartime romance by self-consciously refusing to comply with their conventions. In crucial ways, then, she is more a "master" of the symbolic order than is her male lover/employer. On the other hand, Linda Voss's integrity as a self-determining agent and narrative escape artist is obviated by the film's climactic final action sequence and contained by closure of its narrative frame. Both of these plot choices seem to represent surrender to the symbolic orders — narrative and psychosexual — that Voss's voice-off narration otherwise conspicuously repudiates. The slippage between woman as Subject, master of sign systems, and woman as feckless Object of representation may be typical of contemporary efforts to impose feminist consciousness into the indelibly mythologized past.

Of the three films under discussion, *For the Boys* most clearly illuminates the ongoing cultural and theoretical battle to define the "truth" about psychosexual identity, social formations, the symbolic order, and war. The fact that Dixie Leonard's story spans three wars, from World War II to Vietnam and beyond, enables it to underscore the ideological relevance of the Vietnam War for contemporary World War II films. Like the other two, this film lays claim to a woman's point of view and narrative authority. Once again, the war stories are told in flashback, punctuated and framed by the present, which underscores the films' shared "concern with the present under cover of the past."[25] As a showcase of ideology-in-conflict, *For the Boys* makes explicit the foundations of the gender struggle – the formation of gendered subjectivity – and its mutually sustaining relation to war, a relationship the other films demonstrate but repress.

Specifically, *For the Boys* depicts one woman's struggle against perpetuation of the Law of the Father, and its chicken-and-egg cultural masculinism, within the seemingly ineluctable drama of Freudian family romance. The battle for meaning and value comes down to a war between the sexes for the heart and mind of the heir apparent, a son. The resolution of his Oedipal crisis, or forging of his psychosexual identity as against "woman," posits a web of causal connections among mastery of the Symbolic Order, the sexual objectification of women, and the making of war.[26] Although this "woman's film" censures and mourns the tragic consequences of this arrangement, it finally, if reluctantly, participates in the outcome's apparent inevitability. In this way, it continues the disabling tradition of the "woman's film" of an earlier era, "activat[ing] a pathos which embraces and celebrates loss, reconciling the spectator to the terms of the given social order."[27] In its contemporary form, as if to voice the frustration of women constrained by the givens of phallocentric theories (in particular, psychoanalysis), *For the Boys* articulates its woman's story from within a set of assumptions that renders her objections beside the point. As if untenably squeezed by the contradictory demands of feminist insight and a compulsion to "heal the wounds" of the Vietnam era, this Allgirl Production ironically succumbs to its own Catch-22.

The embattled relationship between "girl singer" Dixie Leonard, a working mom, and Eddie Sparks, a Bob Hope-like entertainer, paradigmatically figures the war between the sexes (and its popular representation) from the start. Initially eager to please, Dixie turns wary and defiant when Eddie, an on-stage charmer, back stage becomes a "two-bit Napoleon" and a "Führer," who is jealous of her success with "his boys" (troops) and enraged by her ribald humor. Eddie prefers women to be silent, long-suffering absences — like his wife — or infantilized, adoring sexual commodities — like his girlfriend, whose on-stage cheerleading antics and mock innocence only thinly disguise her spectacular sexual objectification. Dixie's savvy sexuality and self-possession threaten Eddie's sexual politics and world view. His arrogance and disregard for people's feelings offend her sense of human decency. Nevertheless, (in an unintentionally ironic meta-comment) they are manipulated into pairing up by a *script writer*, who appreciates their popular appeal. Their ongoing conflict, the center of their act, becomes a cultural "industry." The jocular battles Dixie and Eddie "perform" in public sublimate their private, gender-based animosity, rendering it a familiar and ostensibly harmless joke. The audience loves it. Thus, their relationship embodies popular entertainment's ability to manufacture "reality" on the one hand and to erase all signs of its construction on the other, and simultaneously to represent conflict and defuse it.

The dueling duo is crucially transformed when, after Dixie's husband is killed in the war, Eddie becomes surrogate father to her son Danny. At the funeral, Eddie steps up to join mother and son at the coffin, as if to fill an untenable void, and lays physical and verbal claim to Danny. From the moment Danny responds to Eddie's commands, while ignoring his mother's, the outcome is foreordained. Dixie will lose her son, who seems instinctively to recognize Eddie's linguistic and familial authority. Eddie neglects his repressed wife and pitifully dolled-up daughters, but lavishes attention on Danny, whom he teaches, through example and advice, that women are nothing but sexual prey or, in the case of Dixie (who repeatedly refuses Eddie's sexual advances), spoilers of real manhood.

An argument over Eddie's influence reveals that there is more at stake here than Danny's affections. Eddie's "man-to-man bullshit" is filling Danny's head with "crap," Dixie complains. "You're gonna kill him," she concludes in a seeming non sequitur. Eddie insists that "the boy needs a father" to teach him "what his thing is for," in short, how to be a man. Scornful of Dixie's feminizing influence, Eddie asks, "Why don't you put a dress on him?" "I would," Dixie retorts, "but you'd probably make a pass at him." The only psychosexual identities available in this exchange, and as modeled by their own relationship, are male aggressor and female quarry, Subject and Other, Phallus and Lack — that is, according to the inexorable Law of the Father, devotedly passed down by Eddie Sparks.

In Danny, Eddie not only has an appropriate heir to male sexual dominion, but someone through whom he can compensate for his own missed opportunity to guarantee masculinity via the classic role of warrior. Encouraged by Eddie, always the paternal looker-on and never the soldier, Danny chooses a military career. Dazzling in his dress uniform, Danny sincerely mouths the patriotic rhetoric that conjoins the patriarchal family and state: "I believe in freedom and honor . . . in the genius of the American system . . . in the wisdom of our founding fathers. I believe in America . . . [and pledge] to defend it as my father did with the ultimate sacrifice. . . . I believe in the importance of family." While Eddie beams, Dixie mourns; she watches helplessly as her fears that Eddie's fathering will "kill" Danny are realized step by step. A veteran of a different kind, she has discerned that sons too often accept their sacrifice on the altar of masculine identity and privilege, forged in the family and rebuilt war after war.

The Vietnam sequences brilliantly reveal the "intimate" foundational relationship between war and psychosexual identity.[28] As Cynthia Fuchs argues in " 'Vietnam and Sexual Violence': The Movie," war as a form of violent sexual aggression became shockingly visible in Vietnam films.[29] In contrast with the "specialty dancer" from World War II, whose body is passed from man to man only in private, the go-go dancer of the Vietnam era is publicly threatened with sexual assault. Her requisite "innocence," signaled by her white dress, is strenuously denied by its minilength and, most emphatically, by a gaping circular cut-out over her midriff. As she dances, half-clad soldiers join her on stage, grabbing and thrusting, until simulated gang rape threatens to become the real thing and the frightened young woman must be rescued. When the Viet Cong attack, the dancer, now abandoned, is killed by an exploding artillery shell. We observe a spray of projectiles penetrate, in slow motion, her arched back; she is thrown into the air, a faceless casualty, with the multitude of bright red holes all too visible against her pristine white costume. The war fatally completes the assault the soldiers had begun. The hapless young woman's costume, which so graphically figures her as sexual Other — a hole inviting penetration — both perfectly represents and seals her fate. In Vietnam, our most overtly gender-encoded war zone, she never stood a chance.

To be sure, Vietnam has disabused Danny of his notions of honor in war, unblemished American virtue, and death as meaningful sacrifice. When Dixie and Eddie bring their USO show "in country," to Eddie's naive "man-to-man bullshit" about "mixin' it up" and "beat[ing] those little bastards," Danny can only respond with hopeless irony: "Yes, sir. As soon as we find 'em." When Danny tells his mother, "He just doesn't get it, does he?" she reminds Danny of his own role in perpetuating "the old lie" scorned by Wilfred Owen. By his own admission, Danny's letters have told Eddie only "what he wanted to hear." When Dixie suggests telling Eddie "the truth," Danny tells her about a "sweet kid" who "collects ears" to sell stateside after the war. "It's a nightmare," Danny concludes. This horror story is meant to capture the truth of Vietnam and war in general: It is senseless, ignoble, and dehumanizing; nobody wins. The obliqueness of Danny's response to Dixie's desire that *Eddie* hear "the truth" suggests that "the horror," like Kurtz's deathbed epiphany, best remains largely unspoken.

Like Marlow's, however, Danny's selective silence, his rationalized lie, is more self-serving than he admits. He does not hesitate to tell his *mother* the story. A woman's knowledge apparently does not signify; the master narrative is out of her hands. Even as he refuses her comforting caress, he admits that he wouldn't leave Vietnam if he could, for he wouldn't abandon his men, to whom, as their commanding officer, *he* has become surrogate father. Besides, it would "break Eddie's heart." Thus, although he realizes that Eddie is tragically deluded, that even while constructing masculinity war destroys men, he must maintain both a safe distance from his mother and fidelity to the "father," a role he has taken on. To do otherwise would be to repudiate the Law of the Father, which would jeopardize his Oedipally forged male subjectivity on the one hand, and his institutionally reinforced male privilege on the other. To tell the "truth" about war is to betray the father(s), which is to betray the son(s). It is in this sense that war is unspeakable.

Of course, Dixie does "speak" it. Again and again as she tells her story, she reveals her understanding of this deadly "reproductive" process and its consequences. The whole point of her story, in fact, is to explain why she refuses to accept the President's medal with Eddie, to whom she hasn't spoken since Danny's death in Vietnam. But her narrative keeps coming back to the same conclusion: Women are essentially helpless against the Freudian psychosexual dynamic. Eddie, she declares, was "invincible. How the boys loved him." "I never had a chance." Throughout, her tale seems to bear this out. Boys "normally" identify with the fathers against the mothers, who represent lack and, as fetishized sexual others, are the objects of both male desire and aggression, of fear and contempt. Not only was Freud right, but so is Lacan — or so the film as a whole implies. For to protect the integrity of the patriarchal Symbolic Order and his position within it, Danny chooses not to speak, and Eddie, not to listen. Moreover, Dixie, whose desire to expose and subvert that Order seemingly impels the narrative until its closure, finally opts to "speak" against herself and thus to undermine her whole endeavor.

Whereas Dixie cannot effectively speak against the established order, Eddie can neither speak opposition nor hear it: "You don't have a sex problem," she tells him, "you have a hearing problem." After twenty-five years of guilt and frustrated, bereft silence, Dixie wants Eddie to own up to their shared responsibility for Danny's death: "We did it. We put a uniform on him. We loved him and put him in the ground." As Berg and Rowe have noted in a discussion of the relationship between the crisis of the American middle-class family and the Vietnam War, "However it has been normalized as part of the western rite of passage to adulthood, Oedipal conflict and its gendered hierarchies of father, son, and mother involve modes of domestic aggression that may play formative roles in forms of more public violence."[30] But Eddie refuses to acknowledge his part in the reproduction of fathering or the family's role in the production of war, still insisting that his service to the troops has been a "sacred honor." For Dixie this "honor" signifies not only failure and loss, but a treacherous collusion between the state and its subjects.

Appropriately, Eddie's acceptance speech echoes Danny's graduation speech of an earlier era: he's proud to "share this honor with all the young Americans who lay down their lives for the greatest country in the world. Normandy, the Philippines, Korea." Eddie's metonymic litany of war falters, however, when he gets to Vietnam. He stumbles over this signifier repeatedly, as if the elusive and contradictory meanings of the war it names fundamentally disrupt the chain of signification. Eddie's words cannot make sense of "Vietnam," not because it represents loss of his "son" (for all wars signify this loss), but because he doesn't speak its language. Indeed, the ideological contradictions disclosed by the Vietnam

War threaten to annul the Law of the Father by admitting a "meaning" that cannot be. The war thus threatens his conceptual framework.

For one tense moment, the process of ideological reproduction and its cultural dissemination is suspended in midenunciation. The award ceremony's star-spangled spectacle threatens to become empty, absurd, and visibly manipulative. The film promises to "[break] the sentence . . . the sequence" and thus, finally, to break the *Law*.[31] But, moved by Eddie's anguish and isolation, by his undeniable love for "their son," Dixie "saves" him and, concomitantly, rescues the ceremony and all that it represents. Torn between "truth" and compassion, she acquiesces to her own complicity in the mermaid and minotaur pact described by Dorothy Dinnerstein, the perversely symbiotic gender arrangement that, Dinnerstein argues, lies at the heart of patriarchy and war.[32] Despite the intervening episode of the Vietnam era, the questions it raised, and the insight it promised, fifty years after World War II, Dixie and Eddie's characteristic banter still exposes and conceals the ideological underpinning of their "act." Dixie half-seriously boasts of having taught Eddie "how to impersonate a human being." Eddie deflects this, putting her in her apparently inescapable place with a familiar rejoinder: "For an old broad, you're still pretty sexy." Neither the script nor the dynamic has changed a jot. Both Eddie and Dixie seem reconciled to this outcome as they do the old softshoe, a "danse macabre" that publicly "heals the wounds" of all the wars by masking the symptoms and ignoring the disease.[33] As they walk off arm in arm, they disappear behind larger-than-life images of a younger Dixie and Eddie, face to face in timeless confrontation. The past, apparently, repeats itself endlessly.

Presumably, *For the Boys* has the best of intentions. Its daughters and sons, mothers and fathers are all victims of a patriarchal order to which war and the sexual objectification of women are fundamental and mutually constituent. Nevertheless, the film's fidelity to two of Hollywood cinema's most salient characteristics totally subverts its antiwar, woman-as-subject sentiment: the spectacularity of its Vietnam combat scene and, more comprehensively, the overtly psychoanalytic logic of its narrative. In "Anti-War Film as Spectacle," Claudia Springer has argued that films cannot rely on combat scenes, however gruesome, to convey an antiwar message, because the spectacle typical of such scenes paradoxically evokes emotional satisfaction and visual pleasure by providing vicarious thrill and heightened sensation.[34] The crucial combat scene in *For the Boys* accomplishes this through the usual filmic techniques, including sound and light effects, music, and, most conspicuously, slow motion. As in the death scene described earlier (in which the grisly object of spectacle is the fetishized, violated female body), Danny's death, choreographed as a macabre ballet, becomes a perversely pleasurable moment of cinematic excess. The heightened emotional significance of the combat scene is further enhanced by the sequence immediately preceding it. Dressed in fatigues, Dixie sings a moving rendition of "In My Life" for the boys at the firebase. This number (*and* the film, as its title indicates) becomes a tribute to all the soldiers she has known, a memorial to the dead and the soon-to-die. Incoming rocket fire brings a final shot of Dixie and the boys, tenderly saluting each other with the peace sign, to an explosive end. This combat scene ironically establishes the futility of their symbolic gesture.

The picture's second and more significant self-subversion is its total reliance on the Oedipal family romance to structure and motivate its plot. *For the Boys* would seem to support Raymond Bellour's observation that, by and large, "American cinema finds itself enacting . . . the most classic paradigm elaborated for the subject of Western culture by Freudian psychoanalysis." American film, he continues, is therefore "dependent on . . . a system of representations in which the woman occupies a central place only to the extent that it's a place assigned to her by the logic of masculine desire."[35] Tania Modleski and others have demonstrated that not all Hollywood narratives trace the "male oedipal journey."[36] Jackie Byars, among others, argues that even if "Freud's Oedipal family romance . . . generates and drives the narratives of Hollywood film," a dissenting female voice can still be the "primary discursive agent."[37] Perhaps most encouragingly of all, B. Ruby Rich reminds us of "the possibility for texts to be transformed at the level of reception."[38] And, in fact, up to a point these films tend to support such contentions.

Nevertheless, in one way or another all these films ultimately contain their "primary discursive agents" on both the thematic and formal levels. To begin with, although explicitly militarized, the narrators are also re-feminized, so they present no threat to the conventionally gendered structures of war and/or the family. In addition, in no case does the female narrator speak directly to the spectator (while male voice-over narrators often do, thus presenting a disembodied, unequivocally authoritative speaking subject). Rather, and quite typically, as Kaja Silverman has explained, she speaks to a male auditor, who initiates, authorizes, mediates, and, I would add, passes judgment on her narrative.[39] On its completion, moreover, her story is invariably subsumed by dominant phallic discourses and co-opted *(Women of Valor)*, reconfigured *(Shining Through)*, or altogether sacrificed *(For the Boys)*.

All in all, then, fifty years since World War II and in the shadow of Vietnam, these films suggest that our gender-inflected cultural narratives, quintessentially manifest in plots of war and romance, exert a continuing and perhaps renewed tyranny on Hollywood's cinematic imagination. To no small degree, this follows a movement toward recuperation in two senses of the word. First, I am referring to the inevitable tendency for the mechanisms of social production to recuperate resistance to or deviation from dominant ideology, thus demonstrating the efficiency with which that ideology "can incorporate a wide variety of critical perspectives in an enveloping . . . [discursive] system designed to maintain traditional order and values."[40] The second form of recuperation evidences an understandable desire to recuperate from the psychosocial wounds ideological wars induce on the mundane battleground of human relations. There are, of course, indications that narrative tyranny and the "mythological mechanism" of absolute sexual difference that engenders it can be resisted and subverted, even in Hollywood cinema.[41] The most recent re-shootings of World War II (like those of Vietnam) indicate, however, that this particular battle is far from won.

NOTES

1. In addition to the three I discuss here, recent American World War II films (major releases) include *Swing Shift* (1983), *Empire of the Sun* (1987), *Memphis Belle* (1990), and *Swing Kids* (1993).
2. Linda Dittmar and Jean Michaud, "America's Vietnam War Films: Marching toward Denial," in *From Hanoi to Hollywood: The Vietnam War in American Film*, ed. L. Dittmar and J. Michaud (New Brunswick, NJ: Rutgers University Press, 1990), 12.
3. Steve Neale, "Aspects of Ideology and Narrative Form in the American War Film," *Screen* 32 (1991): 53.
4. Kaja Silverman, "Dis-Embodying the Female Voice," in *Re-Vision: Essays in Feminist Film Criticism*, ed. Mary Ann Doane, Patricia Mellencamp, and Linda Williams (Frederick, MD: University Publications of America, 1984), 132.
5. "China Beach," a dramatic television series, more or less focused on the

experience and concerns of American women in Vietnam, although often from a male-defined perspective. To my knowledge, no fictional films about Vietnam have done even that. See Carol Lynn Mithers, "Missing in Action: Women Warriors in Vietnam," in *The Vietnam War and American Culture*, ed. Rick Berg and John Carlos Rowe (New York: Columbia University Press, 1991), 75–91.

6. According to Jeanine Basinger, Lieutenant Davidson "is in the catatonic state of the movie-story woman who tried to be a man, but found she was a woman after all." *The World War II Combat Film: Anatomy of a Genre* (New York: Columbia University Press, 1986), 229.

7. Women reviewers for the Office of War Information objected to the "derogatory portrayal of women" in *So Proudly We Hail:* "The nurses seemed most concerned with having a man around; if he wasn't, they collapsed. 'The worst feminine characteristics have been emphasized,' said [Nelson] Poynter," head of the Office of War Information Hollywood office. Clayton R. Koppes and Gregory D. Black, *Hollywood Goes to War: How Politics, Profits and Propaganda Shaped World War II Movies* (Berkeley: University of California Press, 1990), 100.

8. In a discussion of *Tender Comrade*, for example, Michael Renov argues that a war widow's infant son "holds the place of the father *for* the father" and "the place of the father *for himself.*" *Hollywood's Wartime Women: Representation and Ideology* (Ann Arbor: UMI Research Press, 1988), 220.

9. Ibid., 122.

10. This point is complicated by the fact that the commander is a Japanese-American who was pressed into serving the Emperor because he happened to be in Japan when the war started. His emotional outburst follows the news that his parents died in an American "relocation" camp. His decent treatment of the prisoners and regard for Jessup can too easily be attributed to his American-ness, for by and large the Japanese are depicted as cruel, insecure, emotional, or, in the case of the one humane prison guard, childlike.

11. Dittmar and Michaud, "America's Vietnam War Films," 12.

12. Susan Jeffords, "Reproducing Fathers: Gender and the Vietnam War in U.S. Culture," in *From Hanoi to Hollywood*, 205.

13. I am *not* suggesting that becoming "militarized" is the best — or even an acceptable — way for women to gain/demonstrate "equality." To do so is highly problematic for a number of reasons, including the fact that such a move accepts, once again, the masculine as the universal standard, to which women must aspire.

14. *Shining Through* readily lends itself to class analysis. Linda is at first not considered for the job because she has not attended Vassar. She throws this insult back into her interviewer's face, not because she is ashamed of her origins but because she is angered by the snobbish elitism. She prefers Chaplin, who is "for everybody," to opera, which Ed admits is not "for everyone." Later, one of the "guys from Harvard" describes her German accent as that of a "Berlin butcher's wife," thus drawing attention to her class

status. This seems to work to her advantage, for she eventually infiltrates Nazi households by working as a domestic, first as a cook and, later, a nanny. Her deceptions are ultimately discovered, however, precisely because she steps over the class line, attending an opera as the escort of a high-ranking German officer. And the woman who betrays her is upper class. Thus, class difference constantly works to her disadvantage.

15. In addition to Linda Williams's "When the Woman Looks" (*Re-Vision*, 85), for further discussion of the woman's cinematic "look," see Mary Ann Doane, "The 'Woman's Film': Possession and Address" (*Re-Vision*, 69). Doane argues that "the woman's exercise of an active investigating gaze can only be simultaneous with her own victimization" because of the "phallocentric organization" of the "classic Hollywood text."

16. Jackie Byars, "Gazes/Voices/Power: Expanding Psychoanalysis for Feminist Film and Television Theory," in *Female Spectators: Looking at Film and Television*, ed. E. Deidre Pribram (London: Verso, 1988), 123.

17. Susan Jeffords, "Masculinity as Excess in Vietnam Films: The Father/Son Dynamic of American Culture," *Genre* 21 (1988): 489.

18. Mary Ann Doane, untitled response, *Camera Obscura* 20–21 (1989): 144; and B. Ruby Rich, "In the Name of Feminist Film Criticism," in *Issues in Feminist Film Criticism*, ed. Patricia Erens (Bloomington: Indiana University Press, 1990), 278.

19. This notion, introduced in 1975 by Laura Mulvey, has become the stepping-off point for an ongoing dialogue within feminist film criticism. See, for example, Teresa de Lauretis, *Alice Doesn't: Feminism, Semiotics, Cinema* (Bloomington: Indiana University Press, 1982); Mary Ann Doane, "Film and the Masquerade: Theorizing the Female Spectator" (in *Issues in Feminist Film Criticism*, 41–57), and the special issue of *Camera Obscura* (1989), "The Spectatrix," ed. Janet Bergstrom and Mary Ann Doane.

20. See, for example, Janice Radway, *Reading the Romance: Feminism and the Representation of Women in Popular Culture* (Chapel Hill: University of North Carolina Press, 1984); and John Fiske, *Understanding Popular Culture* (Boston: Unwin Hyman, 1989).

21. One review in *Variety* summarizes *The Mortal Storm*'s two lead roles as follows: "James Stewart is the courageous individualist who refuses to join the Nazi party. . . . Miss Sullavan carries the romantic interest" (*Variety Film Reviews 1938–1942*, vol. 6 [New York: Garland, 1983], June 12, 1940 [n.p.]).

22. Linda Voss's discursive authority was further undermined by the decision to give the part to Melanie Griffith, whose voice has a conspicuously soft, tentative, childlike quality.

23. de Lauretis, *Alice Doesn't*, 131–32.

24. For a discussion of this same phenomenon in another recent World War II film, see Mimi White, "Rehearsing Feminism: Women/History in *The Life and Times of Rosie the Riveter* and *Swing Shift*," *Wide Angle* 7, no. 3 (1985): 34–43.

25. Dittmar and Michaud, "America's Vietnam War Films," 10.

26. Claudia Springer argues that three other recent World War II related films — *Empire of the Sun* (1987), *Hope and Glory* (British, 1987), and *Radio Days* (1987) — "associate a boy's Oedipal crisis . . . with war. By placing the boy at the age when he discovers sexual difference, the films conflate wartime and sexual trauma." "The Boy at the Keyhole Watching Bombshells," *Literature and Psychology* 34 (1988): 16.

27. Doane, untitled response, 144.

28. Susan Jeffords writes that a "study of the structural relations between warfare and gender reveals them to be intimately connected, so much so that one does not survive without the other." *The Remasculinization of America: Gender and the Vietnam War* (Bloomington: Indiana University Press, 1989), xv.

29. See Owen W. Gilman, Jr., and Lorrie Smith, eds., *America Rediscovered: Critical Essays on Literature and Film of the Vietnam War* (New York: Garland Publishing, 1990), 120–33.

30. Rick Berg and John Carlos Rowe, "The Vietnam War and American Memory," in *The Vietnam War and American Culture*, 4.

31. Virginia Woolf, *A Room of One's Own* (New York: Harcourt Brace Jovanovich, 1957), 85.

32. Dorothy Dinnerstein, *The Mermaid and the Minotaur: Sexual Arrangements and Human Malaise* (New York: Harper Colophon, 1977).

33. I have borrowed the phrase "danse macabre" from Jean Bethke Elshtain, "Women as Mirror and Other: Toward a Theory of Women, War and Feminism," *Humanities in Society* 5 (1982): 40.

34. Claudia Springer, "Antiwar Film as Spectacle: Contradictions of the Combat Sequence," *Genre* 21 (1988): 479–86.

35. Janet Bergstrom, "Alternation, Segmentation, Hypnosis: Interview with Raymond Bellour," *Camera Obscura* 3–4 (1979): 93.

36. Tania Modleski, "Hitchcock, Feminism, and the Patriarchal Unconscious," in *Issues in Feminist Film Criticism*, 59.

37. Byars, "Gazes/Voices/Power," 114, 124.

38. Rich, "In the Name of Feminist Film Criticism," 278.

39. Kaja Silverman, *The Acoustic Mirror: The Female Voice in Psychoanalysis and Cinema* (Bloomington: Indiana University Press, 1988).

40. John Carlos Rowe, "Bringing It All Back Home: American Recyclings of the Vietnam War," in *The Violence of Representation: Literature and the History of Violence*, ed. Nancy Armstrong and Leonard Tannenhouse (New York: Routledge, 1989), 200.

41. Jurij Lotman, a Russian semiotician, finds that in narrative a "mythical mechanism produces the human being as man and everything else as, not even 'women,' but non-man" (quoted in de Lauretis, *Alice Doesn't*, 121). De Lauretis goes on to conclude that "in its 'making sense' of the world, narrative endlessly reconstructs it as a two-character drama in which the human person creates and recreates *himself* out of an abstract or purely symbolic other — the womb, the earth, the grave, the woman; all of which, Lotman thinks, can be interpreted as mere spaces and thought of as 'mutually identical.' "

PART TWO

Rebelling Man

Some Perversions of Pastoral: Or Tourism in Gide's *L'Immoraliste*

Jonathan C. Lang

Illness is the night-side of life, a more onerous citizenship. Everyone who is born holds dual citizenship, in the kingdom of the well and in the kingdom of the sick. Although we all prefer to use only the good passport, sooner or later each of us is obliged, at least for a spell, to identify ourselves as citizens of that other place.
— Susan Sontag, *Illness as Metaphor*

Visitors to Algeria may be divided into two categories, the tourist and the invalid.
— Lt. Col. R. L. Playfair, *Handbook for Travellers in Algeria and Tunis* (1878)

Je veux dire qu'un pays ne me plaît que si de multiples occasions de fornication se présentent. Les plus beaux monuments du monde ne peuvent remplacer cela; pourquoi ne pas l'avouer franchement?
[I would like to say that a country pleases me only if multiple opportunities for fornication present themselves. The most beautiful monuments in the world cannot replace such a prospect; why not frankly admit it?]
— André Gide, "Carnets d'Égypte" [Egyptian Notebooks] (1939)

In an incident that the French used to justify their conquest of Algeria, the Dey of Algiers, Hussein Pasha, inhospitably struck the French consul across the face with a peacock feather fly swatter in the spring of 1827. In spite of the hot blood that the Dey's insult must have stirred, it was not until three years later that French troops, after having instituted a block-ade of such inefficiency that Turkish officials continually mocked it, landed on Algerian soil in June 1830, forced the abdication of the Dey, and established a colonial presence that lasted for 130 years. Between the capitulation of the Dey and the revolution of which Frantz Fanon in *A Dying Colonialism* and *Toward the African Revolution* was the famous scribe, Algeria served as an place where Frenchmen might flee increasingly uncomfortable sexual prohibitions of the mother country, ill Englishmen and ill Englishwomen might trade the inclement weather of Great Britain for the tonic that the balmy climate of Algiers offered, sportsmen might test their masculinity by bagging big game in the wild, and tourists of all nationalities might be lured by the general exoticism of Africa to disport themselves in the security of what was, finally, another French province.

In *L'Immoraliste*, Gide represents Algeria as a vacation paradise where his central character, Michel, escapes civilization for nature; that is, he leaves behind the discipline he associates with work in the metropolitan centers of Europe in order to enjoy the carefree state of being he finds in a pastoral world of sunlight and water. Michel lapses from an arduous life of discipline and embraces instead the idleness and pleasures of the vacation world; he must devote himself to seeking a cure from a life-threatening case of tuberculosis that requires him to regenerate himself out-of-doors. While the narrative sequence that describes Michel's illness, subsequent recovery, and newly triumphant hold on life possesses such an obviously literal dimension, it is also a thinly veiled allegory for Michel's sexual awakening. His illness is a metaphor for sexual repression; the cure requires that he accept a life of the body driven by its instinctual passions, and that he acknowledge his (homo)sexual nature.[1]

In fact, from the very days of its conquest, Algeria was known to tolerate — even facilitate — the homosexual relations tabooed in the mother country. In an infamous terminal essay to the *Thousand Arabian Nights and One Night*, British luminary Sir Richard Burton described with great relish the dizzying outbreak of sodomy among the French troops in Algeria:

Under Louis Phillippe, the conquest of Algiers had evil results, according to the Marquis de Boissy. He complained *sans ambages* [in plain language] of *moeurs Arabes* [Arabian habits] in French regiments, and declared that the result of the African wars was an *éffrayable* [*sic*] *débordement pédérastique* [frightening explosion of pederasty]. . . . From the military the *fléau* [scourge] spread to civilian society, and the Vice took such expansion and intensity that it may be said to have been democratized in cities and large towns; at least so we gather from the *Dossier des Agissements des Pédérastes* [*Dossier of the Intrigues of Pederasts*].[2]

Its convenience established by short journeys on Compagnie Transatlantique steamers from Marseilles, Algeria continued to serve as a sanctuary from bourgeois restraints well into the twentieth century, despite the growth of local European communities. Guy Delrouze, a contemporary of Gide's, testifies that

les moeurs soi-disant coloniales sont jugées sans grande rigueur. Otez l'individu de son cadre, des rainures où glissent son activité et sa pensée, il s'adapte à un ordre de choses qui le heurtait d'abord. Toute l'histoire des compagnes d'Afrique le prouve. La facilité des communications, l'importation d'éléments féminins n'a rien changé depuis les premiers jours de la conquête; bien plus, une race nouvelle se forme dans l'Afrique du Nord, énergetique, active, peu scrupuleuse, yankees latins non handicapés de puritanisme, et qui porte dans son sang les fatalités sexuelles des latitudes où elle naquit.
[so-called colonial customs are judged without great severity. Take the individual from his surroundings, from the place where his activity and thinking are formed; he will adapt himself to an order of affairs that would otherwise upset him. The entire history of the African campaigns prove it. The ease of communications, the introduction of feminine influence, has changed nothing since the first days of conquest; moreover, a new race is forming in North Africa: energetic, powerful, practically unscrupled, latin yankees not handicapped by puritanism – a race who carries in its blood the sexual destiny of the latitudes where it comes to life.][3]

In coordinating the plot of Michel's recovery from illness with his sexual awakening, Gide situates Michel's discovery of his sexual nature against pastoral landscapes whose sole function is to solace the body of the visiting bourgeois. Although Algeria, in the period Gide represents it, underwent social and economic upheavals as a consequence of the intrusions of colonialism – the French colonial administration, for example, seized the lands of traditional Algerian families, disrupted their traditional patterns of subsistence, and effectively forced rural women into prostitution in the cities – Gide entertains a vision of the country reduced to the elemental components of a Mediterranean environment: sunlight, water, desert, and oasis.[4] Michel can thus safely maintain the illusion of the benevolence and healing he associates with a timeless pastoral landscape inhabited by perpetually smiling children and itinerant goatherds. What Gide must ultimately acknowledge in *L'Immoraliste*, however, is how the pleasures Michel discovers in North Africa belong to him by virtue of his privileged access to the tourist economy of colonial Algeria.[5]

If North Africa permits Michel unparalleled access to the twin pleasures of idleness and deviancy, it sanctions values directly counter to those of the metropolitan culture where discipline and monogamatic sexuality rule workaday life. Retaining from his journey to North Africa an orientation toward pleasure in a metropolitan society obsessed with productivity and re-productivity, the bourgeois homosexual becomes an embodiment of social and sexual license. Under the sway of the dark continent and suffering an atavistic regression to a putatively base sexual nature long forbidden in Europe, Michel violates his own heritage in forming identifications across lines of class that deliberately engage fears in the bourgeois of social and economic decline.

CLUB MED, OR VACATION IS VOCATION ENOUGH

Michel's marriage to Marceline induces him to take a journey that introduces into his workaday life an ostensible departure from the austere pattern that entirely governs it: "Pour la première fois . . . je consentais d'être privé longtemps de mon travail. Je ne m'étais accordé jusqu'alors que de courtes vacances." [For the first time, too, I was willing to be deprived of my work for an extended period. Heretofore I had permitted myself only brief vacations.][6] The journey to North Africa undertaken in the early pages of the narrative, explicitly presented by Michel as offering unaccustomed leisure occasioned by his marriage, is, however, conceived to meet the demands of his work. Although Michel possesses great resources of time, he cannot free himself from an unremitting discipline that contains the stray forces of his being even when released from the burden of work. In fact, his primary defining trait, prior to the self-transformation he describes in *L'Immoraliste*, is his unyielding fidelity to the bourgeois work ethic, his insensible devotion to a life of the mind: "j'atteignis vingt-cinq ans, n'ayant presque rien regardé que de ruines ou des livres, et ne connaissant rien de la vie; j'usais dans le travail une ferveur singulière" (20). [I turned twenty-five, having looked at almost nothing but ruins or books, and knowing nothing about life; I lavished on my work a remarkable fervor (9–10).] Upon his arrival in North Africa, his academic interests in philology and archaeology thus immediately draw him to the ruins of antiquity: Carthage, Timgad, the mosaics of Sousse, and the amphitheatre of El Djem. He is so absorbed by his work that the "Orient" can claim Michel's attention only insofar as it reveals the history of Western civilization.

The journey in and of itself is thus insufficient to dislodge Michel from the order of his workaday life. The leisure he finds in North Africa is not a consequence of the vacation he takes but of the sudden catastrophic illness that befalls him and forces him to lift his sights from archaeological sites by requiring him to dedicate himself seriously to seeking a cure. As a consequence of a conventional understanding of the nature of tuberculosis, which teaches him to associate well-being with an athletic affirmation of an out-of-doors ethic, Michel makes his first excursions to Algerian oases where he discovers "une sorte d'extase, d'allégresse silencieuse, d'exaltation des sens et de la chair" (50) [a kind of ecstasy, a silent happiness, an exaltation of the senses and of the flesh (39)].[7] By contrast, in a case of the jitters Michel comes to associate death with the monuments he visits: "Je ne pouvais voir un théâtre grec, un temple, sans aussitôt le reconstruire abstraitement. A chaque fête antique, la ruine qui restait en son lieu me faisait me désoler qu'elle fût morte; et j'avais horreur de la mort" (61). [I could not see a Greek theater or temple without immediately reconstructing it in my mind. At each ancient festival site, the ruin which remained in its place made me grieve over its death — and I had a horror of death (50).] He ultimately prefers the leisure he finds in the pleasant quarry gardens called "les Latomies, où les citrons ont l'acide douceur des oranges, et les rives de la Cyané qui, dans les papyrus, coule encore aussi bleue que le jour où ce fut pour pleurer Proserpine" (62) [*latomias*, where the lemons have the sweetness of oranges, and the shores of the Cyane, which flows as blue through its reeds now as when it wept for Persephone (50; italics in original)]. Michel's experiences allow Gide in turn to describe a type of tourism centered not on journeys to the past (i.e., a tourism whose primary and preferred activities include visits to the monuments and ruins that offer authentic vistas onto the past), but on the bodily pleasure of the bourgeois subject, who by happy circumstance is taken ill in a vacation paradise.

Although the pleasure Michel takes from relinquishing the instinctual repressions formed in the service of his work to regress happily to a state of eros appears to be primarily a privilege of illness and only coincidentally the privilege of his extended leisure, illness often provided a convenient screen for the pursuit of pleasure. In the late nineteenth and early twentieth century Algeria not only served as a haven for those who required the tonic the colony's bracing climate supplied their sickly frames but also introduced them to a leisurely life far from the hustle, bustle, and expense of Europe. Books that purported to be of specific utility to invalids also doubled as tourist guides to Algeria's tranquil environs (viz., the Reverend E. W. L. Davies's *Algiers in 1857: Its Accessi-*

bility, Climate, and Resources, Described with Especial Reference to English Invalids. Also, Details of Recreation Obtainable in Its Neighbourhood, Added for the Use of Travellers in General). In 1881, a scant two years before Gide's first journey to North Africa and twenty years before the publication of *L'Immoraliste*, an Englishman by the name of Alexander A. Knox called Algeria "the new playground" and promoted its climate to the bourgeois who might comfortably weather the stresses of the workaday world or the strains of illness: "On the whole, . . . Algiers [offers] the best quarters on the shores of the Mediterranean for elderly people, for semi-invalids, for those who have done with political ambition, business flurry, and social fuss, – for all who would spend pleasant warm hours in the open air, which would otherwise be cold and unpleasant hours indoors."[8] The fact that Algeria was a French colony of course played no small part in its success as a draw. The cost of living was so reduced that the invalid of small means could afford to rest there, and the healthy bourgeois could escape from the demands of the "civilized" world that might otherwise make him ill.

In *L'Immoraliste*, Gide underscores how health serves as a ruse for pleasure. Michel's attention to his body no longer belongs, as the narrative progresses, to a regimen of health whose function is to recondition the body for socially productive labor. In the long run, Michel becomes re-invigorated less by the cure for tuberculosis he manages to effect than by the golden suntan he obtains as he threads his way through Greece and Italy on his return journey to France. While he borrows on the moral imperative of the cure and emphasizes the therapeutic quality of the suntan – its function is to decrease the nervous aftereffects of his illness, his so-called "sensibilité maladive au moindre changement de la température" (66) [morbid sensitivity to the slightest change in temperature (55)] – he must admit that he can advance no authentic medical reason for the therapy he prescribes for himself because his lungs have been healed. The cure that Michel seeks from the suntan clearly serves as a license for the increasingly unabashed pleasure he finds in his body. If his illness teaches him to register unaccustomed sensitivity to the claims of his body ("Il me semblait avoir . . . si peu senti pour tant penser, que je m'étonnais à la fin de ceci: ma sensation devenait aussi forte qu'une pensée" (47). [It seemed to me that . . . I had felt so little by virtue of thinking so much that I was astonished by a discovery: sensation was becoming as powerful as thoughts (37).]), he becomes fascinated by the "being" that brims to the surface of his skin, that is, by a self wholly consecrated to pleasure.

Although Michel's suntan is undoubtedly the consequence of his new-found devotion to leisure, what he explicitly proclaims as his new ethic does not, as a matter of fact, belong to the syntax of a leisured class that maintains class distinctions through ritual exposure to the sun — a ritual often elevated to the central activity of the contemporary holiday. In their remarkable history of international tourism, *The Golden Hordes*, Louis Turner and John Ash assert that the "deliberate cultivation of a darkened skin tone by a leisured class is not to be found before the 1920s," because fair skin functioned symbolically to reinforce a racial and class hierarchy: "In general, the ruling classes of white imperialist states avoided darkened skin tone when this was possible. Any deliberate cultivation of a tan would have savoured too much of identification with lower (largely rural) classes and coloured subject peoples."[9] Indeed, the overly effete Michel emphasizes the sensuousness of his tanned skin because he identifies with and desires those who, characteristically of lower class or inferior race, supposedly embody stronger claims to a life of the body and whose dark skin is the sign of their eroticism.[10] His admiration for the great vitality of the bronzed Italian peasants working in the countryside initially inspires him to offer his own body to the flames of the sun: "La vue des belles peaux hâlées et comme pénétrées de soleil, qui montraient, en travaillant aux champs, la veste ouverte, quelques paysans débraillés, m'incitant à me laisser hâler de même" (66). [The sight of the splendidly tanned peasants whose sun-drenched skins I glimpsed when they threw off their jackets in the fields encouraged me to let the same thing happen to me (55).] In a parallel passage of *L'Immoraliste*, Michel likewise cherishes the "life" (an ambiguous term: on the one hand, praiseworthy example of health and, on the other, the appealing fact of brute sensuality) embodied in one of his favorite Algerian boys before he is fully on the mend:

Le lendemain Bachir revint. Il s'assit comme l'avant-veille, sortit son couteau, voulut tailler un bois trop dur, et fit si bien qu'il s'enfonça la lame dans le pouce. J'eus un frisson d'horreur; il en rit, montra la coupure brillant et s'amusa de voir couler son sang. Quand il riait, il découvrait des dents très blanches; il lécha plaisamment sa blessure; sa langue était rose comme celle d'un chat. Ah! qu'il se portait bien. C'était là ce dont je m'éprenais en lui: la santé. La santé de ce petit corps était belle. (34)
[The next day, Bachir returned. He sat down as he had before, took out his knife, and in trying to whittle a hard piece of wood stuck the blade into his thumb. I

shuddered, but he only laughed, holding up the shiny cut and happily watching the blood run out of it. When he laughed, he showed his brilliant white teeth, then licked the wound with delight; his tongue was as pink as a cat's. How healthy he was! That was what beguiled me about him: health. The health of that little body was beautiful. (24)]

It is significant that Gide should fail to stage the story of Michel's sexual awakening within the social landscape of Algeria but instead should insist that he discover what he comes to understand as his sexual nature *within* nature (as it is signified by sunlight and water). Michel's rejection of sexual repression and acceptance of the life of the body is represented by his flight into a pastoral world, into a sheltered hollow near Ravello close to a spring of clear water, where he strips off his clothes and sunbathes in order to lose the pallor of illness and regain the metaphorical pink of health; he tries to produce a body that is, in his own words, "harmonieux, sensuel, presque beau" (68) [harmonious, sensual, almost beautiful (57)]. The site in Ravello is the logical successor to a series of serene Algerian oases and palm groves where Michel encounters young goatherds whose salutary influence lies in the intense feelings they arouse in the repressed bourgeois; this feeling is then attributed to the climate itself, which becomes the source of Michel's exaltation. The restorative value of the pastoral landscape, which clearly belongs to the plot of Michel's illness and recovery, is linked to the story of his sexual liberation as well so that Gide might more fully associate the virtuousness of nature's healing qualities with Michel's discovery in the self of natural forms of human sexuality.[11] Gide uses the positive meanings attached to nature as a place of escape from the artificiality of and onerous discipline enforced within the civilized world in order to counter the negative meanings attached to nature represented in primitive forms of human sexuality, which was as often as not conceived of as fundamentally *unnatural.*[12]

Within a stereotypical understanding of the so-called perversions that persists, in similarly fallacious form to this very day, both the sexuality of the Algerians Michel admires and the homosexuality it awakens in him were conceived of as pernicious deviancies. In the constructions of anthropological or psychological theory, each represents a "primitive" rather than a "civilized" form of human sexuality.[13] Insofar as the bourgeois, to the credit of his class, supposedly internalizes the norms and restraints of Western civilization to a distinctive degree, it is clear that the identification Michel forms with Algerian natives indicates how far he slips from the conventional moorings of class and therefore from the moorings of civilization itself. For Gide, however, who is intent on removing the stigma attached to the perverse, Michel's discovery of his homosexuality does not mean a decline into deviancy but the recovery of a "natural" self. In a justifiably famous metaphor of a palimpsest used to conceptualize his sexual awakening, Michel describes how in Algeria he recovers an authentic being beneath the encrustations of his education and upbringing:

L'amas sur notre esprit de toutes connaissances acquises s'écaille comme un fard et, par places, laisse voir à nu la chair même, l'être authentique qui se cachait.
   Ce fut dès lors *celui* que je prétendis découvrir: l'être authentique, le "viel homme," celui dont ne voulait plus l'Évangile; celui que tout, autour de moi, livres, maîtres, parents, et que moi-même avions tâché d'abord de supprimer. Et il m'apparaissait déjà, grâce aux surcharges, plus fruste et difficile à découvrir mais d'autant plus utile à découvrir et valeureux. Je méprisais dès lors cet être secondaire, appris, que l'instruction avait dessiné par-dessus. Il fallait secouer ces surcharges. (62–63; italics in the original)
[The layers of acquired knowledge peel away from the mind like a cosmetic and reveal, in patches, the naked flesh beneath, the authentic being hidden there.
   Henceforth this is what I sought to discover: the authentic being, "the old Adam" whom the Gospels no longer accepted; the man whom everything around me — books, teachers, family and I myself — had tried from the first to suppress. And I had already glimpsed him, faint, obscured by their encrustations, but all the more valuable, all the more urgent. I scorned henceforth that secondary, learned being whom education had pasted over him. Such husks must be stripped away. (51)]

Just as a palimpsest reveals infinitely more precious texts in its hidden layers, so too does culture, by repressing human desire, paradoxically confirm its value, truth, authenticity, and naturalness. Gide thereby gives priority to human sexuality in its natural rather than its civilized forms.[14]

   Yet, the "natural" world Gide depicts in *L'Immoraliste*, which serves merely to facilitate Michel's own psychological awakening, appears wholly implausible as a representative metonymy for Algeria. In his autobiography, *Si le grain ne meurt*, Gide cannot sustain the vision of the beneficent pastoral paradise he portrays in the narrative, but confronts what it means to belong to the colonial social world in which tourists like himself circulated. In the following scene, he symbolically illustrates the expensiveness of the European's desire to resuscitate himself in the colonies:

Puis, tandis que je restais assis près des verres à demi vidés, Daniel saisit Mohammed dans ses bras et le porta sur le lit qui occupait le fond de la pièce. Il le coucha sur le dos, tout au bord du lit, en travers; et je ne vis bientôt plus que, de chaque côté de Daniel ahanant, deux fines jambes pendantes, Daniel n'avait même pas enlevé son manteau. Très grand, debout contre le lit, mal éclairé, vu de dos, le visage caché par les boucles de ses longs cheveux noirs, dans ce manteau qui lui tombait aux pieds, Daniel paraissait gigantesque, et penché sur ce petit corps qu'il couvrait, on eût dit un immense vampire se repaître sur un cadavre. J'aurais crié d'horreur . . .

[Then, while I remained seated near half empty glasses, Daniel seized Mohammed in his arms and carried him over to the bed which sat in the corner of the room. He placed him on his back, close to the edge of the bed although across it; and soon I didn't see much more than two slender legs hanging on each side of a panting Daniel, who hadn't even bothered to take off his coat. Very large, upright against the bed, poorly lit, viewed from the back, his face hidden by the curls of his long black hair, in a coat that fell to his feet, Daniel appeared gigantic; and perched over this little body which he covered, he appeared to be a vampire of immense proportions feeding off of a corpse. I could have cried in horror . . .] [15]

If in *L'Immoraliste* Gide insists on the healthful quality of sexual pleasure for the bourgeois, it is striking how in his autobiography he reckons the cost of his regeneration by figuring the Frenchman, Daniel, as a vampire whose health depends on sapping the very life of the native, Mohammed. In characterizing the Frenchman as a dandy through the telling metonymies of his elegant dress and coiffure, Gide establishes Daniel as the depraved product of civilization, the representative of a decadent culture who preys on and destroys the life of the native.[16] This scene clearly reflects larger anxieties formed by Gide's recognition of what it means to belong to invading hordes of tourists who, in living out their fantasies of escape from civilization, consume local forms of material life. Whereas Gide, crying in horror at the sight he describes, would have fiercely resisted identifying with Daniel and the culture he represents, it is difficult to imagine Gide in successful flight not only from French civilization but from its local effects on material Algerian culture that, after all, sustained tourists like him.[17]

Because Michel in *L'Immoraliste* conceives of his flight to Algeria as an escape from the constraints of class, it simply does not occur to him, at this point in the narrative, to question to what extent the politics of colonialism support a racial and class hierarchy that structures his vacation world. And, in fact, Michel's desire for the native and the peasant effaces hierarchical differences between them. When Michel tans his body, he means to signify his desire for the peasant and the native through his identification with them. But he can only do so by repressing the difference between the body tanned through leisure and the body dark-ened from work.[18] In the distance from which Michel pictures their sensual bodies, the Italian peasants belong to a pastoral tableau in which the reality of their back-breaking labor and of the lives that labor saps is aestheticized by his appreciation for their vitality. Yet, in a telling dis-placement that signifies class differences even as the suntan apparently de-stabilizes them, he must remove himself from the laborer's world represented by the field in order to regenerate himself within the vaca-tioner's world of sunlight and water. In effect, Gide recognizes that the vacation world in which Michel finds sanctuary must maintain the appearance of benevolence: he cannot flee Western civilization to en-counter its wounding effects in the place of his escape.

A TOURIST ON HIS OWN PROPERTY

Although the vacation world of colonial Algeria allowed the French bour-geois to reject the often alienating dictates of productivity and sexual conformity and to embrace instead the virtues of idleness and deviancy, it did not necessarily set the stage for his rebellion against the repressiveness of the metropolitan centers. Whereas he might discover how impover-ished the workaday world appears in comparison with the vacation world that permits an unrepressed self to blossom, the bourgeois must return to his place within the economy of the workaday world. Thus, if the bour-geois manages to heal himself from the "wounds of civilization" while he is on vacation, it is only so that he might better steel himself against the tiresome demands made by the life he leads at home. Gide's narrative prepares for just such a conclusion to Michel's journey in delineating his attempts to subsume the license he takes while on vacation to the disci-pline of work and of monogamatic sexuality represented by marriage upon his return. In fact, Michel scarcely skips a beat in moving between what, from one perspective, represents his momentous liberation from repression and, from another, appears to be mere idleness or immaturity.

While the journey to North Africa allows Michel to recover a world of unaccustomed bodily pleasure, his return to France requires him to re-press his deviant sexual instincts; this task is made easier by his association of those instincts with useless childishness.[19] It is no surprise that Michel should reproduce so readily what we have come to know as the Freudian narrative of normative sexual development, because even though he leaves

Europe behind him, he never entirely rejects the norms instilled in him by French society. In falling ill, awakening from repression, and finding sensual pleasure in Algeria, he does not experience the mature pleasures of an adult *eros*; rather, he symbolically regresses to a childhood curtailed by the swift intellectual growth that led him to foreswear and forego childish things too soon:

Je dis: Il me semblait — car du fond du passé de ma première enfance se réveillaient enfin mille lueurs, de mille sensations égarées. La conscience que je prenais à nouveau de mes sens m'en permettait l'inquiète reconnaisance. Oui, mes sens, réveillés désormais, se retrouvaient toute une histoire, se recomposaient un passé. Ils vivaient! ils vivaient! n'avaient jamais cessé de vivre, se découvraient, même à travers mes ans d'étude, une vie latente et rusée. (47)
[I say: it seemed to me; for from the depths of my earliest childhood there awakened at last a thousand glimmerings, a thousand lost memories. My newfound sensual awareness let me acknowledge these for the first time. Yes, my senses, awakened now, were recovering a whole history, were recomposing their own past. They were alive! had never stopped living, had maintained, during all those years of study, a latent and deceitful life. (37)]

His erotic interest in Algerian boys is therefore represented as a form of "play" notably unmarred by the pressures of adult life because it is innocent and, consequently, not open to the scrutiny of potentially suspicious sentries like his wife, Marceline. When Michel regains his health, however, he must dispense with play and reject perverse sexuality as a form of childishness that cannot be integrated into his adult life:

Ashour et Moktir nous accompagnèrent d'abord; je savourais encore leur légère amitié qui ne coûtait qu'un demi franc par jour; mais bientôt, lassé d'eux, n'étant plus moi-même si faible que j'eusse encore besoin de l'exemple de leur santé et ne trouvant plus dans leurs jeux l'aliment qu'il fallait pour ma joie, je retournais vers Marceline l'exaltation de mon esprit et de mes sens. (57)
[Ashour and Moktir accompanied us at first; I still relished their frivolous companionship which cost no more than a half-franc piece a day; but soon, tired of them and no longer so weak that I still required the example of their health, and no longer finding in their play the sustenance I needed for my joy, I focused on Marceline the exaltation of my mind and of my senses. (45)]

The journey to foreign parts, which functions throughout the first part of the narrative to permit Michel's transgression against French moral codes, therefore must end in his commemoration of his marriage to his wife. In one of the narrative's more perverse scenes, Michel becomes so excited by subduing a loutish Italian carriage driver who threatens

Marceline's life, thus proving the power of his newly energized body, that in a fit of machismo that carries over from fisticuffs to the marriage bed, he "possesses" his wife for the very first time. In effect, he withdraws his desire from the Italian, who incarnates the animality he prizes but who cannot serve as a suitable object, and turns for his sexual fulfillment to the docile but available Marceline. The fact that he consummates his marriage to Marceline on his return to France, a consummation clearly deferred from Algerian days, indicates that he is ready to uphold bourgeois norms.

In falling away from forms of transgressive sexuality, Michel rejects as idle his idyllic vacation life. While his illness permits him to temporarily abandon the demands of the bourgeois work ethic, it is one of the ironies of the narrative that the only time his illness claims is the time he legitimately sets aside for leisure. His recovery from his illness while on his vacation indicates that the lapse he commits is well-regulated. The timing of his lapse makes it a matter of course to dismiss as provisional the vagabond state of which he is, for a time, the ecstatic witness. Almost as soon as he sets foot on European soil and on the verge of his return to Paris, Michel re-embraces the virtue of work. He comes to believe this virtue is his own, although he indicates that his wife is the impetus for his recognition of the idleness of his life:

Je pus être étonné d'abord de sentir que notre vie errante, où je prétendais me satisfaire pleinement, ne . . . plaisait [à Marceline] que comme un état provisoire; mais tous aussitôt le désœuvrement de cette vie m'apparut; j'acceptai qu'elle n'eût qu'un temps et pour la première fois, un désir de travail renaissant de l'innocupation même où me laissait enfin ma santé rétablie — je parlai sérieusement de retour. (76)
[I was amazed at first to learn that our wandering life, which I claimed to find so satisfying, appealed to (Marceline) only as a temporary condition; but all at once the idleness of such an existence became apparent to me, and I acknowledged that it was only a phase; for the first time, a desire to work born of the very leisure granted at last by my recovery, I spoke seriously of going home. (65)]

Yet, Michel cannot so easily betray the project of "immoralism" announced in the title of Gide's narrative by lapsing into his old good habits. If his sexual transgression were simply to regenerate Michel for the discipline of the workaday world, it would become a form of "alienated leisure" that supported bourgeois structures rather than undermining them. However, he rejects the *ideology* of the bourgeois class with its emphasis on discipline in order to realize the freedom that his wealth confers upon him to develop an *ethical* orientation to pleasure. In fact, he eventually learns to exploit the very latitude for pleasure that his privileged position within French society permits. Whereas his mother's stern Huguenot teachings induce the discipline that prepares him for an economy of scarcity, his father bequeaths him the fortune that permits him to benefit from an economy of plenty. Even as he readies himself to submit to the alienations of a workaday economy, he can afford to discover how seriously discomforting it is to conform to what was hitherto the discipline of his daily life.

Michel's rejection of the disciplinary ideal of bourgeois culture is represented in *L'Immoraliste* as a gradual falling away from work. At first Michel attempts to reconcile the old discipline of work with his new orientation to life when he gives up the abstract study of archaeology and philology, which can no longer hold his attention. Instead, he turns to the historical narrative of Altharic, a young Italian king who rebelled against conventional values symbolized by his mother and Latin culture in favor of an undisciplined life encouraged by the wild and corrupt Goths. Michel's new studies are clearly motivated by his own recent repudiation of French bourgeois society in favor of the untamed existence he leads in Algeria. However, whatever satisfaction he discovers in lecturing on the primacy of the untamed "life" over the "culture" that would repress it pales in comparison to the possibility of leading the life he publicly champions. Given his recent experiences, he no longer finds the disciplined intellectual work of the past absorbing enough; he can no longer hold at bay those pastimes, typically erotic, that the bourgeois is taught are distractions from serious business.[20]

In his attempts to reorient himself toward pleasure, however, Michel remains fixed in Parisian society and cannot simply discard his bourgeois trappings for the "untamed life" he idealizes in his work. If he wishes to transgress against the bourgeois ideal of discipline, he can only do so initially by gratifying himself with pleasures in their commodified forms.[21] Insofar as such pleasures not only signify the legitimate prerogatives of class but also serve as substitutive gratifications for his wanderlust, they ultimately serve to uphold the bourgeois order. In fact, Michel hopes that the comfortable life, symbolized by the luxurious property in which he and Marceline reside — what Ménalque, the narrative's fictional rendering of Oscar Wilde, derides as his desire for the tranquil happiness of the household — will be sufficient to diminish the lure his past journey continues to exert: "Je ne m'arrêtai . . . devant aucune dépense, me disant, à chacune, que je me liais d'autant plus et prétendant supprimer du même coup toute humeur vagabonde que je pouvais sentir, ou craindre de sentir en moi" (101–2). [I . . . spared no expense, telling myself each time that I was merely forming another tie to control any roving impulse I might feel, or feared to feel (88).] However, the comfort of property (the well-appointed apartment in Paris, the estate in Normandy) and the stable life it underwrites can neither serve as sufficient consolation for the loss of the pleasures he pursues in the colonial world nor dispel the ennui of the dessicated existence he must lead. The social rounds he must make as someone who is more than modestly propertied only deepen his boredom. He finds the Parisian salons and the relationships he must cultivate there predictably sterile, and he is faced with the melancholy prospect of a world devoid of the pleasures to which he has been newly awakened.

If his existence in Paris deepens the conflict he feels between the discipline of bourgeois life and the pleasures of deviancy, his return to La Morinière, his country estate in Normandy, permits him to duplicate the experiences of his North African trip more successfully. Initially, however, the temperateness of the climate in Normandy and the moderation in behavior it requires appear to confirm Michel in the disciplined course to which he directs himself: "Je repris lentement mon travail, l'esprit calme, dispos, sûr de sa force, regardant le futur avec confiance et sans fièvre, la volonté comme adoucie, et comme étouffant le conseil de cette terre tempérée" (83). [Gradually I took up my work again, my mind calm, alert, sure of its powers, regarding the future confidently and coolly, my will apparently chastened, apparently heeding the counsel of that temperate earth (71).] Whereas the wholly benevolent nature of Ravello sustains life without man's efforts to wrest his living from it, in order for him to enjoy the fruits of the Normandy earth he must turn "l'éclatement fécond de la libre nature" (84) [the fecund explosion of free nature (71)] to productive uses, or, in other words, to cultivate the earth. In effect, Michel means to signal his return from a state of nature to the repressiveness of civilization represented by the cultivation of the land, from which he derives an ethic of personal discipline:

Et je me laissais rêver à telles terres où toutes forces fussent si bien réglées, toutes dépenses si compensées, tous échanges si stricts, que le moindre déchet devînt

sensible; puis, appliquant mon rêve à la vie, je me construisais une éthique
qui devenait une science de la parfaite utilisation de soi par une intelligente
contrainte. (84)
[And I let myself dream of such lands where every force was so well controlled,
every expenditure so compensated, every exchange so strict, that the slightest
waste became evident; then, applying my dream to life, I sketched an ethic
which would become a science of self-exploitation perfected by a disciplined
intelligence. (72)]

Yet, as the owner of the country estate, he is not tied to the land as one of
its tenants. In spite of his well-formed intentions to heed the counsel of
the temperate earth, he is free of the discipline he describes. He can
ostensibly reject the stifling bourgeois values typified by productivity and
conformity for the idleness and deviancy of the "underworld" he discovers
on his estate.

Michel's fascination with the underworld corresponds to his falling-
away from his vision of the ideally productive land and consequently
from the disciplined self that the land "chastens." Such a falling away is
symbolically marked by his loss of a gambit initiated by the caretaker's
son, Charles — a gambit in which Michel discourages what he sees as the
inefficient management of the land in the hands of his tenants by threatening to repossess their fallow fields. It is no accident that he loses the
gambit and, in spite of his intention to make his fields more productive,
only manages to turn even larger parcels of his land, abandoned by his
alienated tenants, over to the encroachments of nature. If, as Fredric
Jameson argues, the "emblematic landscapes [of Gide's narrative], the
[North African] oases and the lush Norman farm, are so many forms of a
visible script, in which nature in the guise of spring or annual rainfall, and
culture, in the methods of cultivating the soil, combine to write the
calligraphy of man himself," then in *failing* to encourage the rigorous
cultivation of the soil, Michel establishes an untamed preserve — approximate in its natural qualities to the pastoral landscapes of Algeria — where
the self, no longer disciplined by the need to make the land productive,
might lead a life wholly given over to impulse and untamed instincts, to
deviancy and dissolution: a self closer to its nature.[22]

While Michel's return to nature, symbolized by the pastoral landscapes
of Algeria, serves as an allegory of sexual transgression, it is curious that
the equivalent narrative sequence in Normandy in which the bourgeois
idealizes the untamed preserves of his estate should signify his transgression against the *economic* order. His rejects the primary and most valuable

characteristic of his land — its ability to be cultivated, to be made productive through the concerted efforts of landowner and tenants alike — in favor of his identification with the unproductive deviants, the vagabonds and poachers, who work on his Normandy estate: "Mes deux fermes, il me fallait me l'avouer, ne m'intéressait plus autant que les gens que j'y employais" (136). [My two farms, I had to admit to myself, no longer interested me so much as the workmen I employed on them (122).] In underscoring the shift (or in moralistic terms, the *diminishment*) in his ethical stature, Michel repudiates his positioning in the social world as bourgeois landowner, consequently projecting the ridiculous image of the bourgeois seigneur — "un absurde Monsieur, coiffé d'un ridicule chapeau melon" (136) [a ridiculous Monsieur under an even more ridiculous bowler (123)] — onto the manager's son Charles who is ambitious to make a mark on the management of Michel's estate. In order to complete the transformation of his character, he forms a secret alliance with the adolescent poacher Alcide and poaches on his own preserves.[23]

Although Michel's transgression is foregrounded in the text in economic terms as a violation of the productive ethic of the farm, it possesses an underlying sexual dimension as well. In fact, Michel's transgression against the laws of property symbolized by poaching on his own preserves becomes significant for the bourgeois insofar as it represents a form of pleasure analogous to a *perverse* expression of sexuality, the quality that Herbert Marcuse defines via Freud in *Eros and Civilization:*

In a repressive order, which enforces the equation between normal, socially useful, and good, the manifestations of pleasure for its own sake must appear as *fleurs du mal*. Against a society which employs sexuality as means for a useful end, the perversions uphold sexuality as an end in itself; they thus place themselves outside the domination of the performance principle and challenge its very foundation. They establish libidinal relationships which society must ostracize because they threaten to reverse the process of civilization which turned the organism into an instrument of work. They are a symbol of what had to be suppressed so that suppression could prevail and organize the ever more efficient domination of man and nature.[24]

In other words, just as the perversions sanction pleasurable expressions of sexuality distinct from its generative or reproductive function, Michel gives high marks to poaching on account of its libidinal dimension, the unholy excitement he feels as a consequence of transgressing against the social order, rather than for its productivity, the "goods" supplied by poaching. In any case, the very essence of what it means to poach on his own preserves would preclude Michel from finding much value in the game he captures under shady circumstances, which could never exceed the value of game produced within a licit economy. Lest the ideals of productivity contaminate what must remain a pure diversion, however, Michel relinquishes the rabbits, pheasants, and unfortunate roebuck trapped in his snares to his companion poacher Alcide.

In the figure of the hedonist Michel, Gide duplicates a fearful bourgeois representation of the homosexual who stereotypically embodies an uncontrollable licentiousness. In retaining from his colonial experience an unsuitable orientation toward pleasure in a metropolitan society whose moral touchstone lies in the productivity of its members, Michel attempts to realize the promise of the abundance of La Morinière and convert it wholly to pleasure — even at the risk of depleting his property of its valuable game. Yet, Gide fails to sustain this representation of the bourgeois homosexual as radical libertine. Ultimately, Michel cannot shirk from upholding class interests that he is supposed to represent as a landowner and with which he cannot fail to identify. Thus, he finds himself in the uncomfortable position of protecting his own economic interests when the adolescent Alcide — who initiates the bourgeois into his criminal trade by teaching him how to set traps, but who clearly feels less affinity than a curious aversion for the slumming landowner — double-crosses him without a second thought. Not only does the cunning Alcide earn a tidy profit from turning in their illegal traps for a reward that the owner of La Morinière must pay, but he also forces the bourgeois publicly to commend his diligence in overseeing the interests of property that Michel would rather deny. Though the bourgeois identifies with the poacher because he appears to be closer to the natural order (living as he does off the fat of the land), Alcide disrupts such an idealization by making it clear that he is at least in one sense a paragon of the bourgeois order; he is concerned less with the pleasure of poaching than he is with the profits from his activities. Alcide's betrayal in effect inverts Michel's identification with him by stripping Michel of his status as criminal accomplice and by repositioning the former as hapless bourgeois.

Michel's idealization of a natural order represented by his cross-class identification with the poacher proves illusory in another key sense as well. Although Michel wishes to value nature over culture, pleasure over work by poaching on his own preserves, he must work at poaching *in order to feel* the pleasure of the diversion. That Michel can nonetheless consider the pleasure of poaching to be its central characteristic is a testament to his primary class identification. It is only from the bourgeois' secure position that he can fail to view poaching as a form of work.

While Michel's identification with the poacher proves dismayingly imperfect, his idealization of the vagabond seems to be more successful, because they both share what, from the perspective of an unalloyed conservative, would appear to be a horrifying orientation toward libertinism — Michel in his embrace of sexual pleasure, the vagabond in the dissipation represented by his impulsive drinking:

Un surtout m'attirait: il était assez beau, grand, point stupide, mais uniquement mené par l'instinct; il ne faisait jamais rien que de subit, et cédait à toute impulsion de passage. Il n'était pas de ce pays; on l'avait embauché par hasard. Excellent travailleur deux jours, il se soûlait à mort le troisième. Une nuit j'allai furtivement le voir dans le grange; il était vautré dans le foin; il dormait d'un épais sommeil ivre. Que de temps je le regardai! (134)

[One man in particular attracted me: tall, rather handsome, not stupid but guided solely by instinct; he did nothing save on the spur of the moment, yielded to every passing impulse. He was not from this part of the country, but had been hired for the time being. An excellent worker for two days, he would be dead drunk the third. One night I crept down to the barn to have a look at him; he lay sprawling in the hay; his sleep was the heavy trance of intoxication. How long I stared at him! (120–21)]

Although the appeal that the vagabond holds for the bourgeois is a strong one, Michel's idealization of him is disrupted once again by a powerful class identification: "Ces travailleurs . . . me firent fâcheusement souvenir que je n'étais point là en voyageur charmé, mais en maître" (131). [These workmen . . . reminded me with a start that I was not here as a delighted tourist, but as their employer (118).] As the estate's master and not a tourist on his own property, he is eventually forced to cede to the better judgment of his manager, Bocage, and agree to the dismissal of the vagabond. He is nonetheless secretly delighted that the vagabond's delinquency might infect the other workers and destroy the good name of the farm.

If the text establishes a parallel between sexual and economic activities without productive ends, then what it notably fails to encourage is any equivalence between nongenerative, nonreproductive sexual pleasure and an unproductive or impotent economy represented by the decline of the capitalist farm.[25] In the final analysis, Michel, though he poaches on his own preserves, is checked from bringing about the ruin of La Morinière;

the stalwart stewards of his estate, surrogate bourgeois selves, effectively make Michel's deviations impossible. While the equivalence between sexual pleasure and an impotent economy is *purely metaphorical*, it nonetheless provides the faulty grounds for a commonplace association between homosexual "decadence" and the collapse of society most memorably encapsulated, for example, in Gibbon's history of how degeneracy led to the fall of the Roman Empire; in Marcuse's Freudian account of how perverse "libidinal relationships . . . threaten to reverse the process of civilization which turned the organism into an instrument of work" (Marcuse, *Eros and Civilization*, 50); and most recently in the insistence of the American military brass and their Senate hatchet man, Sam Nunn, that the induction of avowed gay men and lesbians into the armed forces risks undermining the discipline and morale of the ranks.

In an analogous sequence of the narrative, Michel's decadent orientation toward pleasure leads to the decline of the family. The homosexual rendezvous that he arranges with Ménalque — signified in the text by his willingness to arouse the suspicion that the assiduously conventional might attach to his all-night tryst with a man of scandal — requires that Michel neglect his duty to wife who, though she is suddenly taken ill, cannot assert a moral claim on him and dissuade him from abandoning her. When Marceline unexpectedly delivers a still-born child during his extended absence, his indulgence of pleasure *apart* from the family is symbolically connected to its apparent effect *within* the family, where sterility suddenly comes to supplant the promise of new generation represented by their infant. Once again, the symbolic connection depends on a purely metaphorical equivalence between nongenerative, nonreproductive sexual pleasure and impotence or sterility.[26]

Though Michel attempts to reproduce the experience of his North African trip on his country estate, repressive forms of propriety that are attached to ownership of property foreclose such a possibility. In order to free himself from social repression, Michel must return to his travels. Yet, the pleasure that the homosexual might claim as a tourist depends not on his rejection of the principles of productivity, but on his consumption of the surplus value earned within a bourgeois economic regime — one that determines the course and conditions of his deviance. Consequently, the homosexual must endorse the very economic norms against which he attempts to militate but that provide him limited freedom in the institutions of tourism. Within the radical terms that he establishes for transgressive deviance, Michel cannot reproduce the experience of pleasure represented by North Africa as a tourist on his own property or, absurdly enough, as a tourist returning to North Africa.

Michel cannot risk duplicating the condition of the tourist, so he must embrace the condition of another traveller: the vagabond. Michel constructs the vagabond as an alter-ego when he denies all claims of a domestic economy in anticipation of the pleasures awaiting him in Algeria as he backtracks through Italy. By exhausting the surplus value produced by La Morinière and drawing on its capital value, he preserves himself from the repressive economic commitments that might cause him to moderate those pleasures.[27] Moreover, when he places La Morinière up for sale, he not only rejects the ideals associated with productivity of property but he also relinquishes his social place in Normandy, thereby refusing any social commitments that might lessen his erotic drive. In fact, every expenditure of capital he makes is calculated to separate Michel from his social milieu, to divorce himself of familial bonds. He spends lavish amounts on luxurious comforts for the ill Marceline, which actually guarantees his dwindling attachment to her, the spendthrift's transformation into a spindrift beguiled by debauched contact with "life":

[J]'exaspérais ... ma grandissante horreur de luxe, du confort, de ce dont je m'étais entouré, de cette protection que ma neuve santé avait su me rendre inutile de toutes ces précautions que l'on prend pour préserver son corps du contact hasardeux de la vie. (167–68)
[I aggravated my growing horror of luxury, of comfort, of what I had surrounded myself with, of that protection my new health had made useless, of all those precautions one takes to preserve one's body from the dangerous contact of life. (155–56)]

In the end, the suspect juxtaposition of his freedom and her death betrays his desire to kill Marceline in order that he might be released from her moralism; he spends himself so that he might send her to her grave.[28]

Yet, the bourgeois can never spend *enough* in order to achieve the vagabond's extreme state, in spite of his attempt to adopt the vagabond's unrestrained behavior: "J'en venais à ne goûter plus en autrui que les manifestations les plus sauvages, à déplorer qu'une contrainte quelconque les réprimât" (158). [I reached the point of enjoying in others only the wildest behavior, deploring whatever constraint inhibited any excess (146).] If the vagabond is intemperate because he cannot surrender any of his dissipations long enough to be consistently productive, remaining in a perpetual state of alienating impoverishment, the bourgeois homosexual in the service of pleasure cannot consume enough of his worldly goods — even in the mode of "excess" — to find himself in the vagabond's dire straits. That Michel should experience the alienation that is the vagabond's lot as a form of freedom from the constrictions of his own is evidence of how class differences divide them. Even at the moment when he appears most successfully to have transgressed against the boundaries of class and to have overcome the distance between himself and a delinquent subculture of stevedores, tramps, and drunken sailors, Michel acknowledges that he retains the perspective of one who fails to be defined by the condition he idealizes; it is as though he intimates that by relinquishing the *responsibilities* that define his bourgeois life he cannot quite divest himself of its *privileges:*

La société des pires gens m'était compagnie délectable. Et qu'avais-je besoin de comprendre bien leur langage, quand toute ma chair le goûtait. La brutalité de la passion y prenait encore à mes yeux un hypocrite aspect de santé, de vigueur. Et j'avais beau me dire que leur vie misérable ne pouvait avoir pour eux le goût qu'elle prenait pour moi . . . (167; ellipsis in original)
[The dregs of society were delectable company to me, and what need had I of understanding their speech when my whole body savored it! Here too the brutality of passion assumed in my eyes a hypocritical aspect of health, of vigor. It was no use reminding myself that their wretched lives could not have for them the savor they assumed for me . . . (155; ellipsis in original)]

It is thus significant that the focus of the previous passage on Michel's acquired taste (goût) for debauchery as he hovers, his own flesh aquiver, before the "dregs of society" should recall the vampirish dandy characterized in *Si le grain ne meurt*, who, as a tourist enacting his fantasy of escape from the metropolis, devours local forms of material life.

While Michel's liberation from the restraints of productivity means he can commit himself to pleasure without the limitations imposed on the bourgeois tourist, the privilege that remains his nonetheless defines him as the cosmopolitan citizen of a leisured society. It is this privilege that forces Michel to consider the economic character of a world he had previously conceived of as "natural." Upon his return to Algeria, Michel must recognize an economic dimension to his experience when he acknowledges the toll that life in Algeria takes on the local children, whom he once adored for their vitality but who no longer belong to the natural landscape. In his absence, the children, too old to enjoy the leisure that is the prerogative of their childhood and enjoined instead to assume their places within a work economy, have become fully integrated into the *social* landscape:

[Q]uelles fatigues, quels vices, quelles paresses, ont déjà mis tant de laideur sur ces visages, où tant de jeunesse éclatait? Quels travaux vils ont déjeté si tôt ces beaux corps? Il y a là comme une banqueroute ... Je questionne. Bachir est garçon plongeur d'un café; Ashour gagne à grand-peine quelques sous à casser les cailloux des routes.... Sadeck s'est rangé; il aide un frère aîné à vendre des pains au marché; il semble devenu stupide. (172; second ellipsis mine)
[What exhaustion, what vices, what sloth had already imprinted such ugliness on these faces in which so much youth once had bloomed? What servile labors had warped these lovely bodies so quickly? It was a kind of bankruptcy ... I asked questions. Bachir was washing dishes in a café, Ashour earned a few sous breaking stones on the highway.... Sadeck had reformed; he was helping an older brother sell bread in the market; he seemed to have lost his wits. (160–61; second ellipsis mine)]

His ethical orientation to pleasure teaches Michel to discern and to denounce the dreaded productivity that Western culture enforces not only in its metropolitan subjects but also in its colonials — those children who are destined to lead meager and penurious lives in an economy functioning to buttress France's interests.

Michel's commentary on the meagerness of the lives the inhabitants of Algeria are destined to lead and on the penuriousness of their fates serves as a potentially powerful criticism of colonialism. Yet, such criticism is muted because Michel does not fully question the degree to which he inherits the bounty colonialism provides leisured Europeans like himself: this bounty is made evident by how Michel, unlike the children, can return to a vacation economy in North Africa whose comforts will ironically preserve him from what he imagines to be precarious contact with the "life" he seeks.[29]

IT'S A SMALL WORLD AFTER ALL

In underscoring how the bourgeois' commitment to the values of the mother country is undermined by his exposure to a life of idleness and deviancy in the colonies, Gide foregrounds the potentially subversive effect of the journey to Algeria. The ultimate degradation of such a journey is to drain the life-blood of the European who proves himself more interested in the pursuit of pleasure and of deviancy than in maintaining bonds to family and nation. Yet, the subversiveness of Michel's decision to leave his restrictive life behind is mitigated by the closure of the narrative, in which the lapsed bourgeois seeks to be reincorporated into the community.[30] In a diagnosis of his condition produced for the small coterie of friends whom he invites to Algeria to witness his change of heart, Michel learns to construe the story of his liberation in its most chastised form as a cautionary fable. Coming to reflect the repressive viewpoint of Western society, Michel equates his liberty with licentiousness and claims that as a consequence of the license he takes, he must suffer a self perpetually diminished by pleasures that are too readily available.

Although Michel succeeds in freeing himself from the shackles of the conventional life for the erotic splendor of Algeria, the narrative closes not on the ardent prospect of a paradise regained, but instead on Michel's diagnosis of a sudden onset of anomie within himself:

J'avais quand vous m'avez connu d'abord, une grande fixité de pensée, et je sais que c'est là ce qui fait les vrais hommes; — je ne l'ai plus. Mais ce climat, je crois, en est cause. Rien ne décourage autant la pensée que cette persistance de l'azur. Ici toute recherche est impossible, tant la volupté suit de près le désir. Entouré de splendeur et de mort, je sens le bonheur trop présent et l'abandon à lui trop uniforme. Je me couche au milieu du jour pour tromper la longueur morne des journées et leur insupportable loisir. (180)
[When you first knew me, I had a great steadfastness of mind, and I know that's what makes real men — I have it no longer. But this climate, I believe, is what's responsible for the change. Nothing discourages thought so much as this perpetual blue sky. Here any exertion is impossible, so closely does pleasure follow desire. Surrounded by splendor and by death, I feel happiness too close, and the surrender to it too constant. I lie down in the middle of the day to deceive the dreary prospect of time and its intolerable leisure. (169–70)]

Having reached the ostensibly blissful condition where pleasure so closely follows desire, Michel fails to find the life "plus spacieuse et aérée" (105) [more spacious and exposed (92)] that he had projected in its absence. Instead, he discovers the curious emptiness of fulfillment, for he lives in a world where being satiated, he finds his will diminished to such an extent that the only claim he can make on his own attention is to divert himself with endlessly monotonous pastimes:

J'ai là, voyez, des cailloux blancs que je laisse tremper à l'ombre, puis que je tiens longtemps dans le creux de ma main, jusqu'à ce qu'en soit épuisée la calmante fraîcheur acquise. Alors je recommence, alternant les cailloux, remettant à tremper

ceux dont la froideur est tarie. Du temps s'y passe, et vient le soir . . . (180–81; ellipsis in original).
[I keep here, look! some white pebbles that I leave in the shade to steep, then I hold them a long time in the palm of my hand, until the soothing coolness they've borrowed is . . . used up. Then I begin again, alternating the stones, putting back in the shade the ones whose coolness has been exhausted. That's how time passes, and evening comes . . . (170; ellipsis in original)]

Michel explicitly repudiates the life of excess he initially elects to pursue and indicates that he wishes to recommit himself to some sounder course of conduct.

In *L'Immoraliste*, Gide thereby registers how difficult it is for his protagonist to speak on behalf of pleasure in an erotophobic society. The possibility of liberation from sexual repression coexists uneasily with dispensations from economic norms that nonetheless stigmatize pleasures destined to appear, from within those norms, as "immoderate," "decadent," or "exploitative." Although Michel's fervent attempts to embrace erotic excess lead him to make the subjective *judgment* that confirms erotophobic constructs, it is noteworthy that he lacks the *will* with which to certify that judgment by putting it into action. While the text cannot ratify Michel's erotic excess, no sound course of conduct, no social prescription, emerges in the text whose ideological function would be to validate the prohibitions and discipline associated with the workaday world. The immediate dissatisfactions that Michel associates with the life he leads in Algeria are insufficient to make palatable, or even less burdensome, the bourgeois existence with which he proves himself so easily discontented. The end to which Michel comes in *L'Immoraliste* can, in fact, only represent one more disenchantment – a disenchantment, however, that makes the world seem like an infinitely smaller place.

NOTES

I would like to express my appreciation to Michael Lucey and Lee Clark Mitchell for their attentive readings of an early draft of this chapter and for their useful suggestions for revising it.

1. See Susan Sontag: "As much as TB was celebrated as a disease of passion, it was also regarded as a disease of repression. The high-minded hero of Gide's *The Immoralist* contracts TB (paralleling what Gide perceived to be his own story) because he repressed his true sexual nature; when Michel accepts

Life, he recovers." *Illness as Metaphor* (New York: Farrar, Straus and Giroux, 1978), 21.

2. The Sotadic Zone (New York: Panurge Press, n.d.), 94. For a fussy account of sodomy in Algeria, see E.-A. Duchesne, *De la prostitution dans la ville d'Alger depuis la conquête* [About Prostitution in the City of Algiers since the Conquest] (Paris: J.-B. Baillière, Garnier Frères, 1853), 35–46. Duchesne's book ranges beyond a simple consideration of prostitution in Algeria to comment on sexual manners in the Eastern world.

3. Guy Delrouze, "Le Préjugé contre les moeurs: Son origine, sa valeur, ses dangers" [Prejudice against Custom: Its Origin, Value, Dangers], *Akademos: Revue mensuelle d'art libre et de critique* 7 (15 July 1909): 21–22; my translation.

4. Winifred Woodhull, "Unveiling Algeria," *Genders*, no. 10 (spring 1991): 121.

5. Although *L'Immoraliste* is clearly about the transformation its protagonist undergoes in Algeria, only a few critical studies foreground the colonial context. See Jonathan Dollimore, *Sexual Dissidence: Augustine to Wilde, Freud to Foucault* (Oxford: Clarendon Press, 1991), particularly chap. 1, "Wilde and Gide in Algiers," 3–18, and chap. 21, "Desire and Difference," 329–56; Michael Lucey, "The Consequences of Being Explicit: Watching Sex in Gide's *Si le grain ne meurt*," *Yale Journal of Criticism* 4 (fall 1990): 174–92; and "Gide Writing Home from Africa, or from Biskra with Love," *Qui Parle* 4 (spring 1991): 23–42; and Mary L. Pratt, "Mapping Ideology: Gide, Camus and Algeria," *College Literature* 8, no. 2 (1981): 158–74.

6. André Gide, *L'Immoraliste* (Paris: Mercure de France, 1902), 21. *The Immoralist*, trans. Richard Howard (New York: Vintage Books, 1970), 11. All further references, first to the French edition then to the English translation, are made parenthetically in the text.

7. The most prominent British and French tourist firms represented the French colony as the ideal place to recover from pulmonary diseases. See *Cook's Practical Guide to Algeria and Tunisia, with Maps, Plans, and Illustrations* (London: Thomas Cook & Son, 1903), 6; Lt. Col. R. L. Playfair, *Handbook for Travellers in Algeria and Tunis, Algiers, Oran, Constantine, Carthage, etc.*, 2nd ed. (London: John Murray, 1878), 4. The French Guide Joanne, moreover, represented the healthiness of the Algerian climate as a direct consequence of colonization. "Le climat de l'Algérie est très-sain. L'inculture du sol et la présence des marais étaient, dans l'origine de l'occupation, les principales causes des maladies pour les Européens. Ces causes ont disparu en grande partie, et elles auront bientôt disparu entièrement, grâce aux travaux de colonisation." Louis Piesse, *Itinéraire historique et descriptif de l'Algérie de Tunis et de Tanger* [Historical and Descriptive Itinerary of Algiers, Tunis and Tangiers], 2nd ed. (Paris: Librairie Hachette et Cie, 1874), xxxiii. [The climate of Algeria is very healthy. From the period of the occupation, illness in Europeans was principally caused by the lack of cultivation of the soil and the presence of swamps. Thanks to the work of colonization, these causes have disappeared in large part, and soon will have disappeared entirely (my translation).]

8. *The New Playground, or Wanderings in Algeria* (London: C. Kegan Paul & Co., 1881), 9.
9. "Thus the ladies of the British Empire in India did not relax the cumbersome proprieties of Victorian dress to suit the climate. Similarly, for the females of the landed aristocracy in Europe, a pale complexion was the symbol of their superior delicacy, their idleness and seclusion. When these aristocracies and their empires became decadent and began to collapse, this hierarchic attitude to skin tone also began to collapse." Louis Turner and John Ash, *The Golden Hordes: International Tourism and the Pleasure Periphery* (New York: St. Martin's Press, 1976), 78–79. For the travelling sophisticate seeking to experience the simpler life, at least in its largely romanticized forms, Italy serves in the narrative as a symbolic way station between metropolitan France and colonial Algeria.
10. "In a culture that since the eighteenth century has massively depreciated male embodiment — as Elaine Scarry reminds us via Marx, it is not the capitalist, but only the worker, who 'suffers, desires, and risks in his body' — we must register the distinctiveness of those practices of post-Stonewall gay male culture whose explicit aim, uncompromised by weather or fashion, is to make the male body visible to desire." D. A. Miller, *Bringing Out Roland Barthes* (Berkeley: University of California Press, 1992), 30. Gide might be cited as the signal instance, prior to Stonewall, of a strategy to make the gay male body visible to desire following the example established not only by the worker but also by the native. In the process, however, Gide *authenticates* the stereotype of the lascivious native. See, for example, Frantz Fanon's protest against such European representations in *Black Skin, White Masks* (New York: Grove Press, 1967). Robert Mapplethorpe's photograph, *Man in Polyester Suit* (1980), produces an image of the natural man as a cliché. For a relevant discussion, see Kobena Mercer's "Skin Head Sex Thing: Racial Difference and the Homoerotic Imaginary," in *How Do I Look?: Queer Film and Video*, ed. Bad Object-Choices (Seattle: Bay Press, 1991), 169–210; see particularly 175–77.
11. See the following passage where Gide describes the quality of his sexual experiences in sub-Saharan Africa also in relationship to a landscape, the swiftly disappearing equatorial forests of the Congo: "[J]e ne m'y cantonne pas dans la seule jouissance charnelle: celle-ci m'invite à me fondre et confondre dans la nature environnante. C'est bien aussi pourquoi mes souvenirs de volupté les plus parfaits sont ceux qu'accompagne l'enveloppement d'un paysage qui l'absorbe et où je me paraisse me résorber. Dans celui que je viens d'évoquer de ces transes de Mala [Gide's lover from Cameroon], ce n'est pas seulement le beau corps pâmé de cet enfant que je revois, mais tout l'alentour mystérieux et formidable de la forêt équatoriale." *Ainsi soit-il ou les jeux sont faits* (Paris: Gallimard, 1952), 151. [I do not intend thereby to confine myself to mere carnal pleasure which invites me to merge myself and to be joined with surrounding nature. This is why my most perfect memories of voluptuousness are those enveloped in a landscape which absorbs it and in which I

seem to be swallowed up. In the landscape which I have just evoked of Mala's transports, it is not only the beautiful swooning body of the child I see again, but the whole mysterious and fearful surrounding of the equatorial forest.] *So Be It, or the Chips Are Down*, trans. Justin O'Brien (New York: Alfred A. Knopf, 1959), 126–27. (Translation is occasionally modified without comment.)] Though this memory dates from Gide's journey to the Congo in 1925–26, it was not published in *Voyage au Congo* or *Le Retour du Tchad*, the journals that recount that trip.

12. Stuart Marshall makes a parallel claim about Magnus Hirschfeld's attempts to problematize nature:

> Hirschfeld made use of a contradiction internal to the discourse of deviancy in order to construct a reverse discourse of resistance to the process of social stigmatization. The contradiction that lay at the heart of criminal anthropology and the new psychiatry was the problematic status of nature itself. The concept of nature was highly unstable: on the one hand, it represented the truth of human society uncorrupted by the artificiality of developed industrial capitalism; on the other hand, it represented the dark forces of uncivilized primitive man, which had to be transcended in order to perfect human society.

"The Contemporary Political Use of Gay History: The Third Reich," in *How Do I Look?*, 73–74. For a more general account of the ideology of nature, see Neil Smith, *Uneven Development: Nature, Capital and the Production of Space* (Oxford: Basil Blackwell, 1990), 15–16, in particular.

13. For a similar claim, see how Simon Watney traces complex parallels

> between the anthropological attention to African sexuality, illustrated in the lantern-light of eugenic theory, and the equally spectacular inventory of "the perversions," so painstakingly catalogued by the early sexologists. Blacks and "perverts" alike were held to share the characteristics of unbridled sexual rapacity and low cunning. They might also, however, be led to at least the semblance of normality — the former as a result of missionary zeal, and the latter by "therapeutic" initiatives.

"Missionary Positions: AIDS, Africa, and Race," in *Out There: Marginalization and Contemporary Cultures*, ed. Russell Ferguson, Martha Gever, Trinh T. Minh-ha, and Cornel West (Cambridge: MIT Press, 1990), 98.

14. "For Michel in *The Immoralist* and to an extent for Gide himself, desire may be proscribed but this does not affect its authenticity or its naturalness; if anything it confirms them. It is society which is inauthentic." Dollimore, *Sexual Dissidence*, 15. Dollimore provides an extended commentary on how Gide undermines the traditional understanding of the nature of nature in the construction of an authentic self, but fails to consider why Algeria should be the site of the self's discovery of its nature.

15. André Gide, *Si le grain ne meurt* (Paris: Gallimard [Collection Folio], 1955), 345; ellipsis in original, my translation.

16. Michael Lucey has mapped the terrain of decadent homosexual culture before me. See "The Consequences of Being Explicit," 186–87.

17. In the words of Réda Bensmaïa, Algeria functioned within "the imagination

of a decadent [French] elite . . . as a preserve where one might experience otherness under the protection of the French flag." "The School of Independence," in *A New History of French Literature*, ed. Denis Hollier et al. (Cambridge: Harvard University Press, 1989), 1018.

18. Even though the Algerian's body is dark before work, Gide is nonetheless capable of envisioning how the sun transforms the already darkened body into an object of his desire. In his autobiography, Gide makes an effusive point of his own attraction for dark skin: "Disons encore et plus précisément que je suis attiré par ce qui reste de soleil sur les peaux brunes." *Si le grain ne meurt*, 305. [Let me say once again and more precisely that I am attracted by what remains of the sun on brown skins (my translation).]

19. See the diagnosis of French psychoanalyst, Jean Delay, of Gide's own pedophilia as a problem of arrested development: "[L]e problème est de déterminer quelles influences ont empêché la maturation de l'instinct et arrêté [le] développement normal [de Gide]." *La jeunesse d'André Gide*, vol. 2 (Paris: Gallimard, 1957), 528. [[T]he problem is to determine which influences retarded the maturation of the instinct and arrested Gide's normal development (my translation).]

20. Andrew Holleran is the contemporary American inheritor of the narrative of sexual liberation Gide inaugurates when, through his character Michel, he promotes the value of eros over labor. See, for example, the following passage:

[T]he entire realm of daytime existence became meaningless to Malone, and he wondered how it was possible for men to do anything but pursue amorous interests; how it was possible for them to found businesses, build buildings, play squash. He found himself coming home on the subways in the morning, with crowds of people on their way to work — and while the man hanging onto the strap beside him was on his way to the headquarters of Citibank, he was coming home from a long night of love with one of its tellers.

Andrew Holleran, *Dancer from the Dance* (New York: William Morrow and Co., Inc., 1978), 127.

21. Other pleasures that Michel might have enjoyed in commodified forms include the spectacle of the "*danse du ventre*" at the Parisian *exposition universelle* in the 1800s. The exposition represented stereotypes of Eastern exoticism for a leisured European audience. See Zeynep Çelik and Leila Kinney, "Ethnography and Exhibitionism at the Expositions Universelles," *Assemblage* 13 (December 1990): 35–59.

22. *The Prison-House of Language: A Critical Account of Structuralism and Russian Formalism* (Princeton, NJ: Princeton University Press, 1972), 178.

23. If the bourgeois homosexual in *L'Immoraliste* forms cross-class identifications and values experiences that require him to transgress against norms of bourgeois conduct, his behavior appears in accordance with contemporary police accounts, as Alain Corbin represents them:

To the police the homosexual was a person who disdained social barriers. His "unnatural" activities were no longer the exclusive province of the aristocracy. The grande bourgeoisie and artistic circles had allowed themselves to become contaminated. Police records indicated that people of this class often associated with proletarians. Pederasts were even more susceptible to fascination with the lower orders than were men who frequented prostitutes. Homosexuals felt no compunctions about crossing boundaries of class and race. For all these reasons, homosexual behavior seemed abominable to members of the bourgeoisie, who worried about preserving their bodies from contamination and who were as devoted to the purity of sex as aristocrats were to the nobility of blood.

"Backstage," in Vol. 4 of *A History of Private Life: From the Fires of Revolution to the Great War*, ed. Michelle Perrot, trans. Arthur Goldhammer (Cambridge: Harvard University Press, 1990), 640–41.

24. Herbert Marcuse, *Eros and Civilization: A Philosophical Inquiry into Freud* (Boston: Beacon Press, 1955), 50.

25. For an interesting discussion of the metaphorical association between homosexuality and an impotent economy in the context of contemporary American photography, see Allan Sekula, "Some American Notes," *Art in America* 78 (February 1990), 143.

26. The attempt to develop a counterdiscourse or ideology might be attributed to Edward Carpenter, who undermines the equation between reproduction and productivity by making reproductive sexuality a sign of materialism: "it is not unlikely that the markedly materialistic and commercial character of the last age of European civilized life is largely to be connected with the fact that the *only* form of love and love-union that it has recognized has been one founded on the quite necessary but comparatively materialistic basis of matrimonial sex-intercourse and child-breeding." *Homogenic Love and Its Place in a Free Society* (London: Redundancy Press, n.d.), 23; italics in original.

27. "For most people the financial aspects of tourism parallel the symbolic. One accumulates enough money with which to vacation, much as one progressively acquires the worries and tedium of the workaday world. Going away lightens this mental load and also one's money. Running out of money at the end of the holiday is hopefully accompanied by running out of cares and worries — with the converse accumulation of new perspectives and general well-being. The latter counteract the workaday worries with memories of more carefree times. In turn, they stimulate the anticipation and planning for the next vacation." Nelson H. H. Graburn, "Tourism: The Sacred Journey," in *Hosts and Guests: The Anthropology of Tourism*, ed. Valene Smith (Philadelphia: University of Pennsylvania Press, 1977), 23. Graburn offers a cheerful account of tourism, the antithesis of Gide's, in which pleasure is tidily subordinated to the discipline of economic commitments.

28. Roland Barthes offers a relevant description of a perverse economy of desire:

In Werther, at a certain moment, two economies are opposed. On the one hand, there is the young lover who lavishes his time, his faculties, and his fortune without counting the cost; on the other, there is the philistine (the petty official) who moralizes to him: "Parcel out your time . . . Calculate your fortune," etc. On the one hand, there is the lover Werther who expends his love every day, without any sense of saving or of compensation, and on the other, there is the husband Albert, who economizes his goods, his happiness. On the one hand, a bourgeois economy of repletion, on the other, a perverse economy of dispersion, of waste, of frenzy *(furor wertherinus)*. (Ellipsis in original)

A Lover's Discourse: Fragments, trans. Richard Howard (New York: Hill and Wang, 1978), 84–85.

29. Barbara Harlow offers a different reading:

Michel, the hero of Gide's *L'Immoraliste*, [refuses] to recognize in the Algerian landscape the life and historical presence of a people. The children, whom the ailing Michel had met on his first visit to Biskra, are no longer interesting to him on the occasion of his second encounter, when he finds them to have grown two years older and to have developed new activities and habits binding them to the social life of the oasis. . . . "And was this all that remained?" Michel responded to the changes in the Algerian youths, "All that life had made of them?" The children's very claim to a historicity of their own is anathema to Gide's aestheticism.

"Introduction," in *The Colonial Harem*, trans. Myrna and Wlad Godzich (Minneapolis: University of Minnesota Press, 1986), xix. Though Michel does in the end choose to distance himself from the social landscape of Algeria, Gide reveals the *tension* between the privilege that awaits Michel in Algeria and the fate of those children who have no choice but to commit themselves to conventional lives or face the more seriously debilitating miseries that might otherwise be their lot. It is thus possible to read the ending of *L'Immoraliste* in other terms besides the aesthetic – a position or value that Harlow is in any case too hasty in ascribing to Gide.

30. Michel's decision proves less than subversive in another sense. In the act of claiming the pleasure that makes him renounce the bonds imposed by family and nation, he must confine himself to the distant place where the choice he makes to transgress against bourgeois morality fails to challenge, in any substantial way, the official values of European society.

The Dangers of (D)alliance: Power, Homosexual Desire, and Homophobia in Marlowe's *Edward II*

Albert Rouzie

"Dalliance dangereth our lives"

— Matrevis, *Edward II* (V.iii.3)

In *Edward II*,[1] Derek Jarman's film adaptation of Christopher Marlowe's play, the passionate love affair between Edward and Gaveston is played to the hilt. The men embrace, kiss, and declare their passionate love in speeches taken verbatim from the text. In Jarman's hands these speeches ring with an authenticity of feeling that is difficult to imagine while reading the play. Jarman's openly gay interpretation transcends the ago-nized conflicts among scholars over whether Edward and Gaveston can be said to be truly homosexual, whether such a consciousness of different sexuality existed in 1590s England. The prevailing opinion is, for reasons I examine later, that contemporary conceptions of gay consciousness had not yet emerged. Edward and Gaveston could love each other and die in part for that fact, but they could not have seen themselves as part of a gay subculture, nor would their sexual identities have been formed in the crucible of hetero- versus homosexuality.

In an interview, Jarman said that "*Edward* is an obsessive, gay love story. When you first read it, you don't realize it. But it is so shocking when you actually get down to it."[2] Jarman is more interested in the project of "reclaiming a whole history for gay people" than in recreating the play's meanings in its ostensibly original milieu (Grundmann, 26). His film is a work for the present that seems blithely indifferent to scholarly condemnation of anachronism. Ignoring historical and literary critical opinions to the contrary, Jarman brings twentieth-century sexuality into the sixteenth and vice versa, substituting Edward's army with a queer nation of OutRage activists and dressing the nobles in suits and contemporary military attire. Colin MacCabe writes that the film presents "homosexuality as the key term in the understanding of the structure of English society."[3] Rather than condemn its strident anachronism, MacCabe suggests that the cultural work of Jarman's film is a continuation of "a debate about national and sexual identity that goes back four centuries to that moment at the beginning of the 1590s when the Elizabethan stage became the privileged symbolic space for a whole society" (13). Within this "symbolic space," the culture elaborates "definitions, both political and sexual, which will define what it is to be English" (13). The cultural work that was accomplished by theater in Elizabethan England is now played out on movie (and TV) screens across the globe.

Jarman's reading of the play emphasizes its subversive elements. The fact is that Marlowe's play would never have been made into a film by a Kenneth Branagh, for example, because Jarman's reading of it as an "obsessive, gay love story," which exposes the recognizable homophobia of the elite and the interanimation of sexual and class politics, is what makes the play relevant and attractive to audiences today.

Traditional readings of *Edward II* have predictably obscured, downplayed, or reviled the Edward/Gaveston love affair, reading the homosexuality as pathological, when recognizing it at all.[4] The explosion of more recent criticism has fared better at understanding discourses of gender, sexuality, and power in Elizabethan theater. Though, according to Jonathan Goldberg, much recent New Historicist work on Marlowe approaches the intersection of gender and sexuality with (probably unwitting) contemporary heterosexist assumptions.[5] Given the problems of addressing Renaissance sexuality, the critical debate surrounding Marlowe's *Edward II* seems to coalesce around the question of how central the play's homosexual relationship is and therefore to what extent the play can function as a founding text for current attempts within the academy to rewrite gay history outside of dominant "heterosexist" discourses. The gap between the artistic license of Jarman's *Edward II*, a production that embraces what Tom Stoppard called "the cavalier spirit of theater," and the "anxiety of anachronism" widely exhibited in academic criticism of the play, indicates how the roles and goals of academic reading and research differ from those of contemporary artists such as Jarman.[6] This difference rests in part on the varying needs and desires of the audience and the rules governing these not-entirely-distinct "interpretive communities."

Whereas academics write principally for each other, Jarman and his audience's approach to old texts is frankly polemical and nonscholarly (though by no means anti-intellectual); they identify Edward and Gaveston primarily as victims of homophobia and take pleasure in the film's *engagé* exploration of a highly visible homosexual relationship, a treatment that frankly and unflinchingly depicts homoeroticism (unlike the 1993 film, *Philadelphia*). Many critics might object to Jarman's version as a distortion of Marlowe's play and an attempt to revise Elizabethan sexuality for contemporary consumption, but I would like to suggest that the gulf between Marlowe's *Edward II* and Jarman's version may not be as difficult to reconcile as it first appears. Few academics would read the play as justifying Jarman's anachronisms, but I am claiming that the gist of Jarman's reading gets to the heart of the question of how central Edward and Gaveston's homosexual relationship is to the conflict that drives the plot.

I have used the term "homosexual" somewhat anachronistically to describe Edward and Gaveston's relationship. Today we cannot read this word (or "gay") outside of contemporary reifications that do not hold for Elizabethan England. To comprehend the emerging "(no) place"[7] of homosexuality in Renaissance England requires attention to the play between the ordering principles of gender and class[8] and the potentially disordering force of transgression against those constraining categories. As both a man and the ruler of the realm, a king ought to be more interested in war than poetry and pageantry; his loyalties [as expressed in his (d)alliances] should lie more with the aristocrats than the gentry or the peasants. Prescriptions and proscriptions such as these, designed to protect the traditions that maintain the power hierarchy, are usually expressed in terms that signify eternal, natural laws rather than interested and contingent political relations. Homoeroticism (particularly male/male) and homophobia do not become visible as distinct from the structuring power of gender and class, but within it as the thrust and parry in the battle for control and maintenance of established order.

I hope this chapter establishes that, in Marlowe's *Edward II*, Edward's elevation of male lovers in the power hierarchy creates a crisis of definition that simultaneously threatens ostensibly stable categories of class, gender, and sexuality, and that the response to this threat reveals a subtle but virulent homophobia signaling the beginnings of an incipient homosexual subjectivity and identity.

Though homosexuality as such was not yet the distinct category we have today, the centrality of the homosexual relationship in Marlowe's *Edward II* forces the reader and the play's audience to confront an apparent contradiction. Marlowe, a reputed "sodomite," writes a play in which homosexual passion is plainly established and brutally put down. If the category "homosexual" has not yet solidified, we may not read Marlowe as a gay figure/playwright in the modern sense. But to place his play's male-to-male love affair in its proper relation to the power struggles it presents, we must stipulate the beginnings of the category "homosexual," however inchoate. For what better way to make homosexual transgression visible than to locate it in the King, apogee of power and center of symbolic authority? What better way to expose and dramatize the mystification of homophobia than first to implicate it in class and political conflicts, and then to reveal the possibility of seeing it as a reaction to an emergent sexuality?

Analysis of Renaissance homosexuality in England by recent writers in Gay Studies reveals that homosexuality as a specific sexual behavior, identity, and lifestyle was perhaps incipient, but for many reasons ambiguously defined during the period.[9] It was not until the nineteenth century, according to Michel Foucault, that the homosexual became

a personage, a past, a case history, and a childhood in addition to being a type of life, a life form, and a morphology. . . . Nothing that went into his total composition was unaffected by his sexuality. . . . It was consubstantial with him, less as a habitual sin than as a singular nature.[10]

This explosion of discourse positing a "singular nature" enabled greater social control of "perversity" but simultaneously allowed a "reverse discourse" to form in opposition to its claims (Foucault, 43). The lack of such a defining and controlling discourse for the category "homosexual" in Renaissance England prevented any appropriation of those discursive strategies for its defense. There was no "deployment of sexuality" (Foucault, 106) at work in the Renaissance within which the binary opposition homosexual/heterosexual could operate.

Implicit in this recent discourse of homosexuality is the modern assumption of sexuality's fundamental role in the constitution of individual identity: sexuality as the self's deepest secret and key. Though Foucault's analysis is technically accurate, it is misleading to assume by this that a sudden onslaught of homosexual subjectivity came into being with the nineteenth century's binarization into hetero- versus homosexual identity. Claude Summers suggests instead that the "invention" of the modern concept of the homosexual was "a more gradual and more complex historical development."[11] He adds that

homosexual subcultures have been identified in medieval and Renaissance Europe; and, long before the nineteenth century, at least some (and probably many) individuals developed what we would today define — admittedly anachronistically — as a homosexual identity, marked by a subjective awareness of difference and a sense of alienation from society however securely ensconced within it the subject might appear to be. (Summers, 4)

Summers rightfully warns against an extreme "anxiety of anachronism" that would deny any homosexual subjectivity whatsoever in the Renaissance (5). As Foucault suggests, homosexual subjectivity depends for its development on a defining discourse that distinguishes it. If we can trace the presence of homophobia in Marlowe's play, that trace could signal the beginning contours of homosexual subjectivity.

The problem of uncovering a defining discourse is exacerbated by the apparent lack of discrete terms for homosexuality per se in the Renaissance: homosexuality was not so much unnameable as it carried many names lacking specific referents. It was part of what Gregory Bredbeck termed "the rhetorical legacy of undifferentiated vice."[12] The terms "sodomy" and "buggery" served to refer to "unnatural" sexual behavior associated with a general human tendency toward transgression of the laws of nature. At times, sodomy specifically referred to anal intercourse between various subjects: men and animals, men and men, men and women; buggery was an umbrella term for any nonprocreative sexual act and so included genital-to-genital sex with animals, the sodomies already mentioned, and masturbation, in descending degree of heinousness.[13] According to Ed Cohen, sodomy also acted as an umbrella term, indicating "a spectrum of nonprocreative sexual practices ranging from the use of a dildo or birth control to anal intercourse and bestiality."[14] Made a capital crime in 1533, "unnatural" sexual practices were considered part and parcel to other heretical tendencies and a variety of transgressive behaviors threatening to the prevailing concepts of order. Alan Bray elaborates:

Homosexuality was not part of Hooker's law of nature. It was not part of the chain of being, or the harmony of the created world or its universal dance. It was not part of the Kingdom of Heaven or its counterpart in the Kingdom of Hell (although that could unwittingly release it). It was none of these things because it was not conceived of as part of the created order at all; it was part of its dissolution. And as such it was not a sexuality in its own right, but existed as a potential for confusion and disorder in one undivided sexuality. What sodomy and buggery represented — and homosexuality was only part of these — was rather the disorder in sexuality that, in principle at least, could break out anywhere.[15]

So sodomy, and homosexuality within it, symbolized for the era a transgression of the boundaries of order into a wild shadow region of contagious desire without end, a malaise whose major symptom, debauchery, was thought perfectly capable of subverting and engulfing the entire body politic. Jonathan Goldberg elaborates on Bray's points:

Sodomy named sexual acts only in particularly stigmatizing contexts [and] is, as a sexual act, anything that threatens alliance, . . . that does not promote the aim of married, procreative sex. . . . These acts — or accusations of their performance — emerge into visibility only when those who are said to have done them also can be called traitors, heretics, or the like, at the very least, disturbers of the social order that alliance — marriage arrangements — maintained.[16]

Just as there was no discrete category "homosexual," sodomy was never considered apart from other forms of subversion.[17]

The case of Christopher Marlowe is instructive here, because the charges brought against him based on the (probably coerced) testimonies of Richard Baines and Thomas Kyd demonstrate similar transgressions. Marlowe was, according to Baines, a sceptic, papist sympathizer, traitor, and sodomite. It is likely that the authorities would have been much more concerned with the heresy and treason than the sodomy, but because these traits were often lumped together, the sodomy charge made the allegations more plausible (Bray, 20–21). Whereas Baines's testimony may not serve as disinterested evidence, Bray and others have concluded that the probability exists for its accuracy, that Baines's documents are based on Marlowe's actual opinions verifiable from sources other than Baines.[18] Marlowe's remark "that St. John the Evangelist was bedfellow to Christ and leaned alwaies in his bosome, that he used him as the sinners of Sodoma" was independently reported by both Baines and Kyd,[19] and, according to Bray, indicates Marlowe's flirtation with, if not adherence to, the Socinianism of Sir Walter Raleigh's circle with which Marlowe was thought to be connected (63–64). Socinianism denied the divinity of Christ, the Trinity, and original sin. This rejection of traditional Christianity and assertion of Christ as sodomite may be viewed as Marlowe's attempt to rupture orthodox proscriptions of male-to-male sexual behavior. In any case, it establishes Marlowe as an iconoclast who thrived on blaspheming traditional moral and religious beliefs.

However troubled we may be by the nature of the evidence on Marlowe's sexual preferences, he stands as a central figure cited repeatedly in work on homosexuality in the Renaissance. Much of this can be attributed to his infamous remarks from the Baines and Kyd sources, but nonetheless ambiguous, though perhaps more compelling, evidence can be found in the blatant homoeroticism of his literary works. Joseph Porter cites *Hero and Leander*, *Edward II*, and *Dido, Queen of Carthage* as works that flaunt Marlowe's sexual preference and feature an "urgent sensuality" that "realizes with peculiar provocativeness the renascent and newly problematic (because newly secular) appreciation of the body that had come up from the Italy of Botticelli and Michelangelo to an England comparatively starved for pictures and statues of nudes."[20]

What is perhaps most significant about Marlowe is that he was made to fit into the prevailing stereotype of a sodomite with its attendant connotations of heretic and traitor. Jonathon Goldberg writes that "Marlowe is charged with *being* what he and his society allowed existence only as *negations* and *fictions*," that he "lived and died in the impossible project — as author, government spy, and homosexual — of the marginalized, negativized existence permitted him" (his italics).[21] Considering his employment as a spy, Marlowe's skepticism, if it was a tactic for dealing with a prevailing order extremely hostile to deviant sexual practices, proved risky and ultimately fatal, shrouded as his death is in violence and mystery.[22] The risks associated with Marlowe's life — identifiable as heretical, traitorous, and sodomitic — resonate thematically with those faced by Edward and Gaveston.

The first scene with Gaveston and subsequent descriptions establish him as a stereotypical sodomite who seems to possess most of the characteristics that Edward Coke attributed to the origin of sodomy: "pride, excess of diet, idleness, and contempt of the poor."[23] He is "wanton" and loves debauchery, as evidenced by his plan for "Italian masques"; he disdains the poor: "As for the multitude, they are but sparks, / Raked up in embers of their poverty."[24] He is foreign (French), dresses like an Italian, and expresses distaste for England: "Not that I love the city or the men" (I.i.12). Though Marlowe's anti-Catholic audience might have enjoyed Gaveston's violent attack on the Archbishop, the stripping of his vestments and imprisonment reveals Gaveston's heresy and his willingness to use his new powers. The audience, even as they reacted favorably to Gaveston's anti-Catholic action, would have to acknowledge his stereotypically sodomitic character. Although the audience's conflicted emotions over Gaveston and Edward come together powerfully in this particular scene, throughout the play Marlowe employs this tactic of audience alienation from and identification with the lovers.

Marlowe's portrayal of Gaveston as a stereotypical sodomite makes all the more significant the play's lack of overt condemnation of Edward and Gaveston's relationship in traditional moral and religious terms. On the contrary, Gaveston's flair for theatrical productions presents homoerotic display in the more positive context of classical legend. This "urgent sensuality" is established early in the play when Gaveston speaks of his plans to entertain Edward; here Gaveston reveals himself to be both intuitive social climber and theatrical producer extraordinaire:

> I must have wanton poets, pleasant wits,
> Musicians, that with touching of a string
> May draw the pliant king which way I please:
> Music and poetry is his delight;
> Therefore I'll have Italian masques by night;
> Sweet speeches, comedies, and pleasing shows;
> And in the day when he shall walk abroad,
> Like sylvian nymphs my pages shall be clad;
> My men, like satyrs grazing on the lawns,
> Shall with their goat-feet dance the antic hay.
> Sometime a lovely boy in Dian's shape,
> With hair that guilds the water as it glides,
> Crownets of pearls about his naked arms,
> And in his sportful hands an olive tree,
> To hide those parts which men delight to see. (I.i.52–65)

What Gaveston and the King find pleasurable is defined in terms of the theatrical: role-playing, mythic transformation, and cross-dressing, all associated with the English Renaissance theater as a site for the allowable expression of the marginal, including homoeroticism. Edward, emboldened by the eroticized theatrical milieu Gaveston presents him, desires consummation of his fantasy life through marriage to his lover, symbolized by Edward's displacing the queen when Gaveston literally usurps her place next to the throne. When the King speaks of it, he binds together pleasure and power: "What, are you moved that Gaveston sits here? It is our pleasure; we will have it so" (I.iv.8–9). Thus the theater fuels and feeds on desires that are normally confined to the "liberties," London's theater district, but are here located at the very heart of the political system. The movement from periphery to center is crucial to accounting for the crisis generated by Gaveston's carnivalesque inversion. Gaveston is the foreign, low-class, sodomitical heretic whose "idle triumphs, masques, [and] lascivious shows" (II.ii.157) transform the court into theatrical spectacle and bring the carnivalesque relativization of roles and genders from periphery to center stage.[25]

As Phyllis Rackin observes, "the English Renaissance theater was an important site of cultural transformation — a place where cultural change was not simply reflected but also rehearsed and enacted,"[26] thus anxieties about emergent sexualities, gender fluidity, and political change could find expression in the only milieu where the culture's countervoices were allowed to speak freely. In this context, Marlowe's presentation of Edward's reign would evoke oscillations between audience sympathy and disgust for Edward in his bid for power and love on his own terms. Moreover, Marlowe seems to withhold final judgment of Edward by undercutting any audience loyalties that may develop during different parts of the play. Emily Bartels suggests that by presenting both sides, Marlowe encouraged "transgressive responses that implicate the audience as disturbingly complicitous . . . in the 'unlawful things' enacted onstage, placing the spectators in a compromised position between cultural standards that condemn and responses that condone."[27] *Edward II*, then, ought not to be read in terms of any final approval or disapproval of the relationship; the play refuses either easy moral condemnation of Edward and Gaveston's love affair, or a romanticized view of it as the innocent victim of a dominant heterosexuality.

The central problematic of sex and power in the play is that it places the homosexual relationship at center stage as the nexus of political and marital conflict, but is performed originally in a culture that apparently denies its distinctiveness and has yet to develop definitive discourses for it. This denial, however, appears to be overridden and perhaps exposed as such when near the play's conclusion, Edward's execution enacts a return of repressed homophobia.[28] So even though we are wise to refuse the homosexual/heterosexual polarity, Edward is clearly sacrificed, in part, for his refusal to back off from public homoerotic behavior; this refusal heralds a crisis of definition threatening to the ostensible stability of gender and class divisions. The audience's dialectic shutting between alienation and identification allows them to perceive this crisis of defini-tion, an insight that may allow them to imagine a subject position less subjected by the usual divisions.

As previously mentioned, subjectivity in Renaissance England was closely tied to a metaphysic that fixed one into social positions reflected in the hierarchical orders of class and gender. In order to define what it is and secure some stability, this metaphysic depends on the binary opposi-tion natural/unnatural. As Jonathon Dollimore put it, "post-structuralism is helping us to see again what the Renaissance already knew: identity is in-formed by what it is not."[29] Or as the witches in Macbeth proclaim: "Nothing is but what is not." This notion approximates Kenneth Burke's "paradox of substance":

To tell what a thing is, you place it in terms of something else. This idea of locating or placing is implicit in our very word for definition itself: to define or determine a thing is to mark its boundaries, hence to use terms that possess, implicitly at least, contextual reference. . . . To define a thing in terms of its context, we must define it in terms of what it is not. . . . Since determined things are positive, we might point up the paradox as harshly as possible by translating it as "every positive is negative."[30]

If this paradoxical definitional mode is fundamental to the constitution of the "natural," defining it in contradistinction to the not-it, then so are the ways of consolidating the power of the natural by maintaining an illusory separation from what it purportedly is not. Thus the nobles often invoke the "natural" to describe the alliance of king and queen and the king's duty to his peers, whereas the "unnatural" denotes any action or senti-ment that challenges this order, including sodomy.

Burke is of further instruction here in his discussion of the "scapegoat mechanism." The scapegoat "combines in one figure contrary principles of identification and alienation."[31] That is, the scapegoat figure and his persecutors must initially share in the qualities wished to be purged; these shared qualities establish an identification between the two. Then his persecutors "alienate from themselves to it their own uncleanlinesses. . . . [A scapegoat] cannot be 'curative,' " Burke writes, "except insofar as it represents the iniquity of those who would be cured by attacking it" (*Grammar*, 406). Although the persecutors and their "chosen vessel" are seen to originally share the iniquity, a purge of the contamination is effected through the sacrifice of the scapegoat, allowing "the unification of those whose purified identity is defined in dialectical opposition to the sacrificial offering" (Ibid., 406). Thus the purgation of a scapegoat both reveals and resolves a crisis of definition. This mechanism cuts across cultures and histories,[32] but is particularly useful for revealing dynamics of power in *Edward II*. Edward's refusal of the preformed roles of husband and king exposes his (and Gaveston's) homosexuality as scapegoat for the instability of the entire political structure, destabilized by the ambition of the nobles and the queen no less than that of the king's "flatterers." Edward's naive refusal to separate sex and politics serves as a revelation of the inseparability of the two throughout the realm, just as Gaveston's flaunting of his position marks the arbitrary nature of the power afforded noble birth. In this speech to the nobles, Gaveston attempts to invert the usual hierarchy:

> Base, leaden earls, that glory in your birth,
> Go sit at home and eat your tenants' beef,
> And come not here to scoff at Gaveston,
> Whose mounting thoughts never did creep so low
> As to bestow a look on such as you. (II.ii.74–78)

Such revelations are bought at a dear price. As the plot unravels, it becomes increasingly clear that the play's homosexuals, as purged scapegoats, have come to represent more than a specific threat to the power of a handful of nobles, that their presence and power threaten not only to expose the constructed nature of aristocratic power and its slippage due to the rise of the gentleman class, but that the sexual valence of power relations, once made so visible, may be seen to apply to barons and "base flatterers" alike. This identification is kept alien from the aristocrats not only by scapegoating, but by a subtle discourse, which seems to make light of homoerotic attachments even as it aligns them with phallic, often feminized images.

When Young Mortimer seems ready to mount a rebellion against Edward, his older and wiser uncle counsels him,

Leave now to oppose thyself against the king.
Thou seest by nature he is mild and calm,
And, seeing his mind so dotes on Gaveston,
Let him without controlment have his will. (II.i.389–92)

These lines lead into one of the play's only overt references to homosexuality, when the Elder Mortimer cites a long tradition of kings, warriors, and wise men's dalliances with their lessers:

The mightiest kings have had their minions;
Great Alexander lov'd Hephaestion,
The conquering Hercules for Hylas wept,
And for Patroclus stern Achilles droop'd.
And not kings only, but the wisest men;
The Roman Tully lov'd Octavius,
Grave Socrates wild Alcibiades. (II.i.393–99)

The modifiers — mightiest, great, conquering, stern, grave — all signify masculinity, the warrior tradition evoked through the legendary and mythic. The results of their loving — weeping and drooping — are misogynistically feminine, with "droop'd" connoting a general and phallic deflation or impotency. The Elder Mortimer appears willing to grant the coexistence of the extremes as a natural stage in a great man's development, qualified by the expectation that "riper years will wean him from such toys" (II.i.404). As long as such a relationship can be seen as a temporarily "wanton humour," its threat to masculinity and order is subsumed within a narrative of the maturing process of the great man.

Young Mortimer (hereafter referred to as simply Mortimer) answers that he is not bothered by the dalliance itself,

But this I scorn, that one so basely born,
Should by his sovereign's favor grow so pert,
And riot it with the treasure of the realm,
While soldiers mutiny for want of pay. (II.i.406–10)

Dalliance is one thing and alliance another. And so the terms of the opposition are set out in contradistinction to any overtly moralistic or religious condemnation; Mortimer charges the king with reckless abandonment of responsibility for the realm, class transgression, and the opening of the system of favor to outsiders. Goldberg reads Mortimer's apparent tolerance of kingly sexual perogative as Marlowe's "radical move" (*Sodometries*, 121); however, this stated tolerance spells out the terms for recognition of sodomy, that male/male dalliance is sodomy only when it connects with power politics and becomes (d)alliance.

The Elder Mortimer's view of the dalliance corresponds with the era's assimilation of homosexuality within patriarchal homosocial structures. Following Eve Sedgwick, Bruce Smith writes that "homosexuality was one of the many symbolic ways in which males could enact and affirm the patriarchal power that dominated the entire culture."[33] Homosexual behavior was therefore "an aspect of maleness," but one both defined and threatened by a feminine other (Ibid., 75). Although anxieties about gender slippage were aroused by theatrical crossdressing — men who dressed as women might become women — similar transformations were associated with the womanizing man whose excessive contact with women might feminize him. Neither seems to quite fit here, since it is apparent that Edward's love for Gaveston threatens the homosocial order. The barons progressively and unmistakably represent the king as feminized because he refuses male bonding with his most vital political constituents and defers his warrior role for that of the lover. Therefore, the homoerotic bond between the king and Gaveston refigures male bonding as sexual and political at the same time that it occasions homophobic responses that restore the homosocial order via scapegoating.

At first the audience is likely to feel repelled by the vicelike grip the Gaveston character exerts on the king. But following Gaveston's banishment and return, the nobles are not reacting to Edward's earlier dispensation of power and titles, a protest most clearly linked to Edward and Gaveston's breach of hierarchy and the rights afforded noble birth; rather, they protest Edward's passion for the man, which, considering the relationship's duration, suggests a level of feeling and a surrender to desire on Edward's part far surpassing youthful indiscretion. "Diablo, what passions call you these?" Lancaster asks at the sight of Edward's extreme longing for reunion with Gaveston (I.iv.321). Isabella remarks in one of the play's few direct references to homosexuality, "never doted Jove on Ganymede, so much as he on cursed Gaveston" (I.iv.181–82). Initially the Barons had assumed Edward's "wanton humour" to be tied to Gaveston's presence; that is, remove Gaveston and the attachment will dissipate. Lancaster assures the queen that "now his minion's gone / His wanton humour will be quickly left"; Isabella, who knows better, replies "O never Lancaster!" (I.iv.98–200). The logic of the plot to bring Gaveston back assumes that his return may restore the King's equilibrium, marriage, and power to the nobles. Gaveston's return would satisfy a desire that had "wax'd outrageous" by Edward's own admission, and if not, Gaveston can be killed by some "base slave."

Because the heterosexual relationship does not function in the play as the normative opposite to deviant homosexuality — Isabella seems prepared to sell the family out in order to consolidate her own power — her adulterous affair with the regicidal Mortimer subverts any notion of a "normal" sexuality. The naturalness of Isabella's bond to her husband symbolizes for the peers the order they wish to maintain, but Edward's refusal of the "natural" prevents this from occurring. The appeal to the order of marriage and family does not finally hold together. Although initially the audience might respond sympathetically to Isabella in her sorrow over her rejection by Edward, as the play unfolds, Isabella increasingly uses their estrangement to fuel the nobles' hatred of Gaveston: "These hands are tir'd with haling of my lord / from Gaveston, from wicked Gaveston" (II.iv.27–28). Though it is at her instigation that the nobles agree to let Gaveston return, her silent conversation with Mortimer leads us to infer that she has also masterminded Gaveston's death. When Kent sees her kiss Mortimer, realizing the error of opposing his brother, he cries, "Fie on that love that hatcheth death and hate!" (IV.v.24) Mortimer's "device" for Edward's "stately triumph," Gaveston's marriage to Edward's niece, is comprised of a "canker" that creeps up to the highest bough of the tree of state. With Mortimer's rising ambition, the worm has turned full circle. Ironically, it is Mortimer who becomes the more dangerous parasite, not Spenser, Gaveston's replacement. Finally, Isabella's full collusion in Mortimer's murder of Kent and Edward alienates her from any audience sympathy. Though at the end the kingdom is restored to the heir, Edward III, no marriages or relationships remain whole. And, as her motherhood "boots not," Edward III has Isabella jailed (V.vi.92).

Even though upon his return Gaveston's power may now be considered significantly curtailed, his titles revoked, and the nobles' power to have him banished demonstrated beyond any doubt, the peers' repulsion for his closeness to Edward seems only to grow. Can this be solely attributed to Gaveston's disrespect, his refusal to submit to "base stooping" (I.i.18) and the other reasons offered by the Peers, many in terms of the kingdom's welfare? Or, is it in response to the threat to order symbolized by the king's refusal of heterosexual alliance? Is it, at bottom, homophobia?

"Homoeroticism in the Renaissance is always circumscribed by homophobia," notes Claude Summers (7). Smith defines homophobia as "a belief that sexual orientation *alone* removes the subject from 'nature,' 'society,' and other totalizing schemas" (25, n. 46; my emphasis). Following this definition, we could not claim that contemporary formations of homophobia stand alone in the play. Why then is there a subtle undercurrent of apparent homophobia? Though homosexuality had not been fully constructed as a separate "structure of feeling," homoeroticism was acceptable within certain bounds and blasphemous within others. And by locating it in the center of power, Marlowe goes to some pains to make the homoeroticism blasphemous. The primary discursive form it takes here is in the Barons's representations of Edward and Gaveston. The discrepancy between overt statement ("His wanton humour grieves me not") and covert representation (images linking the monstrous and sodomitical) belies the terms of the nobles' rebellion against Edward and Gaveston's love affair, and reveals how the subtle linkage between sex and power (in)forms relations in the play.

Most of the epithets applied to Gaveston emphasize his lower-class status in the exaggerated terms of caste: "base peasant" (I.iv.7), "base flatterer" (II.v.11), "slave" (I.ii.25), "base minion" (I.i.133), "ignoble vassal" (I.iv.17), "creeping ants" (I,iv,16). Whereas this may appear to refer only to caste differences and Gaveston's ambition, distinctions between master and minion, according to Bruce Smith, often involve an erotic significance: "Renaissance Englishmen, like the Greeks and Romans, eroticized the power distinctions that set one male above another in their society. Sexual desire took shape in the persons of master and minion; sexual energy found release in the power play between them"(194). The word "minion" occurs frequently throughout the play and is used by nearly everyone, including Edward, to refer to Gaveston. The minions to the masters were usually boys, but not necessarily adolescents; besides referring to a young male child, "boy" could be either a playful term of affection or one of contempt, close in meaning to "base slave" or to the way grown black men were referred to in the American South as "boys" (Smith, 195). Though by his bearing toward Gaveston Edward willfully refuses the master/minion relation, the barons never let the pair forget Gaveston's minion status. Significantly, though Young Spenser's relationship to Edward is probably not sexual,[34] the barons' approach him no differently than Gaveston, focusing, as Bartels points out, on the younger

Spenser as fitting parallel to Gaveston (164). This supports Bredbeck's insight that "once sodomy is constructed as an affront to order, it can then be used to affront order" (75).

The baron's representations of Gaveston center on the intersection of the feminine, misogynistically construed as a repository of evil, with the phallic and monstrous. Lancaster, for example, compares Gaveston to Helen of Troy in a revealing amalgamation of monster, man, and strumpet:

> Monster of men,
> That, like the Greekish Strumpet, train'd to arms
> And bloody wars so many valiant knights,
> Look for no other fortune, wretch, than death! (II.v.14–17)

Clearly, the barons crossdress Gaveston as the symbolic fulfillment of his playing the queen. By investing Isabella with similar traits, Marlowe uses stereotypical misogyny to collapse distinctions between the factions. Because Isabella joins Gaveston in a monstrous assault on natural order, one might conclude that she too is a sodomite, precluding the notion that sodomy can point to a distinctly visible male/male sexual relation as its primary locus. But Isabella remains mostly out of the loop of the play's discourse. Her ambition is not declared unnatural until quite late in the drama when Kent turns his fealty for the last time back toward his brother and against "this unnatural revolt" (IV.v.18). The preponderance of the barons' discourse attacks the sodomitical flatterer. For example, the Barons present their "devices" to Edward for the "stately triumph" with images of dangerous monstrosity (II.ii.11–12). Both images, the creeping canker (glossed as a worm) that climbs up the tree of state and the flying fish, may be considered phallic, invasive in their penetration of taboo territory, and monstrous perversions of nature: fish out of water. Mortimer compares Gaveston to an even more phallic and this time benumbing and deadly fish, the "vile torpedo," an electric eel whose shocking force is invisible to the beholder:

> Fair Queen, forbear to angle for the fish,
> Which being caught, strikes him that takes it dead;
> I mean that vile torpedo, Gaveston,
> That now I hope floats on the Irish seas. (I.iv.221–24)

When Mortimer asserts that the people "cannot brook a night-grown mushrump" such as Gaveston, he hopes public opinion will sway against the couple (I.iv.284). The image richly commingles the sexually deviant and the natural. Taking advantage of the image of a poisonous mushroom and the sodomitic connotations of the Elizabethan "mushrump," Marlowe suggests the meteoric rise of a flatterer who curries favor by night, and mysteriously, as if by magic, appears out of nowhere. As with the other monstrous images attributed to Gaveston, the sexual and homoerotic meanings are inseparable from the monstrosity: deviance from the perceived order of nature inhabits sexual deviance and vice versa. That nature itself contains the very monsters that haunt and threaten the "natural" hierarchy is revised and obscured by the barons' discourse. Recalling Burke's scapegoat mechanism, we can see how Gaveston becomes the sacrificial vessel whose impurity unifies the perpetrators through the purging of their own monstrosity. Whether images of Gaveston are aggressively phallic ("vile torpedo") or gendered female ("the Greekish Strumpet"), his elimination carries generalized horror and monstrosity away from the order of nature.

Within these terms, King Edward has been corrupted and benumbed into effeminacy by the "night-grown mushrump." Here Mortimer notes that Edward plays at battle like it is more of a fashion show than the serious pursuit of a warrior.

> When wert thou in the field with banner spread
> But once? and then thy soldiers marched like players,
> With garish robes, not armour; and thyself,
> Bedaubed with gold, rode laughing at the rest,
> Nodding and shaking of thy spangled crest,
> Where women's favors hung like labels down. (II.ii.178–83)

The king has unmistakably been feminized with this imagery, though the civil war that ensues would seem to prove Mortimer wrong. Mortimer addresses Gaveston as "corruptor of thy king, cause of these broils" (II.v.10). And so all responsibility for strife, competition, favor, and the king's desires become displaced onto the foreigner Gaveston.[35] Once Gaveston is caught and killed, the nobles wrongly assume an end to the problem, underestimating Edward's passion and his willingness to continue his program of favoring the wanton flatterer. Edward's desire for "minions" would appear infinite, as born out by Young Spenser's easy segue into the king's affections.

The homophobia of the barons remains subtextual for most of the play, but it erupts in the ritual symbolic debasement of Edward toward the close; the ultimate feminizing is the shaving of his beard and his bathing in the channel-water — actually the excremental waste-water from the castle — to which his guard, Gurney, remarks he was "almost stifled with the savour" (V.v.9). Finally, his ritual sacrifice by the sadistic Lightborn unmistakably enacts, by thrusting a red hot poker up his anus, the sodomy for which he is at last openly condemned.[36] This execution, like all of Lightborn's tricks, leaves no exterior marking, and like the other methods, involves a sexually sadistic piercing and thrusting. Lightborn tells Mortimer,

> I learned in Naples how to poison flowers,
> To strangle with a lawn thrust down the throat,
> To pierce the windpipe with a needle's point,
> Or, whilst one is asleep to take a quill,
> And blow a little powder in his ears,
> Or open his mouth and pour quicksilver down. (V.iv.30–35)

Lightborn's refusal to reveal his method of penetrating Edward leaves Mortimer/Isabella ignorant of the exact method. Just as Gaveston's foreign origin locates the infectious sodomite outside of the realm, the most palpably homophobic act is displaced onto an outside agent that is presumably low born. Finally, the audience itself, as witnesses to Edward's debasement and sacrifice, becomes implicated in their judgment of the king: they may feel their own fear of and desire for the king's desires.

Through exposing homophobia, homosexual scapegoating, and the defeat of meaningful human relations in a bleak view of political change, Marlowe opens a space for the audience members to feel for themselves the cycle of alienation and identification that converges on figures who transgress boundaries of sexual desire and class hierarchy. From beginning to end, the audience has ridden the vicissitudes of overturning allegiance. The vacillating figure of Kent may indicate the general movements of sympathy and antipathy the audience feels, but there is little doubt that near the end the sympathy has shifted toward Edward and his deceased friends. Kent's beheading by Mortimer and the queen for his failed attempt to rescue his brother may mark the point at which the audience crosses the last roadblock to full sympathy for Edward's side; having shifted their sentiments in a fashion similar to Kent's, they may feel symbolic investment in his fate. The audience, caught and caught up in a voyeuristic gaze, gets torn up by their emotions. The dramatic force of this catharsis purges all sympathy for the perpetrators and prevents any easy objectification of the homosexual lovers. Finally, although only some semblance of homophobic discourse seems to have surfaced, we have characters whose homoerotic desires the audience may come to feel from an inside perspective, especially as they experience their dramatic purgation. As Bruce Smith suggests, "In *Edward II* we not only *see* the conflict between homosexual desire and the social order; we are invited to *feel* it" (223; his italics). Smith tracks a "psychological shift" from the stereotype of the sodomite circulated by social commonplaces to an "interior experience of homoerotic desire" that "introduces us to the possibility of a homosexual subjectivity" (223). Because the audience can now perceive the objectification they have left behind, they can see the lovers as subjects, or at least as occupying a not wholly negativized space. If, as Burke asserts, "every positive is negative," then the reverse is also true: every negative is positive. Edward, as martyr for an incipient sexual subjectivity, brings male/male sexuality out of the void of sodomy and into view.

Earlier, I referred to Foucault's insight that a discourse on the "singular nature" of homosexuality allowed for reverse discourses to form that often appropriate the terms of the discourses they oppose. It appears obvious that Edward cannot escape as he would like; he cannot simply rebel and effect any consequential change. For Foucault, developing a counterdiscourse does not enable escape from a structure that produces resistance in order to better contain it. Marlowe's heroes, as Stephen Greenblatt has depicted them,

imagine themselves set in diametrical opposition to their society where in fact they have already unwittingly accepted its crucial structural elements. For the issue is not man's power to disobey, but the characteristic modes of desire and fear produced by a given society, and the rebellious heroes never depart from those modes.[37]

Edward wants to integrate into the center of power what the order proscribes, and he hopes to do so by the force of a traditional king's authority, the only method available. And so he depends on the terms of hierarchy and privilege even as he insists on their dissolution, for he upbraids the nobles' opposition to his desires as unnatural while invoking the naturally absolute authority of kingship. The more he is denied the freedom to indulge his desire, the more he desires; the more violently the nobles oppose him, the more he threatens and enacts violence and retribution. But despite the limitations Greenblatt cites, the existence of sexual and political choice is itself a destabilizing factor. Choice posits a challenge to authority, and if one can choose to be either Protestant, Catholic, or Anglican, to love men or women or both, then the metaphysical structure upon which authority stands is no longer unified.

One then is faced with a struggle for power between competing authorities, which in the process weakens the very idea of authority. The tragedy of the play may be that its protagonist is incapable of making a choice that can escape "the characteristic modes of desire and fear" of the society. But that choice to rebel is also what sets in motion the crisis of definition that must be resolved by scapegoating, an action that makes both crisis and its resolution more visible. Actions and attempted inversions may have disastrous consequences, but they reveal the dominant culture's means of suppressing knowledge of its own corruption. This revelation offers the possibility of a critically conscious deconstruction of the dominant's binary oppositions.

Perhaps Marlowe's most subversive move is that he not only makes the sensual aspect of the homoerotic highly visible, but also sets up a fearful symmetry between male/female and male/male sexual relations. This ought to be read as establishing a fundamental ambiguity exploited throughout the play.[38] We can see the symmetry as an expression of the English Renaissance belief in the danger of excess in whatever form — love is not the problem unless it leads to "unnatural" excess, that is, nonprocreative sex and transgressive (d)alliances — or we can see this as a self-conscious subversion of the asymmetry between procreative and nonprocreative sex. Marlowe is able to keep his audience members off-balance: they can neither condemn nor praise the homoerotic relationship because to do so would involve a conscious separation of it from the play's presentation of power politics. Yet that relationship is central to the play. Stripped of the homoeroticism, the "lascivious shows," and the heartfelt declarations of love, the play would enact a power struggle between a king who favors the distribution of power based on a new system that disregards traditional power alignment by birthright, and the barons who stand to lose the most in that transformation. Marlowe shows an England in transit from a feudal state to nascent early modern capitalism, resulting in increased social mobility and the more arbitrary social positioning which money and influence can buy. A good example of this is Baldock, another of this new breed of gentleman courtier. Baldock introduces himself to Edward with "my gentry I fetched from Oxford, not from heraldry." Edward replies, "The fitter art thou, Baldock, for my turn"

(II.ii.43–45). Edward's "turn," when he pledges money for Old Spenser to buy an estate and peerage, is just such a move toward the open acknowledgment of the gentleman class as a new power. Edward's (d)alliance with Gaveston serves as a particularly extreme example of the merging of class and sexuality.

Significantly, Marlowe portrays Gaveston as barely of the gentleman class, whereas the historical Gaveston, according to John Boswell, "was not a commoner . . . but an aristocrat of charm and enormous skill and valor."[39] Accentuating the class transgression serves to feed the already alienating force of the explosive homoeroticism and ties it inextricably with the rise of the new class. Lawrence Stone reports that "the most fundamental dichotomy within the society was between the gentleman and the non-gentleman," a distinction founded on whether or not one had to work with their hands.[40] When the nobles exaggerate the class transgression of Gaveston's rise in kingly favor by demoting him to the status of a base commoner, they are, in effect, suggesting the bodily nature of his "work" on the king.

Though visible, the homoeroticism is not privileged as a more pure mode of relation than the heteroerotic; neither is the increasingly powerful gentry inherently superior to the nobles. The gentry lacks metaphysical claims to eternal authority as a discursive resource, whereas the homosexual, embodying both identification with and alienation from the structure, is particularly suited as the sacrificial vessel capable of purging both. Marlowe exposes the material and political motives that make the polis an unsuitable space for human love and friendship. Here ambition pollutes all who play the game, but the traditional power hierarchy alone possesses the tactical and discursive power to establish and maintain the terms for who and what is either defined as natural or purged.

Yet, as we have seen, Marlowe's theater opens the seams of the dominant discursive power to view. Both Edward and Gaveston employ the homoeroticism of cross-dressing in order to both reveal and revel in the dangerousness of their (d)alliance. When Gaveston returns from his second exile, Edward's greeting includes a revealing comparison:

> Thy absence made me droop and pine away;
> For, as the lovers of fair Danae,
> When she was locked up in a brazen tower,
> Desired her more, and wax'd outrageous,
> So did it fair with me. (II.ii.52–56)

Edward figures himself in the tradition of the separated lover, but significantly casts Gaveston as female to his drooped male (echoing the Elder Mortimer). The significance of Edward's allusion goes beyond his playing Zeus to Gaveston's Danae, a play wholly in keeping with Gaveston's shows, for the issue from this particular mythic coupling, Perseus, results in death to the patriarch, Danae's father. Thus, prohibited couplings, especially those that breach hierarchical chasms, threaten the patriarchal family. For the king's amusement, Gaveston will also have "a lovely boy in Dian's shape" bathe in a spring while players enact around him the myth of Actaeon. In this story, the hunter Actaeon is punished for his voyeuristic gaze upon the bathing goddess, Diana, when she turns him into a stag that is then torn to pieces by his own hounds. The Actaeon myth, like that of Zeus and Danae, suggests the inherent danger of male/female sexual relations across the chasm of hierarchy, and because the goddess Diana is here played by a "lovely boy" (just as Edward plots Gaveston as Danae), the danger also extends to eroticizing males and sexual desire in general.

The larger significance of theatrical cross-dressing lies in the increased homoerotic dynamics of both the Edward/Isabella/Gaveston and the Edward/Isabella/Mortimer triangles. Lisa Jardine asserts that the "stage irony" of Isabella's being played by a boy would not be lost on the audience. Thus Edward's supposedly "natural" love with Isabella is called into question by the male/male actor coupling on the stage.[41] If the disparity stays on the audience's mind as Jardine expects it would, it might help foreground the rivalries of the erotic triangles. Thus, Mortimer's wooing of Isabella elicits the same irony, leading one to consider whether Mortimer's protestations against Gaveston are not, at bottom, the jealous curses of a spurned lover.

Isabella's transformation from wronged wife to revenging queen with all her fine dissembling and plotting suggests an increasingly aggressive masculinity. The gendered subtext is inverted: a boy plays the role of Isabella, and Isabella begins to play the role of a man. But in loving Mortimer, Isabella crosses no hierarchical chasms, and her plotting becomes increasingly subservient to Mortimer's ambition and dominance. When, before the invasion, the queen speaks eloquently to the troops about the reasons for the coming war, Mortimer tellingly cuts her off: "Nay, Madam, if you be a warrior, / you must not grow so passionate in speeches" (IV.iv.15–16). Mortimer recognizes the queen's consciousness of her new power, her desire to be warrior and orator, and in one verbal blow, represents it as ineffectual and renders it so. Given to the passions and poetic that helped to spell the downfall of Edward, she is hopelessly gendered female by Mortimer and put in her place. Whereas Isabella's aggressiveness can be officially explained and sanctioned as a necessary and responsible intervention in Edward's refusal to rule, Gaveston's elevation into aristocratic titles and powers, and particularly his satiric disrespect for the nobles, epitomizes the threat of unlicensed inversion. This is not the licensed inversion of Bakhtinian carnival we might normally associate with the theatrical milieu, but a far more threatening contamination. Carnival presupposes a temporary and officially licensed inversion of hierarchy. As such, it can act as a pressure valve that allows potentially revolutionary steam to escape harmlessly, leaving all structures intact. On the other hand, the upheaval in *Edward II*, caused by the conjunction of transgressive sexual desire and the elevation of a lower class, stems from unlicensed inversions that threaten the stability of the hierarchy. Jonathon Dollimore asserts the demystifying, and therefore subversive, potential of inversion in its ability to make visible the workings of definitive discourses and scapegoating: "Even as civil society endlessly displaces corruption from the social body as a whole onto its lowlife, the latter reveals both the original source and full extent of corruption within the dominant itself" (61).

Of course, answers to all questions of subversion and containment remain in a state of perpetual deferment, and perhaps the demystification I impute to the experience of watching and reading *Edward II* is more important in the present moment than in any remote and irrecoverable past. To suggest that Marlowe probably sacrificed his life over the impossible roles he chose, that his last play strongly exposes his own tendencies, that in it the theater's radical possibilities invade the central locus of power, may help alleviate our sometimes dispirited and increasing sense that literature no longer really matters.

NOTES

I would like to thank Leah Marcus, Ed Madden, Linda Brodkey, and Randi Voss for their perceptive responses to early drafts of this chapter.

1. Derek Jarman, director, *Edward II* (Fine Line Features, 1991).
2. Roy Grundmann, "History and the Gay Viewfinder: An Interview with Derek

Jarman," *Cineaste* 18, no. 4 (1991): 24–27. Further references to this work are included parenthetically in the text.

3. Colin MacCabe, "Throne of Blood," *Sight and Sound* (Oct. 1991): 12.

4. For a brief but illuminating survey of critical views since World War II of homosexuality in *Edward II*, focusing particularly on Edward's death scene, see Stephen Guy-Bray, "Homophobia and the Depoliticizing of Edward II," *English Studies in Canada* 17, no. 2 (June 1991): 125–33. Guy-Bray accuses all but a few critics of "critical homophobia." He writes: "The critics deal with the threat posed by Marlowe's presentation of Edward's homosexuality by diagnosing both the writer and the king as neurotic, if not actually insane." These critics "have helped Lightborn do his job" (132).

5. Jonathan Goldberg, *Sodometries: Renaissance Texts, Modern Sexualities*. (Stanford, CA: Stanford University Press, 1992), 105–43. Further references to this work are included parenthetically in the text. Goldberg objects to representations of English Renaissance homosexuality as a "transvestite masquerade." He particularly analyzes work by Orgel, Howard, and Levine and concludes that in their criticism "sexuality is collapsed through the assumptions of modern gender, the presumption that all sexuality is hetero, and that same-sex relations are versions of male/female ones" (111).

6. This phrase is from a 1993 talk Stoppard gave at the University of Texas at Austin. He suggests that it is in the nature of theatrical production (and film, I would add) to assert great artistic license with venerated texts, so much as to render absurd the very notion of a play's text.

7. Jonathan Goldberg, "Colin to Hobbinol: Spenser's Familiar Letters," *South Atlantic Quarterly* 88 (1989): 114.

8. "Class" here refers to an individual's place in the power/status hierarchy, which in Renaissance England resembled a caste system more than it does nineteenth- and twentieth-century class structure. Though the Marxist term may be anachronistic, I prefer "class" to "power status" for its economy, but also because I wish to suggest that increased social mobility was transforming the status system from a birth to an economically driven one.

9. Goldberg maintains that no truly homosexual subcultures existed until the Restoration and the rise of the molly houses where men cross-dressed and enjoyed each other. "In this guise, homosexuality founds itself upon charges of feminization and transfers the misogyny that structures male/female relations to find an identity for itself that paradoxes the supposition upon which an emergent heterosexuality battens." *Sodometries*, 141.

10. Michel Foucault, *The History of Sexuality, Volume 1: An Introduction*, trans. Robert Hurley (New York: Vintage, 1980), 43. Further references to this work are included parenthetically in the text.

11. Claude J. Summers, "Homosexuality and Renaissance Literature, or the Anxieties of Anachronism," *South Central Review* 9, no. 1 (1992): 4. Further references to this work are included parenthetically in the text.

12. Gregory W. Bredbeck, *Sodomy and Interpretation: Marlowe to Milton* (Ithaca,

NY: Cornell University Press, 1991), 16. Further references to this work are included parenthetically in the text.

13. I have seen no references to oral sex, and must assume that it would fit between anal intercourse and masturbation on the scale.

14. Ed Cohen, "Legislating the Norm: From Sodomy to Gross Indecency," *South Atlantic Quarterly* 88 (1989): 187.

15. Alan Bray, *Homosexuality in Renaissance England* (London: Gay Men's Press, 1982), 25. Further references to this work are included parenthetically in the text.

16. Goldberg, *Sodometries*, 19.

17. Besides Bray and Goldberg, Bruce Smith, Eve Sedgwick, and Steven Orgel concur on this point. Steven Orgel states that sodomy "becomes visible in Elizabethan society only when it intersects with some other behavior recognized as dangerous and antisocial; it is invariably an aspect of papistry, sedition, witchcraft" (20–21). For an alternative view, see Claude J. Summers, "Homosexuality and Renaissance Literature, or the Anxieties of Anachronism," *South Central Review* 9, no. 1 (1992): 2–23.

18. See Bray, *Homosexuality*, 117–18, n. 39; also Kuriyama, in *A Poet and a Filthy Playmaker: New Essays on Christopher Marlowe*, ed. K. Friedenreich, R. Gill, C. B. Kuriyama (New York: AMS Press, 1988), 343–61.

19. Marlowe is also reported to have said that "all they that loue not tobacco and boies were fooles"; from the Baines Note reprinted in Thomas Dabbs, *Reforming Marlowe* (Lewisburg, PA: Bucknell University Press, 1991), 142–44. For a discussion of the "self-serving and coercive, if not coerced" allegations by Baines and Kyd, see Emily C. Bartels, *Spectacles of Strangeness: Imperialism, Alienation, and Marlowe* (Philadelphia: University of Pennsylvania Press, 1993), 11–12.

20. Joseph A. Porter, "Marlowe, Shakespeare, and the Canonization of Heterosexuality," *South Atlantic Quarterly* 88 (1989): 128.

21. Jonathan Goldberg, "Sodomy and Society: The Case of Christopher Marlowe," *Southwest Review* 69 (1984): 377.

22. Little certain is known about Marlowe's murder except that he was stabbed to death (possibly in self-defense) by Ingram Friser on 1 June 1593 in a Deptford tavern. Friser was possibly a rival suitor or a government operative. Some critics have speculated that Marlowe was murdered by the government because he knew too much. See MacCabe, "Throne of Blood," 12. Also see Roger Sales, *Christopher Marlowe* (London: Macmillan, 1991), 32–47. For more on Marlowe's death, see Leslie Hotson, *Death of Christopher Marlowe* (Cambridge: Harvard University Press, 1925).

23. Quoted in Bray, *Homosexuality*, 16, from Sir Edward Coke, *The Third Part of the Institutes of the Laws of England* (London, 1797). Coke was an influential jurist who helped codify sexual laws. For an analysis of Coke's role in a general transition from ecclesiastical to state control of sexual regulation, see Cohen, "Legislating the Norm."

24. Christopher Marlowe, *Edward The Second*, in *Christopher Marlowe: The Com-*

plete Plays, ed. J. B. Steane (Harmondsworth: Penguin, 1969), I.i.20–21. Further references to this work are included parenthetically in the text.

25. Jarman humorously intensifies Gaveston's move to the center by having him crouch naked on Edward's throne and hiss at the disapproving Mortimer.

26. Phyllis Rackin, "Androgyny, Mimesis, and the Marriage of the Boy Heroine on the English Renaissance Stage," *PMLA* 102 (1987): 29.

27. Bartels, *Spectacles of Strangeness*, 20. Further references to this work are included parenthetically in the text.

28. Significantly, Jarman frames his film with scenes in which the king's executioner, Lightborn, prepares the red-hot metal spit that was to be thrust up his anus. Lightborn desists and appears to recognize his own erotic bond with the king, reversing Edward's defeat and defeating in turn Mortimer and Isabella's homophobic self-aggrandizement.

29. Jonathon Dollimore, "Subjectivity, Sexuality, and Transgression: The Jacobean Connection," *Renaissance Drama* 17 (1986): 55. Further references to this work are included parenthetically in the text.

30. Kenneth Burke, *A Grammar of Motives* (Berkeley: University of California Press, 1945), 24–25. Further references to this work are included parenthetically in the text.

31. Kenneth Burke, *A Rhetoric of Motives* (Berkeley: University of California Press, 1950), 140. Further references to this work are included parenthetically in the text.

32. For work that productively builds on Burke's scapegoat mechanism, see René Girard, *Violence and the Sacred* (Baltimore: Johns Hopkins University Press, 1977).

33. Bruce R. Smith, *Homosexual Desire in Shakespeare's England* (Chicago: University of Chicago Press, 1991), 75. Further references to this work are included parenthetically in the text.

34. There is some disagreement on this point. Bartels and Bredbeck assert that Spenser was no sodomite. Although the play offers no evidence that he and Edward were lovers, there is some suggestion that Spenser leans in that direction. Younger Spenser tells Baldock that he intends to gain favor with the king through Gaveston, not by becoming his follower, but rather "his companion; for he loves me well, / and would have once preferr'd me to the king" (II.i.12–13). "Preferr'd" is glossed by Steane as "recommended," but could also be glossed as today's dominant meaning of "preferred" as chosen by one over another possibility. At any rate, the ambiguity of the passage is in keeping with the discursive relation of sex and power.

35. The historical Gaveston was English. Marlowe's deliberate revision signals his insight into scapegoating. According to René Girard, the ideal scapegoat is part of the community, but also a marginal or marginalized member. If the scapegoat is central (as Edward makes him), the murder initiates a cycle of vengeance and reciprocal violence. See "The Sacrificial Crisis," in *Violence and the Sacred*, 39–67.

36. Although it is true that Lightborn only orders a red-hot poker to be brought

without there being explicit stage directions for miming its use, the audience would have been familiar with the famous means by which the historical Edward was killed. That Edward's screaming can be heard throughout the area supports the notion that his means of execution went well beyond smothering.

37. Stephen J. Greenblatt, "Marlowe and Renaissance Self-Fashioning," *Two Renaissance Mythmakers: Christopher Marlowe and Ben Jonson*, ed. Alvin Kernan (Baltimore: Johns Hopkins University Press, 1977), 54.

38. For another perspective, see Claude Summers, "Sex, Politics, and Self-Realization in Edward II," in *A Poet and a Filthy Playmaker*, 221–40. Summers offers an insightful reading of Edward as a man frustrated in his love for a man by the social roles imposed on him. I depart from Summers's reading in his insistence that the king "is torn between his social position and his real identity." Summers opposes an "authentic self" derived from Jungian psychology with a social self. In so doing, he appears to accept a romantic conception of the subject I have tried to avoid here.

39. John Boswell, *Christianity, Social Tolerance, and Homosexuality* (Chicago: University of Chicago Press, 1980), 298.

40. Lawrence Stone, "Social Mobility in England, 1500–1700," *Past and Present* 33 (1966): 17.

41. Lisa Jardine, *Still Harping on Daughters* (Sussex: Harvester Press, 1983), 23.

"What Guy Will Do That?" Recodings of Masculinity in *sex, lies, and videotape*

Sally Robinson

In a diary-style chronicle of the making of *sex, lies, and videotape* (1989), writer/director Steven Soderbergh represents himself as a young naif trying to negotiate his way through the power plays of Hollywood. This written text, containing the screenplay and records of the filming and editing processes, does not offer an authoritative reading of the film's meaning; indeed, what is striking about Soderbergh's account is his failure to elucidate the film in any explicit way. Rather, the autobiographical text is interesting as a model for a process of masculine self-representation, whereby the male subject is engendered against traditional codes of masculinity. Soderbergh fashions a narrative self which eschews the culturally dominant representation of masculinity.

Like the character Graham, the narrator of the written text resists occupying the position of "subject who knows." Instead, Soderbergh gives us a performance of nondominant masculinity: the narrator-director is self-effacing, humble, and afraid; up until the moment when the film wins the big prize at Cannes, he fears an imminent "backlash." He resists seeing himself as either an "artist" or a "star," claiming that his "little" film is not "serious" and, in fact, does not feel "like a real movie."[1] When the film is accepted into the U.S. Film Festival, Soderbergh attends, but hangs out with the festival volunteers. This self-conscious posing, or performance, is pretty transparent, given that the text was written after the phenomenal success of the film. But Soderbergh's playful self-feminization, and his arguably disingenuous anxiety about his "manhood," become something more serious in the context of his ambivalent identification with the protagonist of his film, the physically impotent but irresistible Graham. Soderbergh's identification with Graham consolidates his refusal of the dominant signifiers of masculinity, but it also carries with it a threat of castration.

This becomes clear when the text lingers over the problems Soderbergh encounters in attempting to represent the body and sexuality. The first problem occurs when Laura San Giacomo's agent refuses to allow her to sign on as Cynthia without a "nudity clause" in the contract. Cautioned by a woman friend that "women, in general, are put off by female nudity in films," Soderbergh agrees to the clause, noting that he is a "big believer in equanimity. We all know it's not the same for a guy to take his shirt off, so if we're talking about below-the-waist, I don't think it would be fair to ask that of the girl and not the guy, and what guy will do that?" (56–57). What Soderbergh touches on here is a male fear that representing the penis would demystify the phallus, perhaps because "as a cultural object the phallus may attract immense force and charisma while the humble penis carries on as best it can with its usual bodily functions."[2] Giving away the game, showing that the penis is not the same thing as the phallus, threatens the "humble organ," or, more precisely, threatens its overdetermined cultural significance. As Marjorie Garber so succinctly puts it, "The penis is an organ; the phallus is a structure."[3]

Peter Lehman notes that "traditional patriarchal constructions of masculinity benefit enormously by keeping the male body in the dark, out of the critical spotlight. Indeed, the mystique of the phallus is, in part, dependent on it."[4] Soderbergh engages in a parody of this mystique, putting himself on the line when, later, he is not so sure that the film can do without nudity. In order to convince the cast of the harmlessness of nude shots, Soderbergh strips in front of the camera. The text includes an amazing photograph of this episode. We see the (male) first Assistant Camera gawking wide-mouthed in disbelief, and an unidentified man in the background who refuses to look, but crosses his arms in front of his genitals. In the foreground, we see Andie MacDowell looking, as Soderbergh puts it, "unimpressed." What we don't see in this photograph, of course, is the image of Soderbergh's naked body.

Antony Easthope argues that there are two key components to the dominant myth of masculinity: "One is that the phallus must remain unseen if it is to keep its power. The other is that men are more concerned about seeing 'the unmentionable object' than women."[5] The "unmentionable object" remains unseen in *sex, lies, and videotape*, but it is, nevertheless, the centerpiece of the film. And, although the episode I've described above would indicate a more or less explicit castration anxiety on the part of male spectators, Soderbergh's film attempts to negotiate a masculinity that is not governed by the logic of castration — a masculinity, in other words, that is not formed solely in defense against the Others of femininity and of homosexuality, the twin terrors of the unsuccessfully negotiated Oedipal scenario. Not surprisingly, Soderbergh chooses a fetishist as the representative of this alternative to what I will call a hetcromasculinity.[6] Before going on to my reading of the film, however, I want to take a brief detour through recent work on theorizing masculinity in order to situate Soderbergh's exploration of an alternative to hetero-masculinity.

MALE BODIES

Whereas masculinity, men, and male sexuality have always occupied an important discursive space in feminist theory, it is only recently that feminists have begun to theorize the multiple ways in which masculinity is constructed, reconstructed, and deconstructed in culture. While early feminist theory assumed masculinity as a given — as the purportedly "universal" term against which feminine difference is measured — recent feminist theorists, both male and female, have begun investigating masculinities, the multiple ways in which the masculine is represented and represents itself.[7] Often these essays and books contain calls to action, such as the one that begins Easthope's book: "It is time to try to speak about masculinity, about what it is and how it works. . . . Despite all that has been written over the past twenty years on femininity and feminism, masculinity has stayed pretty well concealed. This has always been its ruse in order to hold on to its power."[8] Central to all of this work on masculinity is the seemingly obvious, but historically invisible, fact that masculinity is constructed in particular ways at particular times. This fact has remained "invisible" in much the same way as the penis has remained invisible behind the phallus. As Peter Lehman argues, "We may learn a great deal by reversing our attention and analyzing the representation of the penis rather than the theoretical purity of the phallus" (108).

For film theory, the need to theorize masculinity has surfaced in attempts to specify the male body as it is represented visually in film. These attempts often take off from Laura Mulvey's classic "Visual Pleasure and Narrative Cinema," an article with much to say about the female body but nothing to say about the male.[9] Or, to put it more precisely, Mulvey's theoretical model can only take account of the male body in the abstract. Mulvey's analysis is grounded in a psychoanalytic understanding of masculinity and male sexuality — with its complementary femininity and female sexuality — which sees the threat of castration as fundamental to the formation of male subjectivity. For Mulvey, woman occupies a contradictory position in classic Hollywood cinema: displayed as a passive object of the male gaze, which can be "possessed" by the (male) spectator through his identification with the film's hero, she simultaneously evokes a threat to the spectator's narcissism. That threat, of course, is castration, for the woman signifies difference, "the visually ascertainable absence of a penis." In her readings of several films, Mulvey argues that

the male unconscious has two avenues of escape from this castration anxiety: preoccupation with the re-enactment of the original trauma (investigating the woman, demystifying her mystery), counterbalanced by the devaluation, punishment or saving of the guilty object . . . ; or else complete disavowal of castration by the substitution of a fetish object or turning the represented figure into a fetish so that it becomes reassuring rather than dangerous. (21)

Mulvey's analysis of how male subjectivity is engaged in classic Hollywood cinema assumes an invisibility of male bodies. In order for that hetero-masculinity to retain its signifying power, those bodies must remain invisible.

Steve Neale makes it clear that the threat of the male body's visibility has everything to do with maintaining a heterosexual norm for desire. Taking off from Mulvey, Neale analyzes films that focus on the spectacle of the male body. He notes a crucial difference in signification between female and male bodies displayed for the gaze of the spectator; when, in male action films, "the spectacle of male bodies" is offered, they are "bodies unmarked as objects of erotic display. . . . They are on display, certainly, but there is no cultural or cinematic convention which would allow the male body to be presented" in the way female bodies often are.[10] Further, Neale notes that when the male body is put on erotic display, as in some melodramas and musicals, it is feminized — "an indication of the strength of those conventions which dictate that only women can function as the objects of an explicitly erotic gaze."[11] Any erotic investment in the male body must be disavowed in order that heterosexuality remain intact. If representations of the male body necessarily evoke the specter of homosexual desire, then the male body must remain invisible for hetero-masculinity to remain the norm.[12]

But neither Mulvey nor Neale consider what we see when we look at the male body. In other words, in both of these articles the "male body" remains abstract. Peter Lehman, in an article on "desire, power, and the representation of the male body," breaks out of this abstraction by focusing on the representation of the naked male body in Oshima's *In the Realm of the Senses* (1976). He focuses his attention on the image of the erect penis as the only signifier for the male body, noting that this image works to secure the phallicization of masculinity and femininity — indeed, of all sexuality. It is, of course, in the interests of the patriarchy to equate the penis with the phallus, because this equation insures that male dominance is "natural" and, thus, outside the realm of the cultural and the historical.[13] Lehman's analysis of hard-core porn as "the only genre which literally dwells on the nude male" (92–93), considers the possibilities and impossibilities of representing the male body as anything other than fully potent and, thus, phallic. In pornographic films, "women's pleasure merely becomes the sign of their dependency on the phallus" — equated in the films with the penis, an equation that Lehman seeks to disrupt. He continues: "The shots of women's faces as they receive pleasure affirm the sexuality of the men who give it to them. Women's pleasure thus becomes fetishized" (93). It is by equating the penis and the phallus, and by making the phallus the signifier for both men's and women's pleasure, that these films alleviate any threat that female sexuality might represent for the male subject. Furthermore, the visual representation of the penis does not endanger the male subject, because, as Lehman convincingly argues, in these films the penis *is* the phallus.

Lehman's analysis of pornographic representation is offered as the extreme case of all currently available representations of the male body. Mainstream Hollywood cinema gives us little opportunity to pay attention to the "representation of the penis rather than the theoretical purity of the phallus" (108).[14] In a fascinating article on "Penis-size Jokes and Their Relation to Hollywood's Unconscious," Lehman makes a distinction between literal (visual) and symbolic (verbal) representations of the penis, noting that many recent films "simultaneously foreground the display of the male body while protecting it from view."[15] They do so by speaking about the penis in the form of penis-size jokes, while leaving the penis literally invisible. Such a strategy points to "complex parallels between the literal and the symbolic, making clear that the representation of the male body involves the problematic relationship between the penis and the phallus" (Lehman, "Jokes," 54). It is precisely this problematic relationship that Soderbergh's *sex, lies, and videotape* explores. The conflation of the penis with the phallus is, as Lehman and others have noted, the foundation on which patriarchal power is built. But it is an ideology of heterosexuality — and its practices and enforcements — that works to sustain that power. Thus, in order to fully recode masculinity — and to disrupt the "naturalness" of patriarchal power — it is necessary to move beyond both the equation of penis with the phallus and a normative heterosexual ideology. One might say that the first is the theory, the second the practice. *Sex, lies, and videotape* attempts to displace both theory and practice, and it is to this attempt that I now turn.

FETISHISM, "TRUTH," AND VIDEOTAPE

The four main characters in the film are John (Peter Gallagher) and his wife Ann (Andie MacDowell), Ann's sister Cynthia (Laura San Giacomo), and John's former college friend Graham (James Spader). John is having an affair with Cynthia and Ann is in analysis when Graham appears for a visit. Immediately, the couples are opposed to each other in a binary system that links John with Cynthia and Graham with Ann. We learn that Graham is impotent — or, in his words, he "can't get an erection in the presence of another person" — and that Ann is "frigid." Cynthia is represented as the classic "oversexed" woman, in opposition to Ann, and John's easy deception of Ann contrasts with Graham's disarming honesty.

Ann helps Graham find an apartment, and their friendship develops quickly until she discovers Graham's "perversion": he masturbates while viewing the videotapes he makes of women talking about their sexual experiences. Predictably, Cynthia is intrigued by this, and soon shows up at Graham's apartment to be videotaped, despite — or, actually, because of — Ann's insistence that she leave Graham alone. A short time later, Ann discovers that John and Cynthia are sleeping together, goes to Graham, and makes a videotape. Some way into the tape, she turns the tables, and the camera, on Graham, making him very uncomfortable, and forcing him to make some other kind of contact with her. Meanwhile, Cynthia has told John about Graham's sexual practices, so that when Ann returns from Graham's to tell John she wants a divorce, he concludes that she has made a tape for him. He rushes over to Graham's apartment, beats him up, and locks him outside while he watches Ann's tape. It is in this segment where we see Ann's tape, which fades out as she and Graham make preliminary physical contact. After John leaves, Graham destroys the videotapes and equipment. From here, the film speeds to a conclusion: John loses Ann, Cynthia, and his job; Ann, who now has a job, reconciles with Cynthia; and Ann and Graham are involved in what promises to be a "normal" heterosexual relationship.

Described in these terms, the film appears to be a kind of morality play, whereby the slimy Yuppie womanizing lawyer gets his just desserts, while the innocent bohemian artist-type "gets the girl." Further, Ann is "cured" of her "frigidity," Graham of his impotence, and Cynthia (presumably) of her "nymphomania." Underneath the overt narrative of the film, another narrative can be discerned, one that glues sexual practices to the dominant ideology of heterosexuality: Graham's "problem" is that he is alienated from his sexuality and from the objects of his desire. His masturbation is the sign of a solipsistic sexuality, one that unfolds in isolation from "genuine" human contact. Similarly, Ann's story is a cliche: the reason she "fails" in her sexual relationship with John is that she has never experienced orgasm — a story straight out of the annals of the sexual revolution. The film suggests pretty forcefully that, despite his apparent sexual success with Cynthia, John also fails to make the "genuine" connection necessary for a "fulfilling" heterosexuality — only John is too seduced by a normative masculine script to recognize his failure. Arguably, Cynthia is the only one of the four who has no "problem" with sexuality. Still, she is held accountable for her deception of Ann, and her breaking off with John places her on the side of monogamous heterosexuality.

Yet the film is much more open-ended than this reading acknowledges, and its ambiguities revolve around the desirability of phallic masculinity as it is secured to a normative ideology of heterosexuality. Soderbergh poses a phallic masculinity against a nonphallic one, and attaches the proper body parts to the two. In some sense, Graham occupies a feminine position in the film, but it is certainly not his feminization that Ann and Cynthia respond to so favorably. The film works hard to make sure that Graham is not, in fact, feminized, attempting to represent a masculinity that is neither phallic nor feminized, but something else entirely. This recoded masculinity might escape the recuperation that marks the description of the film I suggested earlier: that is, a realignment of masculinity and femininity under the sign of a "normal" heterosexuality that triumphs in the end. I say "might" escape in the same spirit as Berkeley Kaite's suggestion that "at the risk of sounding too optimistic," the film might point to "a politics of sexual dislocation."[16]

Such an optimistic reading would depend on two things: a demystification of the penis as carrying the symbolic weight of the phallus, and a subversion of the ideology of heterosexuality that gives what Judith Butler calls "cultural intelligibility" to masculinity (and femininity).[17] It is my contention that a recoding of masculinity depends on a subversion of a normative heterosexuality, and that *sex, lies, and videotape* makes some tentative moves in this direction. It does so by entertaining a representation of sexuality as multiple and by de-phallicizing the penis. And, although *sex, lies, and videotape* is almost militantly heterosexual, its representation of hetero-masculinity as a put-on entertains the possibility of a non-normative heterosexuality and masculinity. These transgressive codings can be found in the space where one might least expect to find transgression: in its exploration of fetishism.

In explicitly exploring the fetishization of the female body by the male gaze, the film appears to be a Mulvey-inspired exercise in meta-cinema. The central narrative hook in the film has to do with the male protagonist videotaping women and deriving sexual pleasure from watching the tapes. This is the classic fetishistic scenario, where the image of the woman stands in for the threatened penis, reassuring the male subject and safeguarding the phallus. One could make the argument that Graham's impotence, his symbolic castration, in the face of actual women prompts him to create a fetish object, the videotapes, in order to keep in suspension the "fact" of castration. However, because the film does explicitly foreground the mechanisms by which Graham achieves his pleasure, the cinematic illusions necessary for an unproblematic voyeurism or fetishism are broken in it.

As Helen W. Robbins notes, voyeurism fails as a defense against castration anxiety when it is too "clearly labelled" as such.[18] The same can be said for fetishism. *Sex, lies, and videotape* self-consciously thematizes the mechanisms that Mulvey identifies in classic Hollywood cinema, and, thus "free[s] the look of the camera into its materiality in time and space" (26). Mulvey's point is that through forcing attention to the materiality of the cinematic apparatus, the fantasy structure that enables seamless identification, voyeurism, and fetishism is broken. In Soderbergh's film, this is clearly the case: we watch Graham filming the women, then watch him watching the tapes. This device makes explicit the fetishistic economy of Graham's desire, but with an interesting twist. The allure of the videotapes is dependent on the women's *discourse:* it is the women *talking* about their sexuality that excites Graham. Unlike the fetishism Mulvey describes, then, the fetishism Soderbergh explores depends not on the "silent image of woman still tied to her place as bearer, not maker, of meaning" (15), but on the woman as speaking, desiring subject. I will return to this intriguing question later. For now, I would like to open up the question of fetishism to another reading and suggest how *sex, lies, and videotape* makes use of fetishism in order to drive a wedge between the penis and the phallus in such a way as to deconstruct hetero-masculinity.

Hetero-masculinity describes what psychoanalytic theory designates as the "normal" masculinity that emerges from a successful completion of the male subject's Oedipal dilemma, in which he learns to identify with the father, and desire a female love object as a substitute for the mother.[19] Part of the pay-off in accepting the father's authority, and in giving up his "right" to the mother is that the son becomes the heir to the father's phallic privilege. That privilege, of course, is won only through negation, a negation that institutes a gap between the penis and the phallus — for, it is only in accepting the "fact" of woman's castration (and the "fact" that his organ is, thus, in danger) that the son accedes to phallic privilege. A complete failure of this Oedipal negotiation would result, according to Freud, in the son's homosexuality — his failure to adopt the "proper" (that is, dominant) position vis-à-vis a female love object resulting in a nonphallic, or "feminine," masculinity.

Much has been said of Freud's homophobic theorization of homosexuality, and I take that as a given. What interests me here is the possibility of a middle ground between a hetero-masculinity and a male homosexuality, and that ground is marked by fetishism. The fetishist solution to the problem of castration is to stall the Oedipal moment, to keep the question of castration in suspension; both accepting the "fact" of woman's castration, and disavowing that fact, the fetishist has it both ways. He is neither secure in his hetero-masculinity, nor is he "stuck" with a homosexual object choice. Rather, as Freud makes clear, the fetishist enjoys the best of both worlds:

It is not true that, after the child has made his observation of the woman, he has preserved unaltered his belief that women have a phallus. He has retained that belief but he has also given it up. In the conflict between the weight of the unwelcome perception and the force of the counter-wish, a compromise has been reached. . . . We can now see what the fetish achieves and what it is that maintains it. It remains a token of triumph over the threat of castration and a protection against it. It also saves the fetishist from becoming a homosexual, by endowing women with the characteristic which makes them tolerable as sexual objects.[20]

Given Freud's excitement over discovering this defense against both homosexuality and heterosexuality, one begins to wonder whether "normal" hetero-masculinity is such a desirable state at all. Indeed, Freud's admiration of the fetishist's ingenuity seems to suggest that the fetishistic solution enables the male subject to have his gynophobic cake and his heterosexuality, too. Such a happy compromise leads Elizabeth Grosz to speculate that "the fetishist is the least likely of analysands to enter a psychoanalytic contract. He remains perfectly happy with his love object (an object unlikely to resist his wishes and fantasies)."[21]

The fetish is a substitute for the phallus, not the penis. Unable to successfully complete the Oedipal transition to "normal" masculinity, the fetishist refuses to learn the lesson that guarantees that the penis comes to represent the phallus. As Grosz points out, "The penis (as real organ) can only take on the role of the phallus because it is missing, i.e., because women are castrated" (43). Because the fetishist maintains that women both are and are not castrated, he "disavows any knowledge of genital differences" (44). In other words, what the fetishist disavows is the "fact" of sexual difference, a fact necessary to systems of male domination in which the penis stands in for the symbolic phallus. For the fetishist, the penis is just a penis; the phallus is elsewhere. And, it is in this respect that fetishism distinguishes its subject from hetero-masculinity. By refusing to recognize the "fact" of sexual difference, Graham as fetishist practices a demystification of the "natural" difference between castration and potency, as well as the "natural" equation of the penis with the phallus.

Sex, lies, and videotape decenters the phallus in a number of ways. John, the representative of phallic hetero-masculinity, is relentlessly deprivileged by the film, whereas Graham, in all his "impotence," becomes an irresistible object of desire. The difference between the two characters begins with their respective organs, but is also signified by an entire chain of effects and affects: John is a successful, wealthy lawyer, complete with the "prize" of an ornamental (if "frigid") wife and picture-perfect home; Graham is a drifter, who resists renting an apartment because that would mean he would need two keys. John accrues possessions, including a mistress; Graham wants only his video equipment, and exhibits no desire to "possess" a woman, except to the extent that he possesses her image on videotape.[22] The film, thus, not only risks making nonphallic masculinity desirable, but also risks making physical impotence a heroic quality — a representational strategy geared to elicit a certain amount of anxiety in the male spectator, not far removed from Soderbergh's own anxiety about representing the penis. The film betrays an uneasy obsession with the penis that is more or less parallel with Soderbergh's ambivalence about Graham, as indicated in his quasi-hysterical negotiations with James Spader over who Graham should be. When Spader warns Soderbergh that "there would come a time when Graham would become his and not mine," Soderbergh recounts: "I was excited by that fact. I'm happy to let the fucker go!" (183). Nowhere else in the narrative does Soderbergh have a negative thing to say about his character, but this comment suggests a desire to distance himself from Graham — and particularly from his impotence and his "perversions." Despite this desire, however, the narrator of the text clearly aligns himself with a nonphallic masculinity in an almost hysterical way.[23]

Such hysteria is a sign of the anxiety attendant upon the de-naturalizing of hetero-masculinity. In her analysis of masculinity as multiple masquerade in film, Chris Holmlund notes that, in films featuring the spectacle of male bodies and masculinity, "the inviolability of heterosexuality has a hysterical ring to it. The doubling and hyping of masculinity in these films only highlights how much masculinity, like femininity, is a multiple masquerade."[24] *Sex, lies, and videotape* doubles masculinity, but in a self-conscious and, I would like to argue, critical way. Graham's fetishism is represented as a playful, nonaggressive mimicry of phallic mastery. Up until the time that Graham is "cured," his fetishism presents an alternative to the "real" phallic mastery John commands. Graham appears to enact a phallic mastery through the agency of his camera, but it is a performance, a play, a sham; John's phallic mastery is the "real thing." The sham of Graham's phallic display, then, might suggest that John's phallic mastery is a game, as well — second, rather than "first," nature. John certainly strikes us as a master of the "put-on," and what he puts on is hetero-masculinity.[25] John's masquerade is not self-conscious because "a man who is a 'real man' does not acknowledge that 'having' a penis is insufficient, that it is not the same thing as 'having' the phallus";[26] but the film insistently foregrounds the sham of this "having."

Because the "disavowal of the phallus as signifier of masculinity threatens to collapse gender differences and infect [male relations] with homoeroticism," as Ina Rae Hark argues in another context,[27] *sex, lies, and videotape* must participate in other disavowals — culminating, as we shall see, in the patently artificial ending. The film manages its anxiety over hetero-masculinity by placing the penis center stage; it is almost as if the threat evoked by Graham's impotence necessitates a representational strategy that will reassure the spectator that the endangered organ is, in fact, fully present. The "unmentionable object" gets spoken both directly and indirectly, but never represented visually. In one sequence, we see two scenes cut together, one featuring Cynthia and John in bed, the other showing Ann and Graham at a cafe. As Cynthia enters the bedroom, the camera pans from her face to John laying on the bed naked, with a plant covering his genitals. Cynthia says "Ain't you a picture," and asks John "Is that for me?" As John smiles and nods yes, Cynthia picks up the protruding wire plant hanger and moves the plant. She looks at what is clearly John's erection, and asks "Is that for me, too?" As Cynthia straddles him, he says proudly "Yeah, it's for you." This (invisible) display of John's erect penis is juxtaposed with Ann and Graham exchanging secrets.[28] We see Cynthia admiring John's penis, while Graham tells Ann of his impotence and Ann tells him that she thinks "sex is overrated." We are led to conclude that it is John's proudly displayed penis that is "overrated," especially when compared with Graham's disarming non-phallic behavior.[29]

The scenes in which the film focuses on the penis work to demystify the "unmentionable organ." In short, they separate it from the phallus. The penis is central to the two scenes where we see Graham videotaping women talking about their sexuality. The idea that an erect penis is "for" women is further entrenched when Ann grills Graham about whether or not he "can give a woman an orgasm." The "interview" between Graham and Cynthia quickly establishes the penis as the key to her sexuality. Asked to describe the first time she saw a penis, Cynthia responds:

I didn't picture it with veins or ridges or anything, I thought it would be smooth, like a test tube. . . . It's weird. Thinking about it now, the organ itself seemed like a separate thing, a separate entity to me. I mean, after he pulled it out and I could look at it and touch it, I completely forgot that there was a guy attached to it. I remember literally being startled when the guy spoke to me.

Cynthia describes the penis as what it is not, and what it is not, it would seem, is the phallus. The attribution of "veins and ridges" makes the penis real rather than ideal, what it is rather than what it symbolizes. Cynthia's desire to detach the penis from the man, to see it as simply an organ, hits a snag when the man speaks: in speaking (his desire), the man cuts off Cynthia's objectifying gaze, "startling" and silencing her. This scene focuses on Cynthia's desire for, but not her mystification of, the "humble organ," foregrounding the nonidentity between the penis and the phallus. The film repeatedly questions the conflation of the two, multiplying the possibilities of sexual difference beyond the binary of having or not having the phallus.

Similarly, the videotaping scenes in the film explicitly foreground the dynamics of the gaze as they structure sexual difference. Thus, once again, they work to break the illusion which Mulvey argues guarantees Hollywood cinema's binary system of sexual difference. Whereas Graham's use of the (phallic) video camera appears to be a textbook case of the mechanisms Mulvey analyzes, Graham's objectification of the women whose images are framed by his gaze is made explicit by the film. At one point, Ann catches Graham referring to her as "she," rather than "you," while he is videotaping her. The quality of the images on the video monitor also works against a seamless objectification and fetishism, for they clearly lack the visual plenitude of cinematic images. This lack is made all the more apparent when, in the scene of Ann's videotaping, Soderbergh switches from filming the video monitor to filming the filming of the video.[30] Where the former image is black and white and grainy, the latter is rich in color and tone. Soderbergh foregrounds the context of Graham's viewing, as well: he is watching a videotape in his daylit living room, rather than a movie in a dark theater. All of these elements conspire to foreground Graham's sexual practices as both mandated by, and disruptive of, cinematic conventions.

Such self-reflexive techniques do not necessarily guarantee a deconstruction of the masculine investments thus exposed; it is, of course, possible for a film to expose, and then recuperate, conventional codings of male (or female) desires.[31] What is intriguing in *sex, lies, and videotape* is the precise nature of Graham's fetishism as it depends on the women speaking. Who ever heard of a fetish talking back — and, talking about "humble organs," no less? Cynthia is the object of Graham's gaze in the scene described earlier, but her position as speaking subject places her as the original subject of the gaze; it is Cynthia who gazes on the male body, and it is Cynthia who articulates the meanings of that body, usurping the phallic privilege of speech and definition. There is, of course, another penis in this scene, because Graham's habit is to masturbate in front of the video monitor as the woman speaks her desire. While Cynthia reminisces about (and gets aroused by) penises in her past, the impotent Graham experiences a pleasure which appears, at first glance, to be masochistic. This scenario is more than a little reminiscent of the phenomenon of women uttering penis-size jokes analyzed by Peter Lehman, in which a paradoxical fetishization of the female speaker overwhelms any masochistic positioning of the male subject due to *his* objectification. The verbal substitutes for the visual in these scenes where, despite what we might expect, the male body evades objectification: "In place of the logical objectification of the male body, we have the fetishistic objectification of the woman who looks" ("Jokes," 56). It is woman's desire that is fetishized, rather than the male body. Lehman continues: "When beautiful, desirable women erotically look at and make evaluative judgments about the penis, the structure may be masochistically pleasurable for men. . . . What is seemingly women's desire is drafted into the service of masochistic male pleasure" ("Jokes," 56). Despite, then, the complication of the relations of gazing here, the film seems to subordinate Cynthia's speaking (and her desire) to male pleasure: "the power of the gaze supersedes the power of the penis that is not a phallus" (Lehman, "Jokes," 57). Graham as cameraman retains control.

Furthermore, Cynthia's seeming fetishization of the penis does little to disrupt the structure of sexual difference that the film, at other moments, works against. As Marjorie Garber argues, female fetishism is the norm, for in cultures governed by heterosexuality, women must invest the penis with phallic value:

What if it should turn out that female fetishism is invisible, or untheorizable, because it coincides with what has been established as natural or normal — for women to fetishize the phallus on men? Lacan, in fact, says as much when he asserts that "[woman] finds the signifier of her own desire in the body of him to whom she addresses her demand for love. Perhaps it should not be forgotten that the organ that assumes this signifying function takes on the value of a fetish."[32]

The "fetish," Garber argues, "is the phallus; the phallus is the fetish," and what the woman is left with (in her "fetish envy") is the "desire for desire," the desire (always frustrated) to speak from a position of phallic mastery.[33] Even if fetishism separates the penis from the phallus, then, such a separation is obviated when it is the penis that is fetishized: fetishizing the penis turns it back into the phallus. *Sex, lies, and videotape* does indeed use fetishism to separate the penis from the phallus, but fetishism necessarily reinscribes the importance of the phallic values which mark hetero-masculinity.[34]

It is while watching Cynthia's video that Graham's fetishistic strategy fails him, and thus, the film makes its first move toward "curing" Graham, both narratively and ideologically. In this scene, Graham appears extremely vulnerable, naked in front of the video monitor, caressing his chest. As Cynthia speaks, he turns away from her image, hugging himself. On the tape, Cynthia asks "Do you like the way I look?" Graham's gaze appears incapacitated, as he cringes away from that "look." Thus, even before Ann confronts Graham with his "problem," he has already become uncomfortable with his sexual practices. The film offers no explanation for this new mode of "impotence," but, in retrospect, two reasons suggest themselves. First, once Ann and Graham establish a "real" (as opposed to video) relationship, Cynthia must be off limits if Graham is to remain distinct from John. Second, Graham will no longer be able to find pleasure in the videotapes because Ann will turn the camera on him in a later scene, asking him questions, and forcing him to account for his powers and his pleasures. Ann inserts Graham's actions into a narrative of normative heterosexuality, uttering the same kind of cliches that have marked her dialogue with both Graham and her therapist. This is the pivotal scene in the film, not only because it represents Ann's first effort at speaking her desire, but also because it initiates the "cure" that will mark the film's closure.

SEXUAL AND NARRATIVE "CURES": CLOSURE AND RECUPERATION

In their introduction to the recent collection *Screening the Male*, Steven Cohan and Ina Rae Hark point to the seemingly paradoxical fact that, in Hollywood cinema, masculinity can only preserve its hegemony by confessing its anxieties. Arguing against a theoretical consensus about the power of phallic masculinity in film, they write:

Not much attention has been paid to the problems arising — in texts and for audiences — from the secure and comfortable "norm" of masculinity which, according to the theoretical model that continues to circulate in film theory, drives the representational system and its institutional apparatus only by being disabled. Rather than examine the paradox of a masculinity that derives considerable social and sexual — not to say spectatorial — power from being castrated, wounded, and lacking, film theory has for the most part confidently equated the masculinity of the male subject with activity, voyeurism, sadism, fetishism and story, and the femininity of the female subject with passivity, exhibitionism, masochism, narcissism, and spectacle. . . . But insofar as film theory also maintains that this representational system works by disturbing the symbolic order of patriarchy in order to motivate audience assent to its restoration, just how singular and unified, let alone secure and comforting, is that orthodox masculine position?[35]

The point here is that even the most "conventional" of Hollywood films, such as those institutionalized as "classic" (and classically masculine) by Mulvey's article, entertain a disruption in gender positions and sexual identifications in order to make the restoration of "normality" more forcefully felt.[36] However, as recent readings of masculinity in film suggest, closing down the contradictions entertained by a film does not necessarily defuse the "trouble" caused by those contradictions.[37] Having articulated that disclaimer, I now want to turn to *sex, lies, and videotape*'s resolution of the "trouble" caused by Graham's "perverse" sexuality.

Referring to the scene in the film where Graham destroys the videotapes (after John has watched Ann's) Berkeley Kaite writes: "What threatens Graham's phantasmatic relation to the videotapes, and what causes him to renounce the power and pleasures of them, is the challenge of closure in the phallic economy, put by John. John's viewing of the video, for different purposes and under circumstances contrary to those of Graham, opens up the fetish and fetish relations to the possibility of multiple readings, not just absence recalled, but an excess of presence."[38] Kaite's point seems to be that John's reading of the fetish (the videotapes) competes with Graham's, thus producing more than one meaning. But, I would argue that John's reading effectively closes down the multiple readings that make fetishism such an unstable economy; and, further, that Graham's acceptance of John's reading portends a larger closing down of the film's transgressive coding of masculinity. In short, the fact that Graham gives up his fetishism suggests that he accepts the phallic economy John represents, and the ending of the film bears out this reading.

This turn-about is facilitated, indeed, necessitated, by the narrative trajectory of the film: Graham's sexual practices gain meaning as "perversions" through their insertion into a narrative of sickness and cure. Indeed, all of the characters, with the interesting exception of the hypermasculine John, are "cured" of their sexual ills by the end of the film. The film thus ends with an ideological recuperation whereby all sexual practices and gender positions are securely glued to a normative ideology of heterosexuality. Any transgressive codings of masculinity are reneged on in the film's rush toward closure. The film ultimately suggests that Graham's "perverted" (nonphallic) sexuality is just a temporary lapse, and not an alternative model. In the process, what first appears to be the promise of an interesting recoding of masculinity and male sexuality turns out to be just another affirmation of the old masculinity in new clothes: Graham turns from sexual (and gender) renegade into a cliche of the "new man," who, as Rowena Chapman argues, is "The Great Pretender."[39]

The narrative trajectory of the film places Graham's sexual practices as "perversions" in the sense that he has a "problem" which needs to be cured. Kaja Silverman notes that "perversion," according to the *OED*, is conceptualized as "Turning aside from truth or right." The example given is from Francis Bacon: " 'Women to govern men . . . slaves freemen . . . being total violations and perversions of the law of nature and nations.' " Silverman notes that what "perversion," thus, "turns away from" is the "principle of hierarchy." She goes on to invoke Freud's definition of "perversion," noting that he too "stresses its diversionary and decentering character." According to Freud, in *Three Essays on the Theory of Sexuality*, perversions are "sexual activities which either (a) extend, in an anatomical sense, beyond the regions of the body which are designated for sexual union, or (b) linger over the intermediate relations to the sexual object which should normally be traversed rapidly on the path toward the final sexual aim."[40] Silverman notes that, thus, the only "true" and "right" sexual activity is heterosexual penetration: "All other sexual activities belong either to the category of 'fore-play,' in which case they are strictly subordinated to 'end-pleasure,' or perversion" (31).

What is diverted or delayed in "perversion" is a normative heterosexuality, defined solely through penetration. Perversion is only "culturally intelligible" as the effect of an ideology of heterosexuality which works to stabilize all sexual and gender meanings. Any "sexual dislocation" would contest the laws of heterosexuality, and its maintenance of a singular masculinity and femininity as the guarantee of coherent gender identity. As Judith Butler argues:

The heterosexualization of desire requires and institutes the production of discrete and asymmetrical oppositions between "feminine" and "masculine," where these are understood as expressive attributes of "male" and "female." The cultural matrix through which gender identity has become intelligible requires that certain kinds of "identities" cannot "exist" — that is, those in which gender does not follow from sex and those in which the practices of desire do not "follow" from either sex or gender. "Follow" in this context is a political relation of entailment instituted by the cultural laws that establish and regulate the shape and meaning of sexuality. Indeed, precisely because certain kinds of "gender identities" fail to conform to those norms of cultural intelligibility, they appear only as developmental failures or logical impossibilities within that domain.[41]

Both sexual and textual closure win the day in *sex, lies, and videotape*, where "end-pleasure" rests on the other side of the "perversions" represented within it. The different characters' reactions to Graham's sexual practices indicate that the film tips the balance toward a reinstitution of "normal" heterosexuality after having opened up the possibility of alternative sexualities and gender identities. Even though Graham stubbornly refuses to admit to having a "problem," he nevertheless ends up destroying the video equipment and opting for a relationship with Ann. Ann, for her part, sees Graham as "perverted." When she warns Cynthia against Graham, Cynthia asks "What's this 'strange' bullshit all of a sudden? Is he drowning puppies over there, or what?" Ann replies that he's not "physically dangerous," but implies that he is dangerous in other ways. For Cynthia, drowning puppies is clearly worse than masturbating in front of a TV monitor, but Ann is not so sure. She has, after all, admitted to her therapist that masturbating makes her feel "silly," as if her "dead grandfather is watching her or something." Graham poses a danger to Ann's conviction that sexuality belongs within the confines of marriage, an act shared between two adults, one male and one female. In other words, Graham poses an ideological danger.

Cynthia has no problem with Graham's sexual practices, or her own. She masturbates while he is videotaping her and does so "for the camera." She clearly shares Graham's feeling that the camera can be a participant in a sexual exchange. When, at the beginning of Graham's "interview" of Cynthia, he asks her to describe her first sexual experience, she comes back immediately with the question, "My first sexual experience or the first time I had intercourse?" This is a distinction that Ann would not make, but one that Graham sees as valid. However, Cynthia's performance for the camera and her masturbation, become, retrospectively, a form of foreplay. As soon as she leaves Graham, she calls John and imperiously demands that he come to her. The film leaves little doubt that the intercourse which follows is much more intense than anything Cynthia has experienced with John up until this point. Cynthia is "on fire" from her session with Graham and the camera, and the joke is on John, who does not realize that Cynthia's desire has been aroused through no agency of his. Throughout the film, Cynthia's role has been, at least in part, to demystify the appeal of John's sexuality. Whereas Ann buys into the cliche, uttered early in the film by Graham — that women only become sexually attracted to men when they already love them, while, for men, it works the other way — Cynthia occupies the "masculine" position by demanding satisfaction from John, making him fulfill her desires. After Cynthia experiences orgasm in the encounter after the taping, she tells John, "You can go now." This attitude does not bother John in itself; it is only when he imagines Cynthia (or Ann) talking about his sexuality that he gets disturbed.

John's reaction to Graham's sexual practices is naked incredulity. What Graham does violates every "commonsense" idea of sexuality that John holds. When Cynthia tells him about the videotapes, he says, "Jesus Christ. And he doesn't have sex with any of them? They just talk? . . . Jesus. I could almost understand it if he was screwing these people, almost. Why doesn't he just buy some magazines or porno movies or something?" Cynthia explains that this "doesn't work. He has to know the people, he has to interact with them." But John is unconvinced. For John, having sex means penetration, or failing the opportunity, using culturally sanctioned alternatives such as porn movies or magazines. Predictably, when Ann returns from Graham's apartment and tells John that she wants a divorce, he says, "Well, at least I know you didn't fuck him." When it dawns on him that Ann has made a videotape, he gets violent — more violent, we suspect, than he would have been had she actually "fucked" Graham. He is troubled enough by the idea of that videotape to rush over to Graham's, knock him out, and watch the tape. Graham threatens more than John's relationship with Ann; he threatens what John has been sure is the unquestionable appeal of his own masculinity, signified by his earlier remark to Ann that "I think there are a lot of women that would be glad to have a young, straight male making a pretty good living beside them in bed with a hard on." Importantly, this comment contains the film's only (albeit oblique) reference to homosexuality, and John defines himself against it.

When Ann asks Graham about his problem, he returns with, "Problem? Do I have a problem? I look around me in this town, I see John and Cynthia and you. . . . I feel comparatively happy." Although Graham eventually admits to having "a lot of problems," his reaction makes it clear that the videotaping is not to be counted among them. His refusal to place himself on the side of "perversion" leaves open the possibility of another masculinity, one that is not conceptualized solely through a normative heterosexuality. In fact, what bothers Graham, and what presumably leads him to opt for "videated sex"[42] over heterosexual intercourse, is his fear of having an adverse effect on another person's life. In other words, he eschews the mastery that defines the dominant myth of masculinity. He confesses to being a pathological liar and makes some vague references to regretting having expressed his feelings "nonverbally" in such a way as to scare people he was close to, but the root of his "problem" remains more or less unspecified. When Ann claims that she, and everyone else who comes into contact with him, cannot help but be affected by him, Graham appears to give it up. After John leaves, with a little dig about having slept with Graham's former lover, Graham destroys the video equipment and the tapes. The film ends with the image of Graham and Ann sitting on his front porch, caressing each others' arms. Although they have not yet had sex, the implication is that they are moving toward a "mutually satisfying" and completely conventional relationship.[43] Is Graham "cured"? And if so, what of?

When Graham first confesses his impotence to Ann, he betrays his adherence to a script of normative heterosexuality, an adherence that comes full circle in the ending of the film. The dialogue in this scene conflates the terms "intimate," "sex," and "intercourse." Ann assumes they mean the same thing, and Graham implicitly agrees to that assumption. Graham tells Ann that he doesn't believe it's possible to be entirely truthful with someone he's not "intimate" with, and Ann is confused by Graham's acknowledgment of "intimacy." He quickly tells her that "I haven't always been impotent." He thus assents to Ann's idea that "intimacy" equals "sex" equals heterosexual intercourse. This dialogue has the effect of erasing Graham's sexuality. Specifically, it eliminates the possibility that "sex" might be something other than erections and penetration. Graham is, as he says here, impotent "for all practical purposes." This suggests that masturbation and fetishism are neither "practical" nor "purposeful." Further, Graham claims that this does not "bother" him. The fact that this confession works to undermine the film's exploration of an alternative to normative heterosexuality points to *sex, lies, and videotape*'s unacknowledged anxiety over the threat that Graham might represent: Graham might not be bothered by his impotence, but the film is bothered enough by it that he is magically cured.

The ending of the film is, as one reviewer pointed out, unsatisfactory: "The closer we get to the so-called truth behind Graham's debilitating alienation, the murkier things become. Graham's precise emotional injury is left pretentiously vague. Worse, his sexual awakening is too magical. Soderbergh's cathartic sexual resolution, where all the paraphernalia is shunted aside and love, not sexual fantasy, brings people together, is merely wishful."[44] Although I agree with the spirit of this comment, I would suggest that it misses the ideological significance of Soderbergh's cop-out. What happens at the end of the film is not simply an unconvincing narrative closure; it is also an unconvincing ideological closure. Because the film has glossed over an explanation of Graham's "problem," it has avoided a pat psychodramatic resolution. Nevertheless, the apparent "cure" that marks the narrative's closure makes the film veer away from its critique of normative heterosexuality.[45]

Graham can only destroy the fake phallus, the video camera, when he attains the "real" phallus; he gives up his "perversion" when, as Freud intimates, he reaches the desired end of "normal" heterosexuality. In the final analysis, and in relation to the film's ending, it would seem as if the video camera stands in for the decentered phallus and the limp penis, which is not exactly a radical rethinking of the mechanisms of male pleasure that Mulvey analyzes. Still, Soderbergh's Graham has caused some "male trouble,"[46] particularly for the phallic values that John represents. James Spader, who rewrote via improvisation a good portion of the scene between Ann, Graham, and the video camera, added a line to the screenplay that suggests a self-conscious comment on the film's artificial ending. When Ann asks him why he came back to Baton Rouge, he replies, rather archly, "I moved back for a sense of closure, a resolution of some sort." In the ending of the original screenplay, Soderbergh has Graham leaving town, and Ann back in therapy. He changed the ending because early readers of the script warned him that it wouldn't fly with mainstream audiences. They were probably right, because the ideological stakes involved in recoding masculinity are high. As Soderbergh quips, "And what guy will do that?" (57).

NOTES

I would like to thank Allison Hersh for reading and commenting on drafts of this chapter.

1. Steven Soderbergh, *sex, lies, and videotape* (New York: Harper and Row, 1990), 215. Further citations are given in the text. As should be clear, I am reading this text, not as an authoritative, or even "realistic," representation of Soderbergh or the making of the film. Rather, I am interested in this text as a narrative performance of nondominant masculinity; Soderbergh's construction of a narrative self here parallels his construction of Graham, with all the attendent problems to which I point later in the chapter.
2. Antony Easthope, *What a Man's Gotta Do: The Masculine Myth in Popular Culture* (Boston: Unwin Hyman, 1990), 4.
3. Marjorie Garber, *Vested Interests: Cross-Dressing and Cultural Anxiety* (New York: HarperCollins, 1992), 119.
4. Peter Lehman, "In the Realm of the Senses: Desire, Power, and the Representation of the Male Body," *Genders*, no. 2 (Summer 1988): 105. Further references are included parenthetically within the text.
5. Easthope, *What a Man's Gotta Do*, 16.
6. This term comes from Richard Meyer's excellent article on Rock Hudson's body as it was made to signify a "hetero-masculinity in American film culture of the 1950's." "Rock Hudson's Body," in *Inside/Out: Lesbian Theories, Gay Theories*, ed. Diana Fuss (London and New York: Routledge, 1991), 275.
7. The following journals, for example, have devoted special issues to "Male Subjectivity": *differences* 1, no. 3 (Fall 1989); "Male Trouble": *Camera Obscura* 17 (May 1988); and "Masculine Sexuality": *Oxford Literary Review* 8, nos. 1–2 (1986).
8. Easthope, *What a Man's Gotta Do*, 1.
9. Laura Mulvey, "Visual Pleasure and Narrative Cinema," *Screen* 16, no. 3 (Fall 1975): 6–18. Reprinted in Laura Mulvey, *Visual and Other Pleasures* (Bloomington: Indiana University Press, 1989): 14–26; further references to this article are included parenthetically within the text. At a recent conference on postmodernism, a colleague complained about what he called the "Mulvey syndrome" in feminist film theory. The comment had to do with what he saw as a dead-end mode of analysis, one that has had its day, and could no longer tell us anything useful about films, whether they be what Mulvey terms

"classic Hollywood cinema" or what might be called, for convenience sake, "progressive" films. Whereas the feminists in the audience, myself included, might have agreed that it is time to question the dominance that Mulvey's influential "Visual Pleasure and Narrative Cinema" has exercised over the field, we were also troubled by the rather glib dismissal this colleague was offering. For implicit in his comment was the odd accusation that it is feminist film theory that has, somehow, invented castration, or, at least, that feminist film theorists seem unwilling to let go of castration as a dominant thematic in reading film.

Resisting the temptation to analyze the currents of desire that might lead feminists to foreground castration, and male critics to disavow it, I want to question whether the time has come to move beyond the "Mulvey syndrome." Or, to put it more precisely, Mulvey's piece still functions as a very fruitful stepping-off point for a wide variety of readings, whether the critic at hand accepts, or critiques, her model. Mulvey herself, of course, responded to early critiques of her "Visual Pleasure" in "Afterthoughts on 'Visual Pleasure and Narrative Cinema' Inspired by King Vidor's *Duel in the Sun* (1946)," *Framework* 15/16/17 (Summer 1981): 12–15. Many critiques of Mulvey have taken off from concern over the rather impossible position in which she places the female spectator. See, particularly, Teresa de Lauretis, *Alice Doesn't: Feminism, Semiotics, Cinema* (Bloomington: Indiana University Press, 1984), and "Aesthetic and Feminist Theory: Rethinking Women's Cinema," *New German Critique*, no. 34 (Winter 1985): 154–75; Mary Ann Doane, "Film and the Masquerade: Theorising the Female Spectator," *Screen* 23, nos. 3–4 (Sept.–Oct. 1982): 175–86, and *The Desire to Desire: The Woman's Film of the 1940's* (Bloomington: Indiana University Press, 1987); Tania Modleski, *The Women Who Knew Too Much: Hitchcock and Feminist Theory* (New York and London: Routledge, 1988); and Gaylyn Studlar, *In the Realm of Pleasure: Von Sternberg, Dietrich, and the Masochistic Aesthetic* (Urbana: University of Illinois Press, 1988). Carol Clover, in *Men, Women and Chainsaws: Gender in the Modern Horror Film* (Princeton, NJ: Princeton University Press, 1992), revises Mulvey with an eye to disrupting binary gender identifications, with particular focus on the male spectator.

10. Steve Neale, "Masculinity as Spectacle," *Screen* 24, no. 6 (Nov.–Dec. 1983): 14.

11. Ibid., 14–15.

12. Ian Green responds to Neale's article (and Mulvey's) by questioning the certainty of gender identifications. He argues that a "viewer's particular phantasies will be complex and subject-based and no amount of tutoring, channelling and controlling by cinematic codes and conventions will buy them off totally" (46). Green is particularly interested in cross-gender identifications, that is, male spectators identifying with female characters. Green, "Malefunction: A Contribution to the Debate on Masculinity in Cinema," *Screen* 25, nos. 4–5 (1984): 36–48.

13. A similar argument has been made by Jane Gallop in her *The Daughter's*

Seduction: Feminism and Psychoanalysis (Ithaca, NY: Cornell University Press, 1982), as Lehman notes.

14. Lehman, "In the Realm of the Senses," 108. It is true that recent analyses of the 1980s male action films have changed the post-Mulvey assumption that male bodies are not put on display, but it is also true that the spectacle of masculinity — as constructed in films such as the *Die Hard* films, the *Lethal Weapon* films, and the *Terminator* films — leaves the penis unrepresented. See the essays on "Muscular Masculinities," in *Screening the Male: Exploring Masculinities in Hollywood Cinema*, ed. Steven Cohan and Ina Rae Hark (London and New York: Routledge, 1993), for analyses of the spectacle of male bodies in these films.

15. Peter Lehman, "Penis-size Jokes and Their Relation to Hollywood's Unconscious," in *Comedy/Cinema/Theory*, ed. Andrew Horton (Berkeley: University of California Press, 1991), 51. Further references to this article are included parenthetically within the text.

16. Berkeley Kaite, "The Fetish in *sex, lies, and videotape:* Whither the Phallus?," in *The Hysterical Male: New Feminist Theory*, ed. Arthur Kroker and Marilouise Kroker (New York: St. Martin's Press, 1991), 183. Kaite suggests that fetishism is a sexual economy that resists closure and, as such, can work to destabilize sexual meanings. Blurring the boundaries between the real and representation, between lies and the truth, and, Kaite suggests, between men and women, the fetish initiates an economy of signification "at the cutting edge of fictive coherence and dispossession" (178). Although I am in sympathy with many of Kaite's points, I think her reading of the film is too optimistic in that she upholds the idea that the fetishism necessarily prevents closure. The film, in my view, closes off fetishism, as well as other avenues toward a recoding of masculinity.

17. See Judith Butler, *Gender Trouble: Feminism and the Subversion of Identity* (New York: Routledge, 1990), to which I refer later.

18. Helen W. Robbins, " 'More Human Than I Am Alone': Womb Envy in David Cronenberg's *The Fly* and *Dead Ringers*," in *Screening the Male*, 134–47. She argues that the Elliott character in *Dead Ringers* fails as an ego ideal for the male spectator because Cronenberg self-consciously inscribes his voyeurism. She writes: "Because Ellie's insulated processing of the woman as video image too nearly reproduces the viewer's own cinematic experience, the male spectator who identifies with Ellie will eventually be forced into an unpleasant and unresolved confrontation with his own voyeurism and the castration anxiety that motivates it" (145). The same kind of thing is going on in relation to Graham's fetishism in *sex, lies, and videotape*.

19. Kaja Silverman suggests a strange twist to this formula in noting that identification with the father cannot be complete, for the son must not enjoy all the privileges of the father; that is, the son is prohibited access to the mother. Silverman makes this point in her reading of male masochism in "Masochism and Male Subjectivity," *Camera Obscura* 17 (May 1988): 41. Further references to this article are included parenthetically within the text.

20. Sigmund Freud, "Fetishism," in *The Standard Edition of the Complete Psychological Works*, vol. 21, pp. 147–57, trans. James Strachey (London: Hogarth, 1955), 154.
21. Elizabeth A. Grosz, "Lesbian Fetishism?" *differences* 3, no. 2 (Summer 1991): 42. Further references to this article are included parenthetically within the texts.
22. John might be considered a fetishist in his own right, for the objects and products he consumes clearly function to prop up his power and masculinity. The film seems dimly conscious of this possibility, as well as the attendant possibility that John and Graham might be seen as different versions of the same thing. Consider Soderbergh's technique of twinning scenes featuring the two characters. Yet, John's fetishism, if it can be described as such, appears to function outside the realm of sexuality, more as a symptom of what Berkeley Kaite suggests is the film's general representation of a postmodern economy of fetishism. Drawing on Marx's, rather than Freud's, theory of fetishism, Kaite points to the general seductiveness of "trafficking in symbols" (179) and the film's indulgence in such seductions.
23. As I indicated in my introduction, I find Soderbergh's self-representation at least slightly disingenuous. That aside, he seems invested in performing a kind of nondominant masculinity, perhaps in an effort to distinguish himself from what he sees as the mainstream of Hollywood movers and shakers. The hysteria arises when this investment comes into conflict with a contradictory desire to distance himself from Graham, who is physically, as well as emotionally, marked as nonphallic.
24. Chris Holmlund, "Masculinity as Multiple Masquerade: The 'Mature' Stallone and the Stallone Clone," in *Screening the Male*, 224. Although Holmlund's analysis is based in a reading of two Stallone movies — movies which could not be more different than *sex, lies, and videotape* — her larger theoretical point seems applicable to Soderbergh's representation of the film's male characters.
25. Yvonne Tasker warns against the assumption that all representations of gender (and, particularly, masculinity) as performance are necessarily subversive. She worries, and rightly so, that the distinction between the "parodic performance of masculinity and the oppressive enactment of that performance" can get lost in celebrations of performance for its own sake. "Dumb Movies for Dumb People: Masculinity, the Body, and the Voice in Contemporary Action Cinema," in *Screening the Male*, 243.
26. Holmund, "Masculinity as Multiple Masquerade," 22.
27. That context is a dazzling reading of *Spartacus*. Ina Rae Hark, "Animals or Romans: Looking at Masculinity in *Spartacus*," in *Screening the Male*, 151–72.
28. In Soderbergh's narrative, he recounts the filming of this scene as follows: "I wanted him naked, but obviously we couldn't have Little Elvis just laying there for all to see" (181). No, indeed.
29. The shot in the film which features Cynthia's intense orgasm might be said to fetishize the woman's pleasure in much the way that Lehman argues

pornographic films do. In Soderbergh's narrative, we learn that this shot was cause for artistic concern: "The Big O Shot, as it was referred to, was not an easy one to accomplish on any level" (187). Interestingly, and without explaining why, Soderbergh confesses that the shot "required a little stylization" (188).

30. Compare, for example, Hitchcock's classic exploration of voyeurism in *Rear Window* (1954), where both Jeffries (James Stewart) and the (male) spectator are implicated in an explicitly thematized voyeurism. See, also, Tania Modleski's reading against the grain of Mulvey's analysis of this film in her *The Women Who Knew Too Much*, 73–85.

31. An astute comment from an anonymous reader of this chapter prompted me to question whether or not "reflexivity" guarantees critical distance. My stance is that it does introduce a wedge into the generally unproblematized mechanisms of desire and pleasure in Hollywood cinema; but that reflexivity itself does not signal subversion of those mechanisms. As this reader reminded me, Jane Feuer has argued that Hollywood musicals use reflexivity to better reinforce identification with the dominant system. See her *The Hollywood Musical* (London: Macmillan, 1982). In *sex, lies, and videotape*, reflexivity does, in fact, function subversively. But this does not keep the film from recuperating any subversive meanings granted by that reflexivity.

32. Garber, *Vested Interests*, 125. The quote is from Jacques Lacan, "The Signification of the Phallus," in *Ecrits: A Selection*, trans. Alan Sheridan (New York: W. W. Norton, 1977), 290.

33. Garber, *Vested Interests*, 120–21.

34. See my "Misappropriations of the 'Feminine,' " *SubStance*, no. 59 (Fall 1989): 48–70, for a critique of recent attempts to valorize fetishism in theoretical discourse.

35. Steven Cohan and Ina Rae Hark, "Introduction," in *Screening the Male*, 2.

36. The films that can be seen as disrupting, in order then to reinvigorate, dominant representations and ideologies are too numerous to mention here. Indeed, as Cohan and Hark suggest, this operation could even be seen as the mark of American mainstream cinema. Still, I would maintain that the disruptions wrought by *sex, lies, and videotape* are not simply in the service of a subsequent realignment of gender and sexuality. I am arguing for a break in the film's narrative trajectory, a tangible turning away from the territory explored through Graham's fetishism.

37. Perhaps the best examples of such work are readings of Clint Eastwood's films. See Paul Smith, "Action Movie Hysteria, or Eastwood Bound," *differences* 1, no. 3 (fall 1989): 88–107; and Judith Mayne, "Walking the Tightrope of Feminism and Male Desire," in *Men in Feminism*, ed. Alice Jardine and Paul Smith (New York: Methuen, 1987), 62–70.

38. Kaite, "The Fetish in *sex, lies, and videotape*," 170; emphasis added. Kaite reads the tapes themselves as the fetish, but I am reading the image of the woman on the tapes as the fetish.

39. Rowena Chapman, "The Great Pretender," in *Male Order: Unwrapping Mas-*

culinity, ed. Rowena Chapman and Jonathan Rutherford (London: Lawrence and Wishart, 1988). Chapman reads images of the "new man" in British advertisements for clothing. See, also, Susan Jeffords's "Can Masculinity be Terminated?," in *Screening the Male*, 245–62, for an analysis of *Terminator 2*'s bizarre inscription of the "new man."

40. Silverman, "Masochism and Male Subjectivity," 31, citing Sigmund Freud, *Three Essays on the Theory of Sexuality*, trans. James Strachey (New York: Basic Books, 1962), 16.

41. Butler, *Gender Trouble*, 17.

42. This is Kaite's term, "The Fetish in *sex, lies, and videotape*," 173.

43. Viewers of the film disagree on this point. Everyone with whom I discussed the film and this chapter hit on this one plot detail as "ambiguous": some agree with me, some disagree. Their decision depends on their desire to see the film as "subversive" or recuperative.

44. Peter Bauman, "Review: *sex, lies, and videotape*," *Commonweal* 116 (6 Oct. 1989): 530.

45. James Spader, according to Soderbergh, objected to Graham turning the camera off before he and Ann make physical contact, because he "was fuzzy on why Graham would even notice the camera" at this point. To which Soderbergh replies: "I agreed, but explained that it was very important that Graham, unconsciously or not, not allow the intimacy between himself and Ann be documented. Graham has finally put the taping thing behind him, I said, and the idea of he and Ann being recorded is now offensive to him" (201).

46. I refer to the title of the special issue of *Camera Obscura*, cited earlier.

PART THREE

Homemade Identities

Nasty Broads and Tender Bitches: The Televising of AIDS Mothers We Love (to Hate)

Kate Cummings

If art is to confront AIDS more honestly than the media have done, it must begin in humour, avoid tact, and include anger. . . . Begin in humour, because humour . . . puts the public on fighting terms with what is an unspeakable scandal: death. Include anger, I say, because it is only sane to rage against the dying of the light.
— John Greyson, *AIDS: The Artist's Response*

God! How many of us [gay men] live in this dreadful anonymous city because we don't want to hurt our mothers? We lose ourselves here. . . . There must be something that connects us. . . . Why can't you hold me?
— *Andre's Mother*

ON THE YELLOWBRICK ROAD

Near the end of *The Wizard of Oz*, Dorothy is disenchanted with the Emerald City, recognizes "there's no place like home," and vows to remain there if only she can return.[1] The upsurge of familial longing succeeds where all else fails; Dorothy awakens in Kansas, safely housed with Auntie Em. Few Americans, I suppose, are unfamiliar with the dream girl's story. However, for those of us who are queer and those of us who are women, her epiphany is more than familiar. The fact is "there's no place like home" and variations upon it are sociopolitical missives that have been aimed at us for years.

The second epigraph is taken from the film *Andre's Mother*; screened

171

on PBS in 1990, it postdates the Hollywood classic by slightly more than five decades. The speaker is a Judy Garland wannabe named Cal, who repeats Dorothy's directive in a bathetic plaint designed to appeal to queers. I ask you to hear it in relation to articulations of "closet-logic" upon which it draws (in romancing the "private" sphere, while repudiating the "public") and which the diegesis of the film repeats and reinforces in melodramatic terms.[2]

Two contemporary articulations of the closet establish a partial context for the film and the genre of AIDS melodramas to which it belongs. One enjoys wide circulation in the world of the everyday. I cite it as the hetero-liberal point of view on the subject of homosex, which is addressed to queers in these approximate words: "What you do in private is your own business; it is the public display of homosexuality that is out of place" or, as some prefer to put it, "it's the sight of homosexual behavior that makes me sick." The other articulation of closet-logic is charged with the juridico-legal force of the Supreme Court. In and partially through the Court's formulation, the signification of "private" acquires an additional valence, as "homosex" is juridically defined as a "dirty secret" that must not be named. I mark this more extensive construction of the closet as the hetero-conservative response to the mere mention of homosexuality in any terms other than aversive ones, and I notate the juridical background to the case of *Bowers v. Hardwick* before quoting from Chief Justice Warren Burger, concurring with the majority opinion.

In brief, the Georgia statute, upon whose constitutionality the Supreme Court was asked to rule, criminalized the *act* of sodomy and not a particular *category* of persons (i.e., homosexuals) who engaged in the act. At the state level, a heterosexual couple accordingly joined Hardwick in challenging the statute's constitutionality, arguing that the criminalization of sodomy exercized a "chilling effect" on their private sexual behavior. When the Supreme Court majority narrowly construed the Georgia statute as criminalizing "homosexual sodomy" alone, they not only rewrote the state law, but they held that the right to "equal protection" under the law did not extend to queers. In so doing, they flatly rejected precedents they had set in interpreting *Eisenstadt v. Baird, Griswold v. Connecticut*, and *Roe v. Wade* as sexual privacy cases.

The case of Griswold is particularly relevant to that of Hardwick, for in it the Court found that the state of Connecticut could not grant married couples the right to purchase contraceptives while witholding the same right from the unmarried. In arriving at this decision, the jurists interpreted the right not to reproduce as a fundamental human right to which all Americans were legally entitled. What the Court refused to see in Hardwick and what his lawyers failed to point out is that sodomy is nonreproductive sex and thus a "fundamental right," as defined by Eisenstadt.

The following is Burger's opinion: "I write separately to underscore my view that in constitutional terms there is no such thing as a fundamental right to commit homosexual sodomy [in private domiciles much less public spaces]. . . . The prescriptions against sodomy have very 'ancient roots' . . . in Judeo-Christian [teaching]."[3] He continues, the unutterability of homosex is a well-established principle of law, and he resurrects a long-dead jurist as an authority on the 1986 case. Thus: "Blackstone described 'the infamous *crime against nature*' as an offense of 'deeper malignity' than rape, a heinous act, 'the very mention of which is a disgrace to human nature' and a 'crime not fit to be named.' "[4]

I also write "to underscore" two aspects of the (moral) majority opinion. One is a paradox in the jurists' construction of privacy, which, on one hand, holds the "right to privacy" does not extend to consensual sex acts between or among members of the same gender and, on the other, imposes a juridico-moral imperative, the effects of which are to privatize queers and (as Burger would have it) censor homosexual representations as "crime[s] not fit to be named."[5] The other aspect of the case against homosex concerns a juridical tradition the "moral majority" opiners conveniently overlook. I remind them that incarceration of the "feebleminded" has "very 'ancient roots' " as well. And were I to follow the spirit of ancient law, I might well propose raving homophobes be given the silence-treatment they prescribe for queers or otherwise be directed to shut up.

When females are the objects of closet-logic, the directive is more likely to be expressed in language recalling the nineteenth-century precept "a woman's place is in the home." Those of us who are middle-aged are likely to have heard variations of this message as a child; those of us who are also middle-class may well have witnessed our mothers enact the same domestic(ating) script; finally, the majority of Americans surely heard the Dorothy imperative resound in the voice of Vice-President Dan Quayle, whose 1992 promotion of "family values" as the antidote to systemic social problems included a particular directive to working women. Draped in the mantle of governmentality, Quayle told us, in effect: it is past time you women left the business world to men and returned to the family you should never have left. The mothers of AIDS melodramas model the Veep's scenario, with a twist. For the homes to which they return will also house their queer seropositive sons, whose every need the moms promise to meet — within the confines of the house. It is a promise bound to delight U.S. constituencies who pray for the day when people with AIDS, homosexuals, and assertive women vanish from sight.

The seropositive women appearing in televized AIDS news genres deliver much the same message on woman's "natural" maternity/domesticity from the opposite angle. In effect, these women, all of whom are poor women of color, are framed as object lessons on how not to behave. Countless documentaries produced by network newsmagazines type seropositive women of color as "breeders" of AIDS and/or "procreators" of AIDS babies in counterpoint, as it were, to the seronegative white women of AIDS melodramas — women whose history of pseudo-male behavior is framed as having bred queer sons. The latter are the abjects of a "judeochristian nation" that has constitutively defined gay men as the "natural" hosts of "unnatural" diseases represented by AIDS. The emplotment of women in each genre follows a similar trajectory until the end, where the paths of third-world peoples, African Americans, Latinas, and Asian Americans sharply diverge from the paths of white women in the United States. That is, where all are initially cast as unnatural mothers who stray from their homes, abandon their families or otherwise prove incapable of maternal love, white women ultimately experience a change of heart that impels their return home.

What is impelled on the level of plot is determined on the level of politics by a strategy entitled "familialism." In essence, the latter is a more comprehensive term for what I have been calling "the logic of the closet." When the subject is AIDS, as in the melodramas, the strategy of familialism involves three discursive operations. First, families are sorted into the healthy and the diseased; next, the healthy are identified as "nation" and the diseased as "family"; finally and most comprehensively, "public" (read "national" and "iterable") concerns are oppositionally distinguished from "private" (read "personal" and "unspeakable") matters.

Distinct from, though currently operating in tandem with this deployment of AIDS familialism is a second family-making strategy to which television productions locating the origin of HIV/AIDS in the "Other" and hyping the so-called spread of AIDS to "the American public" are tactically related. The first of these mediascapes were organized around the subject of "gay cancer." Malignancy is their organizing trope; and the cancerous operation of metastasis emplots all contrafactual stories about AIDS "spread," most of which explicitly oppose malignant agents, who are "not-family," to benign subjects who are. Documentaries encoding women of color as breeders of "heterosexual AIDS" are dramatic expressions of this (un)familial technology. My reading of them is enabled by Simon Watney's classic critique of an ideological formation identifying a mythic family, rather like the Cleavers, with an equally imaginary nation, such as "the back to the future America" of Reagan-Bush. In symptomatic readings of mass-mediated AIDS, Watney further explains how familialism first substitutes the bourgeois family for the nation, then identifies the now enfamilied state as homogeneous, well regulated, and germ free, and so unites a heterogeneous populace against what is envisioned as the ever-present threat of external contaminants: "the foreign, the criminal, the perverted," the promiscuous, the non-white, and the underclass, all of whom are supposed to embody the malignant "AIDS virus."[6]

(The proper name of the virus is, of course, "HIV." As numerous critics have observed, the difference between the two signifiers is far more than nominal; in practice, routinized references to the "AIDS virus" serve to keep three pernicious myths in circulation. One is that AIDS is transmissible; another is that seropositivity necessarily coincides with a variable set of debilitating and ultimately fatal illnesses, collectively represented by "AIDS"; the third is that the moment of HIV transmission is the near moment of death.)[7]

For its part, my essay builds on Watney's deconstruction of familialism to conclude that whereas this formation always equates the nation with the ideological subject of middle-class heterosexual masculinity, it does not necessarily "erase the distinction between 'the public' and 'the private'. . . to establish in their place a monolithic and legally binding category — 'the family' — understood as the central term through which the world and the self are henceforth to be rendered intelligible."[8] On the contrary, where one strategy of familialism does bind family to nation, another supplementary strategy of closet-familialism severs the two. The cover term for what appear to be diametrically opposed configurations of family and nation, familialism is thus a more ambiguous formation than

Watney suggests. And, as I mean to show, it is a more productive apparatus of control than representations of a "monolithic" family alone would allow for.

In reviewing televised productions of "women and AIDS," I aim to challenge the sexism, racism, classism, and homophobia that routinely inform them; to show how AIDS documentaries and melodramas work to enlist the women they represent as accomplices in two strategies of familialism; and to disrupt each strategy by critically surveying the scene of its emergence and by splicing-in (im)pertinent observations, images, and soundtracks designed to open-up television's familial *mise en scène*. My approach, overall, will be to track back and forth between "closed" and "opened" visual fields. In "The Technology of Gender," Teresa de Lauretis describes the first as "the space represented by/in a representation" and the second as "the space[s] not visible in the frame but inferable from what the frame makes visible."[9] Rather than leave these spaces inferable, I have elected to cite them and on occasion to smuggle them into a few frames — in other words, to splice. My use of *The Wizard of Oz* is in this respect paradigmatic. In time, I will be inserting a few soundbites of my own into television productions of "African AIDS," juxtaposing a popular 1980s horror film to the "real-life" documentary "In AIDS Alley," and setting the theme song of the melodrama *Our Sons* to a different set of visuals that challenge the film's construction of privatized AIDS subjects. I will conclude with a coda on Jonathan Demme's *Philadelphia*, which is the most recent in a series of AIDS melodramas. It is also the only feature-length film about the epidemic in which a person of color plays a leading role. How that role is played and with what arguable effects are among the topics of my address.

A moment ago, I indicated my aim in splicing was to open television's scene of AIDS familialism to scrutiny. Let me now add that I also mean to transgress, that is, to turn the logic of AIDS commentary back upon itself by producing a "contaminated" text. Although my choice of what and where to splice is arguably idiosyncratic, the practice of splicing is not. Because watching a show almost always triggers the visualization of other scenarios, the act of viewing involves two screens. One screen is the TV set, which dictates a point of view whose assumption regulates how viewers will watch what is screened. The other is the viewers', which potentially interferes with that reception. More than likely, they are watching with others whose presence multiplies the number of screens and whose representations of television affect their viewing.[10] Thus, whereas footage runs concurrently on all of these sets, neither the images nor soundtracks necessarily mesh. Their potential dissonance produces what Gilles Deleuze and Felix Guattari have termed a "line of flight."[11] By dissonance I do not simply mean the opposition of two scenes, or even their contradiction. Instead, I am thinking more generally of upset or tension induced by the inability to reconcile different views.

At times, the recognition of a literary convention is enough to disturb. The easiest to spot are conventions of detection and horror. Although the two are often masked by and in the discourse of AIDS science, they are hyper-visible in the televisual medium of AIDS news.[12] Viewing fictional and news forms concurrently raises questions about the status of facticity, thereby implicating "truth" in "fiction" without prioritizing either term. Hence, in the signifying relationship I am positing, fiction no more stands behind the production of fact as its animating cause, than horror or detection stands behind documentary or science as its origin or truth. On the contrary, the relations between and among fiction/fantasy, science and news are contiguous. To see them, there is no need for a penetrating gaze; indeed, there is no better way to watch an AIDS program than to look around with a roving eye and see what it functions with. Take Michel Foucault's suggestion and look at the systems of discourse into which its own representations are inserted and by which they are sustained; look also at networks of power (governmental policies, medical practices, social behaviors, etc.) to which the program is linked and by which its effects are extended.[13]

IN THE LAND OF THE WICKED WITCH

I busted my ass with my therapist dealing with all the negative emotions that come with having AIDS. And I had come so far. Far enough to where I was counselling other people. . . . And now this doctor was dancing around willing to let me die because my body was putrid. My blood was tainted and filthy and carried death. . . . I still can't find out if the ovarian abscesses were due to AIDS or just "women's problems." And yeah I'm angry. Blood is dripping from my eyes.[14]

My review of televisual AIDS begins with three newsmagazine documentaries that are "plugged into" a number of other sense-making technologies. Among them are fictional machines of detection and horror; epidemiological machines of classification; libidinal machines of anxiety; and sociopolitical machines of racism, sexism, and familialism whose anxious knowledges and/or phobic projections they mass market as America's defense against (people with) AIDS. The first documentary aired on "Nightline" in the fall of 1986, the second on "60 Minutes" in the fall of 1987, and the third on "48 Hours" in the fall of 1988. All re-present people of color — Africans, African Americans, and Latinas/Latinos — as a different species of being, of no relation to the "civilized" family of man.

As a starting point, consider the framing of "AIDS" on "48 Hours." In a format best described as a peep show, the news crew take "the viewing public" on a tour of Spanish Harlem, which they describe as "infested with junkies" and prostitutes who are carrying AIDS from one subject to the next.[15] As a common signifier in television productions, "the public" hails a homogeneous audience of white middle-class heterosexuals who also make up the enfamilied American nation. Not only are the news teams' "carriers" visibly excluded from this ideological family portrait, by an extension of the same anxious logic, they are cast out of the human habitas and humankind into a (metaphoric) swamp that they "infest" in the form of AIDS-ridden mosquitoes. If anxiety impels the operation of displacement (which is what a psychoanalytic reading would suggest) historical circumstances motivate the substitution of "swamp" and "mosquitoes" for the actual locale and historical subjects under investigation.

Essentially, what the CBS news team uncovers in "AIDS Alley" are prior findings of U.S. journalists on the track of AIDS in Belle Glade, Florida, and in Africa. The American town is an impoverished migrant community whose population is predominantly African American. Its otherwise privatized inhabitants made news headlines in the mid-1980s and periodically thereafter as the enigmatic subjects of heterosexual AIDS in the United States.[16] Mass-mediations of Belle Glade commonly recycled Western fantasies about Africa, three of which are immediately germane. First, the African-American community was imaged as a replica of Conrad's "dark continent" in miniature.[17] Second, his "Horror" was given a modern-day face in the dark visages of heterosexuals with AIDS. Third, two foundational myths about the "nature" of AIDS in Africa were imported to explain the presence of the(ir) epidemic in America. One speculated that mosquito bites were a vector of viral transmission; the other separated non-white from white heterosexuals.[18]

As a rule, the bug-bite scenario was mediated as a highly localized risk

factor, limited to people whose pigments were much darker, sexual practices much kinkier, habitats much filthier, and bodies much germier
than the implied white middle-class audience for whom spectacles of
Africanized AIDS were and are produced. The same scene included peri-
odic lessons in entymology; among them was the fact that females were
the "blood-suckers" of the mosquito species. This sexed opposition between AIDS-bearing females and harmless males would have been of little
import were the same distinction not extended to human beings: in
images of female prostitutes as deadly parasites (read also "vampires")
feeding on hapless male hosts, in projections of recognizably feminized
landscapes as breeding grounds of AIDS, and in portrayals of women's
wombs as viral swamps. Stories of AIDS mosquitoes in Belle Glade also
had another consequence; that is, in their focus on bug bites as points of
viral entry, the actual risk of HIV transmission in unprotected intercourse
between partners of the opposite sex all but disappeared. On one hand,
the sexual oversight imperiled the health of heterosexual women and
men; on the other, it functioned on behalf of the heterosexualized ego in
the manner of a defense, because what was unsaid was effectively spoken
for by the conventional wisdom that heterosexuality was indeed safe (as
a) sex.[19]

Nonetheless, news reticence on the subject of heterosexual transmission was far from total; rather, periods of near silence alternated with
pronounced speech. When stories of heterosexual transmission were set
in impoverished locales within the United States, Western images of
"African AIDS" were projected onto underclass Americans of color whose
heterosexuality they represented in hegemonic terms elsewhere applied
to gay men. Chief among those terms is "promiscuity." How the subject
of African (-American) promiscuity came to be framed within the context
of the epidemic can be seen in "Nightline"'s inaugural newsmagazine
exposé of heterosexual "AIDS in Africa." The framer is a researcher who
explains: "There is no doubt there is a different attitude to sexual intercourse in many of these countries. . . . They are much less chaste than
we."[20] My translation of this statement is that Africans are a different
breed of heterosexual from whom African Americans are descended; neither "African AIDS" nor its relatives in "Africanized pockets" of the
United States have any bearing on white heterosexuals, who can therefore
relax in the knowledge that they are safe — so long as they cleave to their
own kind. "There is no doubt," this safety directive is taken from the

pseudo-scientific manual of eugenics, whose opposition of "degenerate" colored blood to "vital" white blood it reformulates and extends.

Two epidemiological events played a formative role in the emergence of "Africanized AIDS." One was the 1983 discovery that what is now known as HIV is sexually transmissible from male to female.[21] Although the discovery was reported in the most prestigious of U.S. medical journals, it was not considered newsworthy by the networks, who all but ignored the real risk to women in rerunning contrafactual stories on "the spread of AIDS through casual contact."[22] By 1985, the fact that seropositive males were infecting their female sex partners was beginning to receive network attention; so also, if not more so, were the roughly contemporaneous discoveries of AIDS researchers that seropositive women were capable of sexually transmitting HIV to men.

Initial evidence for female-to-male transmission was implicit in 1984 studies of "black African" men and women with AIDS.[23] In 1985, Dr. Robert Redfield provided "documentation" confirming the identification of prostitutes as a "risk group" in a study of seropositive military personnel. What he wrote was that female prostitutes were a potential "reservoir [of HIV] infection for heterosexually active individuals."[24] What Redfield inscribed was an ontological divide between polluted vaginas and (all too) human men contaminated by them. Like the "Spanish Harlem" of CBS, whose prostitute "infested" alleys they anticipate, the doctor's miasmatic reservoirs harken back to the "Africa" of the West. He, unlike the news crews, foregrounds the African connection in two primal scenes.

One scene is speculative and shows that Euro-American prostitutes "probably" acquired the virus from bisexual males of indeterminate nationality and race or heterosexual males from "equatorial Africa" where AIDS is "endemic" (2096). This hypothetical act of infection further implies a chain of transmission running from the bodies of gay men at one end and African women at the other. The women are the subject of Redfield's second epidemiological scene, where they appear to be as efficient transmitters of HIV as their African male cohorts. Both are cited as the subjects of Western researchers in "recent reports from Africa, . . . demonstrating a male-female ration of AIDS of 1.1 : 1" (2096).

It is upon this demonstration that Redfield's speculative identification of prostitutes as the source of HIV infection in male American soldiers partially rests. Additional evidence is provided by the mothers of "newborns" with HIV and AIDS, whose "ability to transmit the virus and disease *[sic]*" warrants their appearance alongside African women and prostitutes (2096). The women's dramatic opposites are military men and the male organ, which appears in the signifier Freud substitutes for it, though not in the (original) fantasies of the subjects he supposes. On the contrary, in Redfield's spectacle, babies "take the place of [the mens'] penis in accordance with an ancient symbolic equivalence" that is symptomatic of the same masculine imaginary that envisioned women as vaginas with legs and vaginas as polluted reservoirs contaminating (baby) men.[25]

The spectacle had two consequences. The first was to transform the image of seropositive G.I.'s from homosexuals, infected through sex with men, to (avowed) heterosexuals, infected by prostitutes. The next and more extensive consequence was to trigger a second set of news stories on the subject of heterosexual AIDS. The first began in July 1985 when it was announced that Rock Hudson had AIDS and concluded with Rock's death on 2 October, shortly before the Redfield news alerts appeared. Together, the Hudson-Redfield narratives make up a transmission sequence, which is briefly related. In essence, the Hudson story located the origin of AIDS in homosexual men, while it represented women who unwittingly had sex with bisexual partners as tragic receptacles of a queer disease. The Redfield story started where its predecessor ends, with a tale of a "polluted female reservoir" that is in the process of contaminating "[hetero]sexually active" American men with the viral run-off of queers and Africans. News bulletins from the Centers for Disease Control warning of a potential epidemic among heterosexuals and reports identifying Belle Glade and Africa as epicenters of the heterosexual epidemic followed the "reservoir" tale.

Before "Nightline" ran its documentary on African AIDS in October 1986, two informatics on the subject of heterosexuals and AIDS were, then, common place. One defines America as a beseiged nation where those prostitutes are "giving AIDS" to our heterosexual men, where people of color are contaminating (the blood of) us whites, where pocket epidemics of "homosexual AIDS" and "heroin AIDS" are no longer self-contained, and where AIDS is thus in danger of striking "respectable" white, middle-class heterosexuals. The other informatic defines Africa as the continent where AIDS was born, the place where thousands of African women are carrying the virus and all African women are either prostitutes or promiscuous, and the scene where "the epidemic" signifies "mass death." In this spectacle of "de-generation," continent and womb are mirror images of morbidity whose value derives from prior understandings of Africa as "the cradle of life" and woman's womb as the "origin" of the same.[26] The cradle image is carried over in spectacular citings of Africa as the birthplace of AIDS, where it appears alongside inverted projections of the continent as humanity's grave. Traditional reproductive tableaux are similarly transposed in two scenes. One attributes the origin of AIDS in babies, men, and women to reproductive sex. Another, which is decidedly more common, builds on that attribution, but "forgets" the seminal role of man and identifies reproduction exclusively with woman; this scene envisions her womb as the apocalyptic site of heterosexual annihilation.

"Nightline," "60 Minutes," and "48 Hours" restage the same apocalyptic spectacle in documentaries whose subjects are the origin and spread of AIDS. The first two productions bear an identical title, "AIDS in Africa"; the third is entitled "In AIDS Alley." As is the case with any narrative of origin, their hunt for the spawning ground of AIDS necessarily reproduces the detective story. Their identification of that ground with the conventionally "uncanny" terrains of Africa, Spanish Harlem, and female bodies, coupled with their focus on AIDS's putative spread, gives their mystery narratives a horrific spin. Indeed, the mere "fact that the geographical source of the virus is alleged to be Africa," as it is in the first two documentaries, "merely feeds into ... monster narratives already available to be mobilized" as Judith Williamson has previously observed.[27] Hence, "Nightline" 's investigative reporter in Uganda points out: "There have been statements made that Africa has presented the world with a horror — a highly contagious and deadly disease with which to contend" (3). The fact that a primary human source of the virus is alleged to be the female body and that her body is subtyped as "sexually primitive"/"colored" has the same horrific effect. Mediated as "filthy," "promiscuous," "predatory," and "polluted," these monstrous incarnations of AIDS represent a subset of nasty broads in my text.

Large portions of all three AIDS documentaries are shot in half light like many detection and horror films. Cameras pan across shadelike figures and close in on shadows. The subjects under scrutiny are women and men of color; the anchorperson, medical "experts," and all but one of the reporters are white. The white folks play the part of disease detectives; with the exception of a few outreach workers and the Ugandan Ambassador to the United Nations, people of color are made to play the diseased or disease. In the following excerpts from the two "AIDS in Africa" shows, watch for the detective plot and horror story. Also look for the "Mother's" return. Dimly present at first in dark images of liquidity, such as the African lake that is imaged as the watery womb of AIDS, the maternal body is more sharply defined in female prostitutes and women who are gynephobically signified upon in the standardized construction of "AIDS-breeders."[28] Prostitutes, themselves, are further (dis)figured as companions of the travelling virus who are truckers by trade.

I quote from "Nightline"'s screening of Africanized AIDS 1986, while splicing in a few soundbites and stage directions of my own. "Researchers attempting to unravel the mysteries of AIDS have increasingly been drawn to their [sic] continent of Africa." There, on the "other" side of our border, "AIDS has the potential of spreading to the entire population." Insert exhibit A in the close-up of "the baby [who] is two months old and dying" and tack on the conventional voice-over: "AIDS transmitted from mother to child, there was no gift of life in this birth" (20). Screen out all images or information that might complicate the transmission scenario, inhibit the possibility of an empathetic response to the birth mother, and show her simply in the loathsome guise of "baby-killer" who deserves a painful death.

Here, is the "dark continent" of "60 Minutes" with my inserts. "They don't often say it, but a lot of scientists around the world have been watching the spread of AIDS in central Africa with a mixture of horror and fascination." The voyeurism thus attributed to the scientists tacitly invites news viewers to watch the televisual parade of AIDS horrors with the same erotic investment. Cut to Robert Gallo, who locates the Monster's lair in the wet surround of Lake Victoria within the heart of central Africa. "When you go there" you can tell She has been there because "in house after house you will find someone dying of AIDS." The death of one of these people, a woman named Florence, concludes the documentary; her death is framed as a grim reminder that AIDS is inevitably fatal and decidedly metastatic: like a cancer, it and promiscuity are said to spread — from "immoral" women, who are misbegotten by Eve, to Adam's sons, who are naturally fallible men. Hence, we hear "the disease didn't stop in the provinces" with Florence. Rather, it "traveled" from her (lair) along "this road toward the capital city because this is the road used by truck drivers." We spy one of them "head[ing] toward the city, stop[-

ping] at four or five truck stops along the way. At every truck stop the women are waiting" for the trucker who turns from continental to cuntinental highway. "By now as many as 76 percent of the women are infected with the virus."[29]

Subsequent visuals and voice-overs show how the women go on to infect. However, they do not begin to address the impact of colonialism on Africa — not the displacement of tribal peoples into urban centers, nor the economic conditions motivating prostitution, by which I mean a global market whose functioning depends on the exploitation of third-world peoples as natural resources and/or cheap labor pools. In short, neither documentary says that if it were not for prostitution, these women would starve to death.

Racism and sexism continue to infect Western coverage of AIDS in Africa. Furthermore, as a recent text, written by the medical historian Mirko Grmek and published by Princeton University Press, illustrates, fictional conventions of horror and detection still regulate the production of AIDS "scholarship." Even more so than the documentaries, Grmek's *History* of the pandemic is hooked on(to) the narrative of a monster's origin and quest for prey. In it, he cites a host of monstrosities "coming out of" Africa; among them are malaria, tuberculosis, various pox viruses, plagues, syphilis, and most probably AIDS.[30] The book alternately depicts African urban centers as womblike locales for the "propitious . . . propagation" of HIV and "nurseries of the AIDS virus" (176). It represents prostitutes and "new categories of 'free women' " as abandoning themselves to "elaborate sexual play" with "a multiplicity of partners" in swelling cities where "overpopulation and overcopulation grow together" (176). It thereby identifies African women with gay men in San Francisco, who are described in analogous terms and both with the "diabolical AIDS virus" that "ricochets outward to disturb [traditional] sexual relations and . . . poison social habits" (xi–xii, 169). In short, as do the documentaries, the book mobilizes a monstrous "Africa" wherein a feminized continent and promiscuous women spawn AIDS.[31]

The depiction of women of color as infected and infecting is represented with a vengeance "In AIDS Alley." Once again, there is no analysis of the systemic causes of prostitution and/or chronic drug use — thus, no mention of institutionalized poverty and racism — nor is there the faintest suggestion that the billions of dollars spent in the so-called war on drugs might be allocated more productively to treatment therapies and needle exchange programs.[32] The documentary segment I have chosen to excerpt begins with a drum beat establishing the African connection, then zooms in on camera crew members, who are playing explorers/ anthropologists on the trail of "restless natives." Camera reticence and references to "unspeakable rites" soon fuse the "Africa" of Western imagination to an equally fantasmatic inner-city scene. As elsewhere, masculine fanstasies about the maternal body play a germinal role. Hence, in an iconic pun on the title, alleys and stairwells are initially screened as birth canals of AIDS. Because some of these alleys are back alleys and all of them are filthy, however, they also ask to be connected to figurations of the rectum. Once the tropological connection is made (and given the media blitz on gay male sexual practices it would be difficult to miss), the bodily presence of gay men can be dispensed with. For they are there metonymically in the rectal sign with which they have been identified, and like the maternal body, they are there to remind the audience that moist bodies (or body parts) breed AIDS. Finally, we are shown the prostitutes; they are explicitly charged as carriers of the deadly virus.

My reading of "In AIDS Alley" is accompanied by a recap of *Aliens*.[33] The monster of the film is a mother whose monstrosity is attributed to physical and sexual difference; equipped with male and female sex organs, the creature breeds to excess. What she breeds is capable of invading human bodies or killing them on contact. By in large, she favors the first solution, for if her brood is to survive and thrive, like HIV, they must "gestate inside a living human host." The alien mother and brood are also reminicent of the so-called AIDS virus in that both are depicted as "being on the move" ("Alley," 2). Finally, neither strain seems to "care if you are gay or straight." Nonetheless, as is commonly alleged to be the case with HIV (just read Jesse Helms, Peter Duesberg, or Cardinal John J. O'Connor), aliens evince a marked predilection for queers. Consequently, in the film's final battle, the dyke and the expedition's "wimpy" commander get it first.

By splicing together *Aliens* and "AIDS Alley," I aim to open the documentary to ridicule, while further indicating how the news program's hook-up with horror regulates its coverage of AIDS. One need not be an afficionado of the genre to recognize that its favorite topic is transgression. Quite frequently, horror trades upon national anxieties that the death or containment of the monster serves to allay; its common coinages are the natural and unnatural. And, though horror may refer to institutional practices, government policies, or the materiality of social life (as *Aliens* does), it tends to do so within an allegorical as opposed to a historical framework.

Here, in brief, is a summary of Cameron's film: The shuttle crew has penetrated the aliens' lair in the hunt for missing colonists. Red in color, the lair is covered with a white viscous substance that oozes from its walls and ceiling. Even its floor is sticky wet. Crew members discover a colonist to interview. Before they can, an alien breaks through her skin. Soon the crew is attacked by a swarm of these creatures, and though a few escape, many more fall prey. Later, a lone explorer returns to the heart of the lair. All around her are eggs; towering above her is the mother alien, who is equipped with a large penislike appendage; she is busy fertilizing what she has bred. The explorer torches the eggs but is pursued by the alien mother, who climbs upon the space shuttle — an airborne invader in search of new prey.

And here is an excerpt from the documentary: "The drums you are about to hear are beating out a warning: [there are] strangers in the neighborhood" (12). The strangers are immediately identified as the "camera crew," after which an on-the-scene reporter explains: "the people here don't want you to see . . . [our] pictures or hear about their business. What went on here last night? . . . Orgies. . . . Sex not for money, but for drugs, in the corners and stairwells, pictures we cannot possibly show" (12), though we will string you along with a gothic cliche. As is also conventional in phobic framings of homoerotic graphics, the place of sexual pictures is taken by the voice of moral outrage. It insinuates the tenement alcoves are bathed in vaginal fluids and sperm. These are the reporter's next words: crack "really stimulates peoples' sex drives. . . . The women who live in crack houses will tell you how it happens" (12) with some prodding from Harold Dow. In essence, one of them confesses to having sex with one partner after another, from which the newscast draws the same conclusion that Redfield did. What we are told is "a number of people . . . with no other risk factors . . . are coming in and they're testing positive because of sexual relationships with prostitutes in crack houses" (13). What the statement recycles is the traditional ontic distinction between heterosexual men who are the "people" (read also "nation") and female prostitutes who are monsters, infested reservoirs, or pathogens. Take your pick. The grand finale accordingly begins: "This is the new wave. . . . The warning is going out. There is a stranger in the neighborhood crack house" (13) and the stranger has been given a new name. Forget the camera crew of "48 Hours," the Alien to watch out for is Mother AIDS. "From [Her] beginnings in New York, the deadly [monster] is on the move [with her promiscuous female brood], headed for America's other big cities" (2).

The travelling AIDS virus calls to mind the subject of another documentary aired on public television in the spring of 1986. Entitled "AIDS: A National Inquiry," the documentary is essentially the exploitative story of Fabian Bridges, a black gay male prostitute with AIDS who continued to have sex after his diagnosis.[34] Here, it is not Fabian's story I mean to tell, but the story of the woman known only as Fabian's Mother or, rather, the tale of their relationship. Under pressure from her second husband, Fabian's Mother bars her son from the family home, thereby refusing to enact her name. The documentary rigorously blames her for this failure to be a "real" mother. In contrast, slight fault is found with the local municipalities, whose only desire is to get rid of Fabian, and no onus is laid on the crew of PBS, who ruthlessly exploits him.[35] The reason has something to do with gender ideology, but more — I think — with the ideology of familialism, which, by deflecting criticism from public to private institutions, ensures that AIDS is depoliticized — closeted within the family as a personal affair. Subject to this logic of the closet, Fabian's Mother makes an obligatory return. I quote from the final exchange between mother and son.

FABIAN'S MOTHER: You gonna need somebody by your side. Without mother, you, you lost.
FABIAN: Yeah.
FABIAN'S MOTHER: Without a mother you lost.
FABIAN: Yeah, without a family.[36]

The very words that convict Fabian's Mother repeat a culturally normative script that is presupposed by the other AIDS documentaries whose cast of women it serves to encode as horrors. I repeat it in the disciplinary rubric of the documentaries whose implied woman is all their nasty broads are not. Most importantly, she is a natural nurturer and sustainer of (family) life, which is why she knows she belongs in the home. By definition, she does not sexually transmit HIV or infect her babies any more than than she abandons or fails to care for those to whom she gave birth, all of which are codified as enactments of anti-nurturance/anti-life. At least, she does not do any of these things without forfeiting "motherhood" and meriting "monsterhood," as the four documentaries demonstrate. Nor does she follow their script by leaving home and family, traveling highways, stalking cities, or haunting crack houses, particularly if she is "harboring" a "lethal virus" as she flits from man to man. Finally, she is never a sexual agent, and she does not have any sex other than reproductive sex or the genital act associated with it; and then she does it only with her husband. More precisely, if she does go astray in any of these ways, she (all but) forfeits her title to womanhood and joins the verminous host of "unwomen" who make up "AIDS Alley" and "AIDS in Africa."

HOME AGAIN WITH AUNTIE EM

These are difficult times for our country and in searching for the causes of our social ills, we could choose to blame the media, or the Congress, or an administration that's been in power for twelve years, or we could blame me [a TV mom, named Murphy Brown].[37]

In AIDS melodramas, the picture looks quite different. Yet the cultural script through which "nasty broads" are made remains much the same. Because the differences in recent made-for-TV melodramas are as striking as they are consequential, they merit attention first. In these films, and unlike the chronicle of Fabian, AIDS mothers effectively steal the show from their gay (wannabe) sons, all but one of whom are played by lesser-known actors. The films are *Mother, Mother*, produced in 1989 and starring Polly Bergen; *Andre's Mother*, first aired on PBS in 1990 and starring Sada Thompson and Richard Thomas (alias "John-Boy Walton"); and *Our Sons*, first aired on network TV in 1991 and starring Julie Andrews and Ann-Margret.[38]

One of the most telling differences between the two AIDS genres is the relentless whiteness of the movies. Admittedly, a Latina/Latino couple make a momentary appearance in the hospital scene of *Our Sons*, where they inhabit the corner of a frame whose center is occupied by two white, middle-class gay males, who are the sons of Julie Andrews and Ann Margaret. The men are also a couple, which is precisely where the other "other couple" comes in. This pair's role is to establish boundaries. As defined by the first boundary, AIDS-related illnesses are both subject specific and "essentially" determined. Thus, the Latino male has Pneumocystis pneumonia (PCP) and the gay male has Kaposi's sarcoma (KS).

Each illness promotes a secondary diagnosis, representing a sociomedical reading of and into the subject's inner being or "truth." PCP accordingly identifies the Latino male as a junkie (note the appellation "junkie pneumonia"), which in the absence of other Latinos equates drug addiction and ethnicity; moreover, because "junkie pneumonia"/"AIDS" is said to be transmitted through "dirty needles," a diagnosis of PCP tacitly identifies Latinos with filth. The scene's other male is gay, which in the absence of other gay male PWAs who manifest different illnesses, equates gayness and KS. This particular representation of the diseased PWA has three other effects. In Simon Watney's words, the standard screen image of Kaposi's renders the gay male body "as repulsive as the task of policing recalcitrant desire requires it to be."[39] Along with numerous indicators of physical weakness and fraility, KS more forcefully encodes this particular body as "pathetic," which is precisely the coding melodramas favor. Finally, and in tension with the boundary separating the two men, the lesions on the gay body are visible markers of its alterity; thus, for the gay body as for the Latino body, difference is represented by skin.[40] The second boundary stipulates that for people living with AIDS, affection is permissible; eroticism is not. That is, it is culturally acceptable for the Latina woman to massage her dying "husband's" feet and for the gay man to follow suit by hugging his dying "friend." ("Naturally," the hug is as hot as the film gets.)

And, finally, there is a third boundary, which is implied by the second. It indicates that on one side, heterosexuals are sexual — meaning, they have husbands, wives, and/or lovers. On the other, queers are asexual — meaning, we have friends. Hence, in the hospital scene, the Latina identifies "my husband" and the gay man "my friend." Because the sole functions of the Latino/Latina couple are to essentialize subjectivity and regulate sexuality, their race is virtually erased. What remains are racist tropes of drugs and dirt.

Still, their depiction might not merit the exposition I have given it were it not for the fact that they and a few African-American walk-ons in *Mother, Mother* are the only people of color in the three films. Although I am far from thinking three movies, much less a single one, can possibly represent the diverse subjects who are living with HIV/AIDS, and although I make no mimetic claims for AIDS melodramas as reflectors of the historical real (quite the contrary), I do read the virtual absence of people of color from fictional films about AIDS as a salient symptom of institutionalized racism. It is in the larger context of their near invisibility in AIDS movies, on the one hand, and the xenophobic conditions under which they become visible in numerous AIDS documentaries, on the other, that I emphasize, walk-ons are the only people of color in the three AIDS melodramas. They are the only representatives of African Americans and Latinos/Latinas, despite the fact that in the United States alone over 40 percent of all males diagnosed with AIDS are African-American and Latino men; despite the fact that over half of these males are men who have had sex with men, while the melodramas are about seropositive gay men; despite the fact that roughly 75 percent of females diagnosed with AIDS are African American and Latina; despite the fact that women of color support and care for seropositive gay sons, while the films allot supportive roles to white women alone; despite the fact that AIDS statistics underrepresent the actual number of AIDS cases among people of color; and despite the fact that men and women of color die even faster from AIDS-related illnesses than do white men and women.

Racism, however, does not entirely explain the absence of people of color from almost all dramatizations of PWAs, the notable exception being Marlon Riggs's *Tongues Untied*, whose subjects are black gay men.[41] In the three television melodramas, as in mainstream AIDS films, considerations of class also dictate which PWAs will and will not be represented.[42] Not only are the melodramas' gay male PWAs and their lovers professional men (upscale artist, architect, writer, and teacher), they are also men of impeccable, if stereotypical, taste. Adept as any "woman" in dressing for occasion, they are more adept than most women in appointing a room. Among the men's avocations are playing the piano, reading Shakespeare, watching old movies, and listening to Bach.[43]

These constructions of gay male PWAs and their lovers produce four "truth-effects." First, the focus on gay men identifies gays with AIDS. Not only does this identification misrepresent the actual sexual diversity of PWAs, many of whom are bisexual and many of whom are straight, it fuels hatred of all queers and thus encourages the bashing of gay men and lesbians. Second, the images define gay males as being artsy, white, and middle class, thereby denying racial and class differences among gay men, while suggesting, as Crimp has said of "AIDS in the Arts," that "gay people have a natural inclination toward the arts."[44] Third, the emphasis on artistic talent implies "gay people 'redeem' themselves by being artists and therefore that the deaths of other gay people are less tragic."[45]

Fourth, and worst of all, the fetishizing of taste fosters the conclusion that people with AIDS whose talents are not artistic and whose tastes are not middle class are not worth caring about; quite possibly they have gotten their "just desserts."

To see how "taste" produces indifference or worse, merely re-envision the impoverished tenements of "AIDS Alley" next to the swank homes of the films' gay men. The contrast between the two domiciles could not be more striking: rotting garbage, used crack vials, and dirty needles litter the one; art objects, books, and flowers accent the other. Each space, and this is the critical issue, encodes a particular reading of AIDS. Briefly, where the tasteful homes exist in what Michael Bronski terms "ironic juxtaposition" to an illness that in its final stages is debilitating, the "infested" tenements exist "as its perfect accompaniment."[46]

Bronski goes on to read the representation of the gay male PWA as belonging to "the *Camille* syndrome: the romance of the outlaw, the misunderstood one who may die, but who dies beautifully and with a great deal of pathos and sentiment. Here is the ultimate and incurable romantic."[47] Here also is the stuff of melodrama. In a formative critique of the genre, Mary Ann Doane identifies melodrama as both the "privileged" cinematic form for "the investigation of issues associated with maternity" and a productive technology of gender whose subjects are always passive or "feminized." She concludes that "whether the character is a man or a woman, 'suffering and impotence, besides being the data of middle-class life, are seen as forms of a failure to be male.' "[48]

The sons of AIDS melodramas invariably fit the specifications of both critics. Where their "artiness" alone hints at "unmanliness," AIDS renders them "feminized" as victims, patients, and losers. In particular, neither of the two PWAs are living with AIDS; instead, they are dying from it. Furthermore, neither is able to do so without his mother's help, as is indicated on one occasion by the cry of Polly Bergen's son: "I can't die without her." The TV lovers of PWAs are also helpless, needy, and dependent on maternal support. Consider the case of Cal, played by Richard Thomas, who spends most of his time trying and all but failing to win acknowledgment from his dead lover Andre's mother. Apart from suffering the death and dying of their lovers, neither he nor Julie Andrew's son, James, do much else.

Let me not be mistaken as objecting to representations of survivors mourning those they have loved and lost. What I do object to is the way in which melodrama works to engender "pathetic" gay subjects, all of whom are seen to suffer from the "failure to be male" and one of whom dies beautifully like Camille. My basic quarrel with pathos is that it enables the operation of familialism. And whereas I recognize mourning is a psychic need, I am convinced AIDS activism remains a historical necessity.[49] Bottom line: Americans are currently faced with a situation in which the signifier, "AIDS," is on the verge of disappearing from the national consciousness, while the syndrome, AIDS, continues to affect increasing numbers of women and men. Bottom line: AIDS melodramas make activism all the more urgent because they work to domesticate their audience, thereby inhibiting critical responses to national mismanagement of the epidemic. To frame my argument against closet familialism, I turn first to the mothers of gay sons in the recognition that it is the mother-son couple who represent the privitizing unit in these films.[50]

With one exception, mothers initially inhabit masculine positions that set them apart from or at odds with their feminized sons. Hence, as Audrey, Julie Andrews of *Our Sons* plays the part of a high-powered business executive who sleeps with a dictaphone beside her bed. Her personal relations resemble her business contacts in being characterized by quiet determination and emotional reserve. Unlikely to ask how others are feeling, she is quick to question what their decisions are and what they have done. In these ways, Audrey's position, behavior, and speech are patterned on those of a typical white upper-middle-class male who is accustomed to having his own way. "Naturally," there is no other man of or in the house.

Polly Bergen of *Mother, Mother* plays a woman who currently runs her own business after years of running her son's life. When he came out to his father against her orders, Mrs. Cutler (Bergen) kicked Jeff out of the house. Having a queer son was too much for Mr. Cutler, who responded to Jeff's news by promptly dropping dead. Since then, the mother's contact with the son has been purely business; on his birthday she mails Jeff a check. The most domineering of the three mothers, Cutler is nicknamed "the Ayatollah," whose misrule and menace are "common knowledge" in the United States. (Incidentally, this knowledge is a product of the Iran "hostage crisis," which was covered as an attack on the American family and featured the Ayatollah Khomeini as threatening the home; as we might expect from Bergen's nickname alone, *Mother, Mother* recovers much the same ground with Cutler starring as the family menace.)

The third mother, played by Sada Thompson, descends from a long line of assertive women. Unlike the other mothers, she is currently married — to a man who is irrelevant to the script. His irrelevance is related to her self-containment, which is a quality she shares with Audrey and Cutler. Thompson's implacability and remoteness earn her the title, "Andre's Mother"; based on the cartoon character, Lulu's Mother, the name signifies a non-woman incapable of emotional display.

Ann-Margret's character, Lu Ann, in *Our Sons* is certainly as unfeeling as any of the other mothers. At least she is when it comes to showing warmth for her son. In fact, were viewers to rank the moms on a scale of empathy or nurturance, she would probably be on the lowest end of the scale, followed by Mrs. Cutler and Andre's Mother; after her, with some space in between, would be Audrey, who plays opposite (to) Lu Ann in the film.

Despite her "unfeminine" lack of feeling, Lu Ann no less poses a partial exception to the masculine rule. The only working-class mother in the AIDS melodramas, she is also the only woman to be figuratively associated with castration. As it happens, the scene of the mother's "castration" coincides with the scene of her son Donald's birth. Lu Ann reconstructs the misbegotten birth for Donald and viewers as he lies dying in bed. Her "maimed equipment" (literally, a broken leg) is thereby connected to his "impaired masculinity" and his debilitation to her "impotence." For Lu Ann's castration to look more than gratuitous, Donald must be cast as the most impaired of the films' sons — which he is. In fact, Donald singularly represents "the AIDS body" as it is conventionally posed to illustrate alterity, disfigurement, and morbidity; moreover, he alone dies during the film. And he does so on cue, as it were, from his mother immediately after her scenic recollection of the castrated/castrating birth.

Lu Ann's motherhood is not exclusively defined in relation to her son, however. It is also defined in relation to her maternal counterpart.[51] The upper-middle-class Audrey has a liberal attitude on the subject of homosexuality: she looks upon gayness as an acceptable "lifestyle" for others, but she resents the sexual "choice" of her son James. Conventionally true to her class position, Audrey has kept her resentment to herself. At her son's request, she flies to Arkansas where Lu Ann lives in order to persuade the "other" mother to visit her dying son (who is James's lover). Lu Ann has had no contact with Donald during the past eleven years, and at first she wants nothing to do with him. To her, Donald is simply "one of them"; nauseating, unnatural and queer, he is obviously no part of Lu Ann's American family. Her initial assessments of his AIDS diagnosis are "it figures," and "you bought [sic] it on yourself."

Lu Ann's language and assessments are as foreign to Audrey as her trailer-park home, bar-maid job, behavior, and dress. Nonetheless, they are not unfamiliar, because everything about Lu Ann is conventionally working class. In essence, the class convention enables middle-class subjects to immediately identify working-class women, in general, by their display of "poor taste," and Lu Ann, in particular, by her excessive smoking, sleazy outfits, heavy make-up, and garish blonde wig. Her flagrant homophobia is perfectly in keeping with the rest of her character, as it appears to be yet another "vulgar" display.

In conjoining "the vulgar homophobe" and "the working-class woman," *Our Sons* provides queer and straight middle-class viewers with a mother who is radically other and therefore easy to hate, while insinuating that straight members of the middle class are incapable of homophobia by virtue of their inherent good taste. Their problem, like Audrey's problem, is institutionalized heterosexuality. If they are parents of gay offspring, they want their sons and daughters to marry and have a family — be, in Audrey's words, "two of us." That is, they want to see themselves reproduced in and through their offspring. The film no more recognizes this self-replicating desire as narcissistic than it visualizes the presence of overt homophobia within the middle class. Instead, it makes an object lesson of Lu Ann in whom Audrey comes to see her own heterosexism mirrored back in grotesque form. Yet heterosexism is not all that Audrey sees; she notices her mistakes in gender as well. With Lu Ann's image before her, she sets about repudiating homophobia/heterosexism while embracing femininity. For Audrey, embracing femininity first means displaying emotion, which Lu Ann has consistently done however "vulgarly." Repudiating homphobia, however, means expressing the "right sort" of affect, which Lu Ann has obviously failed to do.

In *Our Sons* the right affect is maternal love. Here, as elsewhere, maternal love is represented as a primary urge that is more potent than stereotypes of "sick" homosexuals (which it vanquishes), heterosexual anxieties about the other sex (which it displaces with warm affection), and years of culturally supported homo-aversive behavior (which it turns around, more or less instantaneously). In posing mother love as the sole antidote to homophobia, the films further imply the latter was really a personal ailment to begin with; in this way, they serve to veil the productive role of public policies and institutions through which homophobia is culturally transmitted and juridically sanctioned, if not encouraged.

The vaunted power of mother love is perhaps nowhere more apparent than in the tender reunion of Audrey and James. The scene begins with Audrey's confession that she was "devastated" when James came out; she denied what she felt, repressed her maternal instinct, and withdrew emotionally from her son. In an inaugural display of maternal feeling, she goes on to admit she has acted like a father and begs to give motherhood "another try." As an indication of her commitment, Audrey immediately asks James to be tested for HIV. Her request leads to an affecting interlude in which the productivity of mother love is made manifest. Side by side, mother and son talk of a new life together. When James mentions his fear of testing positive, he is enfolded within Audrey's warm embrace; cheek to cheek, the two voice their "need" for each other. A medium distance shot of the couple locked in each other's arms brings the interlude to an end. At this distance, mother and son look exactly like lovers. It thus appears that in surrendering to maternal instinct, Audrey is restored to sexuality *and* femininity, and in recathecting the mother who here replaces the queer lover, James is restored to heterosexual love. This spectacle of the "cured" homosexual is only one component — albeit the privileged component — of the frame; in tension with it, and inseparable from it, is another inadvertent display, namely, the disturbing representation of "sick" heterosexuals. The conjunction of the two images produces an ambivalent tableau whose message is summarily expressed: the taboo against same-sex object choice has been reenforced at the cost of breaking the incest taboo.

The close encounter between James and Audrey typifies melodramatic (re)unions between mothers and sons. There is a slight difference between the scenes in other films and this one in their tendency to dramatize the mothers' more than the sons' transformations. The three conversions can be quickly related. Lu Ann's change of heart occurs soon after Audrey's. Overcome by maternal feeling, Lu Ann reaches out to touch her dying son's hand. In the next frame she leaves for Arkansas with Donald's coffin; that is, she brings him home where he belongs. Mrs. Cutler shows up for her son's birthday party at the urging of his warm woman friend, Kate. Cutler carries with her the teddy bear Jeff always wanted. The mother cries; the son cries. Together, they smile through tears as the film ends. For their part, Andre's Mother and Cal are finally united by a species of transference love at Andre's memorial service. There, Cal turns to his lover's mother for the nurturance his own mother witheld; Andre's mother transfers some feeling for her son onto Cal when she returns his hug.

All three films are thus structurally identical. Beginning with a scene of division or separation, each moves toward reconcilation or unification; more importantly, each locates conflict and its resolution within the family. In their emplotments, AIDS melodramas thus resemble Oedipal dramas with a twist, because the father who is central to Oedipal productions is decidedly decentered here. Whereas the father is missing from three of the melodramas' families, he is represented without power or position in the remaining one. The apparent evacuation of the paternal position is co-terminous with the films' deployment of familialism: that is, the construction of a self-contained domestic unit whose "effeminate" sons and "masculine" mothers differ from the so-called general public and whose boundaries seal it off from the nation or state.

I repeat that the evacuation is apparent. For in the simulated hetero-family containing manly mom and girlish son, the name of the father is assumed by the masculine mother, who performs the paternal function in his stead, thereby averting a definitional crisis in the sex-gender system. Subjected to the diacritical law of gender, the son is made to fill the pseudo-subject position allotted to gay men in the symbolic order, upon whose ideological operation the reproduction and cultural hegemony of heterosex rest. The gay male position is analogous to the impossible place of "the woman [who] does not exist" apart from a heterosexual relation or (in more Lacanian terms) other than as the constitutive outside of the heteromasculine symbolic.[52] The object of masculine desire and/or the projection of male fantasy, the "woman" Lacan inscribes as (a) being "under erasure," grounds subjectivity in the man who is "not-woman," which is also to say "not-feminized" as "queer."

In taking up the name of the father, the films' mothers do not escape the rule of gender to which they — *as paternal place-markers* — subject their sons. On the contrary, the moms are compelled — *as women* — to disinvest in their businesses, surrender to maternal instinct, retire from public life, and return to (safeguarding) the home. In other words, AIDS mothers must recognize their sexual difference from fathers and put an end to all paternal masquerades that cannot be recuperated within the nation's symbolic. When the phallic pretenders recognize they are "essentially" women after all, homophobia and heterosexism disappear from the screen. Thus although masculinity is made to appear as the source of sexual friction between mother and son, it is not masculinity, as such, that is rendered problematic, but only the simulated masculinity of pushy females who are visibly different from "real men." The latter are strong, not pushy; reasonable not vituperative; reserved but not incapable of love. Basically, these men, whose absence is required by the films' twin strategies of privatizing subjects and domiciling AIDS, look rather like Humphrey Bogart. In their masculinized homophobia, the filmic mothers are made to look like horrors or frights. They resemble the Bette Davis of many melodramas, the Joan Crawford of *Mommie Dearest* in the high-bitchiness with which they play their parts.

Still, as opposed to the AIDS documentaries, which ended as they began with the conversion of mothers into monsters, AIDS melodramas merely open with monstrous females; they end by turning monsters into mothers or, as my title has it, "nasty broads" into "tender bitches." Both breeds of women extend the operation of familialism; the "nasty broad" primarily by deflecting attention and anger away from public policies and institutions, the "tender bitch" primarily by channeling energy and affectivity into the home where they are contained and absorbed.

While the constitutive opposition between private (family) and public (nation) has a long history within the United States (where it has determined such public policies as the disfranchisement of women, noninterference in cases of domestic violence, and the recent "don't ask, don't tell, don't pursue" solution to "homosexuals in the military") it was not until the late 1980s that popular AIDS coverage began to set family apart from nation with any kind of regularity. Prior to their discursive separation, the two domains were nevertheless severed in practice. That is, dating from the mid-1980s, at least, mothers especially were being called upon — if not compelled — to care for HIV-infected husbands and children because the nation claimed it could not. Thus, a contradiction at the heart of the national response to AIDS: in daily life, a gulf between an affected family and an unaffected nation; in popular commentary, "instant analogies between the individual family unit and the nation, understood as a familial entity."[53]

These familial analogies were the lynchpin of "African AIDS" and

"AIDS Alley" where, as Watney says, they worked "to shore-up the ideological fortresses of the Nation and the Family, as if they were under a state of unprecedented seige."[54] Though I have focused more on the configured split between family and nation within AIDS melodramas, I am far from thinking their identification *passé*. On the contrary, one of the hottest AIDS stories of 1990–91 assumed that nation and family are equivalent — one in their innocence and one in their susceptibility to foreigners with AIDS.

I refer to the "tragedy" of Kimberly Bergalis, the "demented" dentist who "gave her AIDS," and the evil "bastards . . . that *knew* Dr. Acer was infected and stood by not doing a damn thing."[55] In Kimberly's public letter from which I have quoted, as in the majority of narratives about her, Acer and his cronies are represented as ruining an innocent who "never used drugs, never slept with anyone, and never had a blood trans-fusion" much less a queer thought.[56] They are also represented as ruining the life of her family. Finally, and most importantly, their surrogates in the medical profession, who have always seemed a different breed of individual (by virtue of their relative wealth, professional training, and arcane language, if nothing else) and who have increasingly been identi-fied as "AIDS carriers," their allies, and the cronies of homosexuals, are seen to be threatening "the nation's" health. As readers, we are supposed to identify with this imaginary nation of imperiled innocents, much as we were supposed to identify with Kimberly, whose championship of mandatory "AIDS testing" proved she identified with "us."

At least, we were supposed to identify with her up to a point. For the collective subject represented by "the American public" the point of nonidentification occurred in the late summer/early fall of 1991 and it held through her death. What happened to transform the media's arch champion of seronegative Americans into an Other? The answer has as much to do with Kimberly's deteriorating health as it does with the final episode of her crusade against people (in health care) with HIV/AIDS. When the dying PWA testified before Congress in support of mandatory testing for health care workers in September 1991, she was unmistakably suffering from dementia. At that approximate moment, she became the very abject her image had been defined against. Found monstrous in person, judged malicious in deed, and pronounced all but dead, "she" was placed in the media's gallery of rogues, alongside other conventional criminals with AIDS. When Kim Bergalis died that December, the media moguls who made her famous — and then infamous — gave her passing no more than a word. Their silence returned Kimberly and her family to the private domain from which they had emerged as highly publicized crusaders against people with AIDS in health care settings.

Within the United States, the enfamilied nation model continues to haunt AIDS commentary because it performs two sorts of work. First, its identification of domestic and foreign subjects, coupled with its promise to protect "us" from "them," appeals to a popular imagination that craves distinction and fears difference. Second, the model manufactures a well-behaved subject whose function is to elicit audience identification. The model's appeal is essentially imaginary not only because its distinctions are illusory, but also because the vaunted promise to protect is, on the model's own terms, as fragile as the boundary between inside(r) and outside(r) is frangible. This limitation is compounded by the character of the audience addressed. In theory, an identification with the model subject disciplines audience members; once disciplined, we erect our own boundaries and begin patrolling borders around the body, home, neighborhood, and nation. In other words, we now practice the police work we have heretofore spectated. However, if I'm correct in assuming the "national family" formation imposes discipline whose strategic function is to prevent viral transmission and other social disorders, then its limitations are apparent. Because the model offers no points of identification for subjects who do not see themselves in the nation's innocent "Kimberlys" and because it cannot discipline those it does not address, it is incapable of stemming the so-called spread of AIDS. In particular, the "enfamilied nation" can have no effect on "carriers," that is, those supposed "border-jumpers" who would infiltrate "our" space. Judging by popular support for jailing certain "HIV-infected" individuals, the model's other flaw is that it targets the wrong subjects.[57] In this instance, the fantasy would seem to be that whereas "we" wait nervously within enclosures of our own making, "others" run amuck on the outside.

"Naturally," they must be contained. In the words of then-President George Bush: "In too many places our grandparents and grandchildren lock themselves behind the bars on their windows, afraid to come out from a jail they call home. This must end."[58] It is the troublemakers who belong in the jailhouse; the American family must and will trade places with them. It is in response to this demand that a different ideological relation emerges within AIDS commentary and public policy: an "affected" family, constitutively isolated from an "unaffected" nation, appears to regulate those the family/nation assemblage leaves untouched.

Located within a nation of which it is not a part, the "affected" family functions as a holding tank for infectious practices (i.e., AIDS activism, other antigovernment demonstrations, lobbies for human rights, health care, and housing), widely seen as jeopardizing the socioeconomic well-being of the nation, and infectious persons (i.e., PWAs, queers, people of color, and "unfeminine" women), commonly viewed as threatening the physical and/or moral health of the so-called general population. Though disconnected from the nation, the HIV-infected family is analogically related to constructions of HIV "brooding" within the "host" until it breaks forth and infects other cells.[59] Because the family is both real (that is, made up of actual human beings living with immune systems disorders) and fantasmatic (that is, made out to be a diseased cell), it performs the work of containment spectacularly whether or not it actually works.

If this family cell has not supplanted the family/nation constellation, then that is largely because the "private" practice of volunteerism and its correlate, the privatized individual, have not rendered the "public" practice of force and its correlate, the national good, obsolete. Instead, two constructions of the relation between private and public/family and state — that is, two technologies of familialism integrated into two strategies of containment — are currently regulating opposing policies. For instance, on one hand, state statutes banning sodomy — interpreted and upheld as prohibiting (the practice of) queer sexuality by the 1986 Supreme Court decision in *Bowers v. Hardwick* — along with recently enacted state legislation further limiting women's reproductive rights, and the Senate's decision during the summer of 1991 to impose heavy fines and/or jail sentences upon seropositive health care workers who perform "exposure prone procedures" without disclosing their antibody status, equally rest upon the proposition that body and home are public sites.[60] As such, they are held to be subject to juridico-legal intervention.[61] On the other hand, and under the rubric of traditional values, federal, state, and municipal governments repeatedly appeal to the private sector for charity, as though the solution to institutionalized poverty, inadequate public health care, severe housing shortages, and so forth lay in private help. In these appeals, in the proliferation of anti-gay initiatives bent on returning queers to the closet, as in situations where family members are themselves seen as "undesirables" and their privatization as curbing public expenditure and/or inhibiting public unrest, family and nation/"private individual" and "taxpaying public" are expeditiously severed. My contention has been that these privatized subjects and dis-ease containing families are strategic assemblages AIDS melodramas put to work.

In each film we are initially distracted by footage of maternal misbehavior. As a result, we overlook governmental indifference to the epidemic, along with state and federal statutes discriminating against foreign visitors, immigrants, prisoners, sex workers, and queers. Inadequacies in health care coverage for all people living with immune system disorders and the devastating impact of health care costs on the poor pass us by, as do the profits of pharmaceutical companies marketing AIDS-related therapies, not to mention the sexism of a medical system that has virtually ignored women's specific illnesses and health care needs. We do not notice life-threatening opposition to explicit safe-sex education, particularly education produced by and for queers, or the scapegoating of minority populations affected by AIDS. In short, public institutions and their representatives go about their business effectively, secure from challenge and exonerated from blame, while our attention is fixed on the wicked witch whose performance evokes and contains our rage.

Certainly, few viewers willingly embrace containment. Rather, the witchy mother is such a "perfect" villain because she takes and holds us unaware. She does so, moreover, by exerting a variety of appeals, any or all of which might be felt by individual members of the audience. First, and most generally, viewers fix on the mother because she is visible as diffuse networks of power are not. As a focal point for those of us who are frustrated with and outraged by systemic inequalities and institutionalized discrimination, the mother does more than absorb our affects. She also provides a cognitive service in lending the "enemy" a face. Second, the mother's power is restricted to witholding love. Though she can hurt, she cannot silence, incarcerate, or materially damage dissenters; consequently, she is relatively easy to fight as public institutions manifestly are not. In effect, hating her gives wounded egos and flagging spirits a needed boost. Third, the mother is a woman in a sexist culture. As such, she will affect her audience differently in accordance with their specific histories. Some, I imagine, will judge her harshly for abandoning the home. Others, I assume, will find against her for succeeding in the workplace or usurping a position rightfully belonging to man. But here again, the mother is a politically convenient scapegoat for the nation's economic recession and the concomitant rise in unemployment with which women, as a class, had nothing to do. Many more viewers, I am fairly certain, will condemn the mom's lack of nurturance as they would not a father's or man's. Although they are likely to sympathize with her situation, actual mothers will be found among her detractors — at least, if they respond as cued, in which case they either will censor her unmaternal behavior early on or undergo, as she does, a change of heart in the end. Fourth, the mother is straight, which makes her a tempting target for queer viewers, precisely because many of us see (something of) our own heterosexual mothers in her. At bottom, it is our own mothers we cannot forgive for failing to understand us, accept us, mother us, once we told them we were queer; and it is our own mothers we therefore love to hate in and through the nasty broads on screen. It is past time we let go, left the family enclave, and allowed our mothers to leave as well.

By family enclave I mean the enclosed domestic unit as conceptualized within the discourse of "separate spheres" and not open systems of affiliation or alternative kinship networks. In distinguishing between them, I am further suggesting that the ideology of private life be resisted and the family be recognized as a borderland, conjoining private and public space. That recognition informs the work of "Mothers' Voices," a coalition of diverse women who are AIDS "activists" in the extensive sense of the word.[62] Caretakers, lobbyists, and demonstrators, they present themselves as "the mothers of adult people with AIDS." As their self-presentation suggests, the women's strategy is to use their cultural cachet as mothers to effect material change in the daily lives of people with HIV/AIDS. Two actions of the coalition serve to illustrate. In May 1994, teams of mothers in the nation's capitol delivered roughly a million cards to congressional representatives, inscribed with the message: "Mothers Day can never be the same until there is a cure for AIDS." The women have further politicized motherhood in taking to the streets with other AIDS activists. Months prior to the Mother's Day action, they marched behind their mothers' banner, and they raised their voices with ACT UP in a street protest against planned cutbacks in New York City AIDS services. When ACT UP shouted "They say cut back"; the mothers responded: "We say *fight* back." In effect, their collective message was: AIDS is a public crisis, which demands public solutions; as mothers and the grown children of mothers, we will not be consigned to the AIDS closet or otherwise shut up in (our) homes.

The difference between these historical activists and the mother-son couple of the melodramas could not be greater, nor could the arguable effects of the two spectacles. It is precisely on the level of their effects on actual subjects that the films must be critiqued and their seduction of queers and straight women into believing "there is no place like home" resisted. Ultimately, the success of the melodramas' seduction depends on the charm of the tenderized bitches who embrace mother love *and* queer offspring in the end. Together, the two set up house; in loving and caring for the other person, the deepest needs of each are spectacularly fulfilled. In Freud's parlance, the mother gets the "little boy who brings the longed-for penis with him" and the son his "original love-object" who seems to have one.[63] Indeed, she who appears to him as the sublime incarnation of potency and plentitude, is the penis in phallus drag. She/he "is the first object of . . . [the boy's] love, and . . . remains so . . . in essence all through his [adult] life."[64] Their final coupling is presented from the child's perspective as an Oedipal dream come true. Incestuous "pictures [the films] cannot possibly show" are safely relayed by two of their theme songs ("AIDS Alley," 12).

In the one, which accompanies the reunion of Mother Cutler and son Jeff and continues through the closing credits of the film, the singer soulfully repeats: "Mother, Mother keep me safe from harm. Come into my room tonight and hold me in your arms. I am still your shining child, the one you know by name." In this sanitized plaint of young Oedipus, queer subjects and queer desires are supplanted or erased; mother and son-lover fill soundtrack and screen; between them Oedipal desire circulates and the heterosexual contract is secured. At this moment, it would seem that nothing but the twin desires of limiting public health costs and inhibiting AIDS demonstrations separates the containing family from the homologous family-nation. For outside the domestic unit as within it, the only sex is heterosex — another wholly fantasmatic unit(y) whose diversity must continually be disavowed in order to produce the "same."

The other theme song, entitled "Someone to Watch Over Me," performs the identical work of Oedipus *and* familialism in naming the mother-lover as provider of all needs. Early in *Our Sons*, James performs the song in a piano bar where Audrey is seated. Bathed in blue light, he sings: "There is a somebody I'm longing to see, I hope that she turns out to be the someone to watch over me. . . . Although I may not be the man some girls think of, . . . to my heart she carries the key. Won't you tell her please . . . how I need someone to watch over me." The same lyrics accompany the film's closing credits, by which point Audrey has responded to James's "need." The door is about to shut behind them on an enclosed domestic scene; but at that moment, the repetition of "someone watching" intervenes. As I listen, visions of protection *and* surveillance proliferate; representations of mother (love) and home within the melodramas are recast in relation to representations of government figures, voyeurs, and disciplinary apparatuses of the state; on the television screen the credits continue to roll, but superimposed upon them, another virtual videotrack takes shape. In it, an establishing shot of James performing is spliced to a newsclip of Richard Nixon at the White House piano; an image of a peeping tom accompanies the view of Mrs. Cutler and Jeff peering at each other through house blinds; documentary footage of death row, the Justice Department, and the Centers for Disease Control is intercut with clips of Donald's coffin on route home and the front of Audrey's monumental white house; a close-up of an eyeball ends the tape. In effect, the visual re-presentation of "someone watching" spoils the mood of pathos and displaces the family scene with a visible network of surveillance in which private is connected to public and home to nation.

The lyrics of *Our Sons*'s theme song do not constitute a momentary rupture in the signification system of the film. Rather, they instantiate the rule of repetition in the genre of AIDS melodramas, where building a case for familialism involves multiple representations of the domestic. Because reiteration introduces variation and because viewers re-present or imagine more than is aired on screen, AIDS melodramas can only encourage a return to the heterosexual family and the passive acceptance of one's Oedipal/medical fate. In the end, they cannot secure an audience of familied subjects any more than they can shut-up "undesirables" under domestic quarantine. Rather, in this genre, whose *mise en scéne* is confinement, repetition produces significatory slippages, dissonant messages, and "asignifying ruptures" that open up a "line of flight." Taking it, we exit the family unit and network with AIDS activists and other progressive populist movements in a struggle against privitization.

"SOMETHING TELLS ME WE'RE [STILL] IN KANSAS"

I wake up every day and if I turn on the television set or look through a magazine . . . or go to the movies, I see [almost] no representation of my sexuality. I see

heterosexual plots and subtexts in every media form and it is enraging to feel
homosexual longing toward another person in this context.
— David Wojnarowicz, "Do Not Doubt the Dangerousness
of the Twelve-Inch Politician"

In narrating the short gay life of Andrew Beckett, the film *Philadelphia*
reproduces "heterosexual plots and subtexts" in much the same melodramatic script I have rehearsed.[65] The melodramatic script is equally the
script of liberal humanism, whose timeless tale of universal mankind is
more precisely defined as the narcissistic story of white, middle-class
heterosexual masculinity gazing upon reflections of itself. Because the
humanist's mirror is ancient, it needs refurbishing from time to time. In a
word, "refurbishing" is the job Jonathan Demme's recent film and all
prior AIDS melodramas periodically perform. Generically, they do so to
the apparent advantage of AIDS sympathetic and queer tolerant heterosexuals who are flatteringly set against those who are not; to the presump-
tive benefit of ignorant and inhumane heterosexuals who are enlightened
and humanized in identifying with ideal imagos of themselves; to the
evident profit of institutionalized heterosexuality whose cultural capital is
thereby increased; to the narcissistic delight of heterosexuals whose sexuality is mediated as virtually universal and visibly lasting in contrast to
homosexuality whose subjects are degayed and dying; and to the contingent advantage of people with HIV/AIDS and "homosexuals" whom
moviegoers learn to see as everyman (nowhere more so than in *Philadelphia*), and toward whom indifference and malice are therefore censured.

These are the highlights of Andrew Beckett's story. In the starring
role, Tom Hanks is conventionally pathetic and dies "beautifully" — after
proving he is almost just as good as heterosexual men and nothing like
those vulgar queers who flaunt their sexuality in heterosexuals' faces and
push their "homosexual agenda" at Americans' expense. When queried
about his sexual history on the witness stand, Andy admits to having had
three sexual encounters in a porn theatre, all of which are safely situated
in his past.[66] In the dramatic present, the buttoned-down, white, upper-
middle-class lawyer is in a long-term monogamous relationship that is
framed as a copy of heterosexual marriage. Queried about "gay rights"
outside the courtroom, he responds "I am not political." He is not concerned with the pressing concerns of civil rights, the specific needs of gay
PWAs, or the particular forms discrimination takes against them. Indeed,
Mr. Beckett makes a Mr. Bennett point of framing his suit against the law

partners who fired him because he was a homosexual with AIDS in "purely" humanistic terms. Like William, what Andrew wants is to uphold the founding principle of "human rights"; with his express desire to safeguard man's constitutional liberties, conservative alliances opposing "queer rights" on the spurious grounds that they are "special rights" would in principle agree.

Does this mean that *Philadelphia* is merely the latest installment in the melodramatic serial of heterosexualized gay PWAs who are dying and their virile heterosexual helpers who endure? Not exactly. Though another episode in the book of heterosexual humanism, Andrew Beckett's life is no less related with two twists, effectively distinguishing it from made-for-TV AIDS melodramas. One is Miguel, the lover of the gay PWA, played by Antonio Banderas. The other is the public setting of the courtroom in which conflict over AIDS and homosexuality is primarily staged.

An obvious difference between the other lovers and Miguel is that he is a Latino in a sexual relationship with a white man. Apart from its function as one of many multicultural signals, the interethnic relation serves no purpose. The dramatic difference between Miguel and his TV predecessors has more to do with the way in which he supports his lover; in essence, he does so with unremitting strength, acquired AIDS expertise, and an activist approach to AIDS treatment and care that is unequalled by the gay male characters of the earlier films. If no TV AIDS melodrama does as much, neither does any represent a primary relationship between men as *Philadelphia* undoubtedly does. Hence, instead of the mother love that comes first and displaces queer love in the end, Demme's script insists on the constant love of Andy and Miguel. The gay man dies with his lover beside him; there are no family members present. Moreover, Miguel has pointedly closed the door behind them before returning to Andy's bed.

The final scene between the couple acquires some of its power from the familial subjects it excludes. They are the dramatic opposites of the standard AIDS melodrama family; father, mother, siblings, and their spouses are universally supportive of Andy, Miguel, and their struggle against AIDS. Notably, the entire family attends the trial along with Miguel, whose centrality is further marked by his prompter position behind Andy at the counsel table. Their collective attendance visibly bridges the ideological divide between private and public that the genre of AIDS melodramas has worked to maintain. Of equal importance in this regard is the extended family pretrial discussion; its joint subjects are the publication of private matters in the courtroom and the effects of public proceedings on the family.[67]

The co-implication of the two domains signposts a more dramatic departure. For in an apparent reversal of tradition, *Philadelphia* drags AIDS, homosexuality, and homphobia out of the family closet that its TV antecedents aimed to secure them within. Thus, AIDS is positioned where I have said, on the border between the public and the private, whereas homosexuality is largely and safely (re)situated in the body of a dying PWA who is the near image of a heterosexual man. This situation is akin to another closet, and though homophobia is somewhat less locatable, it will appear to be at least partially rehoused in a conveniently less-than-public domain. That is, although homophobia is explicitly marked as a common public disorder in one critical trial sequence, it is elsewhere dramatized and thereby relocalized in two classes of subjects. One is represented by the flagrantly homophobic law partners; so cartoonlike do Jason Robards and his slimy sidekick appear that it is impossible to see them as realistic figures. No white person, I am sure, would view either as standing for white heterosexual men as a class. The other homophobic figure is the same subject who outed the public's homophobia in the courtroom; he is played by Denzel Washington, the melodrama's leading African-American man.

Joe Miller's court outing begins with a stream of homophobic invectives ("faggot," "punk," "pillowfighter," "rumproaster," etc.) hurled at a closeted gay witness on the stand. The courtroom audience is as universally appalled as it is astounded. Only now does Joe explicitly frame his cross-examination as a performance of "what this case [against the PWA] is really about: the general public's hatred, our loathing, our fear of homosexuals, and how that climate of hatred and fear translated into the firing of this particular homosexual, my client Andrew Beckett." Miller's point is well taken, and through his critical exposé of "the general public's" homophobia, Demme transmits one of the primary lessons of his film. Apart from its reliance on an invidious term simultaneously marking all subjects excluded by it as "singular" and "private," I applaud the lesson.

Nonetheless, I want to revisit the preliminary scene of homophobic outing by which the moral of the story is framed. Consider these questions: Whose subjectivity is being performed here? What are the arguable effects of that performance, or what purposes are being served? That is, what purposes apart from shock value, whose capital is soon exhausted in the audiences' "ah-ha" response "so this is what homophobia is?" Were the performance to elicit an aftershock of recognition — as in, "so, homophobic is what I am" — its use value would be substantially higher. Though I have no way of knowing who actually experiences such a shock in watching the film, I venture two unlikely classes of "public" candidates, one being women and the other white men. In the end, if Joe's rant is an exemplum of what homophobia is, it is all too easy for viewing subjects who are not black men to disavow the presence of the same condition in themselves, not only because of the visible difference of gender and skin, but also because of the audible difference in speech.

In virtually all other public performances, many of which are punctuated with comic articulations, Demme's regular Joe talks the talk of standard white English. Coupled with other more private performances of "sissy-bashing," "homosexual panic," and the like, his code shifting into black vernacular during the outing performance works to encode homophobia as "a black male thing." In effect, the Joe Miller character thus offers straight white men the same escape hatch that the Lu Ann Barnes character afforded straight white middle-class women; speaking conventionally, they would "never say such things." By granting white middle-class subjects this escape valve, AIDS melodramas neglect a critical opportunity to confront the "fear" and "loathing" of homosexuals in the very subjects who have the socioeconomic captial to mass-mediate homophobia, to legislate on its behalf, to work systematically on dismantling the libidino-political machinery of homophobia, and to repudiate its less obvious, thus more insidious, forms.

NOTES

I dedicate this essay to Ken Koehler, the movie mogul at my shoulder. For my recaps of AIDS news, I am indebted to the excellent bibliographic and taping services of Vanderbuilt University Television News Archive.

1. *The Wizard of Oz*, dir. Victor Fleming, 1939. The film is an adaptation of L. Frank Baum's novel. According to the writer, the wicked witch of the west is based on his wife's mother, whose politics were the opposite of the book's. A leading suffragette and staunch feminist, Mrs. Gage fought for women's right

to a place in the public domain and against the ideology of separate spheres. Needless to say, she is not a sympathetic figure in the novel/film, nor are the cast of AIDS news harpies I subsequently affiliate with her.

2. For a compelling study on the formative role of the closet in Western discourse, see Eve Kosofsky Sedgwick, *The Epistemology of the Closet* (Berkeley: University of California Press, 1990).

3. *Bowers v. Hardwick*, 478 U.S., 106 S.Ct. (106 B, October 1986): 2847.

4. Ibid. As I write in the spring of 1994, the closing remarks of America's Chief Justice are again posing a material threat to queers, whose utter silencing is among the objectives of "family-value" campaign initiatives sweeping the states. One of the two currently gathering signatures in Washington is representative. I quote from section 3 of the "Minority Status and Child Protection Act" as drafted by the Citizens Alliance of Washington who resemble their liberal brethren in one respect: that is, in the conclusion that the public domain belongs exclusively to heterosexual subjects.

> *THE PUBLIC EDUCATIONAL SYSTEM SHALL NOT PROMOTE OR EXPRESS APPROVAL OF HOMOSEXUALITY.* The people [here defined as heterosexual] establish that no person representing the common schools or institutions of higher education . . . , as an employee, student, volunteer or guest may undertake any activity that would in any manner advise, instruct, teach or promote to a child, student or employee that homosexuality is a positive or healthy lifestyle, or an acceptable or approved condition or behavior. State of Washington, Initiative 610, 1994.

> A recent statewide poll found 47 percent of Washington voters support this mandate; in what is generally seen as a "liberal" state, only 36 percent of voters oppose a legal gag order on (the subject of) queers. The Elway Poll was conducted during April 1994; the results I have cited appeared in the *Seattle Post-Intelligencer*, 4 May 1994, A 1.

5. Identical sentiments have shaped congressional debates on the "public-funding" of safer-sex intervention efforts targeting gay men (1987); (queer) recipients of NEA grants (1989–90); and the "adolescent sexuality survey" (1991), which was framed as the latest episode in an ongoing "homosexual plot" to "destigmatize homosexuality by presenting it as normal," *Congressional Record* (12 September 1991), S12861. In this debate, scientists and queers were cast as co-conspirators. Their coupling would appear to be overdetermined by co-temporaneous mediations of the David Acer–Kimberly Bergalis case, because one effect of the infected dentist media blitz was to link health care workers, homosexuals, and HIV. In the foregoing congressional debates, Senator Helms played a pivotal role, and in all three he repeated the same gothic cliche. You have heard it in different words from Blackstone/Burger and you will hear it reiterated in televised productions of AIDS where gothicism inflects conventions of horror and detection and where grotesque fictions/phobic fantasies work to disfigure cultural and racial minorities (suspected of) living with HIV/AIDS. On the subject of Robert Mapplethorpe's retrospective collection, funded in part by the National Endowment for the Arts

(NEA), these are Jesse's Walpoldian words: "There are unspeakable portrayals [of homosexuals] which I cannot describe on the floor of the Senate," *Congressional Record* (26 July 1989), S8807.

6. Simon Watney, *Policing Desire: Pornography, AIDS and the Media*, 2nd ed. (Minneapolis: University of Minnesota Press, 1989), 84. But see also, Watney, "The Spectacle of AIDS," *AIDS: Cultural Analysis/Cultural Activism*, ed. Douglas Crimp (Boston: MIT, 1989), 71–86; and Introduction, *Taking Liberties: AIDS and Cultural Politics*, ed. Erica Carter and Watney (London: Serpent's Tail, 1989), 11–57.

7. For the single best critique of "AIDS virus" and other epidemic misnomers, see Jan Zita Grover, "AIDS: Keywords," in *AIDS: Cultural Analysis/Cultural Activism*, 17–30. On the "erotics of political voyeurisms and moralisms" that motivate the conflation of possible acts of HIV transmission with certain death and that enable readings of unsafe sex as (attempted) murder, see Cindy Patton, "Visualizing Safe-Sex: When Pedagogy and Pornography Collide," in *Inside/Out: Lesbian Theories, Gay Theories*, ed. Diana Fuss (New York: Routledge, 1991), 379–85.

8. Watney, "Spectacle," 86.

9. Teresa de Lauretis, "The Technology of Gender," *Technologies of Gender: Essays on Theory, Film and Fiction* (Bloomington: University of Indiana Press, 1987), 26.

10. As an illustration of how collective screenings of AIDS films can work in practice, see my "Of Purebreds and Hybrids: The Politics of Teaching AIDS in the United States," in *American Sexual Politics: Sex, Gender, and Race since the Civil War*, ed. John C. Fout and Maura Shaw Tantillo (Chicago: University of Chicago Press, 1993), esp. 367–79.

11. Deleuze and Guattari's "line of flight" presupposes an understanding of texts as "multiplicities" or "planes," which intersect with other (a)signifying planes: that is, texts, subjects, practices, bodies, institutions, social formations, etc. As I intend it here, a line of flight both marks an "asignifying rupture" within a text and connects that multiplicity to other multiplicities, some of which are signifying apparatuses and some of which are better described as "intensities" or affects. See, Gilles Deleuze and Félix Guattari, *A Thousand Plateaus: Capitalism and Schizophrenia*, trans. Brian Massumi (Minneapolis: University of Minnesota Press, 1987), 8–9, 24–25.

12. The intrication of cultural fictions and narrative conventions in "factual" coverage of AIDS has been addressed by such writers as Douglas Crimp, who critiques the "thriller" plot of Randy Shilts's *The Band Played On* ("How to Have Promiscuity in an Epidemic," in *AIDS: Cultural Analysis/Cultural Activism*, 238–46); Jan Zita Grover, who points to the inevitability of metaphor in AIDS discourse, while condemning dominant metaphors of contagion ("Constitutional Symptoms," in *Taking Liberties*, 152–59); Brian Patton, who addresses the function of military metaphors in various contexts ("Cell Wars: Military Metaphors and the Crisis of Authority in the AIDS Epidemic," in *Fluid Exchanges: Artists and Critics in the AIDS Crisis*, ed. James Miller [To-

ronto: University of Toronto Press, 1992], 272–86); Paula Treichler, who argues that cultural myths are inscribed within AIDS "facts" ("AIDS, Homophobia, and Biomedical Discourse," in *AIDS: Cultural Analysis/Cultural Activism*, 31–70); and Judith Williamson, who spotlights the recurrence of horror and detection conventions within AIDS commentary ("Every Virus Tells a Story: The Meanings of HIV and AIDS," in *Taking Liberties*, 69–80).

13. On the topic of discursive productivity (networks of power/knowledge and their effects) see, for instance, Michel Foucault, *Power/Knowledge*, trans. Robert Hurley (New York: Random House, 1978); *The History of Sexuality*, vol. 1, trans. Robert Hurley (New York: Random House, 1978), esp. 92–102; and Gilles Deleuze and Félix Guattari, who advocate reading books as assemblages "in connection with other assemblages." In their Introduction to *A Thousand Plateaus*, they model a functional approach to reading: "We will never ask what a book means as a signifier or signified. . . . We will ask what it functions with, in connection with what other things it does or does not transmit intensities, in which other multiplicities its own are inserted and metamorphosed. . . . [W]hen one writes the only question is which other machine the literary machine can be plugged into, must be plugged into in order to work" (4).

14. Iris De La Cruz, "Invasion of the Patients from Hell at New York University Hospital or How I Spent My Summer Vacation," in *Positive Women: Voices of Women with AIDS*, ed. Andrea Rudd and Darien Taylor (Toronto: Second Story Press, 1992), 114–16.

15. "In AIDS Alley," "48 Hours" (New York: CBS News, 13 October 1988); rpt. Television Transcript (New York: Journal Graphics, 1988), 2. All further references are cited parenthetically in the text.

16. In 1985, network news named Belle Glade as the site of the highest incidence of AIDS per capita in the United States. (See, NBC evening news, 7 May 1985, and CBS evening news 25 October 1985.) On 19 June 1986, CBS evening news reported on the national implications of heterosexual AIDS in Belle Glade in a story that implicated mosquitoes in the spread of the epidemic. The conjecture that AIDS is "insect-borne" was advanced as "fact" by Whiteside and MacLeod, then co-directors of the Institute of Tropical Medicine in North Miami. In July of the following year, the *Atlanta Constitution* ran a feature story on the deadly bite of mosquitoes that was picked-up by other news agencies. The story implied that Robert Gallo had taken-up the Whiteside-MacLeod cause. Populist disseminators of the AIDS-mosquito hypothesis include Lyndon B. LaRouche, whose 1986 campaign literature for California Proposition 64 identified mosquito bites and aerosal spray as the causes of AIDS in heterosexuals (whom he conventionally defined as subjects who never used injection drugs, never had sex outside of marriage, and stuck to missionary sex within it); and Corey Ser-vaas, Ronald Reagan's addled appointee to the President's Commission on AIDS, whose AIDS Prevention Column advised: "If you are going to Central Africa or the habitats of gays and drug users during the mosquito season, take plenty of insect repellent,"

"Help Prevent the Spread of AIDS," *Saturday Evening Post* 258 (January/
February 1986), 107.

17. Simon Watney has commented at length on the reemergence of Conradian
precepts within Western discourse on "African AIDS" in "Missionary Positions: AIDS, Africa and Race," *differences* 1, no. 1 (1988): 83–100. In his
Introduction to *AIDS: The Literary Response* (New York: Twayne, 1992), 1,
10, Emmanuel S. Nelson stages the epidemic among American gay men in
the same spectacular terms, and in the HBO adaptation of Randy Shilts's *The
Band Played On* (12 September 1993) Africa returns as the scene of horror
repressed. The scene's traumatic figure is the body of an African woman
whom Dr. Francis visits in her village hut. She is out of her head, speaking
gibberish, and as she draws her dying breath, blood gushes from her fevered
body onto his. He cannot forget her death (from the Ebola virus), nor can
viewers who see much of the AIDS epidemic among gay men in the United
States through the straight (read also sexually conservative) eyes of the CDC
epidemiologist. Near the end of the docudrama, the body of the African
woman reappears as a kind of feverish transparancy through which we appre-
hend the body of the film's leading gay man. Like her, Bill Kraus is also
speaking gibberish; and like her, in his dementia he grasps the doctor's hand.
Shortly afterward, he also is dead.

18. The heterosexual distinction and AIDS-mosquito hypothesis are components
of "Nightline" 's "AIDS in Africa."

19. In 1993, the reported rate of new U.S. AIDS cases among heterosexuals
infected through sex exceeded that of men who have sex with men for the
first time.

20. "AIDS in Africa," "Nightline," prod. Richard N. Kaplan (New York: ABC
News, 20 October 1986); rpt. Television Transcript (New York: Journal
Graphics, 1986), 3; all further references are cited parenthetically within the
text. The foregoing comparison was advanced by Dr. Lucas; "Nightline" 's
anchor, Timothy Johnson, anticipated his colleague's conclusion in his opening remarks that juxtaposed the epidemiological situation in the United States
to that in Africa, "where the patterns of disease transmission are intriguingly
different" (2). Mass mediations of "Africanized AIDS" have been forcefully
contested by critics in Africa and the West. Criticism produced by Africans
can be found in Richard and Rosalind Chirimunta, *AIDS, Africa and Racism*
(London: Free Association Books, 1989); Joseph Palca, "African AIDS:
Whose Research Rules?," *News and Comment* 12 (October 1990); and essays
collected in Renee Sabatier, *Blaming Others: Prejudice, Race, and Worldwide
AIDS* (Panos, 1988). For deconstructive readings of African AIDS, see also
Mehboob Dada, "Race and the AIDS Agenda," in *Ecstatic Antibodies: Resisting
the AIDS Mythology*, ed. Teresa Boffin and Sunil Gupta (London: Rivers
Oram, 1990), 85–95; Cindy Patton, "Inventing 'African' AIDS," *Inventing
AIDS* (New York: Routledge, 1990), 77–97; and Watney, "Missionary Posi-
tions."

21. Carol Harris, Gerald H. Friedland et al., "Immunodeficiency in Female

Sexual Partners of Men with the Acquired Immunodeficiency Syndrome," *New England Journal of Medicine* 308 (19 May 1983): 1181–84.

22. In May and June, the networks aired fifteen reports on the subject of AIDS. All but one were about "casual contact" and ensuing "AIDS hysteria." Within this context, the issue of male-to-female transmission was mentioned three times: on 18 May by ABC and CBS and on 24 May by NBC. For particulars of what they term the "epidemic-of-fear" news cycle, see Timothy E. Cook and David C. Colby, "The Mass-Mediated Epidemic: The Politics of AIDS on the Nightly News," in *AIDS: The Making of a Chronic Disease*, ed. Elizabeth Fee and Daniel M. Fox (Berkeley: University of California Press, 1992), 99–101.

23. See Nathan Clumeck et al., "Acquired Immunodeficiency Syndrome in African Patients," *New England Journal of Medicine*, 310 (23 February 1984): 492–97; and Nathan Clumeck et al., "Acquired Immunodeficiency Syndrome in Rwanda," *The Lancet* (14 July 1984): 62–69.

24. Robert R. Redfield et al., "Heterosexually Acquired HTLV-III/LAV Disease (AIDS-Related Complex and AIDS): Epidemiological Evidence for Female-to-Male Transmission," *Journal of the American Medical Association*, 254 (18 October 1985): 2096; all further references are cited parenthetically in the text. Here, it should be pointed out that prostitutes were identified as potential vectors of AIDS in the fall of 1982. A month prior to the publication of Redfield's essay, the Centers for Disease Control released the findings of a seroprevalence study that established the presence of HIV in prostitutes as a population and warned Americans about "them." For his part, Redfield provided no evidence that the prostitutes with whom seropositive American soldiers actually (claimed to have) had sex were in fact HIV+. That his conclusions on female-to-male transmission were no less credited owes much to dominant understandings of prostitutes as diseased. Numerous critics have challenged the myth of the AIDS-carrying prostitute. Among them are Priscilla Alexander, "Prostitutes Are Being Scapegoated for Heterosexual AIDS," in *Sex Work: Writings by Women in the Sex Industry*, ed. Frédérique Delacoste and Alexander (Pittsburgh: Cleis, 1987), 248–63; Carol Leigh, "Further Violations of Our Rights," in *AIDS: Cultural Analysis/Cultural Activism*, 177–81; Zoe Leonard and Polly Thistlethwaite, "Prostitution and HIV Infection," in *Women, AIDS and Activism*, ed. the ACT UP/NY Women and AIDS Book Group (Boston: South End Press, 1990), 177–85; and Paula Treichler, "AIDS, Gender and Biomedical Discourse," in *AIDS: The Burdens of History*, ed. Elizabeth Fee and Daniel M. Fox (Berkeley: University of California Press), 207–10. On the larger subject of prostitutes and disease, see Allan Brandt's classic history of veneral disease, *No Magic Bullet: A Social History of Venereal Disease in the United States since 1880* (New York: Oxford University Press, 1987).

25. Sigmund Freud attributes the penis/baby fantasy to women in "Femininity," in *New Introductory Lectures on Psychoanalysis*, trans. James Strachey (New York: Norton, 1965), 128.

26. The spectacle's gynephobic configuration of "womb" is historically overdetermined by mass mediations of the (gay male) anus as the origin of AIDS/death. My reading of the African scene as a spectacle of "de-generation" is borrowed from Lee Edelman's deconstruction of the anus origin myth in "The Mirror and the Tank: AIDS, Subjectivity and the Rhetoric of Activism," in *Writing AIDS: Gay Literature, Language and Analysis*, ed. Timothy F. Murphy and Suzanne Poirier (New York: Columbia University Press, 1993), esp. 14–17.

27. Williamson, "Every Virus Tells a Story," 73.

28. Paula Treichler has also pointed to the recurrence of water metaphors in AIDS coverage, reading them as gynophobic responses to the female body in "AIDS, Gender, and Biomedical Discourse," 190–92, 208, 220–21.

29. "AIDS in Africa," "60 Minutes," prod. Anne deBolsmilon (New York: CBS News, 8 November 1987); rpt. Television Transcript (New York: Journal Graphics), 10–11.

30. Mirko Grmek, *History of AIDS: Emergence and Origin of a Modern Pandemic*, trans. Russell C. Maulitz and Jacalyn Durfin (Princeton, NJ: Princeton University Press, 1990), 99–108, 148–50; all further references are cited parenthetically in the text.

31. For a more recent redaction of Africa as the breeder of HIV and/or the original locale of "viral traffic" in the annals of "AIDS-science," see Stephen Morse, "AIDS and Beyond: Defining the Rules for Viral Traffic," in *AIDS: The Making of a Chronic Disease*, 24, 32–33. In the late winter of 1994, U.S. news crews returned to the subject of African AIDS. Their focus was the crisis in Zaire, where the epidemic was said to be raging out of control — again. Political unrest, poverty, and a sharp decline in intervention programs were duly listed as contributing to the new "outbreak"; however, the people cited as ultimately responsible for the "spread of AIDS" were prostitutes. Variations on the infectious prostitute story are the focal point of American news on AIDS in the Philippines, Thailand, India, and other third-world countries. In the United States the same story is produced in waves.

32. Currently, federal funding of needle exchange programs is prohibited by law, and despite a well-documented demand for services, relatively little money is allocated for drug treatment. For instance, for the Fiscal Year 1991, the administration proposed a budget line of approximately $10.6 billion to combat drug addiction. Approximately 80 percent of that amount was to be set aside for law enforcement and interdiction, with the remainder going to treatment and prevention. In practice these allocations meant "less than 12% of the more than 12 million drug-dependent people needing treatment . . . actually receiv[ed] treatment services." Larry Gostin, "The Interconnected Epidemics of Drug Dependency and AIDS," *Harvard Civil Rights–Civil Liberties Law Review* 26 (1991): 173. The national situation has not changed significantly with the shift in administrations. And in New York City, where "AIDS Alley" is set, the chance of receiving immediate drug treatment is roughly comparable to the chance of winning the state lottery. "State officials estimate that there are about 500,000 drug addicts *[sic]* in New York City,

and they say there are spaces to treat about 10 percent" of them, if they can wait. They add, the state's drug policy does not even make fiscal sense. A "year in a residential treatment center costs $20,000, for example, while corrections officials say it costs $60,000 a year to keep a prisoner at Rikers Island," which is where convicted injection drug users are commonly housed, regardless of whether their charge is a mere "possession" offense. Joseph B. Treaster, "Giuliani Pits New Strategy against Drug Scourge," *New York Times*, 11 April 1994, A 13.

33. *Aliens*, writ. and dir. James Cameron, prod. Gale Anne Hurd, 1986.

34. The narrative of Fabian is related to the horror tale of "Helen," which preceded it on "60 Minutes," prod. Harry Moses (New York: CBS News, 19 Feb. 1984). Throughout his commentary, a representative of anxious heterosexual males with the appropriate name of "Morley Safer" presents "Helen" as an object of utter aversion who, unlike Fabian, refuses to be interviewed on screen. Her name is Safer's coinage; that his subject is a vulgar copy of the siren who destroyed Troy is apparent from the script. Thus, in the absence of the historical woman, the newsman constructs a seamless narrative of a black heroin addict and prostitute whose baby lies languishing with AIDS in the hospital while its mother sells her body on the streets; public officials are powerless to stop her, and as she moves from client to client, she infects another with AIDS.

35. Douglas Crimp delivers an impassioned critique of the media's exploitative use of Fabian in "Portraits of People with AIDS," *Cultural Studies*, ed. Lawrence Grossberg, Cary Nelson, and Paula Treichler (New York: Routledge, 1992), 121–23. What I have called the "slight fault" of public institutions, for the sake of brevity, might better be characterized as "mixed reviews," corresponding to competing constructions of Fabian. At first, he seems to be the victim of institutional discrimination and neglect; however, once the camera crew learns about his prostitution, the viewpoint "suddenly change[s]. . . . No longer just a victim," Fabian has become a menace whose "lifestyle" calls for a reassessment of medical and juridical institutions. Midway through the film, the latter appear "soft" on AIDS and queers — unwilling or unable to protect the well (adjusted) from the "sick." By the end, the viewpoint has shifted again. Police and health departments have placed Fabian under surveillance, and quarantine is in the planning stages; thus plotted against, Fabian grows more sympathetic, though not entirely at the plotters' expense. Rather, the film suggests from the time his mother refuses to take him in until the time he is housed in the gay community law and health officials are stuck with Fabian by default. For that reason their censure is less than his mother's.

36. "AIDS: A National Inquiry," "Frontline," dir. Christopher Arthur, prod. Michael Kirk (Boston: WGBH, PBS, 25 March 1986); rpt., WGBH Transcripts, no. 408 (Boston: WGBH, 1986), 14.

37. "Murphy's Revenge," *Murphy Brown* (New York: CBS, 21 September 1991).

38. *Mother, Mother*, writ. and dir., Mickie Dickoff, prod. Judy Miller, 1989; and

Our Sons, writ. William Hanley, dir. John Erman (New York: ABC, 19 May 1991).

39. Watney, "Spectacle," 82.

40. I am indebted to Carolyn Allen for pointing out the skin connection between the two males.

41. *Tongues Untied*, dir. Marlon Riggs, assoc. prod. Brian Freeman (1989). In citing *Tongues* as a "dramatization," I am distinguishing the "experimental" video from the genre of documentary "realism" whose rules it visibly transgresses. Riggs describes the video as a hybridic formation. "It is documentary. It's personal biography. It's poetry. It's music video. It's vogue dance. It's 'vérité footage.' " (Marlon Riggs, "Tongues Untied: An Interview with Marlon Riggs," by Ron Simmons, *Brother to Brother: New Writings by Black Gay Men*, ed. Essex Hemphill [Boston: Alyson, 1991], 193). Homophobia and racism ensured *Tongues Untied* was not aired on 174 of the 284 PBS stations originally scheduled to do so on 16 July 1991. Among the PBS affiliates opting to broadcast was KCTS, Seattle, which aired *Tongues* at 3:00 A.M., based on the rationale that this was "a time when it was least likely to be inadvertently seen [by the general public]." Tom Howe, KCTS Sr. Vice-President and Station Manager, as cited by John Engstrom, "Talking on 'Tongues,' " *Seattle Post-Intelligencer*, 16 July 1991, C1. In 1994, within months of each other, Randy Shilts and Marlon Riggs died of AIDS. The first had condemned gay male promiscuity; the second had celebrated sexuality and eroticized safe sex; both had earned national recognition for their work. Notably, the white man's death was extensively covered by the mainstream media and in the gay press; the black man's death was not.

42. Since the official beginning of the epidemic in June 1981, three American movies "about AIDS" have been made for theater release: *Longtime Companion* (1990); *The Living End* (1992); and *Philadelphia* (1993). With the exception of Washington and possibly Banderas, whose role in *Philadelphia* is more appropriately described as "supporting," the films' stars play the parts of gay white men; most of the men represented are seropositive; and all but one who co-stars as a drifter and petty criminal in *Living End* are middle to upper middle class. Though I have excluded *Parting Glances* (1986) from the list of theater "AIDS movies" on the grounds that AIDS is not its focus, its leads are white and middle class as well. Nick, who is the film's PWA, is by turns campy, angry, affectionate, and depressed; he is also unmistakeably queer as the melodrama's assimilationist gay characters are not.

43. *The Wizard of Oz* is part of their film library. In fact, one of the campier lines in *Our Sons* is taken from the Hollywood classic and reframed as Donald's response to his illness. Turning to his lover, he quips: "Toto, I have a feeling we're not in Kansas anymore." Donald's line and a sprinkling of other queer humor are welcome interruptions in the pathetic tone of the film.

44. Introduction, in *AIDS: Cultural Analysis/Cultural Activism*, 4.

45. Ibid.

46. Michael Bronski, "Death and the Erotic Imagination," in *Taking Liberties*, 225.
47. Ibid.
48. Mary Ann Doane, *The Desire to Desire: The Woman's Film of the 1940s* (Bloomington: Indiana University Press, 1987), 71, 73.
49. Douglas Crimp has spoken eloquently to the need for both in "Mourning and Militancy," *October* 51 (1989): 3–18.
50. *An Early Frost* employs a different couple with much the same effect. In this 1985 televized AIDS melodrama, the setting is the family, as per usual; however, the central drama turns on the conflict between father and son. Their struggle is precipitated by the son's dual announcement that he is gay and has AIDS. It is resolved when he is uncoupled from his lover and denuded of sexuality; only then is he reunited with his father in the bosom of the family where he is seen to belong. Though the film alludes to the son's life in Chicago, neither this life nor the gay community's response to AIDS is shown on screen. Rather, here, as in the mother-son AIDS melodramas that are partly based on it, "homosexuality" and AIDS are exclusively represented as domestic crises with domestic resolutions. The salient difference between *An Early Frost* and its spin-offs is that the latter are more productive because they also work to remove women from public life and return them to the home. For a symptomatic reading of *An Early Frost* and *Our Sons* as expressions of the liberal humanist response to AIDS, see Paula Treichler, "AIDS Narratives on Television: Whose Story?" *Writing AIDS*, 161–99.
51. Relational definitions of motherhood are a feature of both *Mother, Mother* and *Andre's Mother*. The first film opens with a tender scene between Jeff and his dead lover's mother, Martha Cousins. The woman is nurturing, supportive, protective; she is true to her biblical namesake and familial surname as Mrs. Cutler is to her title. The second film juxtaposes *Andre's Mother* to her own mother, who, for all her wry wit and acerbity, accepts her grandson and his lover as her daughter does not.
52. Luce Irigaray, "Cosi Fan Tutti," in *This Sex Which Is Not One*, trans. Catherine Porter (Ithaca, NY: Cornell University Press, 1985), 89. Here, Irigaray restates Lacan's theorem: "There is no such thing as The woman, where the definite article stands for the universal. There is no such thing as The woman since of her essence. . . , she is not all." Jacques Lacan, "God and the Jouissance of The Woman," in *Feminine Sexuality: Jacques Lacan and the École Freudienne*, ed. Juliet Mitchell and Jacqueline Rose, trans. Jacqueline Rose (London: Macmillan, 1982), 144. Here and in "A Love Letter" (reprinted in the same text), Lacan posits a signifying relation between the Other that is man's unconscious and the other sex who represents his desire to him and for him. "Truly a confirmation that when one is a man, one sees in one's partner what can serve, narcissistically, to act as one's own support" ("A Love Letter," 157).
53. Watney, *Policing*, 48.

54. Simon Watney, "Photography and AIDS," in *The Critical Image*, ed. Carol Squiers (Seattle: Bay Press, 1990), 174.

55. Kimberly Bergalis, Letter to Florida Health Officials, 6 April 1991; rpt. *Newsweek*, 1 July 1991, 52.

56. Ibid.

57. These individuals include seropositive prostitutes, sex offenders, and medical practitioners who perform "invasive procedures" without disclosing their status. Calls for their incarceration presuppose that HIV positivity is a criminal offense. Such calls have led to the enaction of state legislation mandating HIV testing of convicted sex and drug offenders and allowing the quarantine of seropositive subjects whose behavior places "us" at risk of infection. Moreover, in a few states, the mere charge of a sex offense is held to be "sufficient reason" for subjecting alleged offenders to an HIV test. On 4 February 1994, a sex offender who had tested HIV+ was convicted by a Miami jury of attempted murder; soon afterward in Spokane, Washington, prosecutors upped the charge against a seropositive male from first-degree assault to first-degree murder, alleging he had exposed a female sex partner to HIV/death. Reported in *The Advocate*, 17 May 1994, 21.

58. The "free-our family" appeal was part of an anti-crime campaign speech in which the president also promised to work for legislation mandating "AIDS tests" *[sic]* for all those arrested on a sexual offense. As reported by Gwen Ifill, "Bush Cites Arkansas Crime in Attack on Clinton," *New York Times*, 29 September 1992, A 11.

59. I am indebted to Bob Neveldine for suggesting the viral analogy.

60. Amendment No. 734 specifically stipulates that "such a person . . . shall be fined not more than $10,000 or imprisoned not less than 10 years, or both." *Congressional Record* (11 July 1991): S9778.

61. The majority opinion against Michael Hardwick illustrates:

> Plainly enough illegal . . . conduct is not always immunized whenever it occurs in the home. . . . And if the respondent's submission is limited to the voluntary sexual conduct between consenting adults, it would be difficult, except by fiat, to limit the claimed right to homosexual conduct while leaving exposed to prosecution adultery, incest, and other sexual crimes even though they are committed in the home. (*Bowers v. Hardwick*, 2846)

62. My discussion of the mothers is based on Georgia Dullea's feature story, "Confronting Pain with Undying Hope," *New York Times*, 20 April 1994, A10. In it she cites a self-description of the mothers' coalition written by Florence Rush for *The People with AIDS Coalition Newsletter*. It reads in part: " 'We range in age from 40 to over 80. We are working-class, white collar, business and professional women. . . . We are black, white [and] Hispanic. . . . Our sons and daughters, gay and straight have AIDS, and that is all that matters.' "

63. "Femininity," 118, 128.

64. Ibid., 118. In contrast, the phallic mother is rendered monstrous in Cameron's *Aliens* and the brood of seropositive women, analogically related to Her in AIDS commentary.

65. *Philadelphia*, dir. Jonathan Demme, writ. Ron Nyswaner (1993). Though released to a handful of theaters in December 1993, the melodrama was not screened nationally until 1994. From the tenor of Joe Miller's opening remarks to the jury, framing "panic" as a "normal" response to AIDS and the classic "flight reaction" of anxiety as a "reasonable" defense against PWAs, one would never guess that the narrative year is 1991 nor that the jury members being addressed reside in an urban center disproportionately affected by HIV/AIDS. Nor would one reasonably infer the time frame of the story from its presentation of HIV facts, all of which are variations on the hypermediated truth, "casual contact is safe." If Americans knew anything about AIDS in 1991, they surely knew you cannot get it from a toilet seat, through the air, or by shaking hands. And surely filmgoers can do without the repetition of these educational chestnuts in 1994. At a time when mediations of "chastity," "marital monogamy," and "sobriety" as the only real HIV prophylactics remain commonplace, what *Philadelphia* might have effectively repeated are messages about safer sexual and safer injection practices. However, the film ignores injection use, and on the subject of safe sex it is utterly silent. Its silence sends a double message that *Longtime Companion* rendered explicit in the musings of a seronegative gay man who longs for a time when AIDS is a disease of the past and he can have sex again. That message is: Abstinence is the sole form of safe sex and any sexual contact with someone HIV+ is unsafe. Not.

66. In this flashback sequence the film envisions an act of HIV transmission that could not possibly have occurred as implicitly staged; in fact the only act that could have occurred between two men seated in adjoining movie chairs is masturbation, and, in fact, masturbation is safe sex.

67. *Longtime Companion* is at best a partial exception to the melodramatic rule. Like the TV films, the private is its *metier*; unlike them, the private responses it records come from a small community of white middle-class gay New Yorkers who live and die during the 1980s. By the end of the decade, the AIDS survivors are involved in private fundraisers and AIDS Service Organizations (GMHC). In the penultimate scene, dated 19 July 1989, two of the men and an obligatory heterosexual woman friend discuss an ACT UP demo they plan on attending the next day. The most overtly political of the melodrama's scenes, the segment is dramatically undercut by the finale, which portrays its inhabitants as beings transported outside historical time and the mundane world of politics. In this spectacular dream sequence, a crowd of dead PWAs return to life (before AIDS) and take-up partying on the beach. The mentioned demo is never shown on screen; instead, the dream fades out, and the three figures are finally seen in private musings on the Fire Island shore. For a sustained reading of the film's melodramatic storyline, see Beaty,

who critiques it for reasons I have indicated in "The Syndrome Is the System: A Political Reading of *Longtime Companion*," in *Fluid Exchanges*, 111–34; and James Miller, who lauds the same plot as a humanist testimonial to love in "Dante on Fire Island: Reinventing Heaven in the AIDS Elegy," in *Writing AIDS*, esp. 297–303.

Fig. 8.1. Courtesy of Kraipit. Copyright © SIPA Press.

EIGHT

The Family Romance of Orientalism: From *Madame Butterfly* to *Indochine*

Marina Heung

THE PHOTOGRAPH THAT STARTED IT ALL

On an October afternoon in Paris in 1985, Claude-Michel Schönberg, the composer of the successful musical *Les Misérables*, was looking through an issue of the magazine *France Soir*, when a photograph caught his attention (Fig. 8.1). The photograph showed an Asian woman standing half-facing a young girl. Although a group of men is pressed up tightly around them, the woman and girl seem oblivious to everything but each other. The woman wears plain dark clothes and has her hair pulled back. Her furrowed brows and drawn mouth give her face a pained expression, and — although one has to look closely to see this — her downcast eyes are focused intently on the girl. The girl is wearing a T-shirt; her left hand is being held by someone in the crowd behind her. Her mouth is widened in a grimace, and she is sobbing.

This is the photograph that inspired Claude-Michel Schönberg and his collaborator, the librettist Alain Boublil, to write the hit musical *Miss Saigon*. Later, Richard Maltby, Jr., who was brought in to contribute English lyrics, acknowledged that "the entire show was in that photo."[1] The woman in the photograph is a Vietnamese mother saying goodbye to her daughter. As Schönberg explains, "The little Vietnamese girl was about to board a plane from Ho Chi Minh City Airport for the United States of America where her father, an ex-G.I. she had never seen, was waiting for her. Her mother was leaving her there and would never see her again."[2] For Schönberg and Boublil, the photograph resonated with the devastating pathos of the Vietnam War and its still unexhausted legacy in human trauma: "The silence of this woman stunned by her grief was a shout of pain louder than any of the earth's laments. The child's tears were the final condemnation of all wars which shatter people who love each other."[3] Propelled by their reaction to this image, Schönberg and Boublil went on to write *Miss Saigon*. When the musical opened in New York City, the same photograph was featured prominently in the production *Playbill* and reproduced as the frontispiece in the souvenir program in recognition of its impact on the writers.

But for Schönberg and Boublil, the photograph had a further, decidedly more gendered, significance, one that centered on the figure of the mother. Referring to the nameless woman, Schönberg adds, "She knew, as only a mother could, that beyond this departure gate there was both a new life for her daughter and no life at all for her, and that she had willed it. . . . I was so appalled by the image of this deliberate ripping apart that I had to sit down and catch my breath."[4] Thus invoking the archetype of the self-sacrificing mother, Schönberg and Boublil were led finally to the inspirational intertext for *Miss Saigon* — Giacomo Puccini's *Madame Butterfly*. In Puccini's opera, the geisha Cio-Cio-San (Madame Butterfly) gives birth to a son after Lt. B. F. Pinkerton, an American naval officer, has abandoned her after a brief "marriage." Three years later, when he returns to Japan with his new American wife, Cio-Cio-San agrees to give up her child to the couple and then commits *seppuku* (ritual suicide). For Schönberg and Boublil, the mother in the "Miss Saigon photograph" comes to incarnate the same awe-inspiring maternal selflessness: "Was that not the most moving, the most staggering example of 'The Ultimate Sacrifice,' as undergone by Cio-Cio-San in *Madame Butterfly*, giving her life for her child?"[5] With "a heartbreaking photograph and a potential connection with a famous opera to start from,"[6] Schönberg and Boublil began writing *Miss Saigon* as a contemporary musical, one that reframed the story of *Madame Butterfly* against the backdrop of Vietnam in 1975, when the U.S. military evacuated Saigon on the eve of the Communist takeover.

It comes as no surprise that *Madame Butterfly* should offer a ready-made reference point for the writers of *Miss Saigon*. Puccini's popular opera is in many ways a foundational narrative of East-West relations, having shaped the Western construction of "the Orient" as a sexualized, and sexually compliant, space that is ripe for conquest and rule. Many scholars have analyzed the ways in which race and gender are mutually imbricated within Orientalist discourse and practice, constituting a nexus along which sexual and racial domination operate reciprocally.[7] Central to the Western Orientalist imaginary, the figure of the geisha (whose most notable incarnation is Cio-Cio-San/Madame Butterfly) epitomizes an exoticized and subservient femininity that is leavened with a tantalizing mix of passive refinement and sexual mystique. As a master-text of Orientalism, *Madame Butterfly* confirms the Asian woman's perpetual sexual availability for the Western male even as her convenient demise delimits such liaisons; in the end, Cio-Cio-San's suicide recapitulates the fate of the expendable Asian whose inevitable death confirms her marginality within dominant culture and history.[8]

At the same time, Schönberg and Boublil's conflation of an Orientalist myth with the flesh-and-blood realities of the Vietnam aftermath necessarily reflects the ideological exigencies of a specific cultural moment. In this respect, both the photograph and the musical it inspired are artifacts of the post-Vietnam era. As such, their ideological effects should be understood in relation to the many literary works, autobiographical and documentary accounts, and mass media representations seeking to re-enact, rationalize, and mythologize the experience of the war in order to install it within the collective memory. But, as has often been noted, the problem of representing Vietnam is fundamentally that of representing history.[9] Mass media images of the war, in particular, perform the work of selective remembering and erasure, or what Michael Klein has termed "historical amnesia."[10] Exemplifying the operations of "ideological condensation,"[11] they smooth over moral ambiguities and ideological contradictions by mythologizing history; they assuage the pain of military defeat through cathartic displays of spectacular excess and physical violence. To account for how these representations operate, therefore, one must recognize what they conceal as well as what they contain. In other words, in reading Vietnam representations, one cannot, to use Abigail Solomon-Godeau's phrase, "stop short at the framing edge."[12]

Recently, Susan Jeffords has demonstrated how displacement and repression are the very organizing principles of Vietnam representation. Specifically, Jeffords argues that gender difference is both what Vietnam representation is "about" and, paradoxically, that which it cannot represent directly. Thus, "in Vietnam representation, gender is rephrased as sexuality and presented as its own spectacle."[13] In other words, gender difference is never the overt subject of Vietnam representation; instead, these narratives reaffirm masculinity through an intricate relay of displacements and repressions, for instance, by projecting sexual excess onto women while dissociating them from their power to reproduce. As Jeffords suggests, the figure of woman in Vietnam narrative is radically split according to her sexual, biological, reproductive, and nurturing functions. As a result, the most visible female presence is the hypersexual stereotype of the Asian prostitute; the "unrepresentable" female presence, on the other hand, is the woman as biological mother. Not only this, but the maternal archetype is further polarized into the mutually exclusive categories of the biological/reproductive mother and the mother as nurturer. Based on her reading of Tom Mayer's short story, "A Birth in the Delta," for instance, Jeffords concludes that "the repressed is not the mother *or* the whore, but the mother/whore from reproduction itself."[14] Thus, she asserts that reproduction "may be *the* repressed of Vietnam representation," and " 'mothering' is . . . reduced . . . to a biological act alone, one that can be easily appropriated by technology, one in which bonds between the masculine and technology — the technological body — are foregrounded over and above bonds between the feminine and the child."[15]

Jeffords's analysis rightly recognizes the heavily mediated nature of representation in general, and of the gendered bias of Vietnam representation in particular. However, an account of the signifying effects of a text such as the "Miss Saigon photograph" must also consider how its meaning is generated not only textually but as a result of reading practices brought to bear by its interlocutors. Such reading practices, as Solomon-Godeau notes, are never neutral: "The dynamic act of reading a photograph and producing meaning from it animates trajectories of power and desire, mastery and projection, that run between the perceiving eye, the subjective I, and the visual field, all of which must be factored into our understanding of photographic production and reception."[16]

For Schönberg and Boublil, the "Miss Saigon photograph" encodes an ideologically motivated reading that fixes the figure of woman within the limits of a familial discourse, thus displacing the hypersexual archetype of Asian femininity. Within the specific context of the Vietnam aftermath, this gaze effectively keeps one historical dimension of the Vietnamese woman's experience outside the photograph's "framing edge" and occludes the material circumstances most likely to have led up to this wrenching scene between mother and daughter in the first place. In other words, although it is common knowledge that the large number of Amerasian children abandoned in Vietnam after the war resulted from births to Vietnamese prostitutes catering to U.S. military personnel, the story of the sexual exploitation of Vietnamese women remains the still-unwritten chapter of the history of the war.[17] In the case of the "Miss Saigon photograph," this history continues to be suppressed because the visual text is now dominated by a hypermaternalized icon. Indeed, while accepting Susan Jeffords's contention that "Vietnam narratives are replete with sexual encounters, pornographic images, and sexually motivated vocabularies,"[18] one could argue that the overinvestment in sexualized representations of the Asian woman is simply the preferred strategy in masculinizing the war. It is my contention, then, that Schönberg and Boublil's response to the "Miss Saigon photograph" exemplifies the tactics of a no-less revisionary reading practice, one that engages an elemental trope that I have termed "the family romance of Orientalism."

MADAME BUTTERFLY AS MATERNAL MELODRAMA: FROM INTERRACIAL ROMANCE TO FAMILY ROMANCE

For the United States, the end of the Vietnam War represented a profound trauma to the collective national psyche. Not only were the conduct of and justification for the war deeply contested within American society, but the subsequent defeat of the U.S. military also challenged fundamental beliefs in technological superiority, governmental authority, and, above all, the inviolate nature of masculinity. Postwar cultural representations have entertained a proliferation of images of maleness, whereby the fetishized male, metonymically associated with warlike violence and technological competence, replays battlefield encounters, usually in the absence of women.[19] Within the same period, fundamental changes in gender relations in American culture contrived to create a "backlash" in the form of a rash of popular images seeking to shore up the traditional nuclear family and reinstall paternal authority.[20] In the post-Vietnam era, therefore, anxieties about military and masculine prowess have coincided with a pervasive societal insecurity about maleness and paternal legitimacy, providing the context for an insistent, even obsessive, revalorization of the patriarchal nuclear family. In this context, the Orientalized family romance offers a paradigmatic narrative for "rebinding" wounded masculinity by incessantly rehearsing the saga of recovering lost fathers.

In its original meaning as used by Sigmund Freud, the "family romance" refers to the (male) child's imagination that he has been adopted. In one version of the romance, called the "foundling myth," the child imagines that, unlike the parents who have raised him, his "real" (biological) parents are from a socially elevated, aristocratic class. In a second version of the romance, called the "bastard myth," the child imagines that he is the illegitimate son of his mother, who has conceived him through an extramarital affair. In this second version, the child imagines a biological father whom he has never met and now longs to identify.[21] In Freud's view, the "neurotic's family romance" expresses hostility toward fathers, and is thus typically a male fantasy.[22] The bastard myth in particular speaks to the male experience of the Oedipal crisis, in that the child can, by disavowing the father that he knows, create the imaginary possibility that he can possess his mother in his father's place. Because the mother's identity is not in question, this scenario is teleologically oriented toward the recovery of paternity.

Both versions of Freud's family romance are recapitulated in post-Vietnam representation. Marthe Robert's paraphrase of the "bastard myth," in which a (boy-)child imagines a "royal, unknown father who is forever absent" and "relegat[ed] . . . to an imaginary kingdom beyond and above the family circle . . . but whose vacant place cries out nonetheless to be filled," distills the essence of a narrative about the abandoned Amerasian child within the current phase of postcolonial discourse.[23] Further, in the Orientalized family romance, issues of class difference take on overtones of racial and cultural difference. As Richard de Cordova has noted, because the child confers aristocratic status on his "lost" parents, there is a built-in class dimension in the foundling myth beyond its libidinal and psychic dimensions.[24] In the post-Vietnam narrative, this social dimension of the myth receives a cultural inflection as well, so that distinctions of proletarian/aristocratic are mapped onto an assumed polarity between East and West; as a result, the Amerasian child's search for a lost paternal figure incorporates an unspoken affirmation of the cultural superiority of the West.

And this discourse is by no means a purely fictional construct. Recently, the mass media abounds with news reports on the plight of abandoned Amerasian children and stories of their adoption by American families, especially as a result of the Homecoming Act of 1988.[25] These accounts typically rehearse the story of how these children are obsessed with finding the fathers whom they have never seen; their common refrain is a desperately voiced desire to escape to the United States, where they will find their fathers and enjoy the material riches. In these narratives, the theme of missing fathers implies an uncritical affirmation of American cultural and economic superiority. Further, what is prioritized is the nexus between father and child, and scant attention is given to the situations and subjectivities of the children's mothers.[26]

In this context, the significance of the "Miss Saigon photograph" emerges fully only when we recognize the implied presence of the father as a figure of desire. We will recall that Schönberg's immediate response seems to dwell on the phenomenon of maternal self-sacrifice. However, even as his imaginary scenario foregrounds mother/child relations to obscure and displace the background memory of a prior sexual liaison, its narrative resolution is projected into a future scene of reconciliation between daughter and father, as suggested in these remarks: "The little Vietnamese girl was about to board a plane from Ho Chi Minh City Airport for the United States of America where her father, an ex-GI she had never seen, was waiting for her."[27] Schönberg's emotional response to the actual scene of maternal sacrifice thus forms a preamble to an imaginary scenario in which the Western male reenters the narrative and reattaches himself to the girl as her father. With the male/paternal principle informing the "Miss Saigon photograph" as a structuring absence, the image's primal power clearly derives not only from its inscription of maternal nobility, but also the circulation of the paternal at its edges. At this point, we begin to make further sense of the unexpected connection between the photograph and *Madame Butterfly*. What the photograph traces, albeit in strikingly oblique and deglamorized terms, is a nexus of relations involving mother-child-father, constituting the family romance deeply embedded in the inaugural narrative of *Madame Butterfly*.[28]

To date, *Madame Butterfly* exists in the popular imagination as the quintessential interracial romance, one that depicts the collision of cultural differences within what Mary Louise Pratt has termed the "contact zone."[29] However, an examination of the opera and of its literary and dramatic antecedents shows the extent to which its central myth is dominated by the trope of the family romance. Although Puccini's opera is by far the best known, multiple versions of the *Madame Butterfly* story exist (both in literary form and in staged and filmed versions). The story first appears as the French novella *Madame Chrysanthème* written by Pierre

Loti. It was then rewritten in English as a short story entitled "Madame Butterfly" by the American writer John Luther Long. The popularity of the short story led the successful American playwright David Belasco to write and produce a one-act version for the New York stage. It was this play, which Puccini saw, that inspired the Italian composer to create *Madame Butterfly*.[30] Among these versions, only one, the opera, foregrounds the elements of the interracial romance. And even here, the romantic plot figures prominently only in the first half of the work, which narrates Cio-Cio-San's marriage to Lieutenant Pinkerton, his departure, and her patient longing for his return. Cio-Cio-San's transformation from a lovelorn romantic object to a noble maternal figure occurs in a revelatory moment halfway into Act II (almost exactly at the opera's midpoint). At this juncture, in response to Consul Sharpless urging her to remarry, Cio-Cio-San reveals a secret: she leaves the stage, returns with a child, and, with a flourish, introduces him to Sharpless as her son. From this point on, Cio-Cio-San's tragic status is inseparable from her maternal role. Indeed, the romantic plot quickly retreats, as underscored by the fact that after Act I there is no further direct contact between Cio-Cio-San and Pinkerton.

Among the opera's antecedents, only Loti's *Madame Chrysanthème* dwells to any extent on the romantic relationship between Butterfly and Pinkerton, though in this case, the story of a French officer's liaison with a geisha during a shore assignment is narrated with such a tone of revulsion and contempt that it is a stretch to term the story a romance at all.[31] In both the Long novella and the Belasco play that follow, Pinkerton's presence is significantly more attenuated. In Long's novella, only the first three of the fourteen chapters depict the relationship between Butterfly and Pinkerton; Pinkerton, in fact, never reappears after his departure. Belasco's play, which is directly based on the Long short story, even dispenses with the romantic prologue: the play opens with Butterfly already a mother and awaiting Pinkerton's return.

In each of these versions there is no renewed contact between Butterfly and her lover/husband after he abandons her. Instead, Butterfly's discovery of Pinkerton's treachery takes place through her encounter with Pinkerton's American wife, who asks Butterfly to give up her son. Each version therefore foregrounds Butterfly's doomed struggle to sustain her own claims and desires against the forces ranged against her: the prerogatives of male paternal authority, Western cultural superiority, and a familialist ideology.

As originally coined by Michèle Barrett and Mary McIntosh, the term "familialism" encapsulates the biological (and historically based) bias that elevates the notion of "family" defined in terms of blood kinship and paternal control.[32] The familialist slant of the family romance operative in *Madame Butterfly* is confirmed through Mrs. Pinkerton's appearance at the end of the Long, Belasco, and Puccini versions. Once Mrs. Pinkerton appears as the "legitimate" spouse, Butterfly's claims as wife and mother are immediately diminished, because only as a legitimate wife can she place her son in a "proper" family (which, in this case, also draws legitimacy from its designation as "Western.") Mrs. Pinkerton is the legitimate spouse, so familialist ideology implicitly shores up her position within the triad constituted by recognized father and mother figures and a child. In the drama's resolution, the terms of interracial conflict are thus shifted and reconfigurated around the figure of the child and reframed in terms of a familial problematic.

In each version of *Madame Butterfly*, dramatic tension revolves around contesting maternal and paternal claims on the child, which are then resolved through Butterfly's surrender of him and her ensuing death. By committing suicide, Butterfly defers to paternal and familial prerogatives, and the extremity of her two sacrificial acts — giving up her son and her death — seals her iconic destiny as the embodiment of fanatic excess and self-abnegation.

Butterfly's enduring mythic stature is earned, then, not only as the wronged woman of interracial romance, but also the sacrificial heroine of maternal melodrama. In the maternal melodrama, the woman as mother falls and then redeems herself, usually through a sacrificial act committed for the good of her child. Characterized as an "apologia for total renunciation, total sacrifice, total self-abnegation,"[33] the maternal melodrama ennobles the mother by chronicling how she "reconquer[s] her dignity while helping her child re-enter society thanks to her sacrifices."[34] The familialist and patriarchal tendencies shared by the family romance and the maternal melodrama have been duly noted. Geoffrey Nowell-Smith, for instance, has remarked on how "melodrama enacts, often with uncanny literalness, the 'family romance' described by Freud."[35] As with the classical family romance, the maternal melodrama allows a particularly male-oriented enactment of the Oedipal plot despite its ostensible focus on female protagonists. As E. Ann Kaplan comments, the maternal melodrama enacts "the little boy's fantasies about an adoring, beautiful Mother [in which] the Mother often gives birth out of wedlock, sacrifices herself for the welfare of her (usually in this film type) *male* child, seeking to elevate him in society or to return him to his noble lineage (through his Father), while debasing and absenting herself."[36] Arguing that the maternal melodrama is a male Oedipal drama, Kaplan concludes that the "maternal sacrifice theme was addressed to male needs, desires and fantasies, as much (if not more than) to female desires."[37]

Despite its implicitly male focus, the maternal melodrama plot in *Madame Butterfly* nevertheless creates an interesting tension between the patriarchal stereotype of the self-denying mother and the Orientalist portrayal of the Asian woman as a marginal figure lacking in psychological dimension or moral agency. Numerous writers have demonstrated how the textual invisibility and silence of the third-world woman provide the necessary conditions for the formation of first-world female subjectivity.[38] For instance, Jenny Sharpe acknowledges that the Indian woman appears in colonialist texts as an "absence," "negation," "screen," or "subaltern shadow"[39] precisely because the conferral of authority and individualism upon the English woman depends on the "distancing of the English woman from her Eastern sisters."[40] In a deployment of what Sharpe has termed a "national and racial splitting of femininity,"[41] the perceived subjugation, victimization, and oppressed status of the third-world woman accrues to the white European woman's attainment of individual self-definition and female agency.[42] In this context, by incorporating the outlines of the family romance and the maternal melodrama, *Madame Butterfly* would seem to provide a departure from the schematic distinctions between first- and third-world women evident in the typical colonialist text. No longer the faceless victim whose anonymity and victimization reflect the backwardness of an alien culture, Cio-Cio-San now emerges from the "subaltern shadow" to occupy center stage. With the cloak of Victorian domestic virtue falling on her shoulders, she comes to embody the moral ideal of female self-sacrifice. In this light, the myth of *Madame Butterfly* appears as an exemplary text extolling the female virtues of domestic duty and self-sacrifice, except that these are now figured through the travails of an Asian woman. Whereas on one level this reveals the pervasive reach of Western patriarchal definitions of femininity that apparently recognizes no national or racial boundaries, one would at the same time acknowledge how *Madame Butterfly* offers a rare instance in which the "other" woman is envisioned as possessing a degree of selfhood and agency, even if these qualities are at once diluted by their being subsumed under patriarchal notions of women's place.

Indeed, the conclusion of John Luther Long's short story offers a provocative, if ambiguous, suggestion of Butterfly's assertion of will and self-determination. After an accidental meeting with Mrs. Pinkerton when she is mistaken for a sweet, pretty "plaything," Cho-Cho-San (as her name is spelt in this work) learns of Mrs. Pinkerton's wish to take her son away with her to join her husband. In the last chapter, Cho-Cho-San makes preparations to commit suicide. But, after she stabs herself and blood begins to flow, we read: "The baby crept cooing into her lap. The little maid came in and bound up her wound." And in the last sentence of the story, Mrs. Pinkerton comes to the house and finds that "it [is] quite empty."[43] The silence in the house resonates with the possibility that Cho-Cho-San has chosen to exercise her maternal instinct in favor of saving herself and her son rather than surrendering herself to the fate that awaits her literary avatars.

THE DRAMA OF THE "OTHER" WOMAN

Despite its open-ended conclusion, the Long story is the only version of *Madame Butterfly* hinting that Butterfly might resist the demands of self-sacrifice. Instead, the most striking common denominator among all the versions, from Long to Puccini, is a dramatic denouement precipitated not by a reunion between Butterfly and her faithless husband, but rather by a crucial encounter between her and Pinkerton's wife. The question thus arises as to the symbolic or ideological significance of Kate Pinkerton's intrusion in the text. That Kate's insertion is both overdetermined and integral seems evident because it has persisted through all of *Butterfly*'s permutations, and because it has continued to represent somewhat of a "trouble" in the narrative in its various permutations.[44]

Kate Pinkerton's appearance mobilizes the exclusionary effects of familialist ideology, insofar as the two women are now shown to be vying for a place within the Pinkerton "family." As I have already argued, this issue is resolved by placing the child within a legitimate family, one that is in turn designated by the father's location. By the same token, as each other's rivals, Butterfly and Kate Pinkerton are placed in a situation of mutual "lack" and disempowerment that only one of them can convert into a position of legitimacy, but only at the expense of the other. Butterfly's defeat in this tug of war is, of course, a foregone conclusion, and her surrender confirms her subordinated status as the "other" woman.

As Christian Viviani has noted, the theme of the "other" woman is a familiar subplot of the maternal melodrama.[45] Historically, this figure has functioned to signify female difference and all that is inassimilable and "other" about femininity. As Helena Michie notes, the other woman as mistress is "locate[d] outside the family; the mistress, as the not-wife, becomes the locus of all that is troubling, problematic, and unfamiliar about female sexuality and sexual difference."[46] In *Butterfly*, as both the displaced wife/mistress and the non-European, Cio-Cio-San is of course doubly "other," and her rivalry with an Anglo-American woman only underscores her familial and cultural marginality. Yet the very fact of Butterfly's defeat by an Anglo-American woman brings into focus issues of sexual and racial difference forming the crux of patriarchal and Orientalist discourse.

Although it would be in keeping with the text's simplified politics to cast the rivalry between Butterfly and Mrs. Pinkerton only in terms of East-West conflict, the relationship between first- and third-world women has ramifications irreducible to monolithic categories of difference and hierarchy. Thus, in considering the "problem" of the Western woman within colonial discourse, Laura E. Donaldson has identified "the Miranda complex" as symptomatic of the multivalent intersections of race and gender in first- and third-world relations. Basing her analysis on Caliban's attempted rape of Miranda in *The Tempest*, Donaldson notes the contradictory distribution of power between an enslaved subject and his mistress and the "peculiarities of Miranda's position [emerging from] her status as the sexual object of both the Anglo-European male and the native Other and as the loyal daughter/wife who ultimately aligns herself with the benefits and protection offered by the colonizing father and husband."[47] Donaldson's exploration of the differentials of race, gender, and power between the Western woman and the colonized male forms part of a growing body of work analyzing the ambiguous position of the Western woman in relation to imperialist politics, and especially vis-à-vis third-world women.[48] Extending Donaldson's analysis to consider the relationship between Western and non-Western women, then, we may begin to address a complex interplay of sameness and difference based on a set of overlapping interrelationships at once marking the women as distinguishably different (based on race) and yet apparently the same (based on gender).

It is just such a contradictory interplay between sameness and difference that is activated through Kate Pinkerton's entry into *Madame Butterfly*. First, as already noted, Kate's designation as "Mrs." Pinkerton brings into play a familialist discourse whereby legitimacy is based on familial status. At the same time, Butterfly's encounter with her sexual rival occasions the ultimate test of her willingness to play a sacrificial maternal role. Butterfly's apotheosis as expendable subaltern and noble mother gains both poignancy and urgency because Mrs. Pinkerton's claims are taken as having an irrefutable priority over hers. However, as suggested earlier, it would still seem that this outcome presents a noteworthy instance within Orientalist discourse when the Asian woman, despite her victimization by external forces, nevertheless attains a degree of moral stature and agency by playing a self-sacrificing role. But closer analysis reveals how the play on racial and gender sameness and difference initiated by Kate Pinkerton's entry results in diluting and displacing the very agency that would otherwise enshrine Butterfly as a paragon of Victorian domestic self-immolation.

Generally speaking, the racialist logic implicit in Orientalist texts demands the activation of a discourse naturalizing racial difference.[49] All the versions of *Madame Butterfly* perpetuate the notion of racial difference by emphasizing the intractable differences between East and West, a simple dichotomy that is neatly introduced through the subplot of the "other" woman. At the same time, notions of irreducible differences are also underscored through the ironic device of having Butterfly wear Western clothes, her dressing her son in an American sailor suit, and her naive remarks on American culture confirming her alienation from it.

However, whereas these dramatic touches dwell on racial difference as a given, the text also invokes another, parallel, discourse elevating the maternal as the universal attribute of femininity. Although differentiated by race and divided in sexual rivalry, the encounter between the two women in every case reaffirms the subordination of female desire and individual will — *of both women* — to the claims of a selfless and transcendent maternality. Above all, the meeting between Butterfly and her rival is remarkably permeated with good will and mutual recognition of common ideals. In the Belasco play, the meeting of the two women begins with the exchange of a long look, followed by Kate Pinkerton's embrace of Butterfly. Mrs. Pinkerton then gently persuades Butterfly that they should "think first of the child" and pleads: "For his own good . . . let me take him home to my country. . . . I will do all I would do for my own." This exchange ends with Butterfly in essence expressing her consent and her forgiveness, telling her rival that she is the "bes' lucky girl in these whole worl'."[50] In the opera, there is a brief exchange between the two women in which Kate asks for Butterfly's forgiveness and Butterfly agrees to give up her son, avowing: "Beneath the great bridge of Heaven / there's no happier woman than you / May you always be so . . . / Don't be sad for me." As before, the exchange between the women is strikingly free of rancor, with Kate exclaiming about Butterfly: "Poor little thing!"

Toll of the Sea, the 1922 silent Hollywood film that adapts *Madame Butterfly* to a Chinese setting, condenses even more succinctly the tone with which Butterfly and her rival are reconciled. In the film's last moments, a title card introduces the scene when Lotus Flower (Butterfly's incarnation, played by Anna May Wong) gives Elsie, the American woman, her child: "The sympathy and understanding between good women the world over, brought Elsie back into the garden and led Lotus Flower to tell all." This melodramatic conclusion culminates with Lotus Flower confiding her sorrows to Elsie, pleading with Elsie to take her son to America, and telling her son that she is only his "little Chinese nurse" and Elsie is his real mother.

The paradigmatic narrative of *Madame Butterfly* thus mobilizes a strategically contradictory discourse of sameness and difference as an instance of what Jenny Sharpe has termed the "textual displacements enacted through figures of resemblance."[51] In the many versions of the drama, implications of racial and cultural difference are generally naturalized, elaborated, and exaggerated; however, during the pivotal encounters between Mrs. Pinkerton and Butterfly, notions of difference ultimately yield to an assertion of a commonality based on femininity and domestic mission. So, whereas Laura Donaldson has cited instances of how colonial discourse has at times expediently engaged anti-sexist rhetoric to displace questions of colonialism,[52] in *Madame Butterfly*, an assimilationist discourse subsuming difference and hierarchy is activated to neutralize the bad conscience of domination and exploitation. Under this guise, the Pinkertons' expropriation of the child is "naturalized" away, its inherently imperialist stance softened and rationalized through the camaraderie created between mothers across national and racial boundaries. And insofar as Pinkerton is portrayed in every instance as a callous bounder,[53] his American wife becomes his good conscience and alibi, who, through her benign identification with Butterfly, disarms attributions of plunder and dispossession forming the dark subtext of the Orientalized family romance.

INDOCHINE AS POSTCOLONIAL FAMILY ROMANCE

In the late 1980s and early 1990s, three works — a play, a musical, and a film — achieved enormous popular success in the United States. In 1988, David Henry Hwang's *M. Butterfly* opened on Broadway and went on to win a Tony Award for Best Play that year. In 1991, *Miss Saigon* began its current, very successful, New York run. Then, in 1993, *Indochine*, a French film directed by Régis Wargnier, won the 1992 Academy Award for Best Foreign Film. Despite their radically different contexts of production and authorship (a Broadway play written by an Asian American, a musical written by two Frenchmen and an American, and a French "art" film), these productions shared critical and/or popular acclaim and at least one other similarity: each appropriated the myth of *Madame Butterfly* as an explicit intertext or implicit subtext.

Of the three, *M. Butterfly* and *Miss Saigon* offer polar extremes relative to the politics of representation. Termed a "deconstructivist *Madame Butterfly*" by its author,[54] *M. Butterfly* uses the mythical framework of the Puccini opera self-reflexively to expose the shifting intersections of race and gender embedded in the Orientalist gaze.[55] On the other hand, *Miss Saigon* uncritically adapts the Orientalizing assumptions of its operatic source to the "topical" setting of the Vietnam War, subsuming the material facts of politics and history to the demands of popular consumption and theatrical appeal. But perhaps precisely because its historical vision is so shallow, *Miss Saigon* marks a critical juncture when the family romance within post-Vietnam representation begins to be foregrounded. This is signaled not only in the prominence given to the "Miss Saigon photograph," but also in a notable dramaturgical moment in the production. The second act begins with a musical interlude that has no precedent in any previous version of *Madame Butterfly*. Here, the character John (an army buddy of the male lead) stands facing the audience in front of a lectern on a dimly lit and bare stage. As he sings the number "Bui Doi" ("dust of life"), a collage of children's images are projected onto a screen suspended above the stage. John's song, presented as an address to delegates gathered at an international conference, makes a plea for the Amerasian children who have been abandoned in Vietnam. When the number ends, some titles flash onto the screen identifying the children as orphans looking for their fathers, ending with the appeal: "Please help us to help them." The political register of this interlude is all the more striking because it disrupts the representational codes of theatrical illusion operative elsewhere in the production. Unfortunately, in the context of a work that reduces both politics and history to theatricality and sentiment, its ultimate effect is that of an excrescence at best, and at worst, of opportunism posing as topicality.

As we have seen, *M. Butterfly* treats the prototypical narrative of *Madame Butterfly* as pure myth transcending the bounds of individual or localized histories, and *Miss Saigon* invokes history only as a pretext for theatrical gimmickry. *Indochine*, however, departs from its companion pieces as the only work among the three to deliberately engage the specificities of a particular historical era. Narrating the end of empire, *Indochine* spans the late phase of French colonialism in Indochina, from the rise of a nationalist resistance movement in the 1930s to the 1954 signing of the Geneva Agreement, which formally ended French involvement and, by partitioning Vietnam into north and south, set the stage for American intervention in the region. In this postcolonial allegory, the historical processes of colonial annexation and decolonization are enacted through a maternal melodrama doubly charged with the aura of colonial nostalgia and the mythic resonance of the Orientalized family romance. Although at least one critic has found echoes of *Madame Butterfly* in *Indochine*,[56] the film's most striking departure is in sidelining colonialism as a male enterprise, so that the problematics of race, gender, and colonial disengagement are framed through the relationship between a white European woman and the "native" woman as colonial subject.

In *Indochine*, individual histories and political relationships are configurated within the limits of the family romance, and a critique of colonialism is conveyed through the depiction of aberrant familial and sexual relationships. In an apparent corrective to the male bias of the Oedipal family romance, female-to-female relationships form the central focus. Although the film retains the basic ingredients of interracial romance, that relationship is completely divested of racial or sexual overtones. Instead, tensions between East and West are played out as disturbances between a white European mother and an adopted Asian daughter, and the generic tensions inherent in the drama of the "other" woman, the mother/daughter melodrama, and the classic stepmother tale[57] provide the framework for rationalizing the essentialist schematics of gender, race, and colonial relations.

From its first moments, *Indochine* is infused with the ambience of remembrance and loss that is the signature of postcolonial nostalgia. The credit sequence shows a riverborne funeral procession for a Prince from Annam and his wife, who have been killed in an accident. Their orphaned daughter stands at the head of this procession, holding hands with Eliane Devries (Catherine Deneuve), a French colonial whose father owns one of the largest rubber plantations in Indochina. Eliane's voice-over relates that she has adopted the little girl as her daughter. As a teenager, Camille (Linh Dan Pham) falls in love with Jean-Baptiste Le Guen (Vincent Perez), a French naval officer who is also her mother's ex-lover. In order to separate her from Jean-Baptiste, Eliane arranges to have him reassigned to the north, but Camille runs away to join him. They are reunited, but start living as fugitives after she kills a French officer. Camille becomes pregnant and gives birth to a son; soon after, she is forced to flee alone after Jean-Baptiste and their son are captured. At the end of the film, Jean-Baptiste commits suicide, and Camille leaves to join the resistance fighters, turning her son over to Eliane. In the last scene, Eliane has left Indochina, and she is with her adopted (step-)grandson, Etienne (Jean-Baptiste Huynh), in Geneva on the day of the signing of the Geneva Agreement.

Indochine, then, is "book-ended" by two adoptions across racial lines, both times with Eliane as the adoptive mother. Viewed historically, both adoptions have overtones of colonial expropriation, but their different circumstances parallel the historical process of colonial investiture and its subsequent unravelling: Eliane's first adoption posits a utopian alliance between the French colonial and local ruling class, but her second "adoption" of her step-grandson is a direct aftermath of anticolonialist resistance. The staple plot of the maternal melodrama, based on the disidentification between mother and daughter, subtends the political inevitability of Camille's alienation from Eliane, whereas the generics of the family romance and the narrative of the "other" woman are played out through a dizzying interlacing of multiple roles: Camille is the "other" woman (as Eliane's racial other and sexual rival) and both the adopted child *and* the self-sacrificial Asian mother of the Orientalized family romance.

Within the framework of maternal melodrama doubling as postcolonial critique, Eliane's characterization as "phallic mother" supplies the moral and psychological rationale for the demise of colonialism. Although Eliane's relationship with Camille is initially presented as intimate and warm (the first scene opens with the sound of their intermingled laughter off-screen), Eliane's will to possess and control, her sexual manipulativeness and emotional coldness, and her suppressed tendencies toward violence and cruelty, cast her in the archetypal mold of the "phallic mother."[58] In one scene, she is shown whipping one of her workers who has tried to run away. Eliane then asks the man: "Do you think a mother likes beating her children?" to which he replies: "You are my mother and my father." This episode unmasks not only the violence inherent in employer/employee and colonizer/colonized relations, but also Eliane's conception of mothering as control through physical punishment.

At the same time, the "male" flair with which she rules over her domain seems to derive from the authority abdicated by a father who is mainly preoccupied with seducing local young women. She exhibits a pride and protectiveness over her subjects that is both paternalistic and maternal, as when her crew team, with all "native" members, beats another team powered by French rowers, or when she protects a child whose father is an opium smuggler from Jean-Baptiste. When she strides through her plantation in trousers, Jean-Baptiste reminds her that "It's men who do the commanding, you know," and she answers dismissively, "Men usually say that." When Jean-Baptiste then points out how her coolies are staring at her, her curt response is: "I'm their boss, that's all." At one point, Eliane confesses to Jean-Baptiste that she used to dream that she was a boy, and the film pointedly encodes her as "masculine" by having her wear trousers in contrast to Camille's bare-shouldered and "feminine" looks. Finally, in a bizarre extension of this gender schematism, there is a scene during a Christmas party when Eliane does the tango with her daughter and, in a parody of heterosexual courtship, murmurs to Camille: "I'd like to be alone with you in a small mountain chalet — with a smoking chimney — like in a fairy tale" (Fig. 8.2).

But the "phallic mother" of the maternal melodrama is eventually

Fig. 8.2. Eliane (Catherine Deneuve) tangoes with Camille (Linh Dan Pham). Copyright ©
1992 Sony Pictures Classics Inc. All rights reserved.

punished and denigrated for her excessive will to possess and control. In
Indochine, Eliane receives retribution for her maternal fanaticism and her
"phallic" domination, first through the humiliating outcome of her affair
with Jean-Baptiste, and then through her daughter's competition with,
and ultimate rejection of, her. In her brief affair with Jean-Baptiste,
Eliane's veneer of confidence and self-control is unmasked as emotional
dependence and sexual obsessiveness. Thus, there is nothing to disprove
the charge hurled at Eliane by Yvette, the wife of Eliane's manager: "A
lack of love is never good. It's the worst illness. The truth is no one here
likes you. . . . Without love there's a smell. . . . You're beautiful, but your
looks are deceiving."

At one point Jean-Baptiste castigates Eliane, shouting: "A woman decides my fate. Is this how you run your colonies? You won't let others
live. You won't let them breathe. You treat people like trees. You buy
them and drain them. You want to stifle them the way your father stifled
you." With her misplaced fanaticism and suppressed hysteria, Eliane's
portrayal in *Indochine* exemplifies the revisionist tactics of postcolonial
representation by which colonial pathologies are allegorized through the

figure of woman.[59] In this vein, Laura Kipnis has suggested how the postcolonial cinema foregrounds the feminine to acknowledge and assimilate the "historical wound of decolonization."[60] In Kipnis's argument, "a post-colonial revision of history redeems the male experience of colonialism by coding colonialism as female. The filmic spectacle performs the work of disavowal by *gendering* colonialism, by displaying its scandal onto the female. . . . [As a result] colonialism itself is represented in retrospect as a female enterprise — a 'female disease.' " Accordingly, postcolonial representations associate female mastery with diseased sexuality, and corrupted femininity is offered as a historical alibi for the political error of colonialism.[61] Following Kipnis's conclusion that first-world revisionist representations envision colonialism as a *female* pathological desire for control,[62] in *Indochine*, even Eliane's ostensibly sincere maternal devotion to Camille is tainted with hints of psychological aberration and moral blindness. In this light, her very closeness with Camille has the aura of an unhealthy symbiosis, one that is all the more "unnatural" because it is based on a nonbiological bond.

Most of all, Eliane's blindness — and by implication the pitfall of colonialism — is manifested as her failure to acknowledge the hierarchical relations inherent in colonialism or, in other words, her inability to recognize difference as a given. In the film's opening voice-over, Eliane acknowledges her former utopian dream of unproblematic identification by recalling her friendship with Camille's father: "Prince N'guyen and I had been inseparable. In our youth we had thought the world consisted of inseparable things: men and women, mountains and plains, gods and humans . . . Indochina and France." As this monologue suggests, Eliane's initial error (now recognized in retrospect) has been to deny the intransigence of political differences ("Indochina and France"), which form a continuum with other irreducible oppositions of gender, geography, and ontology ("men and women, mountains and plains, gods and humans"), and, by implication, of race and generation. Eliane's blindness to difference is further suggested in another scene in which Camille asks Eliane about French women: "Do all French girls have light skin like you?" Picking up a slice of mango, Eliane replies: "The difference between people isn't skin color — it's this [showing Camille the mango]." Disclaiming her own racial determination, she adds: "I'm an Asian."

From Eliane's perspective, the story in *Indochine* is one in which her wish to erase difference is contested and finally shattered. Giving the lie

to her fantasy of symbiosis and identity with Camille, the film suspends
the two women between attributions of both sameness and difference. On
one hand, Eliane is a French colonial who was born in Indochina and has
never seen France, and Camille is an Indochinese raised as French; thus,
both possess equally marginalized and hybridized identities relative to
Indo-French colonial culture. On the other hand, the built-in polariza-
tions of the maternal melodrama offer a convenient framework to situate
Eliane and Camille along the oppositional axes of mother/daughter, East/
West, and colonizer/colonized. Furthermore, contradicting Eliane's
avowals that differences between people are not based on skin color, stark
visual contrasts of color coding and dress style emphasize essential racial
and generational differences between mother and daughter. Thus, Eliane
wears mostly black tunics and loose-fitting trousers of a "native" cut,
whereas Camille, the true "native," consistently wears Western-style
dresses in white or with a floral design. In this way, Eliane is coded as
"Asian," and Camille's sartorial typing makes her seem more "Westernized" than her mother. By adopting each other's cultural dress, the two
woman in one sense become more like each other. Yet, the schematized
visual coding governing their depiction only results in confirming,
through simple reversal, imputations of essentialized differences (Fig. 8.3).

Thus, by setting up Eliane and Camille as polar opposites — one masculine, powerful, and degraded; the other feminine, dependent, and "innocent" — *Indochine* reinstates the essentializing postures of patriarchal,
Orientalist thinking. Given the mutual imbrication of Orientalist and
patriarchal ideologies, it is not surprising that the film's schematic differ-
entiations between East and West are projected onto the most fundamentally gendered themes of sexuality and reproduction. As we have seen, the
family romance of the prototypical *Madame Butterfly* myth has operated
in contradictory ways, simultaneously invoking and negating differences
between the white European and the Asian woman. In the family romance
of *Indochine*, the distribution of sexual, reproductive, and nurturant roles
are likewise fraught with contradictions. On one hand, the Asian woman
is constructed in terms of both adolescent asexuality and mature repro-
ductivity. On the other hand, the white European woman displays a
heightened and masculinized sexuality that is presented as fundamentally
sterile and nonreproductive. In *Indochine*'s feminized recasting of the
family romance and the maternal melodrama, therefore, there emerges a
division of labor between first- and third-world woman, whereby the

Fig. 8.3. Eliane tells Camille, "The difference between people isn't skin color. . . ." Copyright © 1992 Sony Pictures Classics Inc. All rights reserved.

former bears the taint of neurotic sexuality but gains a degree of heroic grandeur as a maternal figure, and the latter, the Asian woman, is associated with the biological ("primitive") functions of the womb and the breast.

It can be said that *Indochine*, in an unusual departure from Orientalizing representational strategy, fetishizes the white European woman instead of the Asian, because it is Eliane who is sexualized, exoticized, and displayed as an object of the gaze. To an extent, of course, this effect derives from Deneuve's "star" status as a glamour icon, but it is nevertheless interesting to observe how, through the reversal of clothing symbolism already mentioned, it is Eliane who, by adopting the "native" dress of the Asian woman, takes on the fetishized associations of the Orientalized female body.

At the same time, we have seen how Eliane's character is implicated in inappropriate phallic control and unfulfilled sexuality. Further, her sexual masochism seems continuous with a sterility suggested through heavy-handed symbolism. After the failure of her affair with Jean-Baptiste and Camille's departure, her voice-over monologue ("Life continued as before — footsteps on dead leaves, sap oozing from wounded trees, and what I loved more than anything else, the smell of rubber.") is matched with shots of rubber being harvested on her plantation. Here, the sexual symbolism, with the rubber in its liquid form resembling both semen and milk, infuses Eliane's usurpation of the masculine prowess with a sense of inescapable futility and lack of issue. At the end of this sequence, such associations are reinforced in a close-up of the oozing rubber when, before she leaves for France, Eliane goes out to her plantation for the last time and scrapes the latex from a tree and allows it to run into a bowl.

In contrast, as the "other" woman and the native subject, Camille initially possesses an asexual innocence from which she then leapfrogs straight into pregnancy and maternity, with sexuality being almost totally elided in-between. If *Indochine* is to be read as an *ersatz Madame Butterfly*, with Camille as the stand-in for Butterfly, then what is truly remarkable is how her "romance" with Jean-Baptiste is completely devoid of all romantic or sexual resonance. Indeed, only one scene in the film even approaches the status of a sexual or romantic encounter between the two. This is the scene when they meet after he rescues her during a prisoners' escape attempt. And Camille remains unconscious virtually all the way through. After the couple finally escape to a hidden valley in the north, their developing relationship continues to be depicted in a markedly oblique manner. In fact, although this sequence represents the consummation of their romance, it is drastically condensed into three elliptical scenes. After they are led into the valley by a band of itinerant performers, there follows a brief dialogue when Camille tells Jean-Baptiste to leave without her. In the next scene, she wakes up in the morning thinking that he has left, only to find him crouched outside waiting for her. The next time we see her, she is already pregnant.

In simple narrative outline, *Indochine* might invite association with the interracial romance, but this romance is neither truly romantic nor explicitly sexual. Instead, whereas Eliane bears the weight of the film's projection of neurotic sexuality, Camille, on her part, is discursively confined to the biologically reproductive on one hand, and delimited to the familial and the nonsexual, on the other. Thus, in one of the only two scenes that depict a vaguely physical intimacy between Camille and Jean-Baptiste, the two are making their escape from French authorities on a boat drifting in the labyrinthine waters of Ha-long Bay. Weathering storms and harsh weather, Jean-Baptiste holds the unconscious Camille and gives her water from a bottle; when the bottle runs dry, he drains the last drops and drips them from his mouth into hers. His use of the bottle, the gesture of his oral feeding, and even the maternal pose that he strikes with Camille in his arms, all suggest the ministering of a parent to a child rather than man to woman.

Throughout, Camille remains enmeshed in vocabularies and relationships relegating her to the roles of "daughter" and of a young woman who undergoes psychological and revolutionary rebirth. Thus, having separated from Eliane, she leaves for the north to look for Jean-Baptiste and immediately casts in her lot with another family; this time it is a Vietnamese family consisting of a mother, a father, and a son. The whole saga of her northward journey, which ends with her capture and imprisonment, is articulated as a process of rebirth by which she casts off her past as colonial dependent to assume a revolutionary mission. In describing Camille's journey, Eliane uses language permeated with the rhetoric of sexual penetration and impregnation: "I often dreamed about her. . . . I saw her walking through the open countryside. The scenery entered her body like blood. I thought — now she has Indochina inside her." Later, Camille and Jean-Baptiste seek refuge in a secret valley surrounded by mountains and entered only through a hidden entrance that is closed to the outside for part of the year. It is in this womblike enclosure that Camille's revolutionary incubation takes place and where she, literally, conceives her child. Later, Camille's transformation from protected daughter and colonial subject to nationalist fighter is completed inside the Poulo-Condor prison in a process described in explicitly reproductive terms. As Gus, Eliane's friend, exclaims in consternation at one point, Poulo-Condor is notorious as a "breeding-ground" for Communists, and true to his word, Camille emerges from the prison in her new incarnation as the "Red Princess."

A daughter who is reborn into a politically defined identity, Camille is implicated in a nexus of reproductive relations that splits her into a biological mother and an abstract symbol of maternality functioning as an allegorical figure of national destiny. Yet as one who is mothered — literally by Eliane, figuratively by Jean-Baptiste — Camille herself cannot mother. A distinction must therefore be drawn between Camille's reproductive role as one who gives birth and her role as a mother who nurtures. In the same way that her sexuality and impregnation occupy only the negative space of narrative occlusion, Camille's nurturing of her son after his birth is to all intents and purposes completely elided. In fact, after the birth scene, we see her with her son only once, in the scene when Jean-Baptiste comes to pick him up while she is sleeping next to her infant on a blanket. This one and only glimpse of mother and son is immediately followed by the scene when Jean-Baptiste is arrested with their son. After this, there is no further contact between Camille and her son for the duration of the film, thus justifying Eliane's explanation to the grown-up Etienne that his mother "had no time to be attached to you. You had just been born." The bond between Etienne and Camille is finally and formally severed on the day of Camille's release from prison. Rejecting Eliane's offer to restore her "domain" to her, Camille tearfully turns her son over to Eliane, saying: "I don't want him to know how I've lived, how I suffered. I want him to be happy. Take him to France. Your Indochina is no more. It's dead."

A biological mother only in the most limited terms, Camille becomes, more importantly, the allegorical mother of her country's liberation. And in an extension of this vision, the film sees Indochinese women in general as invisible, or else it writes the "native" female body as an undifferentiated signifier of an epic maternity. Thus, it turns out to be "Indochina," rather than Camille, who provides the nurturing milk for the infant Etienne. Near the end of the film, Eliane recalls for Etienne how one day, after he and his father have been captured by the French military, an anonymous Indochinese woman is called on to give him breast milk. From this moment on, Eliane recounts, a nationalist legend about the "red Princess" is born: "At every stop Indochinese women gave you milk. That's how the legend started. All the women claimed they'd fed you — even those who had been empty of milk for years, even those who had never seen you." Through a relay of signifiers, "woman" comes to signify "Indochina," at the same time that Asian femininity is overwritten as a signifier for a subjugated fecundity that does not discriminate as to whom it succors. Ironically, of course, this "Indochina," figured abstractly as a universally nurturing breast, ultimately "reproduces" Etienne, the son of mixed racial heritage whom his biological mother rejects and for whom there is no place in the land of his birth.

As it turns out, it is Eliane who raises Etienne, and so functions practically as his "mother." We see her bringing him home to the plantataion, taking him out for ice cream, and, most striking of all, standing over his crib as "mother" when Jean-Baptiste returns to see his son. As

Eliane tells the grown-up Etienne, "In my little domain, you were my little boy." In the last scene of the film, Eliane's assumption of a maternal role is confirmed. The two are in Geneva in 1954 on the day that the Geneva agreement is signed. Although Etienne goes to the hotel where he knows Camille is staying, he leaves without seeing her. Explaining the incident to Eliane, he says that he could not imagine throwing himself at an Indochinese woman crying "mother!", and adds, "You're my mother."

The last shot in the film shows Eliane from behind, a black silhouette with outstretched arms looking over the waters of Lake Geneva. In this final image, a white European woman stands with a "son," who is not really her own and whose genealogy is perversely and multiply entwined with hers. This ending, permeated with a palpable sense of loss, is, in equal measure, invested with a profound ambiguity. Both Eliane and Etienne have now returned to a "homeland" that is, to all intents and purposes, utterly alien to them. And as Eliane looks into the distance, there is a certain monumental grandeur to her pose, as she seems to survey the history that she has witnessed and helped to create. However, it is suggested that this history, as it continues to unfold, has no place for her or Etienne, just as her affiliation with this "son" cannot ultimately provide solace for that other, greater, loss of a daughter.

At this moment, we recall that other image with which this chapter began. As in the "Miss Saigon photograph," a shadow figure haunts the hidden space off-frame. Camille's absence from this picture suggests that *Indochine*, the most explicit exposition of the Orientalized family romance to date, cannot find the discursive means to incorporate both of the protagonists between whom the dialectics of its drama have been suspended. Having begun with the "Miss Saigon photograph" and ended with this final image from *Indochine*, then, we have in fact traveled the distance between two refusals, two points of recalcitrance generated by Western discourse's refuge in the certitudes of patriarchy and racial hegeomony, and by its enmeshment with the phantasms and blind-spots of Orientalism.

POSTSCRIPT

Fatal Attraction, the very popular film released in 1987, has been denounced as Hollywood's revenge on the independent career woman and lauded for its timely exploitation of the *zeitgeist* of heterosexual relationships in the late 1980s.[63] On a more subtle level, the film's sexual politics are driven by its valorization of the traditional nuclear family. The story is that of a happily married man, Dan (Michael Douglas), who has a brief affair with a single professional woman, Alex (Glenn Close). When he tries to end the affair, Alex is consumed with envy of his happy married life and starts to terrorize him and his family. The now-famous climactic scene takes place when Alex appears in Dan's house and tries to kill his wife, Beth (Anne Archer). This confrontation between the "wife" and the "other woman," which culminates in Alex's fatal shooting by Beth (a cathartic moment that has been greeted with hoots and cheers in all the audiences I have observed), brings home in flagrant terms how the "feminist backlash" has found, in this work, its most insidious manifestation — the fantasy of women locked in a battle to the death over the right to be a wife and mother.[64]

On the other hand, relatively little attention has been given to how Alex's inscription as the "other" woman in *Fatal Attraction* is underpinned by a series of carefully elaborated allusions to *Madame Butterfly*. When Alex and Dan end their weekend by cooking a spaghetti dinner, they listen to an aria from the opera, which Alex mentions is her favorite. Later, she invites Dan to attend a performance of the opera with her. After he refuses, there is another by-now famous scene of her sitting on the floor next to a table lamp listening to another aria from the opera, and her descent into a fatal obsession is signaled by her compulsively turning the lamp on and off. Even more interesting, the original ending of the film (replacing the bathroom confrontation described earlier) shows Alex cutting her own throat while the strains of an aria from — what else? — *Madame Butterfly* play in the background.

Because my preceding discussion has argued for a reading of *Madame Butterfly* in terms of the family romance and the drama of the "other woman," it certainly seems telling that the opera should re-surface in this film in which the "other" woman's threat to the traditional family is played out in such stark and culturally potent terms. At the same time, it is intriguing to observe how the uncontainable danger represented by Alex as the "other" woman is coded as aberrant and alien by associating her with the excessively devoted and fanatical heroine of *Madame Butterfly*. Finally, because we have learned that the original ending was changed in deference to audience objections, one could speculate why *this* ending, in which a woman kills herself out of unrequited love and a unsatiable longing for family, would have seemed so unpalatable to American audiences when the same plot forms the basis of another, all-too-familiar, narrative.

NOTES

1. Edward Behr and Mark Steyn, *The Story of Miss Saigon* (New York: Arcade Publishing, 1991), 176.
2. Claude-Michel Schönberg, "The Ultimate Sacrifice," in the souvenir program for *Miss Saigon* (New York: Dewynters, n.d.), 4.
3. Ibid.
4. Ibid.
5. Ibid.
6. Alain Boublil, "From *Madame Chrysanthèmum* to *Miss Saigon*," ibid., 5.
7. See Malek Alloula, *The Colonial Harem* (Minneapolis: University of Minnesota Press, 1986); Sarah Graham-Brown, *Images of Women: The Portrayal of Women in Photography of the Middle East, 1860–1950* (New York: Columbia University Press, 1988); Rana Kabbani, *Europe's Myths of Orient* (Bloomington: Indiana University Press, 1986), 14–36; John McBratney, "Images of Indian Women in Rudyard Kipling: A Case of Doubling Discourse," *Inscriptions*, nos. 3–4 (1988), 46–57; Edward W. Said, *Orientalism* (New York: Vintage, 1979), 188, 190, 207–8; Edward W. Said, "Orientalism Reconsidered," *Race and Class* 27, no. 2 (autumn 1985), 12; Ella Shohat, "Gender and Culture of Empire: Toward a Feminist Ethnography of the Cinema," *Quarterly Review of Film and Video* 13, nos. 1–2 (winter 1991), 45–84; David Spurr, *The Rhetoric of Empire: Colonial Discourse in Journalism, Travel Writing, and Imperial Administration* (Durham, NC: Duke University Press, 1993), 170–83.
8. See Renee E. Tajima, "Lotus Blossoms Don't Bleed: Images of Asian Women," in *Making Waves: An Anthology of Writings By and About Asian American Women*, ed. Asian Women United of California (Boston: Beacon Press, 1989), 311; James S. Moy, "The Death of Asia on the American Field of Representation," in *Reading the Literatures of Asian America*, ed. Shirley Geok-lin Lim and Amy Ling (Philadelphia: Temple University Press, 1992), 349–57.
9. See Michael Klein, "Historical Memory, Film, and the Vietnam Era," in *From Hanoi to Hollywood: The Vietnam War in American Film*, ed. Linda Dittmar and Gene Michaud (New Brunswick, NJ: Rutgers University Press, 1990), 19–40.
10. Ibid., 34.
11. Harry Haines, " 'They Were Called and They Went': The Political Rehabilitation of the Vietnam Veteran," in *From Hanoi to Hollywood*, 82. See also the introductory chapter in the same volume, "America's Vietnam War Films: Marching toward Denial," by Linda Dittmar and Gene Michaud; and Gaylyn

Studlar and David Desser, "Never Having to Say You're Sorry: *Rambo*'s Rewriting of the Vietnam War," ibid., 1–15, 101–12.

12. Abigail Solomon-Godeau, "Introduction," in *Photography at the Dock: Essays on Photographic History, Institutions, and Practices* (Minneapolis: University of Minnesota Press, 1991), xxiii.

13. Susan Jeffords, *The Remasculinization of America: Gender and the Vietnam War* (Bloomington: Indiana University Press, 1989), 50, 53.

14. Ibid., 113.

15. Ibid., 93, 110.

16. Solomon-Godeau, "Reconstructing Documentary: Connie Hatch's Representational Resistance," in *Photography at the Dock*, 190.

17. This subject has been taken up by Saundra Sturdevant and Brenda Stoltzfus in their book, *Let the Good Times Roll: Prostitution in the U.S. Military in Asia* (New York: New Press, 1992). The videotape by Rachel Rivera, *Sin City Diary* (1992), provides a rare look at the experience of military prostitution from the perspectives of women. *When Heaven and Earth Changed Places: A Vietnamese Woman's Journey from War to Peace*, Le Ly Hayslip's autobiographical account of her experiences in Vietnam during the war, likewise fills in this historical gap (New York: Doubleday, 1989.) Her book (co-authored with Jay Wurts) was adapted into a 1993 film, *Heaven and Earth*, directed by Oliver Stone.

18. Jeffords, *The Remasculinization of America*, 72.

19. See Lynda E. Boose, "Techno-Masculinity and the 'Boy Eternal': From the Quagmire to the Gulf," in *Gendering War Talk*, ed. Miriam Cooke and Angela Woollacott (Princeton, NJ: Princeton University Press, 1993), 67–107; Jeffords, *The Remasculinization of America*; Michael Ryan and Douglas Kellner, *Camera Politica: The Politics and Ideology of Contemporary Hollywood Film* (Bloomington: Indiana University Press, 1988), 194–216; Gregory A. Waller, "*Rambo*: Getting to Win This Time," in *From Hanoi to Hollywood*, 101–128; Krista Walter, "Charlie Is a She: Kubrick's *Full Metal Jacket* and the Female Spectacle of Vietnam," *CineAction*, no. 12 (spring 1988), 19–22; Susan White, "Male Bonding, Hollywood Orientalism, and the Repression of the Feminine in Kubrick's *Full Metal Jacket*," in *Inventing Vietnam: The War in Film and Television*, ed. Michael Anderegg (Philadelphia: Temple University Press, 1991), 204–30.

20. See Ilsa Bick, "The Look Back in *E.T.*" *Cinema Journal* 31, no. 4 (summer 1992), 25–41; Krin Gabbard, "*Aliens* and the New Family Romance," *Post Script* 8, no. 1 (fall 1988), 29–42; Marina Heung, "Why E.T. Must Go Home: The New Family in American Cinema," *Journal of Popular Film and Television* 11, no. 2 (summer 1983), 79–85; Dave Kehr, "The New Male Melodrama," *American Film* 8, no. 6 (April 1983), 42–47; Neil Rattigan and Thomas P. McManus, "Fathers, Sons, and Brothers: Patriarchy and Guilt in 1980s American Cinema," *Journal of Popular Film and Television* 20, no. 1 (spring 1992), 15–23; Vivian Sobchack, "Child/Alien/Father: Patriarchal Crisis and Generic Exchange," *Camera Obscura* 15 (1986), 6–35; Suzanna Danuta Walters, *Lives*

Together/Worlds Apart: Daughters and Mothers in Popular Culture (Berkeley: University of California Press, 1992), chaps. 7–8.

21. Sigmund Freud, *The Standard Edition of the Complete Psychological Works*, vol. 9 (London: Hogarth Press, 1953–66), 238–39.

22. Ibid., 238.

23. Marthe Robert, *Origins of the Novel*, trans. Sacha Rabinovitch (Bloomington: Indiana University Press, 1980), 26.

24. Richard de Cordova, "A Case of Mistaken Legitimacy: Class and Generational Difference in Three Family Melodramas," in *Home Is Where the Heart Is: Studies in Melodrama and the Woman's Film*, ed. Christine Gledhill (London: British Film Institute, 1987), 256.

25. News reports on the plight of fatherless Amerasian children abandoned in Vietnam and other parts of Asia are legion. See, for example, Carol Lawson, "Sheltering Children of the Vietnam War," *New York Times* (18 April 1991), C1; Belinda Rhodes, "Sins of the Fathers," *Far Eastern Economic Review* 156, no. 24 (17 June 1993), 40–41; Lini S. Kadaba, "Her American Eyes," *Boston* 8, no. 12 (December 1990), 107, 149–50, 153–54; Claire Safran, "The Search for Donald," *Reader's Digest* (U.S.) 133, no. 797 (September 1988), 7–14; Jeanne Gordon and Mary H. J. Farrell, "Mary Nguyen's G.I. Dad Has Never Seen Her Face, but Revlon Thinks It's a Winner," *People Weekly* 32, no. 6 (7 August 1989), 54–55; Mike Sager, "The Dust of Life," *Rolling Stone*, no. 617 (14 November 1991), 56–65; Ron Mareau and Nancy Cooper, " 'Go Back to Your Country,' " *Newsweek* 111, no. 11 (14 March 1988), 34–35; Tom Padgett, " 'Like Meeting My Dad,' " *Newsweek* 115, no. 15 (9 April 1990), 65.

26. A typical treatment of the subject is illustrated by the segment on "Bui Doi: 'Dust of Life,' " in the souvenir program for *Miss Saigon*. The excerpts from Larry Engelman's book, *Tears Before the Rain: An Oral History of the Fall of South Vietnam* represent statements by Amerasian children in Vietnam, almost all of whom speak about their intense preoccupation with their lost fathers and their desire to locate them. The 1985 made-for-TV film *The Lady from Yesterday* recounts how a young Vietnamese woman comes to the United States with her son and finds the child's father, who is now married. In the 1990 film, *Vietnam Texas*, a Vietnam vet goes to Little Saigon in Houston to find the woman he left behind in Vietnam, but the primary focus of the film is his reunion with the daughter born of this liaison. In the play *Redwood Curtain* by Lanford Wilson, the leading role is that of a Vietnam vet in Oregon who encounters a young Amerasian orphan who has been adopted by Anglo-Americans and has built a fantasy world around finding the man who fathered her in Vietnam (New York: Hill and Wang, 1993).

27. See note 1.

28. While the trope of the family romance has been applied by many writers in literary analysis, others have explicitly deployed it as a framework for reading history. See Michael Rogin, *Fathers and Children: Andrew Jackson and the Subjugation of the American Indian* (New York: Alfred A. Knopf, 1975); Lynn

Hunt, *The Family Romance of the French Revolution* (Berkeley: University of California Press, 1992).

29. Louise Pratt, *Imperial Eyes: Travel Writing and Transculturation* (New York: Routledge, 1992), 4.

30. Pierre Loti, *Madame Chrysanthème*, trans. Laura Ensor (London: Routledge & Sons, Ltd, 1897); John Luther Long, "Madame Butterfly," in *Madame Butterfly, Purple Eyes, Etc.*, the American Short Story Series, vol. 25 (New York: Garrett Press, Inc., 1969), 1–86; David Belasco, "Madame Butterfly: A Tragedy of Japan," in *Six Plays* (Boston: Little, Brown, and Company, 1929), 9–32. Belasco's play was first performed at the Herald Square Theater in New York on 5 March 1900. Puccini's opera received its world premiere at La Scala, Milan, on 17 February 1904. After a disastrous opening, Puccini revised the work, which was staged again on 24 May of the same year in Brescia. Other changes were made before the Paris production of the opera in 1906. It is this revised version of 1906 that is usually performed nowadays as part of the Puccini repertory. In its 1993 season, however, the New York City opera presented its production of the original 1904 version.

In addition to numerous versions of the filmed opera, dramatizations of *Madame Butterfly* on film include a 1915 silent version based on the Long short story and starring Mary Pickford; a 1932 *Madame Butterfly* (based on the Belasco play and starring Cary Grant and Sylvia Sidney); and *Toll of the Sea* starring Anna May Wong (1922), which transcribed the basic plot into a Chinese setting. *Dream of Butterfly* (1941) is an Italian film in a modern setting about an opera singer who gives birth to an illegitimate son after being abandoned by her pianist-lover; on the night that he returns from America with his new wife, she performs Butterfly on the stage.

31. Loti's novella is strikingly devoid of sentiment and romance in depicting the romance between its protagonist, Pierre, and Chrysanthème (Madame Butterfly's antecedent). Although he is fascinated by her quaint exoticism, he takes pains to reiterate his lack of attraction to her. Rather, he barely sees her as human, and compares her variously to a doll on a teacup and to an animal. At other times, he is plainly irritated by her grotesque habits and is never under the impression that his relationship with her is based on anything other than convenience and curiosity. The lack of sentiment characteristic of this tale is demonstrated in his last encounter with her: when he arrives to bid her farewell, he finds her sitting on the floor using a mallet to test the authenticity of the coins that he has left her.

32. Michèle Barrett and Mary McIntosh, *The Anti-Social Family* (London: Verso, 1982).

33. Christian Viviani, "Who Is without Sin? The Maternal Melodrama in American Film, 1930–39," trans. Dolores Burdick, *Wide Angle* 4, no. 2, 16.

34. Ibid., 14.

35. Geoffrey Nowell-Smith, "Minnelli and Melodrama," in *Home Is Where the Heart Is*, 73.

36. E. Ann Kaplan, "Mothering, Feminism and Representation: The Maternal Melodrama and the Woman's Film 1910–40," in *Home Is Where the Heart Is*, 124–25.

37. Ibid., 123. Both Kaplan and Marthe Robert have noted how the fall of the mother provides the condition for the idealization and fixation on the father. See E. Ann Kaplan, *Motherhood and Representation: The Mother in Popular Culture and Melodrama* (New York: Routledge, 1992), 91; Robert, *Origins of the Novel*, 28–29.

38. See Gayatri Chakravorty Spivak, "Three Women's Texts and a Critique of Imperialism," *Critical Inquiry* 12 (1985), 243–61; Chandra Talpade Mohanty, "Under Western Eyes: Feminist Scholarship and Colonial Discourses," in *Third World Women and the Politics of Feminism*, ed. Chandra Talpade Mohanty, Ann Russo, and Lourdes Torres (Bloomington: Indiana University Press, 1991), 51–80; Laura E. Donaldson, *Decolonizing Feminisms: Race, Gender, and Empire-Building* (Chapel Hill: University of North Carolina Press, 1992), 41.

39. Jenny Sharpe, *Allegories of Empire: The Figure of Woman in the Colonial Text* (Minneapolis: University of Minnesota Press, 1993), 12, 23.

40. Ibid., 52.

41. Ibid., 47.

42. In Sharpe's analysis, for instance, it is the exposure of the "barbaric" ritual of *sati* imposed on the Indian woman that confers on the Victorian mother/wife a degree of dignity and moral stature purportedly denied to her subaltern counterpart. Ibid., 102–10.

43. Long, "Madame Butterfly," 84.

44. The difficulty of "placing" the role of Kate Pinkerton in Puccini's opera has been generally acknowledged, and is reflected by her diminished importance in the revised (1906) version of the opera. See Julian Smith, "Metamorphosis," in *Stagebill* (New York City Opera, Lincoln Center, July 1993), 17. Alain Boublil, the librettist for *Miss Saigon*, was well aware of what he termed "the problem of Kate Pinkerton," and went on to comment: "The problem was inherent in the story, and in the character of Ellen [the name of the "Mrs. Pinkerton" character in the musical]. Ironically, this had been Puccini's problem, too, with Kate Pinkerton." In Boublil's view, the problem in *Miss Saigon* was solved by turning Ellen "into a three-dimensional character and [exploring] the interrelation of characters in more depth." See Behr and Steyn, *The Story of Miss Saigon*, 31, 161, 129. In *Miss Saigon*, Ellen is introduced as a character in Act II: she and Chris appear in pantomime in the spotlit rear area of the set during Kim's "I Believe" solo; also, in Act III, after her meeting with Kim in the hotel room, Ellen is given an extended solo, during which she expresses her conflicted feelings toward Kim.

45. Viviani, "Who Is without Sin?" 11.

46. Helena Michie, *Sororophobia: Differences among Women in Literature and Culture* (New York: Oxford University Press, 1992), 3.

47. Donaldson, *Decolonizing Feminisms*, 17. As Sharpe notes, "The contradictions

to white femininity are more evident in a colonial context where the middle-class English woman, oscillating between a dominant position of race and a subordinate one of gender, has a restricted access to colonial authority." *Allegories of Empire*, 12.

48. See Nupur Chaudhuri and Margaret Strobel, eds., *Western Women and Imperialism: Complicity and Resistance* (Bloomington: Indiana University Press, 1992); Sharpe, *Allegories of Empire*; Vron Ware, *Beyond the Pale: White Women, Racism and History* (New York: Verso, 1992).

49. Thus, in accounting for the "splitting" between white European and Asian women that typifies colonialist texts, Jenny Sharpe concludes that "any resemblance between the two patriarchal systems threatens to collapse the East-West difference on which the social mission of colonialism is based." *Allegories of Empire*, 96.

50. Belasco, *Madame Butterfly*, 30.

51. Sharpe, *Allegories of Empire*, 29.

52. Donaldson, *Decolonizing Feminisms*, 62.

53. See John Louis DiGaetani's discussion, "The American Presence in *Madame Butterfly*," in *Puccini the Thinker: The Composer's Intellectual and Dramatic Development* (New York: Peter Lang, 1987), in which he analyzes Pinkerton's characterization as a imperialist.

54. David Henry Hwang, *M. Butterfly* (New York: Penguin, 1989), 95.

55. The play, which is based on a true story of espionage and mistaken identity, recounts the affair between a French diplomat, Rene Gallimard, and a Chinese opera singer, Song Liling, in Beijing in the 1960s. It is not until years later, after Gallimard has been arrested for passing on diplomatic secrets to Song, that he discovers that Song is really a man. Not only does Gallimard meet Song during her performance of an aria from *Madame Butterfly*, but the play continually invokes and reenacts moments from the opera to drive home its critique of Orientalism. The play suggests that Gallimard's grotesque and incredible ignorance of his lover's gender is only explicable as a manifestation of the Western/male determination to view all Asians as subservient and sexually passive — in other words, as "feminine."

Hwang's play was, of course, based on a real-life story. With the release of the 1993 film version of *M. Butterfly*, the saga of a French diplomat, Bernard Boursicot, and his Chinese lover, Shi Pei Pu, received renewed media coverage. On 15 August 1993, the *New York Times Magazine* featured a story, "The Spy Who Fell in Love with a Shadow," which was excerpted from Joyce Wadler's book on the affair, *Liaison* (New York: Bantam, 1993). On 8 October 1993, coinciding with the release of the film, the television program "20/20" produced a long segment on the story featuring interviews with the principals. All these accounts suggest fascinating ways in which the purportedly real-life details of the scandal followed the outlines of the Orientalized family romance, albeit with bizarre variations. Keeping the paradigmatic narrative in mind, we might not be surprised that, despite the publicity given to the more sensationalistic aspects of the case, which involve sexual disguise and gender misattribution, Wadler's account (which the author claims is based largely on Boursicot's revelations to her) explicitly describes how Boursicot's sexual interest in Shi faded fairly early on in their relationship. In other words, Boursicot maintained an intense involvement with Shi only because of his desire to form a relationship with "their" son, who is born when Boursicot is away from China. Unlike his mythic counterpart Pinkerton, however, Boursicot is a doting father, and he fervently desires to bring his "family" with him to Paris. Boursicot, for instance, is quoted as saying that the "most wonderful day" of his life is the day when he met his "son" for the first time (Wadler, *Liaison*, 123). Much of the succeeding narrative is then focused on his continued loyalty to Shi as the "mother" of his son and on his efforts to bring the boy to France. Later, Shi and the son, Bernard, do come to Paris. In an improbable echo of *Butterfly*, several episodes deal with how Shi and Bernard move in with Boursicot and his new consort, his homosexual lover, Thierry. According to Wadler, however, there was no overt hostility between the two rivals for Boursicot's attentions.

56. Richard Corliss's review of the film is entitled "Mademoiselle Saigon." In it, he compares the role of the "handsome French officer" to "a kind of Lieut. Pinkerton in this *Mademoiselle Saigon.*" *Time* (21 December 1992), 72–73.

57. See Nan Butler Maglin, "Reading Stepfamily Fiction," in *Women and Stepfamilies*, 255.

58. See Kaplan's chapter, "The Maternal Melodrama: The 'Phallic' Mother Paradigm," in *Motherhood and Representation*, 107–23.

59. Recent films include *Heat and Dust* (1983), *A Passage to India* (1984), *Out of Africa* (1985), *White Mischief* (1988), *Chocolat* (1988), *A World Apart* (1988), and *Outremer* (1990).

60. Laura Kipnis, " 'The Phantom Twitchings of an Amputated Limb': Sexual Spectacle in the Post-Colonial Epic," *Wide Angle* 11, no. 4, 50.

61. Ibid., 44, 50.

62. Ibid., 50.

63. See Susan Faludi's discussion of "Fatal and Fetal Visions: The Backlash in the Movies," in *Backlash: The Undeclared War Against American Women* (New York: Crown Publishers, Inc., 1991), 112–39; Richard Corliss, "Killer! *Fatal Attraction* Strikes Gold as a Parable of Sexual Guilt," *Time* (16 November 1987), 72–76, 79.

64. See Helena Michie's analysis in her interchapter, "Eliminating the Other Woman: The Excremental *Fatal Attraction*," in *Sororophobia*, 131–36.

NINE

The Law of the (Nameless) Father: Mary Shelley's *Mathilda* and the Incest Taboo

Rosaria Champagne

> Society expressly forbids that which society brings about.
> — Levi-Strauss, *The Elementary Structures of Kinship* (1969)

British Romanticism, a literary movement spanning from 1790 to 1830, is the only canon to remain almost wholly resistant to feminist challenges. Still represented by six male poets (Blake, Wordsworth, Coleridge, Keats, Byron, and Percy Shelley), Romanticism is really the last bastion of male canonicity. Both a celebration of individualism and a placekeeper in intellectual history marking the historical moment when subjectivity and perception became privileged terms, Romanticism is defined differently by the different Romantic poets. But what happens if we allow another Romantic, Mary Shelley, to define this cultural and literary movement? Because Mary Shelley is marshalled into the canon derivatively, as the daughter of William Godwin and Mary Wollstonecraft and the wife of Percy Shelley, she is only considered a "minor" Romantic, in spite of the fact that *Frankenstein* (1818) is easily the most popular piece of literature to emerge from this time period. And Mary Shelley's minor status invites critics to dismiss *Mathilda* (1819), her unpublished and suppressed novella about father-daughter incest, for a variety of reasons, the most pernicious being that the incest taboo protects and maintains patriarchal culture by rationalizing and downright outlawing certain (feminist) methods of reading. We see this revealed in the suppression of *Mathilda*, a text whose 140-year burial at the hands of hostile fathers (that is, not only Godwin, but also those literary critics who serve as canonical standard-bearers) reeks of the patriarchal privilege to silence incest narratives.[1]

Mathilda radically decenters the power of paternity and the Law of the Father in at least four ways. First, using trauma theory, we see that *Mathilda* reveals how the Law conceals the ineffectiveness of the incest taboo by preventing a woman from reading the text of her sexual abuse. Second, because silence is the daughter's duty to the father, Mary Shelley's autobiographical heroine kills her father twice, first by forcing him to name his incestuous desires, and second, by writing about her body as a text. Third, *Mathilda* presents contemporary readers with a physical document, suppressed by William Godwin until his death and then dismissed by conservative critical standards until its first publication in 1959; this 140-year suppression demonstrates the physical struggles between this father and daughter, a struggle of great cultural and historical merit that has heretofore been untold. And finally, because Mathilda "chooses"[2] neither of the two possible responses to a sexually abusive father — be raped by or kill him — and because, in trying to publish her novel, Mary Shelley transgresses this Law until stopped by her father, *Mathilda* reveals that patriarchy can be restructured, although the impact of this feminist critique of patriarchy depends largely on a woman's ability to write and (be) read.

GODWIN'S *MATHILDA*

Mary Shelley's normal knack for self-repression was slipping during the writing of *Mathilda* (between 4 August and 12 September 1819).[3] She was suffering from an acute depression that was complicated by the actions of her husband and father.[4] The death of her son William on 7 June 1819, initiated her depression. "I shall never recover that blow," Mary Shelley wrote to Amelia Curran two weeks after her son's death.[5] Percy wrote to Godwin asking him to comfort his daughter. Godwin responded with a series of letters that served to retraumatize Mary.

In his letters, Godwin castigated Mary for not rising above her sex, stating that "it is only persons of very ordinary sort, and of a pusillanimous disposition, that sink long under a calamity of this nature."[6] He then threatened to withhold love: "Remember too, though at first your nearest connections may pity you in this state, yet that when they see you fixed in selfishness and ill humour, . . . they will finally cease to love you, and scarcely learn to endure you."[7] Finally, Godwin blamed her problems on her unfortunate marriage to a "disgraceful and flagrant person" (P. Shelley, *Letters* II: 109), and at last demanded that she coerce her husband to send more money to Godwin if she wished to have further contact with her father.[8] Percy speculated in a letter to Leigh Hunt, written 15 August 1819, that Mary's obsession with winning Godwin's love was fueled by Godwin's cruelty to her. He tried to protect Mary from Godwin: "Poor Mary's spirits continue dreadfully depressed. And I cannot expose her to Godwin in this state."[9]

Percy's behavior toward Mary, although not acerbic in tone or selfish in intention, nonetheless lacked direct acknowledgment of her pain. His actions, as indicated through the aforementioned correspondence, involved concealing information from Mary. And, as Paula Feldman and Diana Scott-Kilvert suggest, "this policy of concealing unpleasant facts from Mary, which Shelley was to pursue for the rest of his life, was undoubtedly prompted by the best of motives, but it must inevitably have weakened the relationship of trust between them."[10]

Aside from protecting Mary from herself, Percy was also, as usual, doing his own thing while Mary grieved. But in the summer of 1819, he was grieving too and, together, their coping mechanisms collided. When depressed, Percy wanted more sex, for "death increased his desire";[11] Mary, six months pregnant, rejected him, in part because "making love seemed a cruelly ironic, impossible affirmation."[12] Also, superstitious as they were, Mary and Percy felt that their children's deaths (Clara the year before William) were an act of symbolic retribution for Harriet Shelley's suffering and suicide,[13] a catastrophe that arose from Percy and Mary's relationship and subsequent marriage. Mary turned to her writing in her depression. She began a new "Journal Book" with an entry that was uncharacteristically self-revealing; she began a new novella, "The Fields of Fancy" (perhaps a play on Wollstonecraft's unfinished tale "The Cave of Fancy"),[14] which she later retitled *Mathilda*.

Writing during August 1819 was not an escape from life, it *was* her life: for the first time in four years, Mary Shelley was not a mother; for the first time in five years, she didn't want to have sex with Shelley. In her first journal entry in this state of mind and body, she writes, "I begin my journal on Shelley's birthday — We have now lived five years together & if all the events of the five years were blotted out I might be happy — but to have won & then cruelly have lost all the associations of four years is not an accident to which the human mind can bend without much suffering."[15] Mary Shelley's journal is not the least bit self-disclosing and often it seems intentionally mysterious. In the place of feelings and emotions, readers will find in the journals from the early years (1817–22) page after page of seemingly innocuous lists. Most entries consist of lists of domestic chores and physical wants, books read and translated, the health of the house's inhabitants, walks taken, food eaten, laxatives needed, Percy's mood, and his relationships with others. In spite of these domestic lists and the normalcy they command, we know that during the summer of 1819, Mary Shelley's tight hold on herself was breaking down. Feldman and Scott-Kilvert address this:

> Mary does not dwell in the journal on the two major tragedies of the years 1816–22, the deaths of their daughter and son; Clara's death is briefly noted, but William's is marked only by the breaking off of entries at the end of the second notebook, leaving only the prescriptions for purges and diuretics among the endpapers of the volume as a reminder of their useless efforts to save the little boy's life.[16]

And yet, Mary Shelley's entry on 4 August 1819, asking that the last five years be "blotted out," reveals that her pain was slipping through her tight hold. During August through September 1819, Mary Shelley's rules for writing and for life did not remain in the separate domains she wished them to occupy.

Mary Shelley's desire to publish *Mathilda* and William Godwin's ability to suppress it are documented in the surviving letters and journals of Mary Shelley and Maria Gisborne. Godwin's responses to the novel, the most notable of which is his refusal to return Mary's only fair copy after years of badgering and begging by Mary Shelley and Maria Gisborne, have survived only through the writings of other people. As William St. Clair notes, for a family who threw nothing away, it is significant that important documents of the correspondence between father and daughter have not survived. Although St. Clair makes no reference to *Mathilda* in his "biography of a family" (an important omission in its own right), in its chronological place he observes that Mary's "own letters to her father have, with unimportant exceptions, all been lost, perhaps deliberately destroyed later by members of the family embarrassed by the strength of love they revealed."[17] However, because Godwin apparently wanted to deny and conceal everything that had to do with *Mathilda*, it seems more likely that Godwin himself destroyed this correspondence.[18] To explore my speculation that Godwin destroyed these letters in order to conceal and deny the father-daughter incest that threatened to occur (or occurred? Perhaps Godwin was the one "embarrassed by the strength of love" these letters revealed?), I will piece together the letters and journals of Mary Shelley and Maria Gisborne and recreate the series of events that resulted in the suppression of *Mathilda* from May 1819, until Elizabeth Nitchie edited it for North Carolina Press in 1959.

Mary Shelley gave her only fair copy of *Mathilda* to Maria Gisborne on 2 May 1819, and asked Maria to deliver this text to Godwin.[19] This in itself needs to be examined. The Shelleys never sent their only copy of a newly written work to any publisher, least of all someone as notoriously unstable as Godwin. Mary had available to her the means to have *Mathilda* recopied (or to recopy it herself). That she did not suggests to me that this text functions as a material site for Mary Shelley's self-articulation. (Was this a personal attack on daddy, as in "see you bastard, I haven't forgotten"?) Mary Shelley was not careless. That she sent Godwin her own copy, and did not even deliver the text in person, offers one of the many gaps in Mary Shelley's biography that needs to be examined.

Maria Gisborne was travelling to England, and Mary Shelley told Maria that Godwin would probably read, edit, and publish her novel.[20] On the voyage, Maria read *Mathilda* and was duly impressed. In her journal, she wrote:

I have read *Mathilda*. This most singularly interesting novel evinces the highest powers of mind in the author united to extreme delicacy of sentiment. It is written without artifice and perhaps without the technical excellence of a veteran writer — There are perhaps some little inaccuracies which, upon revision, might have been corrected: but these are trifling blemishes and I am well persuaded that the author will one day be the admiration of the world. I am confident that I should have formed this opinion had I not been acquainted with her and loved her.[21]

Maria delivered *Mathilda* to Godwin, and on 8 August 1820, she recorded his response in her journal:

Mr. G. spoke of *Mathilda*; he thinks highly of some of the parts; he does not approve of the father's letter.... The deception on the part of the father with regard to his real design is too complete; for himself he says he should most certainly not have ordered a carriage to be prepared for the pursuit, after receiving such a letter.... The subject he says is disgusting and detestable; and there ought to be, at least if it is ever published, a preface to prepare the minds of the readers.[22]

It is most interesting that Godwin declares the subject "disgusting and detestable." Curiously, Godwin calls for a preface, perhaps to deflect the autobiographical readings *Mathilda* was sure to generate? Godwin also fails to address (or Maria does not record) the transparent autobiographical connections: the fictional Mathilda is the author's age (twenty-one) in 1819; Mathilda's mother dies giving birth to her, just as Mary Wollstonecraft died giving birth to Mary Shelley; and, Mathilda's father disowns her when a male suitor arrives on the scene, just as Godwin disowned Mary when she fell in love with Percy. Furthermore, Godwin relegates *Mathilda* to a category he does not reserve for other incest tales; certainly, he fails to interpret Matthew Lewis's *The Monk* (1796), Horace Walpole's *The Castle of Otranto* (1764), or Percy Shelley's "Laon and Cynthia" (1817) and *The Cenci* (1819) as "disgusting and detestable" on the grounds that they deal with incest. Importantly — and I will deal with this issue more fully later when I "read" *Mathilda* — *Mathilda* does not just *thematize* incest as do the other Romantic texts. Mary Shelley's text goes further by teasing out the *aftereffects* of incest, which were not in cultural or intellectual currency at the time. By relying on aftereffects and not themes, Mary Shelley anticipates both Freud and the most important gesture that contemporary trauma theory offers feminist therapy: the privileging of the subject's vantage point and way of seeing. One has to ask: how did Mary Shelley know?

After receiving Mary's only fair copy of *Mathilda*, Godwin turned a deaf ear to her request for the manuscript's return. According to Peter Marshall, Godwin "quietly put the manuscript in the drawer. Three years later Mary was still trying to get it back, and the work was not published in her lifetime."[23] U. C. Knoepflmacher puts it this way: "Godwin made sure that *Mathilda* would never be published."[24] Meanwhile, in February 1822, while Mary Shelley was recovering from Percy's affair with Jane Williams (in January 1821) and Emilia Vivianti (in February 1821),[25] she wrote to Maria Gisborne asking her to steal *Mathilda* from Godwin's desk drawer. On 9 February 1822, Mary wrote to Maria: "I should like as I said when you went away — a copy of *Mathilda* — it might come out with the desk."[26] One month later, on 7 March 1822, Mary wrote again: "Could you not in any way write [to Godwin] for *Mathilda? —* I want it very much."[27] Maria's response was not encouraging. Godwin, who was subject to frequent and wild mood swings, was not receiving the Gisbornes. Maria wrote to Mary: "With regard to *Mathilda* . . . as your father has put a stop to all intercourse between us, I am at a loss what step to take."[28]

Three years later, Mary was still anxious for *Mathilda*'s return and apparently concerned that Maria Gisborne was not transmitting her desires to Godwin. On 10 April 1822, she wrote an exhaustive letter to Maria wavering between her desperation to get *Mathilda* back and her concern over Shelley's recent arrest. As in all previous correspondence with Maria, this letter constructs Godwin as audience:

> I wish, my dear Mrs. Gisborne, that you would send Godwin, at Nash's Esq. Dover Street — I wish him to have an account of the fray [Shelley's arrest for cursing at an Italian officer], and, you will thus save me the trouble of writing it over again, for what with writing and talking about it, I am quite tired — In a late letter of mine to my father, I requested him to send you *Mathilda* — I hope that he has complied with my desire, and, in that case, that you will get it copied, and send it to me by the first opportunity.[29]

Significantly, this letter demonstrates, among other things, how Mary weaves *Mathilda*'s absence into the daily fabric of domestic anxiety and life with Percy. In her correspondence, she makes similar gestures to her dead children, alluding to them in such a way that incorporates them into the present. *Mathilda* thus functions in Mary Shelley's letters and journals as a relic of herself, as a dead child (or transmogrification of herself as a child?) like William and Clara, who is allowed to haunt the present. (One can profitably compare this use of "child" with the recent focus in the contemporary recovery movement on "the child within," which describes the abused and stifled child within the body of the adult survivor.) It is only after Percy dies (8 July 1822) that Mary Shelley begins to construct *Mathilda* as a story foreshadowing her husband's death.

In the letter that tells Maria Gisborne that Percy and Edward Williams drowned at sea when the *Don Juan* capsized, Mary Shelley also reveals that she displaces her needs so that the comfort she asks for will not really soothe her pain. In this 15 August 1822 letter, Mary begins by restating a dream that Percy had before he took the fateful voyage. Mary writes:

> [Percy] dreamt that lying as he did in bed Edward & Jane came into him, they were in the most horrible condition, their bodies lacerated — their bones starting through their skin, the faces pale yet stained with blood, they could hardly walk, but Edward was the weakest & Jane was supporting him — Edward said — "Get up Shelley, the sea is flooding the house & it is all coming down." S. got up, he thought, & went to the window that looked on the terrace & the sea & thought

he saw the sea rushing in. Suddenly his vision changed & *he saw the figure of himself strangling me.*[30]

When describing to Maria Gisborne how she and Jane reclaimed their husbands' drowned bodies, Mary relies on Mathilda's experience: "it must have been fearful to see us — two poor, wild, aghast creatures — driving like Mathilda towards the sea to learn if we were forever doomed to misery."[31] Wife-murder is to the present as incest is to the past. Percy's dream and Mathilda's fate foretell the future: even though Mary does not die, her role as Percy's wife dies with him. Likewise, in *Mathilda*, the daughter replaces the mother as object of sexual desire. This displacement cancels out Mathilda's childhood and adulthood simultaneously: the father's transgressive sexuality kills the child, whereas, psychologically, the exchange of the live woman for the dead makes it so Mathilda fears being alive. Mathilda follows her father to the sea, where he has drowned; likewise, Percy follows his 7 July dream to the sea, where he meets the same fate.

By displacing her past and condensing her future, *Mathilda* becomes the site of Mary Shelley's unconscious rereading of her past, especially her adolescence, in an effort to understand how her past has transformed into the present. Its import was not lost on the author herself. One year later, in 1823, she reflects on this: "But it seems to me in what I have hitherto written I have done nothing but prophecy what has arrived. . . . *Mathilda* foretells even many small circumstances most truly."[32] It must have seemed appropriate, given Mary Shelley's obsessions about privacy, concealment, and deception, that her most self-revealing text was never published in her lifetime.

MARY'S *MATHILDA*

Mathilda is a novella about a twenty-one-year-old woman dying of consumption whose "last task" involves breaking the silence of father-daughter incest by writing her history for Woodville, the Shelleyan poet who, had it not been for the sexual stigma of her body, should have been her suitor. After her mother dies giving birth to her, her father departs to wander the world while an elderly maiden aunt raises Mathilda in isolation in Scotland. After sixteen years, her nameless father returns; suddenly, the aunt dies, and Mathilda moves with her father to London. The father sexualizes almost every moment between them until a "young man of rank" visits their abode; this eligible suitor for Mathilda brings the father's sexual desire to a crisis. The father responds by turning the young man away, emotionally battering his daughter, and finally, physically moving with his daughter back to the house that he shared with his late wife, Diana. Eerily, the house has been preserved as a shrine to Diana; everything is as it was sixteen years earlier. Once there, the father explains that Mathilda is to act as Diana once had. That is, his daughter is now to live with him as his wife.

The night after he declares his incestuous plan and before he physically acts on it, the father abandons Mathilda once again, this time leaving behind a suicide note in which he blames Mathilda for his sexual desire. Mathilda reads his suicide note, then follows his track by carriage, only to reclaim his dead body from the sea. After his death, Mathilda runs away from her guardians and lives ascetically in an isolated part of the country. There she meets a poet, Woodville, and rejects him as a suitor because she feels tainted by her father. Wanting a spiritual tie instead, she tries to engage Woodville in a suicide pact (as Percy had suggested to Mary before their elopement); with his rejection comes the onset of her consumption. Attempting to make sense of her life and explain her strange secrecy to Woodville, Mathilda writes her history of incest.

Mathilda's concession to write her history for Woodville initiates the plot of *Mathilda*. Because patriarchy codifies denial by making certain questions and observations "unthinkable" (both consciously, through social pressure, and unconsciously, through denial), Mathilda breaks the silence only when she is free to do so: after her father is dead and she is dying. Momentarily resisting the imposed silence the Law demands, Mathilda can represent the unthinkable. She writes: "While life was strong within me I thought indeed that there was a sacred horror in my tale that rendered it unfit for utterance, and now, about to die, I pollute its mythic terrors."[33] Importantly, her "freedom" comes with the price of death; although her father is dead, the Law still reigns. This is made clear by the father's namelessness: his name is "only" father; he therefore is ever-present, not simply historically specific. He is the Law, the role, the cultural placekeeper.

The incest taboo in cultural, psychoanalytic, and political permutations shows that the father need not seduce his daughter; instead, he imputes his desire onto her. Good daughters obey their fathers; good daughters anticipate and fulfill their father's needs; good daughters seduce their fathers so that their fathers do not have to be the agents of transgression. In this way, the Law restructures and reconstitutes the daughter and her desires.[34] After sixteen years of parental abandonment, with mother dead from bearing Mathilda and himself absent because her presence commands his grief, the father returns. It is he who sexualizes the reunion: "I cannot tell you how ardently I desire to see my Mathilda," the father writes in a letter to the aunt (186). Mathilda tells us: "As he approached, his desire to see me became more and more ardent" (187). Here we see how Mathilda takes over her father's vocabulary, thereby textually enacting the imputation of desire. He cannot (at this point) speak his desire, so she says it for him.

At her father's return, Mathilda is a love-starved child with no concept or framework in which to understand sexuality. Her aunt (who acted as her legal guardian out of duty, not compassion [182]) made herself available only during specific hours and then only twice a day (182). Her anti-Wollstonecraft aunt forbids her to befriend girls her own age because she might "catch" their Scottish accent ("great pain was taken that my tongue should not disgrace my English origin" [183]). When her father arrives, the possibility that he may love her (something Mathilda has never known) makes her feel as if she is a new person: "I felt as if I were recreated and had about me all the freshness and life of a new being: I was, as it were, transported" (188–89). She is not "awakened" sexually, however, and when her desire to be parented comes with the price of sexual abuse, she does not know that her father's lust will appropriate her need for care and protection: "I had no idea that misery could arise from love, and this lesson that all at last must learn was taught me in a manner few are obliged to receive it" (198). Here we see that the father's misappropriation of Mathilda's love confuses her sense of boundaries and reality. By calling incest "love," he teaches her a lesson that not "all" must learn. E. Sue Blume explains this lesson in detail: "As a distortion of intimacy, incest teaches many contradictions: to be cared about is to be taken from, to need someone puts one at risk of being taken advantage of, and to be given to leads to expected payback. For the incested child, intimacy equals danger and damage."[35]

Within the rules of the Law, the father's sexual desire is projected onto the daughter, who does his bidding and takes his fall. As Jane Gallop explains, "The Oedipus Complex, the incest taboo, the law forbidding intercourse between father and daughter, covers over a seduction, masks it so it goes unrecognized."[36] And, Luce Irigaray emphasizes that "the *seduction function of the law* [works when it] suspends the realization of a seduced desire. . . . The law organizes and arranges the world of fantasy at least as much as it forbids, interprets and symbolizes it."[37] Mathilda's power is located in her ability to create her own subjectivity — in trauma theory, to differentiate enough from her abuser so that she knows that there exists a difference between wanting to be loved and wanting to be fucked: "I disobeyed no command, I ate no apple, and yet I was ruthlessly driven from [Paradise]. Alas! My companion did, and I was precipitated in his fall" (198).

Writing about her incest makes the experience of incest real for Mathilda; her naming the event offers a counterdiscourse to the Law. Mathilda takes the risk of writing her own text while reading her father's Law; but because she knows she is dying, she also knows she can afford this risk.

However, if incest is the secret women keep from themselves (although a highly contested figure, Blume states that "half of all incest survivors do not know that the abuse occurred"),[38] then Mary Shelley is playing a much pricier game than her heroine. If, as I suspect, Mary Shelley writes her way into understanding her "excessive and romantic" love for Godwin as incestuous, then her reconstructed memories of love/incest deepen any explanation for why the summer of 1819 was so traumatic. When an incest survivor starts to remember, her memories are accompanied by the feelings of repulsion and terror she was not allowed to "indulge" as a child.[39] Most of what we know about Mary Shelley's depression during this summer we know through reading the absence: no sex with Percy,[40] little correspondence,[41] a journal filled with obsessive-compulsive lists.[42] She made "confessions" only when she thought people were not listening. To Leigh Hunt she wrote, "I ought to have died on the 7th of June last."[43] Mary Shelley "lived" through her writing of *Mathilda*. In the textual embodiment of incest, for whatever reason, she kept herself sane. The irony, of course, is that those around her thought she was going mad. By writing *Mathilda*, Mary Shelley was momentarily freed from the seduction of the Law: "The seduction fantasy is really about seducing the daughter to not read her own text, but instead to obey the law of the father."[44]

The first time Mathilda falls for the seduction of the Law, she unwittingly echoes her father's words spoken sixteen years before regarding the intrusion of third parties. At this point in the text, the father has moved

Mathilda from Scotland to London and, seemingly without conscious intent, is grooming Mathilda to become his wife replacement. Just as sixteen years earlier, when the father and Diana "seldom admitted a third to their society" (180), so, too, now Mathilda says: "It was a subject of regret to me whenever we were joined by a third party" (190). In his life with Diana, the father's spoken aversion to the presence of a third party mystically calls forth Mathilda, whose presence killed his wife. And now, Mathilda's internalization of her father's aversion to outsiders seems to make material a "young man of rank," whose presence galvanizes the father's violent desire.

According to M. M. Bakhtin in "The Problem of the Text," the third party holds a special dialogic relation to the text: "Each dialogue takes place as if against the background of the responsive understanding of an invisibly present third party who stands above all participants in the dialogue."[45] But, in an incestuous household, third parties are not welcome because they threaten to expose how the Law of the Father denies, trivializes, or distorts the daughter's experience; they also threaten to expose the father's desire itself.[46]

The father's behavior toward Mathilda changes in response to her sexual potential, not her behavior: "I now remember that my father was restless and uneasy whenever this [third party] visited us, and when we talked together [father] watched us with the greatest apparent anxiety" (91). The father typifies the behavior of seductive fathers, who

reacted to their daughter's emerging sexuality either with an attempt to establish total control or with total rejection. The message they conveyed to their daughters was, in effect, "As long as you remain my little girl, everything will be fine; but if you try to grow up, there will be hell to pay."[47]

Mathilda is paralyzed by her father's change in attitude and behavior, especially because she cares very little for this "young man of rank." Importantly, this third party becomes significant because of what he does (brings the father's incestuous desire into crisis), not who he is; this third party, like the father, has an unstable relationship to patriarchy. Like the father, his namelessness makes his power to permeate Mathilda's life even greater.

Mathilda blames herself-in-body (the incested daughter knows that her body always-already puts her in jeopardy) and her self-in-narrative for her father's shift: "I seem perhaps to have dashed into the description. . . . In one sentence I have passed from the idea of unspeakable happiness to that of unspeakable grief, but they were this closely linked together" (193). We know her self-blame is repeated in the act of writing, of creating a narrative, because the geography of her terror is the "sentence" that moves too swiftly. The "link" that Mathilda knows but cannot define or see shows that the Law must never be made into narrative; in breaking this commandment, Mathilda has exposed an important connection among narrative, representation, and violence.

Mathilda reads the text of her father's behavior while she writes her own text for Woodville; furthermore, she constructs a reading of her father's text that he would not endorse. Mathilda's grief is thus so "unspeakable" because the Father's Law imposes silence. This textual moment exposes a gap, a stopping of patriarchal momentum: Mathilda has not yet realized that, once the incest is spoken (that is, represented or made discursively "real"), her "desire" will be overlaid by her father's Law. The guilt and terror and filth that she will use to describe herself and her wants are the by-products of desire cut off from its origin.[48]

Equally important, Mary Shelley is also burdened by this convolution of desire and displacement, which explains why the covert incest described in her own admission (her "excessive and romantic" love, which is really her inscription and imputation of his desire according to the Law) can find voice only through the fictional Mathilda's body. Denial is not the simple act of knowing the truth and consciously lying about it to the outside world. Rather, denial is a complicated coping mechanism that relies on and is shaped by the reading and writing of one's own body as text: if I don't name it, it didn't happen; if I don't write about it, I won't make it real; because its reality depends on my reading, I won't read the experiences of my body. Because the Law determines what a woman reads about her body's experiences, it also makes reading and writing unlawful acts for the survivor of sexual abuse: "Laws shape experiences we have before we have them."[49] In the summer of 1819 in the text of Mary Shelley's life, both the "fictional" Mathilda and the "real"[50] Mary Shelley are at the precipice of the Father's Law: although silence no longer seems natural, silence now takes on a greater power. It is both life saving (for the daughter who can never grow up) and life threatening (for the woman who can create herself and her own subjectivity only if she reads the text her father forbids and then writes herself out of the role he has constructed for her).

The father responds to Mathilda's physical maturation by moving her geographically and symbolically backward:

He intended to remove with me to his estate in Yorkshire. . . . This estate was that which he had inhabited in childhood and near which my mother resided while a girl; this was the scene of their youthful loves and where they had lived after their marriage; in happier days my father had often told me that however he might appear weaned from his widow sorrow, and free from bitter recollections elsewhere, yet he would never dare visit the spot where he had enjoyed her society or trust himself to see the rooms that so many years ago they had inhabited together. . . . And now while he suffered intense misery he determined to plunge into still more intense, and strove for greater emotion than that which already tore him. (194)

This passage reveals the father advancing the paternal power to plot the rape of his daughter. First, by fitting his daughter for the role of his dead wife, he differentiates — or fails to differentiate — between mother and daughter. Second, this passage exposes the beginnings of Mathilda's denial. In agreeing to read her father's text and embody her father's reading, Mathilda does not suspect her developing body *also functions* as a third party (along with Woodville) that galvanizes their household crisis.

Whereas a psychoanalytic framework shows how the Law projects the father's desire onto the daughter who does his bidding and takes his fall, an anthropological/sociological paradigm further problematizes the possibility of a daughter knowing or acting on her desire by defining her body as a "gift." By moving Mathilda backward, instead of letting her grow up and out of his house, the father exchanges his daughter for his wife. According to Claude Levi-Strauss, "The prohibition of incest is less a rule prohibiting marriage with the mother, sister, or daughter, than a rule obliging the mother, sister, or daughter to be given to others. It is the supreme rule of the gift."[51] The father who refuses to give to other men the gift of his daughter and fails to exchange her as a commodity in the marketplace of patriarchy commits the ultimate act of narcissism by cannibalizing the "gift." Just as readers cannot help but appropriate texts that they read (this is the cruder rendition of "the reader constructs the text"), so Mathilda's father uses the act of reading as incest foreplay: "When I was last here, your mother read Dante to me; you shall go on where she left off" (195).

The Law of the Father makes possible the daughter's place as gift; but ironically, by fitting Mathilda for Diana's role, the father makes himself vulnerable to parricide. By moving history backward, he moves himself into the territory of the living dead: "Although more than sixteen years had passed since [Diana's] death, nothing had been changed; her work box, her writing desk were still there and in her room a book lay open on the table as she had left it" (194–95). This open book functions as a symbol of textual necrophilia: if reading is like incest because both are acts of the cannibal, then the father is eating and reading and fucking the dead.[52] Most importantly, the exchange of women, although central to the proliferation of culture, is so pervasive that both its agency and its effects go unnoticed. According to Gayle Rubin in "The Traffic in Women," because "women do not have the same rights [as men] either to themselves or to their male kin"[53] women "are in no position to realize the benefits of their own circulation."[54] Of course Mathilda is burdened by a guilt that cannot be expressed; something as routine as the traffic in women becomes representable only when it exceeds the Law of the Father. Ironically, whereas incest is representable to the father, it is often unrepresentable to the daughter ("secrecy, a necessary component of control, is imposed on the victim of incest").[55] This business of who gets to represent the victimization of a woman's body is significant because one's subjectivity depends on the act of representation. Thus, Mary Shelley's disrespect for the Law takes shape in the writing of her fiction, where she commits the ultimate act of bad-daughter behavior: she reads and writes the text of her body, a text that Godwin has censored.

W. Arens has suggested that incest has been linked to cannibalism because, historically, sexual and nutritional excess signified the savage.[56] If "you are what you eat," we can see that the father's Law fashions Mathilda in another way, as murderer. Mathilda unwittingly "kills" her father because the presence of her body makes his role as father untenable. Because "the body is a model which can stand for any bounded system,"[57] we see that the father has cannibalized his way beyond satiation. Laws function not merely to define lawful behavior, but also to inscribe "how, when, [and] in what ways to be lawless."[58] Thus, the father who transgresses the incest taboo has committed a representable crime. Unlike the daughter's, his transgression is not "unspeakable." Mathilda becomes introduced to the connection between reading and cannibalism when she muses: "I did not yet know of the crime there may be in involuntary feeling" (197). Mathilda does not yet know that all reading is an act of appropriation and ingestion and that we are what we read and misread. Therefore, she misreads the limitations of her power to "correct" her father's feelings. Before she knows about her father's sexual desire for her, she thinks, "when I know his secret then will I pour a balm into his soul and again I shall enjoy the ravishing delight of beholding his smile" (197). But after she embodies the text of his sexual desire, she becomes irrevocably and indescribably changed; she feels soiled: "I gained his secret and we were both lost forever" (197). The nameless father rapes his daughter with desire, not touch; only through Mathilda's embodiment (in body and text) of his crime can we find his trace.

Although *Mathilda* is a story of incest that does not involve touch, Mathilda becomes touched by her father's sexual desire when she reads the text of that desire. Just as Mary Shelley lived during the summer of 1819 through the act of writing, it is through the act of reading that Mathilda is raped. The horror of this father's crime is located in its intangibility; because her rape does not fit the socially inscribed "model" standard (vaginal penetration), only Mathilda's aftereffects are materially evident. Mathilda is raped by words, by gestures, by her father's gaze, and by the textual gaps in all of these. Her father says: "You are the sole, the agonizing cause of all I suffer, of all I must suffer until I die. Now, beware! Be silent! Do not urge me to your destruction. . . . My daughter, I love you!" (200–201). The trap here is not lost on Mathilda: she wants her father to love her, but not sexually. Although the Law protects the father by always trivializing incest, in this case, by recognizing physical rape as more "legitimate" than the psychological rape Mathilda endures, the fact that someone else's victimization is more physical does not lessen Mathilda's suffering.[59] There are many ways of minimizing sexual abuse, and one is to change the subject, thereby indicating that, in this case, the construction of Mathilda's subjectivity is "wrong" because she was not physically violated.

Mathilda was betrayed, and then abandoned. The source of both was her father's desire to possess her sexually; although he did not use his penis to penetrate her, the combination of his power and desire penetrated her past and present. His power/desire prevented her entry into a future as an adult because adulthood requires taking stock of one's past, whereas being a good daughter involves keeping the (father's) secret of incest, even from oneself.

Mathilda dies a good daughter. And in an uncharacteristic gesture, I

imagine that Mary Shelley acts like a bad daughter in the summer of
1819. Mary Shelley took stock of her life the summer of 1819. She had
been a good girl, and nevertheless her husband had cheated on her, her
children had died, and, once again, Godwin had threatened to abandon
her if she didn't "cheer up." Because the image she carried of herself and
her life died with her children, Mary Shelley was free to explore this
previously hidden psychological terrain possibly triggered by this loss.
Importantly, she allowed herself this freedom only when she thought
people would not take her seriously, or literally. Thus, her identification
with incest was filtered into the "lie" of her fiction.

This permeation of truth and lies can also be understood as a function
of the Law. Irigaray and Gallop revise Lacan's configuration of the Freudian father's Law, which simplifies the power of patriarchal authority by
separating it from the penis with which it wields its power. According to
Lacan, "The phallus is a signifier . . . intended to designate as a whole the
effects of the signified."[60] Although Gallop contends that "it is only the
law — and not the body — which constitutes [the father] as patriarch,"[61]
she makes the connection between representation and social control that
Lacan bypasses: "as long as the attribute of power is a phallus which refers
to and can be confused . . . with a penis, this confusion will support a
structure in which it seems reasonable that men have power and women
do not."[62] Mary Shelley adds another dimension to the Law by "lying"
about her body, which is to say, telling the construction of the truth the
father will not hear unless it is contextualized in fiction.

Mathilda carefully weighs the differences between the construction/
invention of one's history and the telling of lies. After her father's suicide,
her identity as daughter is also killed; thus Mathilda is not sure what to
do with her past, but she knows she must do something with it. Should
she consciously lie to herself and "over the deep grave of my secret . . .
heap an impenetrable heap of false smiles and words?" (216). She says she
"dare not," because to "do nothing" with her past (that is, to not put it in
narrative and thus construct/record it) or to bury it with false narratives
would allow it to become an unimaginable weight. She considers feigning
her own death, so that her heirs can claim the inheritance she feels has
prostituted her, and decides against this only because self-support would
involve writing, which would necessitate her (even veiled) self-disclosure
of her own history. Mathilda feels stuck because all systems for making

sense of her past seem a lie. Because her father's crime was a crime of desire, Mathilda must name (invent, construct, make up, represent, write) the crime in order to "escape" it (216).

But herein springs the trap of the phallus/penis symbol/body Law. To name the crime is to give it shape and power; not to name it is to be silenced by it, to be the object of the Law's desire and power once again. Unlike Mary Shelley, who risks the Law by writing *Mathilda*, Mathilda decides to not decide. And so, Mathilda copes by never growing up. Mathilda says, "In solitude only shall I be myself" (216). She contrives her own death, which symbolizes her death-as-daughter. In doing so, she leaves herself no place to live within the symbolic or cultural order. Mathilda writes:

I escaped. I left my guardian's house and I was never heard of again; it was believed from the letters that I left and other circumstances that I planned that I had destroyed myself. I was sought after therefore with less care than would otherwise have been the case; and soon all trace and memory of me was lost. (219)

In order to escape to a place where she can write her history, Mathilda must construct the presence of a "third" party who reads her traces, those implications she drops like bread crumbs and "forgets" so that she may eventually remember.

As the penis/phallus conveniently confuses the agency of patriarchal Law, *Mathilda* problematizes another element of the Law, that of the role of the absent mother. In his suicide/abandonment letter, the father writes to Mathilda: "In my madness I dared say to myself — Diana died to give [Mathilda] birth; her mother's spirit was transferred into her frame, and she ought to be as Diana to me" (210). As I argued earlier, the economy of exchange explains and legitimizes the father's brandishing of power so that the incest taboo organizes this exchange by mediating a relationship between the incestuous father and the mother's absence; because Diana died in the process of giving birth to Mathilda, the father has the right (within the Law) to exchange/change daughter for wife. Mathilda "kills" her father by resisting the exchange.

However, Mathilda resists in a complicated fashion. She does not say or do anything. Rather, she disobeys by not taking on her role as seductress, by not anticipating what her father wants and thus saving him the trouble of transgression by embodying his sexual desire. Furthermore, when she orders a carriage and follows her father after his departure, she does so because she finds her identity in her role as daughter: if he "dies" then she "dies." She wants to exonerate herself as her father's murderer; by resisting the Law, she kills his role and because "it is only the law — and not the body — which constitutes [the father] as patriarch,"[63] she has unwittingly found him out, undressed the father, exposed his phallus as penis. Of her tale, Mathilda says "Oedipus is about to die" (176). (And it is worth pointing out that Oedipus, at death, is reconciled to his daughter, but his death also forces her into the market of exchange.) Importantly, Mathilda is too late to fulfill the script of the Law, and therefore Mary Shelley sees to it that she successfully resists the Law. Thus, in reclaiming her father's dead body, Mathilda functions as a Bakhtinian "third party" who serves as the most important reader on the scene.

In constructing herself and inventing her history, Mathilda manifests many symptoms that result from incest: "splitting,"[64] feeling unable to mourn or name her pain, embodying self-blame and guilt, perceiving herself as soiled, and sensing that she has committed some crime that she cannot name. Simply put, Mathilda embodies incest:

My father had for ever deserted me, leaving me only memories which set an eternal barrier between me and my fellow creatures. I was indeed fellow to none. ... Unlawful and detestable passion had poured its poison into my ears and changed all my blood, so that it was no longer the kindly stream that supports life but a cold fountain of bitterness corrupted in its very source. (229)

First, patriarchal societies claim that incest is harmless because children forget or lie,[65] good for daughters because it makes them more sexually open,[66] or simply the victim's deserving fault;[67] next, patriarchal culture makes laws ensuring that legal authorities read the text of a woman's body in these ways.[68] Eventually, women write the texts of their bodies in accordance with this prescription. Because we learn to read and write within culture and ideology, what is most devastating about the lessons that patriarchal cultures teach about incest is that, eventually, the survivor herself does not know how her body could have "allowed" this to happen. And when one feels betrayed by one's body, one feels responsible for the crimes that have been committed. After the intrusion of incest, Mathilda feels that the blood that pulses inside her is not really hers anymore. This creates two related incest aftereffects for Mathilda: self-blame and splitting.

The Law constructs the daughter as always-already at fault. As I have said, she does her father's bidding (by becoming the seductress, if necessary) and takes his fall. Even though Mathilda does not allow the father to project the role of seductress onto her, she nevertheless feels responsible, if not for his sexual desire, then for the fact that she did not sacrifice herself, use her body as a wedge to separate the father from his sexual desire by embodying it, by "wanting" it. She says, "I believed myself to be polluted by the unnatural love I had inspired, and that I was a creature cursed and set apart by nature" (238). Because "the remembrance haunts [Mathilda] like a crime" (218), she responds by splitting, by not matching her depression to its source. She has to force herself to "feel": "I often said to myself, my father is dead. He loved me with a guilty passion, and stung by remorse and despair he killed himself. Why is it that I feel no horror?" (215). Instead of feeling pain and anguish, she bypasses her body, and tells herself what and how to feel.

Mathilda experiences a time-warp between feelings and reactions because splitting reverses the process of reaction. Instead of feeling pain, and then thinking about why she feels this pain, Mathilda inverts this: "I do not weep or sigh; but I must reason with myself, and force myself to feel sorrow and despair" (215). As she becomes more practiced at splitting, she reads history not to understand the feelings of others, but to know how she should feel: "I began to study more . . . to lose my individuality among the crowd that had existed before me" (222). (Importantly, Mathilda is not trying to write her experience into the master-narrative of history — she says, "perhaps a history such as mine had better die with me" [175]; rather, she tries to efface her history by borrowing the feelings of others.) Mathilda becomes so practiced at splitting that she stops living in her body and instead merges with her father; she converts the memory of her father's love into "the life of my life" (223). Eventually, when splitting seems more natural than feeling, Mathilda says, "Even my pleasures were endured, not enjoyed" (223). And finally, splitting from the memory of incest causes Mathilda to "forget." She therefore starts to believe she has made it all up (another aftereffect of incest): "There were periods, dreadful ones, during which I despaired — and doubted the existence of all duty and the reality of [the] crime" (221).

Secrecy, an element always present in crimes of incest, either eliminates or displaces the "third party" who reads and confirms the violation. Woodville exemplifies the displaced third party whom Mathilda allows to read her story only when she is dying. And, because Woodville's power as a third party has been displaced, Mathilda says, in spite of Woodville's place as reader, "Who can be more solitary even in a crowd than one whose history and the never ending feelings and remembrances arising from it is known to no living soul" (216). Mathilda can never grow into the role of adult woman ("I must shrink before the eye of man lest he should read my father's guilt in my glazed eyes" [216]) because, unlike Mary Shelley, Mathilda writes her way into death, not life.

MY MATHILDA

As suggested earlier, as a literary movement Romanticism demanded (and its canonization still demands) the privileging of the father's word over the daughter's; and in fact, it predetermines her silence. But in the summer of 1819, Mary Shelley broke this silence and used writing to heal her pain, specifically by creating an autobiographical character whose pain served to bear witness to her pain. And, whatever the "real" source of Mary Shelley's pain, she chose the theme of incest to reflect it. If, as the recovery movement suggests and Lacanian psychoanalysis declares (and as I believe), writing actually "makes" events narratively real and therefore representable by repairing secrets, impressions, dreams, and other events that occupy unnarrativized psychic places into language, then it is significant that Mary Shelley chose to write about incest — painful, betraying, self-splitting incest — to represent "romantic and excessive" love between a father and daughter. Along with writing, Mary Shelley healed through reading, the other side of the coin. Without reading, even physical trauma is not "real" because it can never be made real by a Bakhtinian third party who reads its place. (Importantly, the reader can be an outside "third party," the writer herself, or both.) When the unnamed subject is incest, the only way to make real one's anger and have an existing document stand in for that pain, even when the subject herself is absent or playing the role of the third party, is through writing and then reading. In fact, without the act of narrative, the body of an incest survivor is forever trapped; by not constructing her anger outside her body, the survivor's body remains only a signifier of despair.

A century after Mary Shelley wrote *Mathilda*, Sigmund Freud and Josef Breuer, in analysis with female hysterics, developed the "talking cure," which is a method through which subjects construct their demons through, and deposit them in, language. Today, a predominance of self-help books recommend that subjects write their way back to psychological health. In Ellen Bass and Laura Davis's *The Courage to Heal*, writing is necessary to healing:

So often, survivors had their experiences denied, trivialized or distorted. Writing is an important avenue for healing because it gives you the opportunity to define your own reality.... By going back and writing about what happened, you also reexperience feelings and are able to grieve. You excavate the sites in which you've buried memory and pain, dread and fury. You relive your history.[69]

Unlike Freud's hysterics, who produced "talk" that became the intellectual property of Freud himself, Bass and Davis suggest that feminist self-help theory restores agency to the writing subject.

There are many ways to minimize or deny the possibility that *Mathilda* may function as the site of Mary Shelley's reconstruction of her "excessive and romantic" (Shelley's words) "love" (to patriarchy; "incest" to me) for Godwin. One way involves declaring that if she were *really* incested by Godwin, then she would have "said" it somewhere else, somewhere more legitimate than in her fiction. Even if enforcers of patriarchal institutions believed sexual abuse survivors, obligating Mary Shelley to "confess" would naively imply that traumatic memories reside in accessible psychic places. In truth, unless the subject reveals signs of psychosis, experiences with past trauma are "civilized" into silent aftereffects so that the body "talks" in disguised ways. This results in behaviors, nightmares, addictions, and a multitude of fears, visions, and panic attacks; these "serve" the trauma survivor by keeping her secret. And, these aftereffects are evidenced in the "gaps" of Mary Shelley's letters and journals.

Mary Shelley manages, and perhaps even conceals, her identification with incest by letting her fiction become the repository for this "excessive and romantic" father/daughter connection. Any reader of Mary Shelley's life (especially during the writing of *Mathilda*) who minimizes the place of telling truths (making self-disclosures) within the narrative of "lies" (fiction) reveals how the incest taboo is a taboo against writing and reading, not against the act of sexual abuse. As W. Arens states, "The literature [on incest] suggests quite clearly that as a rule intellectuals have either ignored or unintentionally denied the existence of incest in propounding their theories about the universality of the prohibition."[70] Arens asks academics to interrogate the intellectual coercion — the Law — which denies the fact of incest (and its privileged place in maintaining patriarchal culture) by accepting without question that the taboo successfully outlaws the crime.

Accepting the spirit of this challenge, Diane Price Herndl focuses on the subject's power to write her way out of the Law:

As the "writer," the woman becomes not just a subject, but a subject who produces that which is visible and which will be visible even in her absence. She produces a discourse which will take her place. . . . Writing can provide an other to "hear" her discourse, even if such another is not present; "she" can be "read." That is, she can be seen. Writing can become the Other, insofar as she inscribes herself, represents herself in her text. Writing separates her from the unbearable presence of experience by re-presenting it as other, as that which is written, as the not-me. . . . But writing is a poison as well as a remedy, because to cure the woman, it must kill the hysteric. Writing takes the place of the hysteric.[71]

This change of focus offers feminist readers an important gesture, one that reclaims bodily experiences through the piecing together of aftereffects. Reading aftereffects as a text appropriates poststructural interrogations of the unified subject on feminist terms.

Mary Shelley's depression lifted temporarily after she finished writing *Mathilda:* she gave birth to her fifth child, she fought with Godwin over his suppression of *Mathilda,* and she returned to her correspondence and journal keeping. It was the "writing cure" that killed Mathilda and temporarily soothed Mary Shelley. A letter to Marianne Hunt dated 28 August 1819, approximately two weeks after Mary Shelley completed *Mathilda,* suggests that this "fix" was temporary. Mary Shelley writes: "Shelley has written a good deal and I have done very little since I have been in Italy."[72] And so, whereas *Mathilda* paves the way for another displacement, for another series of repressions, importantly, it identifies the way Mary Shelley embodied herself in the grips of depression. The coping strategy she advanced anticipates both Freud and the feminist recovery movement, not because Mary Shelley was ahistorically clairvoyant, but because incest and its aftereffects are not contained (or containable) by specific centuries, classes, households, or families.

NOTES

I wish to thank the following friends and colleagues who have read and commented on this chapter, and/or have challenged my ideas about Romanticism, psychoanalysis, and feminism: Laura J. George, Marlene Longenecker, Debra A. Moddelmog, Mark Schoenfield, Linda M. Shires, and Clare Simmons. I also wish to thank Kayann Short, associate editor of *Genders,* who, along with the anonymous readers, gave me excellent suggestions for revision. This chapter is part of my book-in-progress, *The Politics of Survivorship: Incest, Women's Literature, and Popular Culture*, under contract with New York University Press.

1. In accordance with the definition used in contemporary recovery theory, incest does not have to involve touch. The most widely accepted definition of incest is "the imposition of sexually inappropriate acts, or acts with sexual overtones, by . . . one or more persons who derive authority through ongoing emotional bonding with that child" (E. Sue Blume, *Secret Survivors: Uncovering Incest and Its Effects in Women* [New York: Ballantine, 1985], 4). Although touch may be absent, secrecy, which is ever-present, becomes more and more difficult to endure, especially if the daughter's denial has made her "forget" the experience (Blume, *Secret Survivors*, 1–20). According to Judith Herman, "most girls *[sic]* dread discovery of the incest secret and do not reveal it to anyone. . . . They believe that no recourse is available to them and that disclosure of the secret would lead to disaster" (Judith Lewis Herman, *Father-Daughter Incest* [Cambridge: Harvard University Press, 1981], 129). Also, frequency of attack is often used to dismiss the relevance and import of sexual abuse. But, as Bass and Davis suggest, "Betrayal takes only a minute. A father can slip his fingers into his daughter's underpants in thirty seconds. After that the world is not the same" (Ellen Bass and Laura Davis, *The Courage to Heal: A Guide for Women Survivors of Child Sexual Abuse* [New York: HarperCollins, 1988], 22).

2. I put "chooses" in quotation marks, because although it is clearly the wrong word, it is the one a patriarchal culture deems appropriate. No woman "chooses" to be raped; selecting among compromises should never be confused as an act of free will.

3. Elizabeth Nitchie, introduction to *Mathilda* (Chapel Hill: University of North Carolina Press, 1959), vii.

4. Emily Sunstein, *Mary Shelley: Romance and Reality* (Baltimore: Johns Hopkins University Press, 1989), 171.

5. Betty T. Bennett, ed., *The Letters of Mary Wollstonecraft Shelley*, 3 vols. (Baltimore: Johns Hopkins University Press, 1980, 1983, 1988), I:100.

6. Peter H. Marshall, *William Godwin* (New Haven: Yale University Press, 1984), 331.

7. U. C. Knoepflmacher, "Thoughts on the Aggression of Daughters," in *The Endurance of Frankenstein*, ed. George Levine and U. C. Knoepflmacher (Berkeley: University of California Press, 1979), 113.

8. Percy Bysshe Shelley, *The Letters of Percy Bysshe Shelley*, ed. Frederick L. Jones, 2 vols. (Oxford: Clarendon Press, 1964), II:109.

9. Ibid.

10. Paula R. Feldman and Diana Scott-Kilvert, eds., *The Journals of Mary Shelley*, 1814–1844, 2 vols. (Oxford: Clarendon Press, 1987), I:292.

11. Sunstein, *Mary Shelley*, 171.
12. Ibid.
13. Ibid.
14. See *Posthumous Works of the Author of a Vindication of the Rights of Woman*, 4 vols. (London, 1798), IV:97–155.
15. Feldman and Scott-Kilvert, *Journals*, I:293.
16. Ibid., xvii–xviii.
17. William St. Claire, *The Godwins and the Shelleys: A Biography of a Family* (New York: W. W. Norton, 1989), 467.
18. My speculation offers an important contrast to the precision with which Godwin preserved, ordered, and published Wollstonecraft's letters, a contrast suggesting that Godwin concealed *Mathilda* and Mary's letters for the purpose of concealing and silencing Mary's understanding of their relationship.
19. Frederick L. Jones, ed., *Maria Gisborne and Edward E. Williams, Shelley's Friends: Their Journals and Letters* (Norman: University of Oklahoma Press, 1951), 27.
20. As Bennett notes in a footnote in *Letters* (I:68, n. 2), Maria Gisborne (1770–1836) was a lifelong friend of both the Shelleys and the Godwins. She cared for Mary when she was a baby, was courted by and refused to marry William Godwin in 1800, and, with the exception of a one-year estrangement in 1820–21 (due probably to the fact that Maria Gisborne repeated some gossip from Mary Jane Clairmont), they were lifelong friends.

    Perhaps the most notable element of their relationship is that Maria Gisborne is the person whom Mary Shelley trusted the most in the early years of her marriage to Percy. In her letters, Mary shares with Maria her bitterness regarding her stepmother, her anxiety about her father's opinion of her, and her anger toward Percy.
21. F. Jones, *Maria Gisborne*, 27.
22. Ibid., 44.
23. Marshall, *William Godwin*, 331.
24. Knoepflmacher, "Thoughts on the Aggression," 115.
25. Anne K. Mellor, *Mary Shelley: Her Life, Her Fiction, Her Monsters* (New York: Routledge, 1988), xvii; Sunstein, *Mary Shelley*, 193–96, 213, 224, 233, 374.
26. Bennett, *Letters*, I:218.
27. Ibid., I:224.
28. Jones, *Maria Gisbourne*, 76.
29. Bennett, *Letters*, I:229.
30. Ibid., I:245; my emphasis.
31. Ibid., I:247.
32. Ibid., I:336.
33. Betty T. Bennett and Charles E. Robinson, *The Mary Shelley Reader* (New York: Oxford University Press, 1990), 175–76. All further references to this work are noted parenthetically in the text.

34. Jane Gallop, *The Daughter's Seduction: Feminism and Psychoanalysis* (Ithaca: Cornell University Press, 1982), 78.
35. E. Sue Blume, *Secret Survivors: Uncovering Incest and Its Effects in Women* (New York: Ballantine, 1985), 221.
36. Gallop, *Daughter's Seduction*, 75.
37. Luce Irigaray, "The Blind Spot of an Old Dream of Symmetry," in *Speculum of the Other Woman*, trans. Gillian C. Gill (Ithaca, NY: Cornell University Press, 1985), 38.
38. Blume, *Secret Survivors*, 81.
39. Bass and Davis, *Courage to Heal*, 70–92; Blume, *Secret Survivors*, 95–107.
40. Sunstein, *Mary Shelley*, 191.
41. Bennett, *Letters*, I.
42. Feldman and Scott-Kilvert, *Journals*.
43. Bennett, *Letters*, I:108; remember, young William died on 7 June.
44. Irigaray, "The Blind Spot," 38.
45. M. M. Bakhtin, "The Problem of the Text," in *Speech Genres and Other Late Essays*, trans. Vern W. McGee (Austin: University of Texas Press, 1986), 126.
46. The living hell created when third parties are absent is not lost on Bakhtin: "the understanding of the Fascist torture chamber or hell . . . [is] the absolute lack of being heard, as [in] the absolute absence of a third party" (ibid., 126). Bakhtin's configuration helps illuminate Mathilda's isolation: after all, it becomes necessary that she write her history, thereby constructing her subjectivity, only when another displaced third party — Woodville — offers himself as reader.
47. Judith Lewis Herman, *Father-Daughter Incest* (Cambridge: Harvard University Press, 1981), 117.
48. Judith Butler suggests that desire is never one's own, but rather it is something one is forced to "own" when, inevitably, the Law of the Father creates the situation where self-expression is relegated to a series of displacements: "The very entry into the cultural field deflects that desire from its original meaning, with the consequence that desire within culture is, of necessity, a series of displacements" (*Gender Trouble: Feminism and the Subversion of Identity* [New York: Routledge, 1990], 65).
49. Andrea Dworkin, *Intercourse* (New York: The Free Press, 1987), 150.
50. I put both "fictional" and "real" in quotation marks because the separation between the two is both arbitrary and political. Repairing events to narrative makes them fictions; at the same time, narrating a previously unnarrativized experience constructs the event as "real."
51. Claude Levi-Strauss, *The Elementary Structures of Kinship*, trans. James Harle Bell and John Richard von Sturmer (Boston: Beacon Press, 1969), 481.
52. Irigaray's "Women on the Market" offers insight into the father's role: "The society we know, our own culture, is based on the exchange of women. . . . The passage into the social order, into the symbolic order, into order as such, is assured by the fact that men, or groups of men, circulate women among themselves, according to a rule known as the incest taboo" (in *This Sex Which*

Is Not One, trans. Catherine Porter and Caroline Burke [Ithaca, NY: Cornell University Press, 1985], 170).

53. Gayle Rubin, "The Traffic in Women: Notes on the 'Political Economy' of Sex," in *Toward an Anthropology of Women*, ed. Rayna Reiter (New York: Monthly Review Press, 1975), 177.

54. Ibid., 174.

55. Blume, *Secret Survivors*, 51.

56. W. Arens, *The Original Sin: Incest and its Meaning* (New York: Oxford University Press, 1986), viii.

57. Mary Douglas, *Purity and Danger: An Analysis of Pollution and Taboo* (New York: Ark, 1966, 1989), 115.

58. Dworkin, *Intercourse*, 166.

59. Privileging the body over the mind only to "prove" that the bodily damage was minimal offers one of the most harmful effects of patriarchal arrogance to our society. Importantly, someone — either the dominant gaze or the subject in question — always translates the body's pain through categories available to the mind. The separation of mind and body and the convenient focus on the site of a woman's body (whose pain becomes legitimate only when catalogued and understood by others) reveals how Western logic obscures, circumvents, or simply overturns subjective inscriptions of the body in pain.

60. Jacques Lacan, "The Signification of the Phallus," in *Ecrits: A Selection*, trans. Alan Sheridan (New York: W. W. Norton, 1977), 285.

61. Gallop, *Daughter's Seduction*, 77.

62. Ibid., 96.

63. Ibid., 77.

64. "Splitting" should not be confused with split-personality syndrome, although both are dissociative disorders now understood as aftereffects of incest. Because a daughter cannot physically and/or emotionally leave a sexually abusive parent, she copes by splitting, by holding the experience in her mind, but refusing to feel the pain in her body. According to Bass and Davis, splitting refers to both the survivor who remembers the facts of the abuse, but not the feelings, as well as the woman who can, in times of extreme pain or fear, leave her body (*Courage to Heal*, 208–10). Blume defines "splitting" as a cognitive aftereffect and places this in the same category of coping mechanisms as denial, flashbacks, repression, multiple personality disorder, and blocking/amnesia (*Secret Survivors*, 81–97).

65. Herman, *Father-Daughter Incest*, 22–35.

66. Ibid.

67. Ibid., 36–49.

68. According to Lynda E. Boose in "The Father's House and the Daughter in It," the relative openness with which our society now addresses incest does not portend a liberal future; rather, "the subject has changed venues and now rests in the hands of a new and more powerful set of cultural fathers." In fact, these new fathers rule with a more ruthless reign than their predecessors:

In 1987, after a six-year study conducted by doctors from Harvard Medical School and Massachusetts General Hospital, headed by Harvard psychiatrist Muriel Sugarman, a new phenomenon termed "divorce incest" was identified, in which the children typically were not abused *until* the divorce or separation took place. Having followed a group of "19 children age 6 or younger whom the researchers believed had been sexually abused by their biological father during visits after separation or divorce," the study reported that at the court level, in spite of substantial documentation of incest by social-service agencies, "allegations were disbelieved in 73.7 percent of the cases," and not one of the men accused was prosecuted. In fact, the judicial system seemed so loathe to side against the privileges of the father that "in nearly 60 percent of the cases, the children were forced to have [continued] visits with their fathers." (Lynda Boose, "The Father's House and the Daughter in It," in *Daughters and Fathers*, ed. Lynda E. Boose and Betty S. Flowers [Baltimore: Johns Hopkins University Press, 1989], 71, n. 5)

69. Bass and Davis, *Courage to Heal*, 27.
70. Arens, *Original Sin*, vii.
71. Diane Price Herndl, "The Writing Cure: Charlotte Perkins Gilman, Anna O., and 'Hysterical' Writing," in *The National Women's Studies Association Journal* 1, no. 1 (1988): 68.
72. Bennett, *Letters*, I:103.

PART FOUR

Feminisms that Make (a) Difference

Female but Not Woman: Genders in Chinese Socialist Texts

Mingyan Lai

If the critical intervention of feminists of color (from/of/in the "third world" and the "first world") has productively displaced a singular conception of "woman" and called attention to the interaction of gender, race, ethnicity, class, and nation in the social configuration of female subjects, then a continued focus on the pluralized category "women" as the bona fide subject of feminism seems unnecessarily restrictive. And, at least arguably, it is counterproductive for coalition struggles against gender oppression.

Localizing differences in female subject formation within a general category of "women," however one shifts its boundary, risks the reification of a binary sex/gender construct. The strategy also risks foreclosing the possibility of and inquiry into actual historical practices of radically different gender systems that do not constitute sexual differences into a gender binary of man: woman. Or, to argue the issue differently, insofar as genders are produced and maintained in specific political and sociocultural discourses, the relevance and political implications of invoking a category of "women" to encompass all "female persons" would seem to need unremitting deliberation in every instance and context. Without such deliberation and a concomitant attention to the specificity of genders within each social and cultural formation (however the boundaries are drawn), plotting the intersection of gender, race, class, and nation may, indeed, occlude important differences in the gender configuration of female bodies *within* the same race, ethnicity, class, and nation. This may also cover over power relations that are consequential to coalition struggles against gender oppression.

Yet, arguably because of the hegemonic power of "woman" as a gender category, an unproblematized privileging of "women" as the subject of feminism(s) prevails even in third-world feminist critiques of Western feminism.[1] Chandra Mohanty's critique of Western feminism's complicity in colonialist power, for instance, is grounded on a theoretical distinction between " 'Woman' — a cultural and ideological composite Other constructed through diverse representational discourses (scientific, literary, juridical, linguistic, cinematic, etc.) — and 'women' — real, material subjects of their collective histories."[2] Invoking this distinction, Mohanty argues that Western feminism's composite construct of the third-world woman cannot adequately represent the "real, material subjects" of third-world women, because it is based on an indiscriminate objectification of third-world women into victims of oppression. The singular sign of third-world woman, in other words, bypasses the interaction between gender and other ideological structures in the constitution of third-world women in its essentialization of gender differences into a transcendental relation of the oppressor and the oppressed. Whereas Mohanty is thus attentive to Western feminism's elision of differences among women of different ethnicities, races, classes, nations, religions, and so forth, her invocation of a universal category of women as real, material subjects implies a commonality of gender construction in practice that belies her argument of interactive formation of gendered subjects, and leaves unquestioned the general relevance, to third-world cultures and third-world feminisms, of the dichotomous categories that are operative in the Western sex/gender system.

Indeed, the notion of women as real, material subjects seems to suggest a prediscursive foundation for the category of women even as differences are posited for the historically and culturally constituted subjects who inhabit this category. This implicit assumption is particularly revealing in light of Mohanty's explicit rejection of any forms of essentialism for third-world feminist struggles: "it is not color or sex which constructs the ground for these struggles, but the *way* we think about race, class, and gender — the political links we choose to make among and between struggles."[3] There is perhaps no better index of the hegemonic power of the category of women than its unproblematized incorporation into a feminist position that foregrounds the cultural embeddedness of gender and the political constitution of feminist struggles.

The prevailing assumption of a stable relation between feminism and the category of women has recently come under critical scrutiny within Western feminism. Through an analysis of the historical construction of women against different discursive categories in Western sociocultural formations, Denise Riley challenges the apparent continuity in the subject of women and argues the necessity for feminism to unveil the deceptively constant opposition of women to men by confronting discontinuities and instabilities in the category of women.[4] Similarly, Judith Butler's insistent questioning of the political effects of maintaining women as the subject of feminism, by way of a critical genealogy of Western gender categories that uncovers the production of the men: women binary in the regulatory practices of compulsory heterosexuality and phallogocentrism, underscores the embeddedness of gender positions in regimes of power/discourse.[5] If the gender positions available in different historical and cultural formations cannot, then, be presumed without reference to their specific regulatory practices and institutions, it follows that the questions of whether "women" is a culturally intelligible and inhabitable gender category, how it is produced and maintained, whether there are competing and/or complementary gendering practices, and how particular gender categories relate to feminism(s) cannot be bypassed, especially where non-Western societies are concerned.

Regardless of the uncertain and predictably variable trajectory of "women" in non-Western contexts, however, the hegemony of Western modernity, buttressed by the economic and military forces of imperialism, seems to have put this privileged Western sex/gender category irrevocably onto the contested cultural and political terrains of third-world modernity. In spite of, and perhaps even because of, what Riley calls the "volatility of 'women' " in Western cultural formations, the ideological production of "women" has been, and continues to be, appropriated as a problematic sign of modernity in the third world.[6] An instance of such interweaving of "women" into cultural contestations over modernity is analyzed in Tani Barlow's historical study of "women" as a gender category in China.[7] Barlow traces the production of "woman" (*nuxing*, literally female sex) and its oppositional construct, "women" (*funu*), to the iconoclastic cultural displacement that revolutionary intellectual elites engineered for China's modernization in the 1920s.

Through a close reading of late imperial Chinese discourses, Barlow shows that a general category of woman/women is alien to the premodern gender system that produces gender effects on the ground of the patrilineal family rather than the sexed body. In this system, gender identities are enacted in and signified by the performance of specific duties according to behavioral codes that are mapped onto a complex grid of hierarchical kin relationships such as father/daughter, mother/son, and husband/wife.[8] It was against this kinship-framed gendering practice reified as tradition, Barlow argues, that the category of woman was constituted in a textuality of modernity that appropriated Western discourses of the sex binary for, ironically, the project of nationalist liberation from Western imperialism. It was, in turn, against both this category of woman (together with its underlying discourses of modernity) and "feudal traditions" that the Chinese Communists generated the competing category of women in the Chinese Marxist discourses of liberation and socialism.

In positioning the "indigenization" of the category woman/women as a major site of cultural struggles over modernity, Barlow's text opens this hegemonic modern gender category to interrogation against a "context" of multifold contestation with historically dominant cultural practices. Yet the interrogation is significantly short-circuited in her reading of gendering practices in modern China, which, in effect, maintains the hegemony of women as the (modern) gender for females. As Barlow's study stresses the discontinuities among *nuxing*, *funu*, and the late-imperial kinship-framed gender categories, it implicitly maps such discursive discontinuities onto major historical ruptures in modern China: the overthrow of the imperial system and its legitimating discourse of Confucianism brought into play the signs *nuxing* and *funu*, and the eventual victory of the Chinese Communists instated *funu* as the principal female gender. This historical mapping, reinforced as it is by an exclusive focus on *nuxing* and *funu* as the gender categories for females in modern China, elides the possible reconstitution of the late-imperial gendering practice in modern China. That the regime of gendering in and through the performative enactment of kin-inflected behavioral codes may be redeployed to operate in a different form under Chinese socialism, in conjunction and perhaps tension with the constitution of *funu*, although not explicitly denied, is in effect foreclosed. Elided at the same time, then, is the possibility of multiple gender systems operating within socialist China.

This foreclosure of multiple gender systems producing different but coeval gender categories in a specific historical and cultural context is, arguably, effected from and, in turn, maintains the hegemonic power of "women" circulating within and between Western feminism and Chinese socialist discourses of revolution and liberation.[9] "Women's liberation" (*funu jiefang*) has been a privileged term under which Chinese state socialism regulated the renegotiation of gender relations in the course of revolution and socialist construction. Seduced by this discourse of liberation, the subject of which seemed "identical" to their own subject of interests, Western feminists have also discussed the promises and inadequacies of the Chinese experience in terms of women, often with the expressed aim of investigating "socialism's capacity to liberate women."[10]

If Barlow's insightful text successfully illuminates the discontinuities between the Chinese socialist and Western feminist production of the category of women, it also reveals the limits of a critical destabilization of the category across cultures. In focusing on women as the subject of study, it excludes important inquiries into gender constitution and negotiation under Chinese socialism. For instance, if *funu* is produced and maintained as object of political mobilization for socialist liberation and development, then to what extent is it an inhabitable subject position? Insofar as it is not inhabitable, what subject positions are available to females? Are all female sexed bodies equally gendered into *funu?* If not, how and under what conditions are gender differences generated and regulated among females?[11] Given the conflicting demands for female labor in socialist construction, is a general category of *funu* adequate for the mobilization of female labor? Is it enough for the regulation of gender relations for all state interests? If not, what other genders are discursively prescribed to females, and under what conditions? Are any of the kin-inflected gender categories redeployed in the Chinese socialist order? If so, in what terms? To what purposes? These questions bear on our thinking about gender in important ways.

Apart from their immediate relevance to our understanding of gender configuration in China, these questions also have implications for more general issues about gender, such as: What is the relation between sex and gender? To what extent is the usefulness of the notion of gender predicated on a binary frame? What are the limitations of presuming a binary gender system? Are there multiple gendering practices within a social formation? Are female bodies variously constituted into multiple gender identities? And are there power differences among female gendered subjects that may be covered over by the general category of women? To the extent that these questions are closed off, the hegemony of women as a gender category is sustained and alternative visions to gender oppression unduly restricted.

In an effort to keep open some of these questions, this chapter discusses the discursive construction of genders under Chinese socialism through a close reading of selected journalistic and literary texts sanctioned by the Chinese state. My primary objectives are to problematize the prevailing exclusive focus on the category of women in feminist studies and to call attention to the possibility of multiple gender systems and the reconstitution of putatively traditional gendering practice in modernity. Thus no attempt is made here to give a "comprehensive" analysis of gendering practices in modern China. By the same token, this is not a historical project in the sense that it seeks neither to examine the history of gender categories and constitution in China, nor to provide a general or "representative" picture of Chinese gender practices in a specific historical period. Nor is there any attempt to discuss the complex negotiation in and between regulatory practices through which gendered subjects are constituted in actuality, a subject involving issues of desire and agency that require lengthy treatment beyond the scope of this chapter.

For the purpose of interrogating the inhabitability of the category "women" and the availability of other gender categories under Chinese socialism, a good point of entry is the formulation of genders in public texts that form a part of the state ideological apparatus. These include journal articles and novels published under the aegis of the state. To ensure that the gender categories and systems under discussion are indeed coeval, all of the texts analyzed here are taken from the period 1972–74. This period yielded a large number of interesting texts on the Chinese socialist formulation of gender, arguably because the socialist system was in crisis and the state found it necessary to reclaim legitimacy on all grounds after the disastrous events of the Cultural Revolution (1966–69).[12]

As is detailed in the following pages, the Chinese socialist state maintained strong interests in and control over gender constitution in order to legitimize its professed historical achievement of revolution and liberation, as well as to enforce its vision of socialist construction. The multiplicity of these interests generated a complex formulation of sex/gender relations that goes beyond a male/men:female/women dichotomy. In this formulation, even as physiological differences are mobilized to constitute a sex binary of male and female bodies, sex differences are not the primary ground on which gender effects are produced. Rather, it is differential relations to state and party institutions that configure the regulatory practices for a system of performative enactment and signification of genders. Sex is registered in different modalities and to various degrees in this system. Accordingly, multiple female genders are produced that do not add up into a category of women.

WOMEN—FROM DOMESTIC SLAVERY TO SOCIAL PRODUCTIVE LABOR

Women's emancipation is a component part of the proletarian liberation. . . . It is important, as Lenin taught us, "to get women to take part in socially productive labor, to liberate them from 'domestic slavery,' to free them from their stupefying and humiliating subjugation to the eternal drudgery of the kitchen and the nursery." . . . Chairman Mao has said, "Times have changed; nowadays males and females are the same. Whatever male comrades can accomplish, female comrades can as well."

— *Renmin Ribao* editorial, 8 March 1973

The category of women *(funu)* figures rather prominently in the Chinese state discourse of revolution and socialist construction during the Campaign Against Lin Biao and Confucius (1973–74), a major effort to bolster Maoism in the post-Cultural Revolution struggle to (re)define Chinese socialism.[13] The renewal of interest in the women issue in such an ideological endeavor is instructive.[14] It calls attention to the embeddedness of the sign "women" in a discourse of national difference from the past and the modern West. In this discourse dominated by the trope of new versus old, women are situated in a history of, and called on to keep up, the struggle between the new and the old, which are coded respectively as the "revolutionary" Maoist line for socialist liberation and construction and the "revisionist" line of feudal and capitalist exploitation and oppression. The narrative of struggle inscribes woman between two subject positions, the housewife and the worker, marking a passage of liberation from (domestic) slavery to (equal) social labor. Woman in this configuration functions in the same way as "backward elements" do in Ann Anagnost's analysis of China's politicization of the individual body: they "provide the raw materials to be worked on by the machinery of the party organizations. . . . [and] are essential to the party's self-definition as a progressive force in the building of a socialist modernity."[15] In other words, the category of women is produced in Chinese state/party discourses as a sign of backwardness that needs to be erased through, and thus also marks the course and value of, socialist construction.

This configuration of women underlies dominant themes in the state/ party discourse on *funu gongzuo* (literally woman-work, signifying the work of the state organ responsible for organizing and mobilizing women, Women's Federation), an exemplary version of which appears as a *Peking Review* article written by the Vice-Director of the Beijing Women's Federation to commemorate the 8 March "International Working Women's Day."[16] The article's title summarizes the basic proposition of this discourse: "Women's liberation is a component part of the proletarian revolution."[17] Invoking the authorities of the forefathers of Chinese Marxism (Marx, Engels, Lenin, and Mao), the article grounds gender oppression in class exploitation and establishes a metonymic relation between socialist revolution and women's liberation with Mao's thesis that "the political authority of the landlords is the backbone of all the other systems of authority[;] [w]ith that overturned, the clan authority, the religious authority and the authority of the husband all begin to totter."[18] Women, cathected with oppression from all four systems of authority, functions here as a trope for revolutionary need: "women urgently need revolution . . . [and] they are a decisive force in the success or failure of the revolution."[19] Women's liberation, represented by "opportunities to take part in political activities and productive labor," then, becomes a signpost of the progress in socialist revolution: "Times have changed and today men and women are equal. Whatever men comrades can accomplish women comrades can too."[20]

In such a configuration, woman is not an inhabitable subject position under Chinese socialism. Women are "interpellated" precisely for the project of breaking out of gender inscriptions to assume the presumably gender-neutral category of worker.[21] This point is forcefully made in a story illustrating women's liberation into social productive labor in a *Peking Review* article:

Yang Kuo-chen is a *woman worker* in the Red Flag Embroidery Factory in the Hoping District of Tientsin. Soon after liberation, on learning about the significance of women's emancipation, she decided to go out to work and contribute her share to building up the country. She joined an embroidery production group, the predecessor of the present embroidery factory, organized by the women's federation. But her husband, a worker, saw the matter in a different light. His family lived much better after liberation. He considered that since he was working, his wife should as a matter of course do the housework and that it was a disgrace for her to go out to work. They often quarrelled about this. With more and more women taking jobs outside of the home, public opinion changed, and he also changed his attitude. Now Yang Kuo-chen is a *skilled worker* in charge of a small group. Relations in the family changed too. In the past she waited on her husband, but now he does his share of the washing, cooking and other housework. They consult each other about family expenses and get along very well.[22]

This narrative takes the reader through the logic of the discourse of women's emancipation. It makes clear that learning to identify with the subject of women's emancipation means renegotiating one's subject position from housewife to worker. The identification of Yang as a "woman worker" at the very beginning signals that woman is not a subject position to inhabit. In (re)inscribing preliberation female subject formation in terms of division of labor by sex, the discourse of women's emancipation simultaneously excludes sex differences from postliberation female subject configuration. This is, of course, not to argue that sex differences do not matter in postliberation discursive and social practices. Yang's employment in a factory organized by the women's federation to produce the traditionally female work of embroidery certainly suggests a continuation of sex segregation and division of labor after the "liberation" of women from "domestic slavery" into social productive labor.

The point, rather, is that the discourse of women's liberation does not allow sex/gender differences to be constitutive of postliberation subject positions. The term "woman worker" marginalizes "woman" into an attribute qualifying the (new) subject effect of worker, thus signifying the secondariness of sex/gender to class. This marginalization intensifies as the story of emancipation develops, until, in the end, even the gender attribute is displaced by the productivity qualifier of skills, and Yang is completely inscribed in a narrative of social production: she becomes "a skilled worker in charge of a small group." The narrative shift also brings about a negation of the differential relations to housework and social production that have formerly structured the gender positions of husband and (house)wife: now husband and wife each do a share of housework and consult each other about family expenses.

In the narrative of women's emancipation here, women is a gender category under erasure. The simultaneous invocation and denial of women as subject in Yang's story is repeated in the narratorial strategy of the *Peking Review* article as a whole. Even as a footnote foregrounds the gender of the narrator/author and her authority to speak in the name of women by identifying her as "a member of the standing committee of the Tientsin Municipal Women's Federation and Chairwoman of the Hoping District Women's Federation in Tientsin," the narratorial voice assumed is consistently gender unspecific.[23] It distances itself from a woman's voice by maintaining third-person references to women throughout. Even when recourses are made to the personal experiences of the narrator/author to enhance narratorial authority on women's liberation, the "I" who reads and speaks the experience stakes a claim on the subject position of worker rather than women, as shown in the statement: "I was then a worker in Tientsin and had my fill of the sufferings workers had to endure in the old society."[24] The narratorial strategy as a whole, then, suggests that in the state discourse of women's liberation, women are spoken as subjects, yet do not constitute a subject position from which one (can) speak and self-represent.

IRON GIRLS—ACCOMPLISHING AS WELL WHATEVER MALE COMRADES CAN

We, ten young female comrades, have broken out of the fetters of the exploiting classes' and revisionist thoughts to organize a cotton-planting team. . . . Besides working in the main fields, we have planted ten *mou* of high productivity experimental fields.

— Ten Sisters Cotton-Planting Team of Wangjian Brigade

We, the female commune members of the Dazhai Brigade, brave the scorching sun and bitter cold all year round to fight side by side with male commune members, performing all kinds of agricultural tasks.

— Iron Girls Team of Dazhai Brigade

The untenability of women as subjects is perhaps most discernible from their putative self-representations in state discourse. Two such texts were published in the party journal *Hongqi* in the early 1970s, one by the "Ten Sisters" Cotton Planting Team of Wangjian Brigade in Linyi Prefecture Shanxi Province, and the other by the Iron Girls Team of Dazhai Brigade.[25] The very inclusion of these texts in the party journal signals their inscription within the official discourse. They are thus particularly illuminative of the subject positions this discourse makes available to females. Unlike Li Chen's *Peking Review* article discussed earlier, both of these texts assume specifically gender-marked narratorial voices. To register solidarity with women, the collective narratorial voices often prefix references to women with the pronouns "us" and "we." But complete identification is nonetheless lacking, and woman is still not a subject position to inhabit or speak from. In the Ten Sisters' narrative, for instance, "women" repeatedly occupy object positions, both in syntax and signification, whereas females in subject positions are identified as "female comrades" *(nu tongzhi)*. This difference is exemplified in the statement: "When the high productivity experimental fields were first started, not only were there people in society who looked down upon us women *(women funu)*, but we, the few female comrades *(nu tongzhi)* [who started the experimental fields], also underestimated ourselves, still thinking that 'after all is said, women are not as good as men.' "[26] In this rhetorical splitting of female identity, women are metonymically linked to oppressive traditions and ideas, whereas female comrades are associated with socialist production and development. As objects of oppression, women are also subjected to political mobilization and transformation, through which the subjection of women is to be negated: "women are mobilized by the teachings of Chairman Mao to participate in revolutionary struggles and social production," and are taught in the process that "women cannot be completely liberated without struggles against [their] own old ideas."[27] By contrast, the category of female comrade signifies the "progress" of females into subject positions under socialism. Female comrades constituted in social production occupy subject, rather than subjected, positions in the project of building socialism, as suggested in the statement: "We, ten young female comrades . . . organize a cotton planting team to change the condition of production in our brigade, increase production, and win the battle of revolutionizing agriculture."[28]

A similar contrast, though to a lesser degree, is set up between "working women" *(laodong funu)* and "female commune members" *(nu sheyuan)* in the Iron Girls' narrative. There, working women are textually linked to liberation from oppression by Confucianism and its contemporary manifestation in the revisionist line: "Working women have so much hatred to voice, so much bitterness to speak against the feudal shackles and doctrines of Confucius and Mencius."[29] Female commune members, on the other hand, are situated in the field of socialist construction, "performing all kinds of agricultural tasks and working with technicians to conduct scientific experiments" on agricultural production.[30]

The subjects who narrate women's liberation from oppression in these two articles, as already suggested in the authorial names, are the female comrades and commune members. Their narratives not only displace gender from the center of subject formation for females under socialism, but actively and systematically deny the importance of sexual differences even as secondary attributes. This is most apparent in the Iron Girls' emphasis on their comradeship with male commune members and their voluntary performance of all kinds of agricultural tasks without any consideration of their sex. The irrelevance of sex to a commune member's productivity and contribution to socialist construction is, in fact, implicitly offered as a signpost of liberation: "[Dazhai] girls insisted on struggling alongside the male commune members, without ever complaining about hardship or exhaustion. It was thus in struggles that the Iron Girls Team was organized. [The Iron Girls] have become masters (*zhuren*) in the transformation of nature."[31] The necessity for females to transform themselves into socialist subjects through actualizing their potential for performing tasks traditionally reserved to males is also underscored in the Ten Sisters' account of their own self-education and liberation through collective agricultural labor. Their collective narratorial voice cites as evidence of their liberation their "behaving like males," working barefooted in the fields, collecting manure, and even excavating wells.[32]

As foregrounded in the title of the Ten Sisters' article, the master text behind these two testimonies is, again, Chairman Mao's adage that "whatever male comrades can accomplish, female comrades can as well."[33] Thus regulated, the marginalization of gender and sex in the very act of bearing witness to the transformation of "women" is inevitable.

(RE-)PRODUCTIVE MOTHERS AND POLITICAL DAUGHTERS

Gender, however, is not invariably excluded, nor are sexual differences always denied signification in the Chinese discourse of socialist construction.[34] In the "new" subject position of worker or commune member, sex becomes significant again in the other realm of production, that is, reproduction. The regulation of reproduction through controlling the signification of female sexed bodies has consistently been an important component of "women-work" under Chinese socialism. Late marriage, family planning, and other institutions proffered as welfare services for women (such as health clinics, creches, and kindergartens) are integral parts of the state regime for controlling female sexed bodies. Discursively, it is precisely in this regime of control that a disjuncture in the category of women appears and the intervention of different gendering practices becomes evident.

If all females are constituted as women in relation to traditional ideas and practices of oppression according to the state discourse of liberation, they are differently configured in the management of sexed bodies for production and reproduction prescribed by the discourse of socialist construction. The sexed bodies of female urban workers, for instance, are configured into culturally intelligible gender primarily through the state regulation of maternity, as the following statement from a *Peking Review* article shows:

Based on the state's unified stipulations, the city [Tientsin] adopted in 1953 its regulations to protect women workers which clearly prescribed: Both women and men workers should enjoy equal pay for equal work and equal opportunities in jobs and in acquiring new skills. Dismissal of expectant mothers and nursing mothers from jobs are prohibited. Special care should be given to women workers when they are pregnant, confined or nursing. Nursing rooms and creches should be established. In accordance with women's special physiological factors, regulations insist that special consideration be made in four periods — menstrual, pregnancy, maternity and nursing. Pregnant workers get regular free health checks in the hospital. . . . Nursing mothers are given time off to feed their infants twice a day during working hours and they can put their infants in the nurseries run by the mills. Special stand-ins are provided by the mill to look after the machine while a mother is nursing her child. Most mills have creches and kindergartens close by where mothers work. . . . In planning a new factory, the state takes into account the proportion of women workers and due attention is given to setting up creches, kindergartens, primary schools, hospitals and other ancillary facilities.[35]

Insofar as the sex of a female worker assumes meaning in the official discourse, then, it does so through the socialist inscription of motherhood in an urban production unit. In other words, her gender is configured in the institution of motherhood under the socialist factory system and is thereby defined and signified as "mother." The normative behavior signifying her gender, moreover, is predominantly structured in relation to the various institutions and facilities built and maintained by the state. It is in acting her parts vis-à-vis the state provisions of hospital visits, nursing routines, childcare arrangements, and so forth, that the worker inhabits the gender position of mother.

In contrast, unmarried females in the rural areas, such as the Iron Girls, assume gender identity within the official discourse of socialism through the institution of socialist marriage. This is indicated in the Iron Girls' narrative in *Hongqi*:

Because of Confucius' pernicious influence, some people look down upon peasants and do not let their *daughters marry peasants*. So we Dazhai girls struggle against this old idea. Dazhai girls love rural villages and are committed to settling down and making revolution in rural villages. For years, Dazhai girls have not gone [married] into town and quite a few even married into remote mountain villages. . . . Iron Girls lead the way in marrying late.[36]

Gender signification is here effected through the system of patrilocal marriage in socialist rural China. This marriage system is centered not on the heterosexual relations between husband and wife, but on the structures and politics of labor exchange and reproduction in the rural production units. Such politics configures the female bodies of the Dazhai girls into "daughters" who take part in local "revolution" over and through marriage. As such, they are different from the "revolutionary" daughters of the May Fourth era (late 1910s and 1920s), who struggled against individual families for liberation from arranged marriages.[37] The Dazhai girls are not daughters of individual families but daughters of and to a collective unit of socialist production — the Dazhai brigade — whose relation to marriage has been politicized into a transfamilial issue bearing on socialist construction in the countryside. Contributing to the revolutionary cause by delaying marriage and then making a commitment, through the eventual patrilocal marriage, to settle in poorly endowed production collectives in need of their skills and labor is the regulatory practice that engenders them as socialist daughters.

The difference in regulatory practices through which female urban workers and the rural Dazhai girls assume gender identities calls into question the conventional conception of a gender binary corresponding neatly to a sex dichotomy. If, as the commonly accepted distinction between sex and gender implies, there is no necessary linkage between sex and gender, then the possibility that gender may not be confined to two categories predicated on the physiological dichotomization of sex deserves serious consideration. In the case of Chinese socialist practices discussed here, whereas a sex dichotomy is maintained in terms of physiological differences, genders are constituted on grounds other than physiology. Moreover, the behavioral codes that engender female urban workers and the rural Dazhai girls are grounded in institutions so different that they produce distinctive gender effects. They disrupt a unified category of women to effect a more complex order of gendered subjects for production and reproduction prescribed in the state discourse of socialist construction.

The differential constitution of "mothers" and "daughters" through the regulation of normative behaviors suggests a trace of the late-imperial Chinese gender system. It seems pertinent, then, to look beyond the "traditional versus modern" framework to consider the relation between such a gendering practice and the socialist construction of gendered subjects. As evident in the passages quoted earlier, the configuration of urban workers into socialist "mothers" and the rural Dazhai girls into socialist "daughters" takes place in a complex structure of interlocking state, party, and family institutions that is, at the same time, markedly different in the urban and rural areas. The social and political restructuring carried out by the Chinese Communist Party during the revolutionary struggle and early years of state building has radically reconstituted the ground on which a kin-inflected gender system works, to the extent that it does, under Chinese socialism.[38] State intervention into the family system, through the promulgation of new marriage laws and the women-work of the Women's Federation, and economic and political restructuring, such as the land reform, have disrupted the direct familial relationship constitutive of the earlier gendering practice.[39] The husband-wife or father-daughter relationships that produce gendered subjects under the late-imperial system are now mediated by an institution of public patriarchy comprising various party/state apparatuses and functionaries.[40] In other words, the party/state plays a central role in the gendering of socialist subjects. If the late imperial state maintained a legislative interest and power over behavioral codes that regulate gender enactment through the performance of proper duties *within the family* (as in the state promotion of widow chastity, for instance), the socialist state is directly involved in the normative behaviors constitutive of genders. For it is in the nexus of state/family relations that genders are produced and maintained under socialism. This shift in the social ground of gender constitution is evident in the text of the Iron Girls. The behavioral codes that regulate and signify the gender of the Dazhai girls, as we have seen, are woven into the social fabric of revolutionary production collectives rather than that of the individual family.[41]

Public patriarchy's displacement of paterfamilias in the normative practice constitutive of the gender of daughter is clearly foregrounded in a "personal testimony" published under the section "Youth of China" in the *Peking Review*. Like all texts incorporated into an official journal of the party/state, this article is a part of the state discourse of socialism, despite and even on account of its claim to be a "personal testimony." Although this does not mean that the text is nothing but an instance of state discourse, it does suggest that the subject position in this "personal testimony" is one not only inscribed in but actively promoted by state discourse. The gendering of this subject position is thus illustrative of the normative social ground for gender signification. Marked in the text as "young student integrating with the poor and lower-middle peasants," this subject is gendered in and through the politics of patrilocal marriage:

The years passed swiftly; it was time to consider the choice of a life-partner. Some tried to persuade me to choose from among certain friends in the city, but the commune members all hoped that I would settle down in Hsiangkuochang. . . . Once I had thought of marrying a college graduate or a cadre in the city; that would ensure a more comfortable life and I would be able to look after my father who was getting on in years. But considering the significance of living and working in Hsiangkuochuang and the need for educated youth to build up the countryside, I preferred to remain. Moreover, I felt close to the peasants – how could I leave? The poor and lower-middle peasants were overjoyed on learning of my decision. "You've taken the correct path," said Pi Yu-lin, deputy secretary of the brigade's Party branch.

A college student married to a peasant! . . . Had I done the right thing? I tried to find an answer from the writings of revolutionary teachers. *Engels said: "Marriage is a political act." Chairman Mao also pointed out that . . . in solving questions of love and marriage, one should proceed from the proletarian political stand.*[42]

The dominant relations that structure the regulatory practice of Pai Chi-hsien's gendering here – her marriage – are those between her and members of the commune in which she works and lives, especially the local party officials. Through the rhetorical juxtaposition of her concerns for her personal father and the brigade, the narrative effects a tropological displacement of the personal family and signals a shift in the social ground of her constitution as daughter. In place of filial duty to her personal father, the Maoist injunctions that (a) educated youths should be reeducated by poor and lower-middle peasants and (b) marriage should be considered politically from the proletarian standpoint, now constitute the behavioral code that produces and signifies her gender. It is, then, precisely in subjecting herself to the wishes of the public patriarchs and making a politically sanctioned marriage for the sake of building socialism in rural China that Pai inhabits the gender position of daughter. Her constitution as daughter of and for socialist revolution is thoroughly embedded in the patrilocal and patrilineal family structure and interlinking state and party apparatuses in the commune structure of rural China.

If, as I have argued, it is relations to the public patriarchy that produce and signify genders in the Chinese state discourse of socialist construction, then not only are the genders available to females in the urban and rural settings different, but there need not be one gender for all females in either the urban or rural context. In light of this, the emphasis of state discourse on the gender of mother for urban workers and the gender of daughter for rural commune members deserves some attention. It raises the question of why a certain gender is privileged or dominant in a particular discursive and social context. Although the answers to this question are necessarily context specific, the underlying issue of dominance suggests that significant power relations among female genders are being masked in the exclusive emphasis on a particular gender. To explore this, I examine in detail the discursive constitution of female genders for socialist construction in the countryside through a close reading of a socialist realist text promoted by the state and widely circulated in the public.

FEMALE GENDERS AND RURAL PUBLIC PATRIARCHY

The norms that govern the production of genders in the Maoist discourse of socialist construction of rural China can be read from the (in)famous novel *Jinquang dadao* (The Road in Golden Light, 1972, 1974), which is one of the first fictions of length to be published in the wake of the Cultural Revolution.[43] A major work by Hao Ran, a writer of peasant origin officially reputed to be the most representative Maoist author, *Jinguang dadao* is an exemplary exercise in Chinese socialist realism. Confronting the disorientation and disillusionment in the aftermath of the Cultural Revolution, *Jinguang dadao* seeks to reaffirm the values and visions of Chinese socialism through an epic retelling of the foundation of socialism in rural China. In an idealized fictional representation of the experiences and struggles of liberated peasants in a northern Chinese village to consolidate their revolutionary gains through increasing cooperation after the land reform, the novel meticulously lays out the principles, values, and practices of socialism and seeks to provide "regulative psychobiographies" for the subjects of socialist China by figuring a set of characters who embody the normative ideals of socialism in their everyday behaviors. Reflecting the Chinese socialist emphasis on practice as the indicator of intention and desire, the novel gives lengthy and detailed descriptions of the characters' behaviors in lieu of close looks into their psychological and emotional states. So although female characters are, significantly enough, rather secondary, their inscription still shows clearly the regulatory practices that generate different gender effects in support of the normative socialist order.

Woman, signifying the female sex in a general context of sexual division of labor, is a marginalized category in *Jinguang dadao*. The female sexed characters are textually constituted not into women as such, but into different genders through differential relations to the public patriarchy. The gender identities of mother *(niang)*, wife *(xifu)*, and daughter *(guinu)* are separately enacted by female characters who perform different tasks, directly and indirectly, for the state/party organs in the village of *Fangcaodi* (fragrant meadow). And the normative behavior constitutive of each of these gender identities is illustrated through a particular exemplary character.

Grandma Deng *(Deng sannainai)* is the mother par excellence in the novel. A widow since her late twenties, her identity is centered on her only son, whom she has voluntarily given to the revolutionary army during the war against the Japanese (historically, 1937–45). The army, with its engagement in the Korean War in the narrative present (1950–52) textually represented as a defense of the newly established socialist state and the land reforms the state implemented in the countryside, is a privileged symbol of the socialist state in *Jinguang dadao*. Grandma Deng's sending her son to the army, then, effects a transformation of her from an individual mother into a mother of and for the socialist state and the "liberated" community of Fangcaodi. Her continued residence in Fangcaodi, while her son and daughter-in-law stay on the battlefront to defend the state, further enhances the collective nature of her motherhood.

Grandma Deng's subject position as a communal mother is also produced and maintained by her relation to the public patriarchs in Fangcaodi. She considers it her duty to advise, alert, and/or admonish local party members about (political) developments in the village community. For instance, on learning that Zhang Jinfa, the village head and a party member, has compromised the class line by doing business with the village's former landlord, she takes it upon herself to stop him. After trying unsuccessfully to plead with Zhang himself and reprimanding another party member for failing to understand the import of the matter, she approaches the protagonist and remaining party member in the village, Gao Daquan, with words that clearly assert her senior position: "Whenever I see things that don't agree with the wishes of *us* poor peasants, I can't help but interfere. . . . It's *our* Communist Party in power now and *our* Fangcaodi has only the three of you party members" (I:244; emphasis added).

Grandma Deng's repeated references to a collective "we" that shifts easily from the social class of poor peasants to the party and the village community create a circuit of solidarity that allows seniority to flow from one collectivity to another. Through this circuit, the seniority she claims on the ground of experience in class struggle, by alluding to her experience of oppression as a poor peasant in Fangcaodi under the old regime and her stake in the new, also enables her to assume an "elder" position toward the party members. The subject position invoked here is, significantly, not sexed. It is inscribed in terms of class: Grandma Deng is an "elderly poor peasant" who has gathered together the "painful scars of the enslaved and the glorious marks of the creators" and summed up the lessons of life from "the whip of the feudal landlords, the cannons and guns of imperialism," which enable her to "show the future clearly . . . with [her] steps" (I:207).

However, insofar as her political activities are confined to counselling party members, the subject position Grandma Deng inhabits in the public political field is constituted not only by class, but by sex as well. The novel shows no incidents of Grandma Deng participating directly in political struggles. In contrast, the representative figure of male elderly poor peasants, Zhou Zhong, is characterized by a zealotry for direct engagement in political struggles. This is most vividly represented in his midnight chase to retrieve a pair of poorly stitched shoe soles, so as to prevent soldiers in the Korean front from being harmed by substandard equipments and to protect the reputation of the village's mutual aid teams (II:336-47); it is such zealotry that ultimately earns him a party membership.

The signification of sex in Grandma Deng's relation to public patriarchy is most prominent in the division of labor within the village community. Not directly involved in social production, her contribution to socialist construction is different from that of male elderly poor peasants who remain active in agricultural production. She oversees the performance of domestic duties, playing, as her name suggests, the role of a grandmother. It is, however, not in relation to her personal family — which is not even in Fangcaodi — that her position of grandmother is constituted. Rather, she is grandmother to all the families in her mutual aid team (a unit of several households cooperating in agricultural production) headed by Gao Daquan. This makes her not only a grandmother in a quasi-state organizational unit in the village, but a mother to Gao Daquan, who represents the (ideal) party member and cadre in the novel. Her role in informing Gao Daquan's estranged brother about Daquan's decision to give up his better living quarter for his brother's marriage and organizing help when Daquan's wife gives birth substantiates this maternal position.

Grandma Deng's mediated participation in political struggles fits in well with her occupation of a mother position vis-à-vis Gao Daquan in the mutual aid team. As overseer to the domestic sphere, she has no independent institutional base from which to participate directly in political struggles. Within the boundaries set for her in the text, acting indirectly through the party members (especially Gao Daquan) is her most viable option in political participation. The gender of mother as enacted by Grandma Deng is thus constituted, primarily, in relation to the public patriarchal positions of mutual aid team leader and party member/cadre occupied by Gao Daquan.

It is also in relation to Gao Daquan that another exemplary figure in the novel acts out her gender identity. Unlike Grandma Deng, however, Lu Ruifen's relation to Gao Daquan is not completely grounded in his public patriarchal positions.[44] Her gender as wife is constituted in the intersection of Gao Daquan as public patriarch and as husband. The centrality of the intersection to this gender construct and Lu Ruifen's status as its exemplar are brought out in the novel through the contrastive configuration of Qian Caifeng as wife. Having divorced her exploitative and oppressive husband under the aegis of the postliberation marriage law, Qian Caifeng appears in the novel as someone whose "body has been liberated by the new marriage system, but her heart has not" (I:307). She has failed to learn from her "unfortunate" experience and subsequent liberation the bankruptcy of a livelihood based on individual familial relationships and the necessary link between marriage and political struggle. Instead, she remains envious of the rich and plentiful lives of individual households and wishes to find a most loyal and capable husband who not only loves and cherishes her, but "enables her not to worry about food and clothing, to live generously and have everything she desires" (I:220).[45] Like the husband she ultimately remarries (Gao Daquan's brother, who, under her influence, insists on splitting with his self-sacrificing brother to set up a separate household), Qian Caifeng still subscribes to the "traditional custom" and old belief in "familism," thinking that a family of one's own is the only way to ensure a dependable future (I:521–22).

Qian Caifeng's clinging to the old narrative of familism spins a cautionary tale within the novel. Her bid for a better life through a renegotiation of the individual husband/wife relation falls through in the end, revealing, to her and the implied reader, that the vulnerability of the subject position of (individual) wife lies not so much in marital exploitation and oppression as in the weakness of an individual household in guaranteeing a better future for the exploited. In spite of a caring and hardworking husband of her own choice, her new marriage reenacts the old tragedy of exploitative labor because of her failure to discriminate between paterfamilias and public patriarchs; this leads to a mistaken trust in the former and alienation from the latter. Her reading of Gao Daquan according to the narrative logic of familism inscribes him as a paterfamilias whose neglect of his own household would keep it forever poor, and whose anger at his brother's splitting up the household would dispose him to revenge on the brother's family. The same narrative logic leads her to see the calculating and wealthy husband of her sister as a reliable patron who would help her new household prosper, thus taking her further away from the public patriarchal structure Gao Daquan represents. The result of this "erroneous" choice of narrative and reading, as she later finds out, is that she and her husband become little more than servants to the exploitative husband of her sister, who makes use precisely of family relation to trick them into servitude. While her husband is exploited as a cart driver away from home most of the time, "she has to do the housework of two households and experience in [her brother-in-law's] resentful expressions and tone, when negligence occasionally occurs, what it feels like to be a dissatisfactory slave to an exploitative master" (II:601–2).

The untenability of the gender position of wife separate from the public patriarchal structure is finally brought home to Qian Caifeng — and the readers through her eyes — in the tragedy of Liu Mo's wife.[46] Liu Mo's wife presumably acted out the destiny of wife inscribed in the narrative of familism, and her tragedy pushes Qian Caifeng to renegotiate her own relation to that narrative. Liu Mo's wife had initially favored joining Gao Daquan's mutual aid team, but, in order to protect her recently mended marriage, she deferred to her husband who, trusting the resources of his individual household, refused to expose himself to what he considered the risk of being taken advantage of in a mutual aid team. When emergency hit the fields of Fangcaodi and Liu Mo could find no recourse outside of his own family, his wife helped him in the field only three days after childbirth. Caught in a sudden torrent of rain while working, she fell ill and died. Her tragedy moves Qian Caifeng to an impassioned reading of the difference between being a wife in an individual household and in a mutual aid team:

Scenes of the time when her sister-in-law, Lu Ruifen, gave birth flash through her mind: in those few days, people in the mutual aid team all lent a hand in carrying water, cooking, and feeding the baby. People even stayed over to keep her company. Everyone was as affectionate as family. This alone was so different from what happened to Liu Mo's wife. Compared to those in individual households, members of mutual aid teams are indeed living in heaven. (II:587)

What Qian Caifeng learns from the comparison is that a wife's relationship to the public patriarchal structure literally makes a life and death difference. Childbirth and household chores may define the position of wife for Lu Ruifen no less than for Liu Mo's wife, but the practices required of these two wives differ according to their public institutional locations. Whereas support from the mutual aid team enables Lu Ruifen to concentrate on her "wifely" duty of reproduction, Liu Mo's wife has to take up the additional task of working in the field. The latter's consequent death suggests to Qian Caifeng that the position of wife cannot be maintained without the mutual aid team's enhancement of the efficiency and effectivity of intrafamilial sexual division of labor through social cooperation. A wife isolated in an individual household will eventually lose either her life, like Liu Mo's wife, or her independence in becoming a slave to another household, like herself.

If the cautionary tale of Qian Caifeng highlights the normative location of wife in the intersection of the personal family and public patriarchy, Lu Ruifen illustrates the regulatory practices that produce and maintain this gender. What situates Lu Ruifen in relation to public patriarchy is her "domestic" support for her husband's political activism. Her part in the novel (and her relation to Fangcaodi) "originates" in her marriage to Gao Daquan on the eve of "national liberation." The grounding of her identity in the new regime on a marriage arranged by the older generation makes her a crucial link between the "residual" rural order and the emergent socialist structure.

The pattern of behavior that defines the husband and wife relation between Gao Daquan and Lu Ruifen is indeed based on the sexual division of labor underlying the old rural order. For years before their actual marriage, Lu Ruifen has taken care of Gao Daquan's mother and younger brother in his native home while Gao Daquan learned agricultural skills and engaged in class struggles far away in Fangcaodi. With Gao Daquan increasingly engrossed in the struggle to build a socialist order in postliberation Fangcaodi, this pattern of behavior between husband and wife has become normative in the narrative present. Gao Daquan expects his wife to take care of all household affairs so he can devote himself to public duties and political activism. He informs Lu Ruifen that he has "taken little care of [their] own household affairs in the past, and cannot afford to do more from now on, for [he] must work wholeheartedly with [his] comrades to lead the villagers in increasing production and building socialism" (I:293).

This, however, does not make his household a "private" matter and Lu Ruifen its sole "manager." For the household is linked to the public patriarchal structure through Gao Daquan. Lu Ruifen must not only keep the household well, but also contribute to the public structure whatever Gao Daquan requires of the household. When there are not enough grains left in their household to contribute to his mutual aid team's collective purchase of a cart, for instance, she has to give up the eggs reserved for her nourishment after childbirth. Through the mediation of the public patriarchal positions of her husband, what is personal to the wife cannot but become "public" as well.

Conversely, political participation of the wife is also mediated by personal activities for the husband. Lu Ruifen sees her primary responsibility in the socialist construction of Fangcaodi as "giving Gao Daquan a special kind of assistance which no one else can offer," something that includes "doing her best in raising their son, taking care of her husband's younger brother, and managing their household affairs," as well as "relieving [her husband] of all family burdens and worries so he can work as he wishes on the important [public] matters he is enthusiastic about" (I:533, 437). Though formally entitled to her own individual voice in their mutual aid team, she invariably defers to her husband's opinion and decision regarding public matters. "Just follow what you [Gao Daquan] decide" (I:287; II:85, 478) is her common response in these situations. And because of the interweaving of the personal and the public in the public patriarchal structure, this support of and submission to her husband's stand is also extended to public expression of personal affairs. On Gao Daquan's demand, for instance, Lu Ruifen refrains from showing any sign of unhappiness over the split between Gao Daquan and his brother. Her public response to questions about the affair also follows her husband's line of argument about class struggle. As she tells Gao Daquan: "I answered [the interlocutors] with what you told me. I said that it was a problem of . . . the system of private ownership, which could not be changed by individual desires" (I:633).

It is then in her self-abnegating support for her husband's public activities that Lu Ruifen enacts the gender position of wife. Of all gender positions available to females in the novel, that of wife is most embedded in the historically dominant sexual division of labor that confines females to a domestic space. Yet, because of the fundamental restructuring of the public/domestic boundary in the building of Chinese socialism, this sexual division of labor is not a continuation of tradition. It is as much a part of Chinese socialism as the institution of public patriarchy. What the gender of wife constituted in this division of labor does for the Chinese socialist order is perhaps most succinctly summarized in the words of Zhou Zhong's wife: "if we [wives] do not cook to feed them well and sew to keep them warm, can they guys be activists?" (II:417). Her rhetorical statement makes clear that the production of party members/cadres like

Gao Daquan is not possible without the domestic support of wives like Lu Ruifen.

Such a dependence of political activism on female domestic support implies the necessary production of female party members/cadres into a gender radically different from that of the wife. This is most apparent in the gender constitution of the only female in Fangcaodi to become a party member, Zhou Liping, who is repeatedly identified in the novel as "Zhou Zhong's old daughter." The political zealotry that earns Zhou Liping her party membership is rooted precisely in her long-standing rejection of the gender position of wife. She had vehemently declared her resolution against ever becoming a wife when she was sought as a child-bride years before revolutionary victory. She had tried in vain to get an education that would enable her to support herself. "National liberation" turned her frustration and anger into enthusiasm for political struggle, as she learned to see "feudal exploitation" as the real culprit denying her any alternative in the past (I:432). "National liberation" also offers her an escape from the "common female destiny" of being made a wife. For, through the party, she can now get the education that her poor peasant father could not afford and participate in public (political) activities. The new regime thus allows her to inhabit a reconfigured gender position of daughter, which encodes a female "liberation" from domestic confinement in the emergent public patriarchy.

Whereas the gender of wife is grounded in a rigorous division of labor by sex, the antithetical gender of daughter enacted by Zhou Liping displays a variable relation to her sex. With her sexed body not (yet) configured in the institution of marriage, Zhou Liping is not tied to a primary responsibility of childbirth and household chores. She is thus relatively free to participate fully in social production. So, when the needs for more social labor arise, she can take a job as temporary worker in a shoe factory in the nearby market town, while village wives like Lu Ruifen are confined to piecework sewing at home. Yet, insofar as she works in the mutual aid team, her tasks still largely follow a pattern of sexual division of labor. She, for instance, takes up the housework in a poor peasant's family while the males work in his field when the sickness of the peasant and his wife calls the mutual aid team into action. Similarly, she is given the task of taking care of Lu Ruifen and her household needs when the latter gives birth. Even after she becomes a party member, her work in the production cooperative is still sexually determined and segregated: "Another group [working in the storeroom] consists of several maidens *(guniang)*. Zhou Liping is papering the window. . . . Qin Kai's daughter and Su Cunyi's daughter are squatting on the floor, washing teacups" (II:668). A division of labor by sex, rationalized and socialized under cooperative production, thus underlies the gendering practice of Zhou Liping just as it does that of Lu Ruifen, but to a lesser extent and allowing more flexibility.

By contrast, sex is mostly not signified in the political activism that is central to the regulatory practice for Zhou Liping's gender of daughter. As a member of the Youth League and village militia, Zhou Liping's political activities are generally no different from those of a young male activist. Whether in painting wall slogans or guarding harvests, she plays an identical part alongside the males. Her celebration of party membership, especially, lays bare this exclusion of sexual differences from the normative political behavior constitutive of her gender. On the day they are formally admitted into the party, Zhou Liping joins her father on equal terms in voluntarily repairing a stone bridge in the village. She herself initiates the work in order to "do something beneficial to the masses and the revolution to mark [their] first step" as party members (II:422).

Given the prevailing sexual division of labor, Zhou Liping's equal participation in such strenuous physical labor signals the elision of her sex as she joins the privileged fraternity of political activists. In her capacity as party member, the normative behavior is unequivocally male: "to follow single-mindedly the behavior of Gao Daquan, acting as the masses' ox, pulling the cart of revolution" (II:422). However, the ambivalent sex/gender relation Zhou Liping shows in social production is not altogether absent in political activities. Her female sex is (re)signified to make her a reliable representative — presumably of both sides — when a need for mediation between the public patriarchy and female villagers arises. So, in a struggle to block the staging of a "revisionist" play, Zhou Liping's sex is superimposed on her Youth League membership to make her the leader of the village's female youths. Again, when the marriage between Qian Caifeng and Gao Daquan's brother runs into problems, Zhou Liping is called on to do prototypical "women work." She is sent to negotiate with Qian Caifeng as a "representative of the Youth League and the village militia" by "the Youth League branch secretary, Zhu Tiehan, and [her] father, Zhou Zhong, to help Gao Daquan resolve his worry and bring credit to the liberated households" (II:11,18). Her sex is here interwoven into her locations in the public patriarchal structure to determine the political practice required of her.

It is thus through a flexible sex/gender relation in both social production and political activism that Zhou Liping performs her gender of daughter. This flexibility, allowing the daughter a direct participation in public patriarchy, marks a significant difference between the gender of daughter and the other female genders of mother and wife, whose public engagements in the rural community are always mediated by males, especially party members. Such difference calls attention to the discontinuities and power differences in these female genders and reveals a fundamental contradiction in the novel's rhetoric of women's liberation and its presentation of Zhou Liping as the model of emerging socialist female subject. In the figure of Zhou Liping and her "liberation" through engagement in political struggles, the novel suggests that "the road to women's liberation" lies in direct participation in public patriarchy (I:432). What is covered over in this projection of "women's liberation" is the unavailability of such a road to other (married) female figures. As we have seen, the activism of Zhou Liping herself is dependent on the existence of some other females (notably her mother and sister-in-law) who have not been, and are arguably institutionally constrained not to be, so "liberated" as to reject the "wifely" domestic support that political activism takes for granted. Rather than being diachronically related as Zhou Liping's narrative of liberation suggests, the gender constructs of wife and daughter in the public patriarchy of Fangcaodi are irreducibly synchronic and interactive. The active participation in political struggles that characterizes the gender position of daughter cannot be the regulatory practice for all females without unravelling the very social fabric of the (emergent) socialist village. The absence of a politically active wife in the novel is an eloquent reminder of this impossibility. To hold out Zhou Liping's narrative of women's liberation for all village females and to advance her daughter position as the postrevolution subject position for all females are to mask significant differences in power and oppression among female genders in the rural socialist order.

LOOKING BEYOND THE IDENTITY POLITICS OF WOMEN

The discursive production of different female genders, with differential distances from her sex and participation in the public patriarchy, in a state-sanctioned literary representation of socialist construction in rural China suggests a complexity of gender constitution under Chinese socialism that cannot be reduced to a general category of women. In drawing attention to this differential production of female genders, my purpose is not to argue a distinctive socialist gender system that eludes Western feminist categories. Rather, it is to highlight the need to interrogate the relation between sex and gender as part of our (here, I include feminists of all sexes and colors in the first and third worlds) continuous effort to critique and struggle against gender oppression, an effort involving destabilizing the dichotomization, and thus fixation, of gender categories that still underlie the identity politics of "women struggle." The differential signification, both in degree and modality, of the female sexed body in the gender, for instance, of wife and daughter in Chinese socialism indicates that dichotomous sex produced and maintained on the basis of physiological differences is not necessarily the ground on which genders are constituted. No less significantly, the complex and shifting power relations among these female genders call attention to the inadequacy of a strategy of fixing and representing sex/gender identities for building coalition struggles against gender oppression. To reveal and renegotiate the power relations among these genders, it is necessary to resist the deployment of identity categories that neutralize the multiple differences in gender production and signification. Herein lies the importance of problematizing the hegemony of the category of women and foregrounding the absence of a necessary link between sex and gender. Recognizing the possibility of multiple gender configuration for the female sex would enable us to resist the maintenance of gender oppression in essentialized categories and, hopefully, open a more productive space for coalition struggles to be imagined and built on the ground of political projects rather than social identities.

NOTES

1. See Diana Fuss, *Essentially Speaking* (New York: Routledge, 1989) for a discussion of the stakes involved in essentializing the categories of "man" and "woman" for (Western) feminism.
2. Chandra Talpade Mohanty, "Under Western Eyes: Feminist Scholarship and Colonial Discourses," in *Third World Women and the Politics of Feminism*, ed.

Mohanty, Ann Russo, and Lourdes Torres (Bloomington: University of Indiana Press, 1991), 53.

3. Chandra Talpade Mohanty, "Cartographies of Struggle: Third World Women and the Politics of Feminism," introduction to *Third World Women*, 5; emphasis in original.

4. See Denise Riley, *Am I that Name?: Feminism and the Category of "Women" in History* (New York: Macmillan, 1988).

5. Judith Butler, *Gender Trouble: Feminism and the Subversion of Identity* (New York: Routledge, 1990).

6. For a sense of the complexities of the issues involved in the relation between "women" and "modernity" in the third world, see *Third World, Second Sex*, vols. 1–2, ed. Miranda Davis (London: Zed Books, 1983, 1987); and Kumari Jayawardena, *Feminism and Nationalism in the Third World* (London: Zed Books, 1986).

7. Tani Barlow, "Theorizing Woman: Funu, Guojia, Jiating [Chinese Women, Chinese State, Chinese Family]," *Genders* 10 (spring 1991): 132–60.

8. Judith Butler's deconstructive reading of gender as "performatively enacted signification" is a fitting characterization of the gendering mechanism here.

9. Insofar as the kin-inflected gender system has been reconstituted, it is not "traditional"; it undeniably shares the same temporality with the "modern" gender of woman/women.

10. The phrase is taken from Judith Stacey, *Patriarchy and Socialist Revolution in China* (Berkeley: University of California Press, 1983), 1. See also Elisabeth Croll, *Feminism and Socialism in China* (London: Routledge & Kegan Paul, 1978); Delia Davin, *Woman-Work: Women and the Party in Revolutionary China* (Oxford: Clarendon Press, 1976); Phyllis Andors, *The Unfinished Liberation of Chinese Women, 1949–1980* (Bloomington: Indiana University Press, 1983); Kay Ann Johnson, *Women, Family and the Peasant Revolution in China* (Chicago: University of Chicago Press, 1983); and Margery Wolf, *Revolution Postponed: Women and Socialism in China* (Stanford, CA: Stanford University Press, 1986). Although the contributions of these studies should not be denied, Aihwa Ong's critique of their tendency to privilege the concerns of Western feminists is quite pertinent to the issue under consideration. See Aihwa Ong, "Colonialism and Modernity: Feminist Re-presentations of Women in Non-Western Societies," *Inscriptions* 3, no. 4 (1988): 79–93.

11. The distinction between sex and gender in these questions need not imply an agreement with the assumption of a "natural" basis for sex. Rather, it takes seriously the dominance of this assumption in the Chinese socialist formulation of sex/gender relations and foregrounds the importance of the natural versus cultural paradigm in the Chinese socialist formulation of genders.

12. The time-span of the Cultural Revolution is a controversial issue. Although it is generally extended to 1976, the year Mao Zedong died, I find Maurice Meisner's distinction between the end of the Cultural Revolution (in 1969) and the end of the Maoist period persuasive.

13. The campaign was an important part of the intense power struggle between the pre-Cultural Revolution veteran state and party officials championed by Zhou Enlai and the Cultural Revolution beneficiaries led by the "Gang of Four," a struggle waged in terms of ideological differences over the course of socialism in modern China. For a summary of the campaign, see Maurice Meisner, *Mao's China and After* (New York: Free Press, 1986), 413–15; see also Croll, *Feminism*, ch. 11, for a discussion of the state and local activities on the women problem during the campaign.

14. Unless otherwise stated, both "women" and "woman" hereafter in the text refer to the Chinese category of *funu*.

15. Ann Anagnost, "The Politicized Body," *Stanford Humanities Review* 2, no. 1: 91.

16. The most important party journal published in a foreign language, *Peking Review* (later *Beijing Review*) offers a distilled version of state/party discourses for foreign consumption. Setting off discursive constructions in sharp relief, its articles are valuable sources for the analysis of China's state discourses.

17. Hsu Kwang, "Women's Liberation Is a Component Part of the Proletarian Revolution," *Peking Review*, 8 March 1974, 12–15.

18. Ibid., 13.

19. Ibid., 14.

20. Ibid., 15. This is one of the standard Chairman Mao quotations on Chinese women under socialism. For reasons discussed later, my translation of the same statement in the epigraph of this section renders *nan tongzhi* and *nu tongzhi* as male comrades and female comrades, instead of the "men comrades" and "women comrades" used here in the *Peking Review* article and other official publications in English.

21. Whether or not the category of worker is gender neutral is, of course, a loaded and provocative question. It would seem so in the limited sense that it is a subject effect of the state discourse on class. However, to the extent that gender and class are discursively interlaced, class categories are arguably not gender neutral. Moreover, insofar as the explicitly marked gender term is "female" and *funu* has no "male" counterpart, it is highly contentious whether superficially ungendered categories should not be read as implicitly "male." For the complexities of a comparable issue in Western feminism, see Judith Butler's discussion of the different positions Monique Wittig and Luce Irigaray take on the relation between gender and language/philosophy in the West in *Gender Trouble*.

22. Li Chen, "Women Take Part in Productive Labor," *Peking Review*, 22 March 1974, 19; emphasis mine.

23. Ibid., 17.

24. Ibid., 18.

25. Since its inception in 1963, the Dazhai Iron Girls Team has been a model organization within the model agricultural brigade of Dazhai. Exemplifying the idea(l) that given sufficient ideological and political mobilization, females can perform difficult agricultural tasks like males, it has inspired similar

establishment of female "shock workers" teams all over China, of which the Ten Sisters Cotton Planting Team is one. For a brief description of the Dazhai model and its mobilization of female labor, see Andors, *Unfinished Liberation*, 98–99.

26. The Ten Sisters Cotton Planting Team of Wangjian Brigade in Linyi Prefecture Shanxi Province, *"Nutongzhi yeneng ban nantongzhi neng ban de shi"* (Female comrades can accomplish as well whatever male comrades can), *Hongqi* (Red Flag), Oct. 1973, 96–97.

27. Ibid., 95, 96.

28. Ibid., 95.

29. Iron Girls Team of Dazhai Brigade, *"Women geming funu zuihen kongmeng zhi dao"* (We revolutionary women bitterly hate the doctrines of Confucius and Mencius), *Hongqi*, March 1974, 37.

30. Ibid., 38.

31. Ibid., 38.

32. Ten Sisters, "Nutongzhi yeneng," 97.

33. Ibid., 96.

34. I thank an anonymous reader for an incisive critique that enables a clearer formulation of this part of my argument.

35. Liu Chao, "Safeguarding Women's Interests," *Peking Review*, 29 March 1974, 15–16.

36. *Iron Girls*, "Women geming funu," 39; emphasis mine.

37. For a discussion of feminist struggles in the May Fourth period, see Croll, *Feminism*, ch. 4.

38. See C. K. Yang, *Chinese Communist Society: The Family and the Village* (Cambridge. MIT Press, 1959) for a discussion of social restructuring and family reforms in the countryside; and Martin King Whyte and William L. Parish, *Urban Life in Contemporary China* (Chicago: University of Chicago Press, 1984) for changes in the cities. See also Stacey, *Patriarchy*, for a summary account of the differences in family reforms in rural and urban China and their implications for the renegotiation of gender relationships. William Parish and Martin K. Whyte give a detailed description of the maintenance of patrilocality and patrilineality in rural China in *Village and Family in Contemporary China* (Chicago: University of Chicago Press, 1978).

39. See M. J. Meijer, *Marriage Law and Policy in the Chinese People's Republic* (Hong Kong: Hong Kong University Press, 1971) for a detailed account of the marriage laws and their implications for the family system, and Yang (*Chinese Communist Society*), Andors (*The Unfinished Liberation*), and Johnson (*Women, Family*), among others, for the effects of land reform on family relations.

40. I am appropriating Judith Stacey's term here. In Stacey's usage, public patriarchy refers narrowly to the patriarchal aspects of the Chinese Communist Party manifested in the subordination of mass organizations such as the Women's Federation and the supervision over personal lives (*Patriarchy*, 227–35). I argue that state and party institutions are central to the very production

and regulation of genders and use the term "public patriarchy" to signify the collective effects of these institutions.

41. Although the production teams or brigades were often based on existing villages, thus, in effect, consolidating the lineage ties that usually underlaid the village structure, a visible insertion of state and party organizations into the existing structure still made significant differences to relationships in these agricultural production units.

42. Pai Chi-hsien, "Integration with the Poor and Lower-Middle Peasants," *Peking Review*, 26 July 1974, 12–14; emphasis in original.

43. Hao Ran, *Jinguang dadao*, vols. 1–2 (Beijing: Renmin wenxue zhubanshe, 1972, 1974). An abridged version of the first volume appears as *The Golden Road*, trans. Carma Hinton and Chris Gilmartin (Beijing: Foreign Languages Press, 1981). All translations here are mine. References to the novel are hereafter included parenthetically in the text.

44. The surname of Lu Ruifen is almost homonymous with the word for female (*nu*), suggesting a close association between the female sex and the gender of wife that Lu exemplifies.

45. Her surname Qian, which literally means money, indicates her identification with material wealth and preoccupation with monetary consideration.

46. This character's function as a negative illustration of the gender (non)position of (individual) wife is indicated by her lack of a proper name. She is introduced in the novel as "the wife of Liu Mo living in the front yard of Zhang Jinfa; since the boy in her arms is called Xiaozhu, everybody calls her 'Xiaozhu's mom' (*Xiaozhuma*)" (II:483).

ELEVEN

Compulsory Heterophobia:
The Aesthetics of Seriousness and
the Production of Homophobia

Carol Siegel

The last few years have featured what one might call the return of the repulsed, and the repulsive, on a number of fronts in the ongoing battle against homophobia. The year 1992 was one of organized political backlashes against gay and lesbian rights legislation. And no sooner was one anti-gay ballot measure defeated, than several more popped up to take its place. In many areas, reactionary political groups have won serious victories over the extension of constitutional protection from discrimination to homosexuals. As I write, the Oregon Citizens Alliance (OCA) is working in Oregon and the state of Washington to pass legislation with aims similar to those expressed in the infamous Measure 9, which was defeated in Oregon two years ago, and their efforts have met with some success in small cities, suburbs, and rural counties.[1] Living in Portland, Oregon, one of the storm centers, I have been unable to avoid hearing much more than I generally do from homophobes about their concerns and hopes.

One of the most surprising things I have learned is that members of the homophobic extreme right wing no longer want to pretend in front of the children that homosexuals do not exist. Instead, our antagonists seem preoccupied with institutionalizing education about differences in sexual preference. Measure 9 offered the OCA version of sex education. The paragraph of the measure that provoked the most ridicule from educators states:

319

The amendment would require state, regional, and local governments and their subdivisions, including specifically the State Department of Education and the public schools, to assist in setting a standard for Oregon youth that recognizes homosexuality, pedophilia, sadism and masochism as abnormal, wrong, unnatural, and perverse. In addition, the standard would recognize that homosexuality, pedophilia, sadism, and masochism are to be discouraged and avoided.[2]

Following the OCA's unveiling of this plan, there were months of public debate (and merriment) over what the measure implied should be taught by every teacher in our schools. But what interests me most is how far this proposal goes beyond the usual conservative efforts to remove certain books from school libraries and to keep homosexuals from teaching in public schools. I'm also curious about why it takes the direction it does.

The Measure 9 attack on public education shifted the emphasis in legislating "morality" from the usual endorsement of censorship to a plan for dissemination of what must be called misinformation, even according to the conservative terms of the American Psychiatric Association's definition of perversity, which exonerates homosexuality while still stigmatizing other less popular consensual sexual preferences. Note in the text of Measure 9 that recognition of homosexuality is mandated as strongly as condemnation of it. OCA leaders explained that students were to be taught about homosexuality (along with pedophilia, sadism, and masochism), and then taught that such practices are "abnormal, wrong, unnatural, and perverse." The implication seems to be that because homosexuality is such an attractive nuisance, it cannot effectively be opposed simply by privileging the dominant culture's values and sexual practices or even by silencing dissenting voices. In years past, it had apparently seemed to conservatives that children would develop an interest in heterosexual activity without any prompting, but the framers of Measure 9 clearly believe that unless schoolchildren are indoctrinated into heterosexualism by adults in authority, large numbers of them will become homosexuals. The ballot measure attempted to reify into law what has previously been considered a more subtle product of our cultural ideology, compulsory heterosexuality. And, in so doing, it suggested that in times and places where homosexuality is not criminalized, our previous understanding of how and why heterosexuality is compelled may have become inadequate.

Adrienne Rich introduced the idea of "compulsory heterosexuality" into feminist studies in an attempt to explain the difficulty of moving outside the concept of sexuality as a contact between oppositely gendered beings, and thus, the difficulty of moving beyond our culture's pervasive misogyny and homophobia.[3] The difficulty derived, in her view, from cultural naturalization and idealization of heterosexuality, which, as she shows, was maintained in much of the psychologically oriented feminist theory written in the mid- to late 1970s. Both prior to and after the publication of Rich's essay, feminist theorists have extensively investigated the limiting effects on representation in general and on artistic expression in particular of heterosexuality's privileged status as the paradigm for intercourse of all types. However, as numerous theorists, including Rich, have pointed out, a great deal of feminist theory has also been marked by an apparently unconscious or inadvertent privileging of the heterosexual model of difference. Thus what is meant to be a critique of traditional gender norms often ends by reinscribing and essentializing them.[4] For many feminist critics, recent critiques of essentialism and discussions of the construction of gender provide a much-needed escape from entrapment in the tropes belonging to a heterosexist perspective.[5] These discussions suggest that, if we cannot attain a vantage point beyond gender difference and thus envision a world without it, we can at least attain an outside perspective on essentialism in order to subvert the authority of its narratives and the power of its binaries by consciously manipulating the signs of gender.

Nonetheless, deliberate manipulations of the signs of gender are far from universally popular among feminists and others working for changes in gender politics. Heated arguments over the political value of "gender fuck" performances like parodic transvestism and exaggerated sex role playing have continued to divide gay, lesbian, and other feminist communities since the 1970s. The sort of performances least likely to be seen as furthering feminist and gay liberation agendas generally seem to be those that give attention to men's gynophobia, especially when the performances are authored and/or produced by men. Why would critics and nonprofessional audience members feel that a man's dramatization of fear of sexual contact with women — no matter how parodically overdone — can only be read as sexism?

The answer must come from a brief examination of how the gender politics of texts are usually analyzed both inside and outside the academic world. Most feminist discussions of traditional heterosexuality assume that belief in fixed and hierarchic gender difference is fundamental to heterosexist ideology. In gender studies, we usually presume that belief in a fixed gender hierarchy overlies repressed awareness of gender's instability. For this reason, we often tend to see textual manifestations of male anxiety about the instability of traditional gender status and roles either as deliberate expressions of misogyny or as involuntary revelations of male fear of being overcome by woman. Consequently, through a logic of reversal, accounts of men's fear of heterosexual contact are read as allegories in which the real terror is of the unfixing of gender hierarchy.

This reading practice has two major political advantages. First, it exposes the misogyny that often lies at the bottom of what might otherwise be disarming confessions of male weakness and fear in relation to women. Second, it empowers feminist critics to read the repressed, rescuing the texts' unconscious content and so putting what many describe as the feminine back into circulation. But, there is also a problem from the feminist perspective with the practice of reading accounts of male fear of heterosexual contact as misogynist tales in which the unfixing of gender stands for loss. Such a reading practice erases all possibility that the male-authored text might sometimes aim to subvert the hierarchies, might go against gender categories instead of always going against women. If our methodology erases that possibility, then male and female authors are rewritten as absolute, essential enemies.[6] The male who is indisputably different is marked as feminine, so that the diversity within the two officially recognized genders, which should explode them as categories, is recontained into the binaries masculine and feminine.[7] Should the feminist critic claim for herself the role previously reserved for the psychiatrist as decoder supreme, always revealing the unconscious of the text, the hidden, disruptive feminine voice of the masculine text and bestowing authority on that voice? A certain satisfaction can accompany this sort of role reversal. However, it ultimately works to reinscribe gender difference and to mark woman (once again) as a mystical outsider by nature.

So one may come to ask whether a male-authored tale of fear of heterosexuality can be about something other than unconscious fear of gender instability. Rather than coercively idealizing heterosexual relations, as the theory of compulsory heterosexuality claims the dominant culture tends to do,[8] while disclosing a troubled (textual) unconscious hatred of women and thus providing us with material made for deconstruction, some representations of gynophobia display and even flaunt their consistency with a tradition of ridiculing and denying heterosexual love. I turn now to the controversial film *Basic Instinct* (directed by Paul Verhoeven) because it is a case in point.

Films and texts like *Basic Instinct* illuminate the space between the reflexive patriarchal misogyny that attempts to resolve the woman question by repression and a gynophobia that is an open admission of male defeat. Such a text can also help us see how homophobia can come from sources other than devaluation of the feminine. This film not only presents the war between the sexes in a wildly extreme fashion, it also, through this performance of gender difference, provides an exterior perspective on the present legacy of past textual and cinematic construction of gender norms.[9] And, in addition, a close look at the film and its reception illuminate much about how heterosexuality is both embattled and compelled wherever homosexuality falls within the law.

Basic Instinct's commentaries on gender are inextricable from its narrative structure. Unlike easily recognizably feminist films that focus on women's empowerment through control of narrative (such as *Strangers in Good Company* and *Fried Green Tomatoes*), *Basic Instinct* has no pretensions to being a woman's guide to life, nor is it presented as if from a woman's perspective, although it does include a woman's narrative.[10] The woman's narrative is peripheral in the sense that it is almost never heard. Yet from the margin it inhabits, the female narrative's power emanates out informing the film's "own" narrative or major narrative, which could be understood as both a counterstory and as one struggling to contain all that the female protagonist writes.

The film's main method of diegesis might most accurately be described as the would-be dominant narrative, but for brevity's sake I call it the major narrative. This narrative is strongly identified with the male protagonist, Nick Curran (played by Michael Douglas), because it comes to us almost entirely through point-of-view shots and shots in which he is the focus character. On the rare occasions when he is absent both as actor and observer, as in the sequence that goes under the opening credits, what we see is out of focus or shot from a confusingly oblique angle as if his presence were essential to clarity of vision. But despite the camera's endorsement of his vision, the major narrative fails to account adequately for what the audience sees. The woman's narrative rivals the major narrative and challenges it in ways that Nick's point of view cannot seem to fully incorporate into the story we see.

The major narrative's double failure, both to pull all the plot details into coherence and to contain the woman's narrative, is crucial to the film's many plot twists. Like the noir classics it imitates, *Basic Instinct* tells us its story deceptively, almost always as if from within the defective viewpoint of its male protagonist, a stereotypically paranoid, macho, rebellious police detective with the requisite substance abuse problems and haunted past. A technical difference from classic film noir works against narrative coherence. Voice-over is conspicuously absent, leaving the story without an enunciated moral center.[11] The film breaks most decisively from noir conventions in its female protagonist. Catherine Tramell (played by Sharon Stone) is a professional writer who insists on treating both the story we see unfold and Nick as her material to be manipulated into whatever shape best expresses her vision. When Nick (and thus the story line that comes to us through him) fails to account for events, the failure is directly attributable to Catherine's narrative, whose exigencies consistently dominate the action.

In the opening scene, we see a woman astride a man who is tied to the bed posts. At what appears to be their moment of climax, she stabs him to death with an icepick. The woman's face is not clearly visible. The scene then changes to introduce Nick as an investigating police detective. Nick begins the investigation by focusing, logically enough, on Catherine, who is the victim's lover. His suspicions are further, and even more logically, aroused by his discovery that she has published a book in which an identical murder is committed. Although after a fashion she does defend herself by asking whether anyone would so blatantly announce her own murderous plot in advance, she also tauntingly proves, over and over, that she is capable of just such an audacious gesture. She exhibits herself to an interrogation room full of policemen, she socializes with her multiple murderer friend Hazel, she teases her multiple murderer lover Roxy, and she toys outrageously with Nick, and in each case, she luxuriates in her own power and her obvious sense of invulnerability. As she plots out her next novel, which she jeeringly describes to Nick as his own story, Catherine leads him on a wild chase of "clues" that bring him to shoot his sometime girlfriend, police psychologist Beth Garner. She had once, apparently, rejected Catherine's advances and we have also seen her trying to free Nick from his enthralled passion for Catherine. In the last scene, Catherine is once again on top of her lover, now Nick, and seems to be trying to decide when to use the icepick.

The film suggests that Catherine was either directly responsible for or engineered the violent deaths of Johnny Boz, a retired rock star, whom we see stabbed to death in the first scene; Nilsen, an Internal Affairs Officer who has sold Catherine private information about Nick's therapy sessions with Beth; Nick's partner, Gus; and Beth. We may also surmise that before the drama opens, Catherine has killed her parents, her academic advisor in college, and Beth's husband. Part of the confusion of the plot comes from the lack of reasonable motivation for these murders. As soon as a motive is implied, evidence appears that occludes it. For instance, one might think that Catherine murdered her parents to get their money. (She is the heiress to $100 million.) However, because they died when she was a child and she could not have gained autonomy, this complicates imagining the killings that way. Her murder of Nilsen at first seems clear-cut. We know that he knows at least one incriminating thing about Catherine in that he accepted a bribe from her, and we also find out that he was investigating her past. The question of how he could have done her any harm without also revealing his own guilt is left unanswered. Other murders, including Boz's and Gus's, seem absolutely unmotivated. Catherine, too, seems troubled by these unreasonable crimes. She is explicitly said to use knowledge gained from her college double major in English and psychology to explore the violence that flows out of her, befriending/studying multiple murderers and "novelizing" her own crimes.

Whereas the noir heroine is conventionally shallow, mercenary, and calculating, less deep than she seems, Catherine has nothing to gain from her plotting but an insight into the construction of her own identity. Traditional noir heroines are figures for the mystery of the body of woman, that is, the terrible mystery of the *thing* of beauty whose surface draws out the soul through the eyes. Catherine is a new thing in noir: woman as active creator of images. Her manipulation of the world extends beyond presenting her beauty as a lure; she makes Nick as much as she makes herself. Like the author she is, she contemplates a world recreated in her image. Because she is in the process of enmeshing Nick in her fiction, she likewise makes him contemplate the mystery of her mind.

The more Nick strives to resolve her mystery, that is, to contain the mystery of her within the narrative/police report we must assume he is trying to put together, the more surely he is reduced into a character within the story she is writing. In fact, it is in this respect that the absence of voice-over is most conspicuous because the concept of an exterior and containing text, put together retrospectively by the detective, is essential to the truth claims of the contemporary mystery story. Because Nick gives us no overview, we must turn to Catherine for one. Whereas Catherine's novel might be considered to belong to the mystery genre, its mystery cannot be unravelled according to genre conventions.

By the conclusion we know that Catherine was the murderer in the first scene, but the only explanation we get of why she stabbed her lover during the sex act is that this action provides a conclusion to her story about him as the object of her sexual and violent impulses. If one were to insist upon retrospectively reconstructing the plot in order to give each murder a motive, one might come up with something like this: At college Catherine has one sexual encounter with Beth and becomes obsessed with her. (Beth tells this version of their relationship to Nick.) Catherine then kills her advisor, a psychology professor, because he realizes that her feelings about Beth are abnormal and dangerous. Catherine continues to pursue Beth and, when Beth marries, Catherine kills her husband. Then, several years later, when Catherine and Nick become lovers, Catherine gets Nick's attention by murdering Johnny Boz, first detailing the murder in a book and then seducing Boz. Although by the time Catherine's book is published, Nick has already lost interest in Beth, Catherine buys information from Nilsen that enables her to seduce Nick. She then kills Nilsen and frames Nick for the crime. She lures Gus and Beth to a setup so that she can kill him, making it look as if Beth is responsible, and thus causing Nick to kill her. This version of the murders does reflect a somewhat warped sense of poetic justice. However, it seems completely improbable not only because it has gaps (like the omission of any explanation of Catherine's parents' deaths), but also because the number of murders is absurdly excessive if the aim is simply to punish Beth. It is most strikingly unlikely because Catherine never shows any emotion about Beth at all, whereas she clearly mourns the deaths of other characters, like Roxy. Ultimately, the only reason we are given for Catherine's elaborate machinations to get Nick at icepick's point is that she has written the story that way.

Many film reviewers commented on the inadequacy of the film's plot. Terrence Rafferty's complaint that "they tell us who the killer is and leave everything else unexplained" is typical.[12] The source of this general dissatisfaction with the narrative may be that the film ignores the usual questions raised by the noir/mystery genre plot, including what the murderess' motivation is for her crime and for her cold-hearted affair with the male protagonist. Catherine's murderess friends' crimes are described as motiveless, the result of impulses as inexplicable as they were irresistible. Throughout the film, characters comment on Catherine's lack of motivation for the murders. Catherine explains, "I'm a writer, I use people for what I write. Let the world beware." When Nick asks her to substitute a marriage for the murder at the end of her new novel, she says, "It wouldn't sell. Someone has to die." This statement opens up a new frame of interpretation, one in which Catherine figures most significantly not as a noir murderess but as an author. Killing and making love are not sequential means to an end in *Basic Instinct;* plot has become an end in itself for the plotting heroine. Her answer to Nick directs our attention away from the idea that she as woman, the mysterious feminine, is the secret source of death. It is, instead, suggested that cultural and narrative conventions motivate her and explain the story's deadly secret.

The film raises numerous unanswered questions, including the identity of the title's basic instinct. A plausible, but crucially only partial, answer is that it is heterosexuality; after all, Nick and Catherine seem to struggle against and eventually romantically succumb to their attraction to each other. Visual images suggest that we are watching nature working in its rawest form. For instance, Catherine attracts Nick by displaying her body to him. She does this first in the most conventional (and hackneyed) film noir style by undressing in front of a mirror angled so that he can see her. Her next move breaks with traditions outside of pornography. During her police interrogation, she commands his attention with the sort of direct sexual remarks that psychologists tend to categorize as "inappropriate" and then spreads her legs. Her short white skirt rides up and her vulva is visible. Her expression is triumphant. Despite her degree in psychology, she is obviously unaffected by theories of female genital lack. Her certainty that there is something there and moreover something the sight of which will give her power over the male seems more confidently animal than intellectual. She positively sneers with superiority as she displays the power between her legs.

The film's redefinition of heterosexual "instinct" continues with Nick's reaction to Catherine's pursuit of him. He is not only unable to resist her, he is unable to resist submitting to her. Water imagery, which has traditionally been sexualized in both film and literature, is played against close shots of ice to dramatize the power dynamics between Nick and the woman who is writing his story. The waves crashing on the shore at her Stinson Beach house and the deluge of rain outside her Pacific Heights house, alternate with and inflect scenes in which she wields the icepick to break ice blocks just as she will shatter Nick's carefully maintained icy hardness. He gladly, and literally, puts it all, pick and ice, into her hands.

In both the major narrative and Nick's own vision, he is identified with Catherine. Other characters remark that Nick is "as crazy as she is." And, if he solves the crime, then it will be because "it takes one to know one." Nick makes a few feeble attempts to differentiate himself from her but soon gives in to full identification. This is most apparent in their parallel interrogation scenes. The set piece scene in which she wisecracks and spreads her legs as she is questioned about Boz's murder begins with the comment, "This session's being taped." Later, when Nick is questioned in the same room about Nilsen's murder, it is as if the tape is being played back; Nick repeats Catherine's defiant lines verbatim. This odd scene resonates with what is perhaps the strangest line in the film.

In an earlier scene set in a diner, Gus realizes that Nick has been making love with Catherine and tries to warn him from further sexual involvement. Gus is drunk and his obscene turns of phrase elicit angry comments and looks from others seated around them. Nick acknowledges the danger of getting too close to Catherine, but then, as if bemused by his own attitude, remarks that he is not afraid of her. One might expect the foulmouthed Gus to deliver the hardboiled cliche "that's just your dick talking." Instead he says, "that's just her pussy talking." If Nick relishes his role as stand-in for the contemptuously communicative vagina, Catherine insists on the difference between them. She often reminds him of his fictional and her metafictional status. She consistently reminds the audience that we are in a postfeminist world of noir, where woman has access to the script. She not only creates the story in which he is a character, she also knows why the story must be as it is.

What determines the story's conclusion is the open secret at the film's core. In order to understand why the story must end with betrayal or rejection of heterosexual love, it is necessary to understand why homophobes would feel it is necessary to teach children to despise homosexuality, rather than simply continuing, as they always have in the past, ignoring it completely, and treating heterosexuality as if it were the only possible form of sexual expression. The film suggests that the conventions of fiction demand that we see heterosexual love as more fatal illusion than basic instinct. Before dismissing this message as aberrant and discontinuous with literary tradition, we might note that included among the earliest meanings of "romantic" the *Oxford English Dictionary* lists: "having no foundation in fact," "having no real existence," and "going beyond what is customary or practical." These definitions raise some troubling questions about the evolution of the word "romance," which since the middle of the nineteenth century has slowly shifted in meaning so that to everyone except critics it now seems to signify nothing but flowery love stories. "Romantic" likewise has come to mean sentimentalized sexual desire. Because both terms are associated with such low-culture forms as greeting cards, formula novels, and "easy listening" songs, it would seem that the combination of the concept of romance with that of love results in a fantastical construction, one fundamentally divorced from the harsher principles of what we term reality.

Counter to what one might expect, given the dominant culture's demonization of homosexual relations, heterosexual love is particularly culturally marked as unreal. An expressed lack of belief in "true love" is not simply part of the general cynicism of what is currently considered a realistic attitude toward life. It also reflects the logical consequences of a specific part of heterosexist ideology: belief in the inevitability of a war between the sexes as long as civilization interferes with the purely natural, which is conceived of as unthinking acceptance of gender hierarchy. Heterosexist ideology cannot allow for an egalitarian resolution of the conflict between men and women because such a resolution would be deemed unnatural. Therefore, no possibilities are left open for narratives about love except obvious fantasy that romanticizes away conflict or "realism" based on the recording of the battle.[13] Monique Wittig argues that the ordinary positing of two genders that exist in a natural dominant/submissive relation prior to social order makes the social contract a contract with heterosexuality. As she asserts, "Breaking off the heterosexual social contract is a necessity for those who do not consent to it."[14] For this reason, heterosexuality inevitably becomes a battle site for women who refuse passivity. When the penalty for such refusal was death at worst and silencing and extreme marginalization at best, as long as heterosexuality was the only speakable option, texts could mark themselves as sophisticated by doubting the possibility of heterosexual love without suggesting that they advocated anything else. The only recognized area of representation outside high culture's seriousness was low culture's "romantic" heterosexual fantasy.

Linda Williams has pointed out that pornography, women's romance, and horror films are all scorned for being what she calls body genres, that is, genres that stimulate physical responses.[15] Romance and pornography are also very often criticized for offering unrealistic wish fulfillment. If we recognize that so-called romantic love is radically incompatible with art that has pretensions to either realism or seriousness, then we can see why horror and suspense films with a central love story so frequently attempt to redeem themselves as art with the sort of surprisingly open conclusion (The End . . . Or is it?) that *Basic Instinct* presents in exaggerated fashion. *Basic Instinct*'s conclusion follows a full fade to black from Catherine's tender embrace of Nick after his suggestion that they "live [together] happily ever after." After the black out, the picture returns suddenly and, as ominous music on the sound track wells up more and more floridly, the camera tracks down from the entwined couple on the bed to an extreme close up of the icepick under it. This disclaimer of romance is placed in a world where "pussies" talk and women write, where homosexuality has been spoken aloud and so must be recognized even by those who wish it did not exist.

Catherine's combination of bisexuality and murderousness has been read by many critics as a negative depiction of lesbianism harkening back to fifties' film stigmatizations of lesbians as deranged and violent.[16] That Catherine's lover Roxy killed her two younger brothers and that Catherine's friend (and possibly lover) Hazel killed her husband and three children are seen as further indications that the plot crudely equates rejection of the traditional feminine role with viciousness. However, one might keep in mind that whereas all three women have killed their way out of the family, Catherine, unlike Roxy and Hazel, has not completely rejected heterosexuality. She is represented as not just a bisexual, but as that special creature, the San Francisco bisexual. The film makes emphatic reference to its location in nearly every scene, and frequently informs, or more accurately reminds, viewers that homosexuality and bisexuality are neither illegal nor socially stigmatized in the San Francisco Bay Area. We might therefore read Catherine as a contemporary figure, as one who could not have existed openly in many other times or places. Unlike the seeming bisexuals of fifties' cinema who we are invited to see as sneaky homosexuals whose "bisexuality" is itself alternately a disguise and the revelation of hidden evil, Catherine is not one-within-the-other but both/and.

The figure of the bisexual has often been regarded as a representation of flawed or confused gender identification. But it can also be read in a way similar to the figure of the mulatto that Hazel Carby describes "as a convention . . . that enabled the exploration in fiction of relations that were socially proscribed. The mulatto figure is a narrative device of mediation, allowing a fictional exploration of the relation between the races while offering an imaginary expression of the relation between them."[17] As a bisexual, Catherine brings two worlds of gender identification into contact. On one hand, she embodies dissonance. That her body holds heterosexuality and homosexuality in tension gives the lie to the dominant culture's reading of both identities because, as Eve Sedgwick points out, above all else " 'sexual identity' is supposed to organize [difference] into a seamless and univocal whole."[18] In this modality, Catherine's identity multivocally speaks the impossibility of heterosexuality. On the other hand, Catherine as bisexual plays a mediating role, inviting us to look at her not only in comparison to the contextualizing characters Roxy and Hazel, but in contrast to Beth, her foil and the other suspect in Johnny Boz's murder.

Played by Jeanne Tripplehorn, in a wide-eyed pouty little girl style, Beth is the anti-essentialists' nightmare woman. She is a whining embodiment of stereotypical femininity, always defined by powerless maternal flutterings or helpless dependence. As both his psychologist and his girlfriend, Beth is always scurrying supportively after Nick. Some plot details lead us to read her as an animalistically "natural" heterosexual woman; consider her seemingly involuntary submissive response to Nick's sexual violence and dialogue like Gus's comment on her devotion to Nick: "She mates for life." However, other details problematize this reading. For instance, two scenes stress her inability to experience orgasm with a man. Nick attributes this to her tension and lack of self-knowledge, both characteristics one would not expect in a natural woman. More subtly, her worship of the rebellious male is presented as darkly comic through her almost fetishistic attachment to the plastic Bart Simpson on her key ring. She strokes this toy during stressful encounters and it causes her death when Nick mistakes it for a gun hidden in her pocket. In relation to Catherine's story, Beth's seems to be a tragedy based on her rejection of female bonding in favor of self-destructive attachment to the role of the good girl who can only rebel through identification with the rebel hero. Catherine, whose basic instinct seems to be to kill whatever male comes too close, is conversely defined as the sort of survivor whose success comes from understanding culture's script — and who better than she who (re)writes it?

The rivalry over narrative control between Beth and Catherine, both of whom compete to persuade Nick, is reminiscent of the struggle between Janine the psychiatrist and Christine the murderess in Marleen Gorris's *A Question of Silence (De Stilte Rond Christine M.)*. Because Gorris and Verhoeven are the two Dutch filmmakers best known internationally, it is tempting to compare the two films, especially because they are parallel in their use of detective story motifs to present a narrative of an apparently motiveless murder. Verhoeven's film also offers us the same configuration of female characters. Both films pit a lone psychotherapist against a trio of closely bonded murderous women. Gorris's story is informed by collectivist feminist values. In contrast to Verhoeven's, it dramatizes the change in consciousness of the "male identified" woman as the psychiatrist Janine is drawn into a complicitous understanding of the murderesses' need to kill a man who to them represents patriarchal power. Where Gorris's film emphasizes women's enforced silence, Verhoeven's dwells on the dangers women's writing poses to the handmaiden of patriarchy. Where Gorris, with what often seems a pseudo-documentary style, locates the battle between men and women within the material world and its institutions, Verhoeven continually refers to the battle's foundation in textuality and its conventions. The films are alike in their insistence that, as Geetha Ramanathan says of *A Question of Silence*, "the price a female pays for claiming subject status in a violently patristic society [is] murder. For each of the women has to write her name in blood to write it at all."[19]

Basic Instinct resembles most of Verhoeven's earlier films in its wittily self-conscious engagement with the tradition of depicting heterosexual desire as paradoxically both irresistible and deathly.[20] Catherine's little lectures on literary convention emphasize the compulsion, basic to all but the lowest art, to represent heterosexuality as dangerous and distasteful for both partners. The film visually echoes these values. The sophistication that our culture equates with denial of the possibility of fulfilling heterosexual love lavishly varnishes the hard surface of every scene. Whereas both Catherine and Beth complain to Nick that in college the other imitated her, the audience is teased by the remarkably perfect color coordination of Nick's wardrobe to each of the two women's clothing in their respective shared scenes. For instance, in the notorious, violent sex scene with Beth, they both wear identical shades of olive brown and olive green, with his underpants rather arrestingly, because so unusually, matched to her skirt. His shift into identification with Catherine is coded into their next scene by the shift of the color range to steel blue and dark taupe. It is as if the cloth for their clothes has been cut from the same dye lots. Never has heterosexuality appeared more as a life style.

Basic Instinct's design, as well as color, reifies heterosexuality's discontents into visible patterns of unease. In aerial shots especially reminiscent of *Vertigo*, we see Nick's world as a puzzle in which Northern California coastal roads and the stairwell of his apartment building are mazes that he must negotiate in search of the woman and the secret. Nick's desire for certainty and closure appears in his (ungratified) demand that Catherine affirm his sense of their sexual encounter as an experiential peak, "the fuck of the century." His struggle for narrative control is also evident in his insistence that he become her only lover, and, above all else, his commitment to "nailing her" by solving the murder case. The case remains open and she remains free as he circles around and around, with the hilly locale enhancing (as in *Vertigo*) the sense of much movement yielding very little progress.

Similarly, the first close-up of one of Catherine's novels paradoxically evokes both movement and stasis. The book, entitled *Love Hurts*, is one of those garish productions in which a window cut into the front cover reveals the center of the mystery, in this case a bloodied male corpse tied to the bed posts. And, when one opens up the book, a second cover inside reveals the solution, in this case a picture of the murderess. The simple suggestion, open me up and you will see the answer, is simultaneously belied by the author's name, Catherine Woolf, in large letters above the picture. Catherine's pen name seems so offensively inappropriate to an obvious and trashy genre novel that it can hardly fail to make the viewer wonder what she can mean by it. We jump ahead to knowledge; we jump back to question.

In this sort of semiotic play with the viewer, the film de-emphasizes Nick's identity crisis in favor of an admiring contemplation of Catherine's richly full presence. Like the landscape before our eyes, she is twisty and obscure, difficult to read, but omnipresent. All roads lead back to Catherine. Her meaning extends visually beyond being the key to the mystery. In this way, the film differs greatly from the classics to which it refers. Tania Modleski seems right to claim that the structure of *Vertigo* implies that "femininity in our culture is largely a male construct" and, in doing so, taps into a source of male terror because "if woman, who is posited as she whom man must know and possess in order to guarantee his truth and his identity, does not exist, then in some important sense he does not exist either, but rather is faced with the possibility of his own nothingness."[21] *Basic Instinct*, in contrast, identifies authorship as female and femininity as the creation of women, thus the woman who creates has an existence posited even outside the frame. Rather than man fading as he destroys the woman he has made, male presence is shown being effaced by the inscription of the woman writer's name, written in his blood.

Basic Instinct parodies, through self-referentiality, the dominant aesthetics of our era, which, as Jane Tompkins says, define legitimate art in contrast to "sentimentality."[22] Comic love stories can end with marriage because their pretensions to realism are already undercut by their comic tone. They have announced tonally that they are not to be taken seriously. They present themselves as amusement as much as art. A story that demands to be taken seriously as art cannot go too far in indulging fantasies of romantic resolution. The aesthetics of seriousness implicitly demand conflation of the death drive and heterosexual libido because the idea that heterosexual desire can be satisfied is automatically dismissed as delusion. By this logic, to seek to satisfy heterosexual desire is to deliberately maintain a state of delusion, to willfully divorce oneself from reality, from the real, and hence from the world or life. Because the given is that heterosexual satisfaction cannot exist in the world, the pursuit of it becomes a yearning to leave the world. If this seems exaggerated, remember the vast number of "great" love stories that end with the death of at least one of the lovers.

In *Basic Instinct*, the description of a possible future in which Nick and Catherine will "fuck like minks, raise rug rats, and live happily ever after," is repeated three times and dismissed three times. The first time Gus asks if this is what Nick thinks will happen and then comments disgustedly, "Oh, Man!" The second time, Nick proposes it to Catherine, who comments that she hates "rug rats." The third time, when Nick omits the children, we are left to believe that Catherine accepts this comic resolution, that is, until we see the icepick. Being serious and being realistic are euphemisms for being pessimistic in matters of love and romance, so for the film to move firmly into seriousness at its conclusion, it must promise to prick the romantic bubble. And because the story is placed in a context in which women irrepressibly create and choose, a world in which homosexuality has been spoken and cannot be unsaid, Catherine's rival narrative demands that, as a bisexual woman, she puncture an opening in the heterosexual closure that would "nail" her down. With her face full of tender regret, she must still provide the ending that will transform her love story into art.

Basic Instinct suggests that homophobia does not come only from a fear of losing the sense of identity based on belief in gender difference. It suggests that homophobia arises as much from a fear that if ordinary logic and literary realism both dictate that heterosexuality is incompatible with anything but love-death, then homosexual love might be left as the only sane choice. In other words, the film shows that homophobia may be as much the product of our culture's devaluation of heterosexuality as it is of our culture's devaluation of homosexuality. *Basic Instinct* shines a bright light into the corner in which culture has desire boxed, deathly in every direction it turns. The film stimulates rage against traditional representations of gender difference, which was the inevitable result of a design that foregrounds the naturalization of masochism, fatalism, and despair in artistic treatments of heterosexual relations, while recognizing the existence of homosexuality as a hated and feared alternative. Our anger, like the film's own, might best be directed toward this tradition, this message, rather than the messenger that discloses it, because art's endless reiterations that heterosexuality is both basic instinct and deadly madness does much to create the need to maintain the heterosexual couple through compulsion.

NOTES

1. In November 1992, the state ballot initiative Measure 9 was defeated by 54 to 46 percent of the vote, but by March 1994, anti-gay-rights measures had been passed in twenty Oregon cities and counties.
2. Official 1992 General Voter's Pamphlet (Oregon, 1992): 93.
3. Adrienne Rich, "Compulsory Heterosexuality and Lesbian Existence," in *Powers of Desire: The Politics of Sexuality*, ed. Ann Snitow, Christine Stansell, and Sharon Thompson (New York: Monthly Review Press, 1983), 177–205.

4. For an overview of the feminist debate over "essentialism," see Diana Fuss, *Essentially Speaking: Feminism, Nature, and Difference* (New York: Routledge, 1989).

5. See especially Teresa de Lauretis, *Technologies of Gender: Essays on Theory, Film, and Fiction* (Bloomington: Indiana University Press, 1987); Judith Butler, *Gender Trouble: Feminism and the Subversion of Identity* (New York: Routledge, 1990); and Jane Gallop, *Around 1981: Academic Feminist Literary Theory* (New York: Routledge, 1992).

6. For a discussion of some of the costs to feminism of the erasure of male feminism, see Robert Vorlichy, "(In)Visible Alliances: Conflicting 'Chronicles' of Feminism," in *Engendering Men: The Question of Male Feminism*, ed. Joseph A. Boone and Michael Cadden (New York: Routledge, 1990), 275–90.

7. The most extreme version of this sort of recontainment of transgressive sexualities is the concept of sexual inversion, according to which male and female homosexuals are imagined as being of the genitally "opposite" sex inside so that the identity of each is collapsed into that of, respectively, "the" male and "the" female heterosexual. By the same sort of logic, a man's sympathy with feminism feminizes him so that he can never be seen as a man speaking as an advocate of the rights of women just as the male homosexual cannot be seen as a man loving men, but must, instead, be seen as a man becoming woman, or speaking in her place. On the dangers to feminism in the poststructuralist yearning to "become woman," see Alice Jardine, *Gynesis: Configurations of Woman and Modernity* (Ithaca, NY: Cornell University Press, 1985).

8. Rich, "Compulsory Heterosexuality," 183–84.

9. For a feminist defense of *Basic Instinct* (on other grounds than I argue here), see "Icepick Envy," a two-column section consisting of C. Carr, "Reclaiming Our Basic Rights" and Amy Taubin, "The Boys Who Cried Misogyny," *Village Voice* 28 April 1992: 35–36.

10. This chapter does not focus on whether or not the characters in the film are presented as role models, a question raised in reviews in mainstream and alternative papers alike. But, because *Basic Instinct* has been harshly criticized for its negative depiction of women, I do not want to leave the topic of "images of women" without remarking that one might make the argument that *Basic Instinct* really does no less to offer women positive role models than the popular *Fried Green Tomatoes*, which has generally been considered a feminist film. The films are quite similar in their focus on mysterious bisexual women, their emphasis on the importance of bonding to women's survival, and their exploration of the idea of female control of narrative. Central to each film is a woman's grotesque murder of a man. Although *Fried Green Tomatoes*'s female characters are generally more wholesome than those in *Basic Instinct*, and the man's death is depicted as clearly justified in the former film, the cannibalism in *Fried Green Tomatoes* would seem to create some problems if we wish to say that it provides women with guidance on how to live in a difficult world.

11. See Amelia Jones, " 'She Was Bad News': Male Paranoia and the Contemporary New Woman," *Camera Obscura* 25/26 (1991): 301–3, for a discussion of connections between voice-over and male authority in both noir films and the recent films dealing with male paranoia, which Jones terms "new women's films."

12. Terrence Rafferty, *The New Yorker*, 6 April 1992, 83.

13. See Nancy Armstrong, *Desire and Domestic Fiction: A Political History of the Novel* (New York: Oxford University Press, 1987) for a detailed discussion of how "the sexual contract" operates within nineteenth-century fiction to do "much the same work that Rousseau imagined the social contract would perform" (42).

14. Monique Wittig, "On the Social Contract," in *The Straight Mind and Other Essays* (Boston: Beacon, 1992), 40–41, 45.

15. Linda Williams, "Film Bodies: Gender, Genre, and Excess," *Film Quarterly* 44, no. 4 (1991): 2–5.

16. For a discussion of the development of the killer lesbian stereotype in fifties films, see Vito Russo's *The Celluloid Closet: Homosexuality in the Movies* (New York: Harper and Row, 1987), 99–105. One's sense of the retro aspects of *Basic Instinct* may be heightened by noting that among the films Russo discusses is the 1950 *Young Man with a Horn* in which Michael Douglas's father, Kirk, stars opposite Lauren Bacall, who plays a "murderous" lesbian.

17. Hazel V. Carby, "The Quicksands of Representation," in *Reading Black, Reading Feminist: A Critical Anthology*, ed. Henry Louis Gates, Jr. (New York: Meridian-Penguin, 1990), 84. Carby specifies that this is a feature of African-American fiction rather than of fiction by whites about African Americans, which raises the sort of questions about authorial identity and intention that this chapter attempts to address.

18. Eve Kosofsky Sedgwick, *Tendencies* (Durham, NC: Duke University Press, 1993), 8.

19. Geetha Ramanathan, "Murder as Speech: Narrative Subjectivity in Marleen Gorris' *A Question of Silence*, *Genders* 15 (winter 1992): 69.

20. Whereas I am not arguing for a reading of *Basic Instinct* based on auteur theory, the director's previous work is made more relevant to this discussion by his much-publicized refusal to allow Joe Eszterhas to revise his screenplay in response to criticisms from gay groups. Eight other films directed by Verhoeven have been released in the United States. These films span several genres in subject matter and approach. Although *Katie's Passion* (1977) includes some classically naturalistic depiction of poverty in the turn-of-the-century Netherlands, both it and *Turkish Delight* (1974) might be best described as "sexploitation" films. *Soldier of Orange* (1979) is a serious historical film about resistance to and collaboration with the Nazis in Holland during World War II. *Flesh and Blood* (1985), also a historical drama, less seriously frames class conflict in the Middle Ages in terms of a renegade soldier and a young nobleman's competition over a pretty little princess. *Spetters* (1980) looks at the interactions of five young people involved in various countercul-

tural activities in contemporary Holland. *The Fourth Man* (1984), also set in the present, combines surrealism and film noir conventions to tell the story of a bisexual man's flirtation with a deadly widow and her fiance. (Taubin calls *Basic Instinct* "a remake" of this film [36].) Verhoeven's last two films, *Robocop* (1987) and *Total Recall* (1990), are both science fiction dystopias. Of all of these films, only two, *Katie's Passion* and *Robocop*, do not represent marriage as a direct threat to life. *Soldier of Orange, Flesh and Blood, Spetters,* and *The Fourth Man* explicitly contrast homosexual unions with heterosexual ones, valorizing the former as more honorable. Even in the latter two films, where the portrayal of homosexuality is less schematically that of a contrasting good, it is still depicted as creating relationships in which altruistic alliance is possible.

21. Tania Modleski, *The Women Who Knew Too Much: Hitchcock and Feminist Theory* (New York: Methuen, 1988), 91.

22. Jane Tompkins, "Sentimental Power: *Uncle Tom's Cabin* and the Politics of Literary History," in *Feminisms: An Anthology of Literary Theory and Criticism,* ed. Robyn R. Warhol and Diane Price Herndl (New Brunswick, NJ: Rutgers University Press, 1991), 20–23.

TWELVE

The Crisis of (Ludic) Socialist Feminism

Teresa L. Ebert

The relation between feminism and postmodernism continues to be an urgent theoretical and political question. But why does feminism need to be concerned with postmodernism? A common answer is that it is an unavoidable issue for feminist activists and theorists alike. Postmodernism, at least in its dominant forms, has called into question the entire series of fundamental concepts grounding feminism: from identity, difference, and the category of woman/women to the very nature of politics and the "real." But it has created a special crisis for socialist and materialist feminists: it has discredited Marxism and almost entirely erased the issues of labor and production from feminist theory — particularly from those theories that move beyond narrow disciplinary inquiries.

Postmodernism has so changed the frames of knowing and politics that a number of feminists, including socialist feminists, have largely abandoned the fundamental precepts of transformative politics: emancipation, exploitation, revolution. Michele Barrett, for one, finds that her 1980 book, *Women's Oppression Today*, which has helped define contemporary socialist and materialist feminism, "could not be written in the same way now."[1] Its basic terms, like "oppression," she comments in the 1988 revised edition, "look rather crude" in light of recent theoretical developments, and it would "be impossible to write in such a confidently materialist vein" today.[2] However, she goes on to say that "postmodernism is not something that you can be for or against. . . . It is a cultural climate as well as an intellectual position, a political reality as well as an academic fashion."[3]

For the most part, feminists have tended to consider feminism as *outside* postmodernism. Whether the relation between the two is read as one of antagonism and opposition or as one of alliance and affinity, feminism and postmodernism are commonly treated as two distinct but comparable entities. This view informs the diverse discussions of post-modernism by most feminists, as demonstrated, for example, in *Feminism/ Postmodernism*, a heterogeneous, conflicting set of texts on the subject. Linda Nicholson and Nancy Fraser describe the relation between the two in terms that presuppose "outsideness" as well as distance: "feminism and postmodernism . . . have kept an uneasy distance from one another. . . . The two tendencies have proceeded from opposite directions."[4] Although this position is quite common, it is a reductionist understanding of post-modernism as primarily a set of philosophical discourses comparable to feminism narrowly understood as another set of discourses. Feminism and postmodernism, however, are two very different orders: feminism is a theory and political praxis that attempts to understand, explain and, fre-quently, to transform postmodernism as a *historical condition*. Thus con-temporary feminism is not only *not outside* postmodernism, it is funda-mentally situated within the historical condition of postmodernism. The question is, *how* does feminism theorize postmodernism and its position in it? How feminists understand postmodernism is central to the kind of politics we build and the kind of social interventions we can make.

At the core of the problem is the question: What is postmodernism's — and feminism's — relation to capitalism? As Fredric Jameson has pointed out, "Every position on postmodernism in culture . . . is also at one and the same time, and *necessarily*, an implicitly or explicitly political stance on the nature of multinational capitalism today."[5] At stake here is the issue of whether postmodernism involves "superstructural" changes or if it consists, as Donna Haraway argues, of "fundamental transformations in the structure of the world"?[6] It has become commonplace in the domi-nant postmodern discourses to proclaim that we are in "New Times": a post-Fordist world in which consumption replaces production; fragmen-tation displaces centralization; and "diversity, differentiation and frag-mentation" replace "homogeneity, standardisation and the economies and organisations of scale."[7] For these critics New Times require "new poli-tics" to displace the seemingly "old" Marxist paradigm of the mode of production, labor, and class.

Feminists have been making important, often pioneering, contribu-tions to these developments, including the displacement of Marxism and the production paradigm. Donna Haraway's well-known "A Cyborg Manifesto: Science, Technology, and Socialist-Feminism in the Late Twentieth Century" is an exemplary instance of this effort to write a "new" politics *without Marxism* for socialist-feminism in New Times. But are these really New Times and can these new politics and knowledges emancipate women and other oppressed peoples from exploitation? My argument is that these so-called New Times continue many of the same old relations of exploitation and oppression in patriarchal late capitalism — specifically the exploitation of people's labor — and require a very different way of understanding postmodernism and capitalism as well as feminism's relation to them.

Postmodernism, I propose, is the articulation on the level of the superstructure of changes in the social, cultural, political — "in short, ideological forms" — which have come about as a result of new forms of deploying capital and extracting surplus labor around the world.[8] As such, postmodernism is not simply a series of philosophical discourses, shifting aesthetic and architectural styles, proliferating commodifications, split subjectivities, or multiple identities and differences. Instead, postmodernism is a contradictory historical condition: both postmodernism and the theories that try to explain it are divided by the social contradictions of capitalism. In order to understand this condition, we can distinguish between different ways of theorizing postmodernism — what I call *ludic* and *resistance postmodernism* — depending on how they account for these contradictions and the resulting changes.

Ludic postmodernists share the view that unprecedented new social, cultural, and technological forms in contemporary societies are evidence of fundamental structural changes in capitalism and "in the world." Consequently, they see the emergence of what they consider to be entirely new social configurations: variously called New Times, post-industrial society, consumer society, post-Fordism. And all of these are seen as postproduction, postclass, postfoundationalist, and, frequently, posthistory. In other words, ludic critics tend to conflate the economic with the cultural, social, and technological and to (mis)read the considerable changes in the superstructure as indicative of profound economic changes, constituting a "break" in capitalism and the existing relations of production. This position characterizes the dominant theories in/of postmodernism: notably Baudrillard's concept of "consumer society," Lyotard's "postmodern condition," and especially Donna Haraway's "cyborgian" "informatics of domination." It even marks, to a large degree, Fredric Jameson's notion of "postmodernism as the logic of late capitalism," in which the mode of production is almost entirely dissolved into the superstructural processes of consumption and commodification.[9]

No matter how different various ludic feminists and postmodernists are from each other (and the differences are considerable, e.g., among Helene Cixous and Jean Baudrillard; Julia Kristeva and Jacques Derrida; Luce Irigaray and Michel Foucault; Judith Butler and Jacques Lacan; Drucilla Cornell and Gilles Deleuze; Donna Haraway and Antonio Negri), they all share a number of similar presuppositions. Among the most basic of these is a privileging of the semiotic — whether articulated in terms of language, discourse, textuality, codes, or signifying practices — as grounding knowledge and determinining social reality. As Baudrillard says, it is not production, but "the code that is determinant: the rules of the interplay of signifiers and exchange value."[10] The "determining" nature of the code (discourse, textuality) and its "rules" is the core of theories as diverse as Derrida's deconstruction, Lyotard's language games, Foucault's notion of aleatory power, Butler's concepts of "performance" and "citationality," and Haraway's "cyborg semiologies."[11] The "code" and its "rules" are reunderstood by all in terms of the indeterminate *play* (hence the term *ludic*) of its elements. The most common articulation of this play is, of course, the poststructuralist notion of the indeterminate slippage of signifiers. This in particular includes Derrida's trope of *differance*, understood as "supplementarity," as the *difference-within*, as well as Lacan's notion of the sliding signifying chain and the split subject.[12] Whereas Foucault does not deploy these same terms, he does rewrite power as operating primarily through discursive regimes but also as evincing the very character of discourse: as a rule-goverened "chain or system" of differences, which is, as he says, "repetitious, inert, and self-reproducing," aleatory, reversible and basically indeterminate.[13]

The core of ludic logic, then, involves rethinking all aspects of society (the social, cultural, economic) in terms of the indeterminate play of differences articulated through semiotic or discursive codes. One of the more influential developments of this logic is put forth by the post-Marxist, Ernesto Laclau. He insists on "identifying the social with an infinite play of differences" and argues, following Derrida, that "to conceive of social relations as articulations of differences is to conceive them as signifying relations."[14] Thus, not only is the social "de-centered," according to Laclau, but social relations, like all "signifying systems," are "ultimately arbitrary," and, as a result, " 'society' . . . is an impossible object."[15] If social relations are "ultimately arbitrary," they cannot be subjected to such determinations as exploitation and would no longer require emancipation.

Elaborating on this ludic logic, Judith Butler argues that "the term 'emancipation' " is "exposed as contradictory and untenable" and thus "unrealizable."[16] She thus proposes a "post-teleological," "postfounda-tionalist" use of the term as *"citational"* (i.e., as discursive or rhetorical act) "that will mark off the 'playful' use of the category from the serious and foundationalist one." This "playful" (ludic) use of the concept fore-grounds the indeterminate and undecidable "play" of its signifiers and "citations" and means that "the writer," according to Butler, "will not know in advance for what purposes or in what direction the term will come to signify."[17] The "serious," "foundationalist" use that she rejects is, of course, Marxism, in which *emancipation* has a serious, "unplayful" use as a "struggle concept." Emancipation, for historical materialists, is "founded" historically (not ontologically or metaphysically) on the social contradictions of patriarchal-capitalism. Emancipation is not undecidable; rather, it is the specific historical effect of the revolutionary struggle to transform the social relations of production: to change from a society organized around profit and the social divisions of labor and property to one that meets the needs of all people and equally distributes property and social resources without exploiting people's labor. Politics, in the ludic logic, is primarily a cultural politics aimed at semiotic freedom. It seeks to achieve the unrestricted play of differences through the subver-sion of existing significations (representations). This is what Drucilla Cornell (following Derrida) calls the "dream of a new choreography of sexual difference" in which we "dance differently with the old distinc-tions."[18] Whether these political strategies for realizing the unrestricted play of differences are called "resignification" (Butler), "re-metaphoriza-tion" (Cornell), or "recoding" (Haraway), they are all semiotic practices confined to the superstructure.

Instead of the semiotic or discursive materialism of ludic theories with their exclusive attention to the superstructure, resistance postmodernist theories work dialectically between base and superstructure.[19] They artic-ulate a historical materialist understanding of the changing sociocultural conditions and argue that there is *no break* in capitalism. That is, extraordinary superstructural changes that we mark as postmodernism are simply new articulations of the fundamental social contradictions resulting from the relations of production, specifically the divisions and exploitation of labor in late capitalism. Resistance postmodernism, in short, is a contesting way of explaining and intervening in the changing social, cultural, and political (i.e., the ideological forms) of imperialist and racist patriarchal-capitalism. It takes as its point of departure the fundamental, objective reality of capitalism, the extraction of surplus labor for profit, and argues that as long as surplus labor continues to be the base for the accumulation of capital (profit), then there are no fundamental structural changes in capitalism. Labor, of course, refers not only to wage labor, but to the (historical materialist) feminist retheorization of "surplus labor" to include the "superexploitation" of subsistence, nonwage labor: particularly in terms of the gender and race divisions of labor. In other words, the global accumulation of profit and property in imperialist patriarchal-capitalism is based not only the extraction of surplus value from wage labor (in which women are quickly becoming the majority of workers), but also from the nonwage, subsistence labor of women, peasants, and the colonized.[20]

Resistance postmodernism, like other forms of postmodernism, foregrounds the importance of difference. But in doing so, it radically reunderstands difference itself. It is not simply difference between, or as poststructuralist notion of difference-within (that is as differance), but rather difference is always *difference in relation to the system of exploitation* — specifically, the relations of production and divisions of labor. The social differences of gender, race, and sexuality are historical effects of the changing divisions of labor.[21] This means that any explanation of differences at this historical moment must attend to the production of difference-in-relation to the system of exploitation and relations of production that is capitalism.

Resistance postmodernism does not deny the emergence of new *cultural* forms (variously called "virtual reality," "hyperreality," "cyberspace," and so on), nor does it dismiss the excessive cultural significations, discursive performances, textual reproductions, and fragmentations of subjectivities so widely heralded as postmodern. It does argue that these are *not autonomous* practices. For resistance postmodernists, these are, instead, highly mediated and layered articulations *on the level of the superstructure* of the social contradictions arising out of the relations of production. The superstructure, for resistance postmodernists, is the scene in which people become "conscious of this conflict" between labor and capital and "fight it out."[22]

The opposition between ludic and resistance postmodernism is a form of this "fighting out" in the scene of theory. Ludic postmodernist theory primarily advocates the standpoint of the consumer — of consumption, of desiring — thereby supporting the "interests" of capital. This privileging of the desiring consumer informs theories as diverse as Baudrillard's rewriting of late capitalism as the new "consumer society" and the ludic feminist politics privileging the liberation of the unconstrained pleasures, *jouissance* of sexual differences (what Gayle Rubin calls "lust," which is discussed later). In contrast, the "standpoint" of resistance postmodernism is production and the struggle to end the exploitation of labor. It is, in short, the standpoint of revolutionary class struggle in its *broad sense:* not class as identity politics, but class as the conflict over the appropriation of surplus labor. The broad notion of *class* then does not treat class, gender, race, and sexuality as distinct, equal identities or essences, but rather it is the contestation over the divisions of labor in which class divisions of labor are historically imbricated with gender, race, ethnic, and sexual divisions of labor. The issue of *class* in capitalism unavoidably includes the way gender and racial divisions of labor have been and continue to be fundamental to capital accumulation and the expropriation of surplus labor. A crucial issue of class struggle, thus, has been and continues to be the way the ruling class and the hegemonic ideologies attempt to separate class and labor from gender and race — suppressing the former and de-materializing the latter.

Socialist feminism has largely abandoned historical materialism and a revolutionary theory of class struggle and social change. Most Anglo-American socialist feminists have by and large substituted Foucault for Marx, discourse for ideology, and joined other ludic feminists in embracing a cultural or discursive materialism. Perhaps the best-known socialist feminist to make this shift is Michele Barrett, who announces that she is moving from Marx's "*economics of untruth*" — "being," as she says, "Marxism's account of ideology, used to show 'the relation between what goes on in people's heads and their place in the conditions of production' " — to Foucault's "*politics of truth*, being his own approach to the relationships between knowledge, discourse, truth and power." In so doing she says, "I am nailing my colours to the mast of a more general post-Marxism."[23] At

first this move seems at first to be the result of ludic postmodern discourses on feminism, but a more careful analysis shows that feminist
theory has itself played a highly influential role in the articulation of the
ludic logic, especially the erasure of the mode of production and the issue
of labor from theories of gender as well as from postmodern social theory,
in general. (Former) socialist-feminists, such as Drucilla Cornell, have
taken the lead in arguing (along with Seyla Benhabib) that "the confrontation between twentieth-century Marxism and feminist thought requires
nothing less than a paradigm shift . . . the 'displacement of the paradigm
of production.' "[24] Having rejected Marxism, Cornell's most recent work
seeks a "feminist alliance with deconstruction" on which to build an
"ethical feminism."[25]

The new commonplace among ludic (socialist) feminists is to dismiss
the priority of labor and the relations of production — and with them,
Marxism — as not only economic reductionism but also as "out of date,"
"obsolete," and as "past" knowledges that are superseded by the "new"
post-al knowledges (poststructuralism, postmarxism, postmodernism,
posthistory, post-lesbian/post-gay queer theory, etc.). This is, for instance, the core argument against historical or dialectical materialism and
for cultural materialism in Donna Landry and Gerald MacLean's *Materialist Feminisms.*[26] But this logic of outdatedness conceals a political contestation; it covers over the social struggle in the site of theory. In this way,
it is able to represent ludic knowledges as new boundary knowledges that
are self-evidently true. They are true, not because they have access to any
core of the real (a possibility they have already denied), but because they
are new, exciting, and ultimately pleasure-full. And, most important,
they represent the winning side: free market economy and bourgeois
democracy. Contesting knowledges, such as those produced by historical
materialism, are simply erased as outdated. Consequently, knowledge is
itself represented as that which is the newest, that which is at the "end"
of thought.

I put aside here the contradictions in the ludic representation of itself.
On one hand, ludic theory denounces "progress" as a modernist metanar-
rative and, on the other hand, it represents itself as the outcome of
progress, that is, the transformation of the "old" into the "new." The
ludic "argument" about the outdatedness of historical materialism "wins"
in the postmodern academy because of its *truth* not because of its *appeal.*
In the academy where one's worth (marketability) comes from the "new-

ness" of one's knowledges, there is little room for whatever is designated as "old." Like capitalists, whose survival depends on their ability to out-new their competitors, the ludic academy constantly seeks new forms of commodifying knowledge. By erasing historical materialism from the scene of theory, theory itself is represented not as a historical construct that is, ultimately, a response to the contradictions of the social division of labor but as a form of immanent knowledge produced by language in a panhistorical "always already."

Why should this ludic displacement of labor and the production paradigm matter? It matters because the ludic logic — with its proliferating multiplicities and deconstructed binaries — becomes an elaborate alibi that conceals the increasing economic divisions (the very real historical binaries) between the "haves" and "have nots." Ludic theories are becoming hegemonic at the very time when *inequality* is gaining social popularity and legitimacy, especially in the United States, and is "now being widely defended as a source of productivity, economic growth and individual striving for excellence."[27] The "real" economic inequality between the privileged classes in the West and the exploited classes both in the West and globally, whose surplus labor is appropriated to produce that privilege, is increasing.

In the United States alone, according to the Economic Policy Institute, there has been a substantial redistribution of wealth. As reported in the *Washington Post*, the share of the nation's wealth owned by the top 10 percent of its households rose from 67.5 percent to 73.1 percent between 1979 and 1988. The share of after-tax family income earned by the top 10 percent rose from 29.5 percent in 1980 to an estimated 34.9 percent in 1990. In the same period, the income share of the bottom 10 percent dropped from 1.7 percent to 1.4 percent. The broad middle class (the 60 percent of Americans between richest and poorest) saw its share of family income decline from 50.2 percent in 1980 to an estimated 46.5 percent in 1990.[28]

The displacement of labor and the production paradigm denies feminism the basic "struggle concepts" it needs to explain and transform the relations of exploitation in capitalism. The so-called New Times and changing superstructural forms of postmodernism have not altered the fundamental, "invariant" element of capitalism: the organization of all social and economic life according to *profit*. And profit in capitalism, as one Marxist critic points out, *"rests on the exploitation of living labour in production*. . . . Capitalism is founded, in short, on a class relation between capital and labour."[29] As Marx has argued, "the free development of each is the condition for the free development of all," and there can be no "free development" unless the fundamental *needs* of each person are met: unless production fulfills needs instead of making profits.[30] Making profits, in short, is the denial of the needs of the many and the legitimization of the desires of the few. As a revolutionary (not a ludic) socialist feminist, Nellie Wong argues,

Without overthrowing the economic system of capitalism, as socialists and communists organize to do, we cannot liberate women *and* everybody else who is also oppressed.

Socialist feminism is our bridge to freedom. . . . Feminism, the struggle for women's equal rights, is inseparable from socialism — but not identical to socialism. Socialism is an economic system which reorganizes production, redistributes wealth, and redefines state power so that the exploiters are expropriated and workers gain hegemony.[31]

The struggle to end the exploitation and oppression of *all* oppressed people — especially women and particularly those who are workers, women of color, and lesbians — within the metropole as well as the periphery, is not simply a matter of discursive or semiotic liberation. Rather, it requires the transformation of the material conditions — the relations of production — producing these forms of oppression.

The class struggle in the scene of theory between ludic and resistance postmodern feminists means, at the very least, that we need to critique-ally reconsider the feminist dismissal of the production paradigm; we need to reopen the debate over historical materialism in feminism, which is a debate that has been largely silenced in favor of the hegemony of a semiotic or discursive materialism.

One way of beginning this debate is to critique-ally reexamine one of the inaugural arguments made against the production paradigm and to address its consequences. I am, of course, referring to Gayle Rubin's "The Traffic in Women."[32] We readily see the impact of Rubin's argument, for example, in the recent anthology *Women, Class and the Feminist Imagination: A Socialist-Feminist Reader*, which is based in large part on a year-long forum over the "impasse of socialist feminism" in *Socialist Review* (which is singularly antagonistic to the "production paradigm").[33] The editors, Karen Hansen and Ilene Philipson, rehearse a common narrative about the demise of the production paradigm in feminism. In this story a flawed and inadequate dual systems theory, which represents the failure of feminist efforts to theorize the condition of women in terms of relations of production and reproduction, is successfully vanquished by Gayle Rubin's sex/gender system and her critique of Marxism. Quoting Rosalind Petchesky, who claimed Rubin created "a genuine Marxist-feminist methodology . . . a kind of watermark for Marxist-feminist's theoretical growth," Hansen and Philipson go on to add that Rubin's paradigm of "sex/gender system" offered a "truly materialist means of understanding how sex and gender are produced [that] transcended the specific content of marxist categories."[34]

But how is materialism understood here? Rubin displaces the fundamental materialist categories of labor, class, and relations of production. Her effort to, as she says, "isolate sex and gender from 'mode of production' " is based — as Nancy Hartsock effectively argues in her critique of Rubin — on a misreading of Marx "that undermines the value of Rubin's theory: [her] inadvertent redefinition of production as exchange."[35] This is then compounded, Hartsock argues, by another "abstraction: [her] transformation of the kinship system into a symbol system."[36] In other words, Rubin dissolves the relations of production into an abstracted notion of exchange that is then replaced, through analogy, with the symbolic production of gender in a kinship system of exchange. She thus offers a cultural understanding of the production of gender in place of an economic explanation and substitutes a version of cultural materialism for historical materialism. She is, in short, rewriting the sex/gender system as entirely superstructural.

Rubin is quite explicit in calling on feminists to cut off the analysis of sex from its material conditions. First she asserts that "the needs which are satisfied by economic activity even in the richest, Marxian sense, do not exhaust fundamental human requirements. . . . The needs of sexuality and procreation must be satisfied as much as the need to eat."[37] Then she argues that analysis of "sex . . . as social product" requires that "we need to understand the relations of its production" (by which she means cultural and symbolic not economic relations), "and forget, for awhile, about food, clothing, automobiles, and transistor radios."[38] This is quite an idealist argument. It elides and covers over the basic issue; all needs, sexuality as well as nutrition, are material, which is another way of saying that economic practices are the condition of possiblity for all other human practices. Futhermore, her argument draws a populist and ahistorical equation between very different levels of needs. The fundamental needs of food and the protection of the body are not at all the same as the commodified consumer needs of automobiles and transistor radios.

There is no question that Rubin's concept of a sex/gender system has been very influential in feminist theory, informing the work of feminists as diverse as Sandra Harding and the postmarxist, Chantal Mouffe. Andrew Parker, for one, claims that it "has become nothing less than indispensable, forming indeed one of the cornerstones of the field of Women's Studies."[39] Many of these feminists and postmodern critics have followed Rubin's lead, especially in the humanities and cultural studies. They have not just forgotten "for awhile," but have almost entirely rejected and suppressed any knowledge of the economic relations of production in their theories of gender and sexuality. If they deal with the economic at all, it is in terms of an ahistorical and abstracted notion of commodity consumption and exchange or an abstracted notion of technology cut off from economic relations of production (as in Haraway's cyborgian "informatics of domination"). Thus, a major reason Rubin's work has been so influential, I argue, is because it has played an instrumental role in isolating feminist understandings of gender construction from the material, economic conditions — the division of labor and relations of production — crucial to (re)producing gender and sexuality and determining the exploitation of women, lesbians, and gays. But the cost of isolating feminism from a historical materialist socialism has been very high indeed. As Lynne Segal points out, "It is certainly true that twenty years of feminism has *failed* to improve the economic and social position of all women, although it has brought about many gains for some. . . . Nowhere is it quite so clear, nowhere are the constrasts between the lives of women . . . quite so stark, or the conflicts within feminism and their declining relationship to socialism quite so dramatic, as in the United States."[40]

This separation of gender/sex from economic practices and the erasure of historical materialism legitimates the class interests of ludic feminists (nearly all of whom are middle- and upper-middle-class professionals), who would, for the most part, like to see some measure of gender equality, but who argue for this equality to take place within the existing class relations so as not to disturb their own class privileges. They do so usually by omission, that is, the complete neglect of any critique of the existing class and labor relations in the theorization of sexual differences. We need only turn to Judith Butler's *Bodies that Matter*, or Drucilla Cornell's *Beyond Accommodation*, to see the articulation of theories of subversion that suture over (and thus maintain uncontested) the existing class relations.

This issue of the class politics and social consequences of feminist theory is a difficult one. Basically, it comes down to the following question: where and how are feminists situating themselves and their work in the class struggle? Obviously most feminist theorists (including the writer and most readers of this chapter) are knowledge workers and, frequently, university professionals; thus they are part of the privileged, and newly empowered, "aristocracy of labor." How does this privileged class position affect the way feminists and postmodern critics understand and explain the real? When ludic theorists displace issues of class, labor, and exploitation — substituting instead a politics of desire ("lust") and multiple (deconstructing) "undone" or "cyborg" identities, along with a (Foucauldian) notion of power as nondeterminate, shifting, and reversible — are they not misrecognizing some of the historically specific effects of class privilege as *universal* conditions, which they impose on the very different class realities of others, and do so all in the name of difference? The issue here is not so much how feminist theorists "earn a living" as it is about our "class consciousness." Do we identify with and reproduce the interests of our own (mostly) privileged position in the division of labor, or do we — to paraphrase Marx in the *Communist Manifesto* — cut ourselves adrift from the interests of the ruling class and join in solidarity with the most exploited?[41] Do we try, in short, to raise ourselves "to the level of comprehending theoretically the historical movement as a whole" in order to act to change it?[42] Certainly this is the most urgent question for any *socialist* feminism in postmodernity.

But Hansen and Philipson do not address this question in their "history" of socialist feminism. Instead, they replay Rubin's idealist argument. They assert, for example, that "as feminists have come to recognize that women's desire to marry and raise children cannot be explained in exclusively economic terms, socialist feminism defined as dual systems theory appears to be at an impasse."[43] Such statements, which are frequently taken at face value, employ the same false logic as in Rubin's essay. The "production model," even in the problematic form of dual systems theory, does not try to explain subjectivity and desire "in exclusively economic terms." Rather, it insists on the necessity of understanding and explaining these desires in dialectical relation to the material conditions, the division and exploitation of labor producing them.

Women's sexual desires, especially the very possibility of breaking the bounds of heterosexuality, are determined by the material conditions by which they produce the sustenance of their life. As Marx writes, "The first premise of all human existence and, therefore, of all history . . . [is] that men must be in a position to live in order to 'make history' " or, we can add, to fulfill their desires. "Life involves before everything else eating and drinking, housing, clothing and various other things. The first historical act is thus the production of the means to satisfy these needs, the production of material life itself."[44] In other words, both the fulfillment of bodily needs and the *ways* in which these needs can be satisfied (the paths of "desire") are first contingent on the relations of production sustaining the body. Thus, a woman's very sexuality — the ways in which her desires are constructed and the ways in which she is able to act on them: to be heterosexual, to be lesbian, to be a mother or not — are all conditioned by her position in the histocially specific gendered division of labor. The parameters of desire and the possibilities for fulfilling them are quite different for a woman whose means of sustenance depends on her taking up a rigidly gendered position of domestic labor and (re)production in a heterosexual marriage (as in many precapitalist, or partially capitalist societies), than they are for a woman who is able to meet her needs in advanced capitalism through access to one of the relatively gender-flexible positions in wage labor (e.g., a highly paid professional, such as a university professor).

Recent ludic theories of sexuality, especially queer theory, try to separate sexuality itself into yet another independent realm, distinct from any causal determinants. Again, Rubin's writing is exemplary here. In another influential essay, she has largely repudiated her own "concept of sex/ gender system" put forth in "The Traffic in Women" because, as she now says, "I did not distinguish between lust and gender."[45] She thus argues "that it is essential to separate gender and sexuality analytically to more accurately reflect their separate social existence."[46]

Rubin not only breaks off gender/sexuality from Marxism and the material conditions of production, but she also breaks off sexuality from gender and, in effect, advocates a form of what I call "post-al feminism." Post-al feminism is the post-gender feminism founded upon the autonomy of what Rubin calls "lust." Lust in post-al feminism becomes the allegory for the sovereignty of the subject of desire whose "excess"ive-ness is uncontainable within a historical category such as gender. The subject of lust is truly the deregulated subject of late capitalism where there are no limits on her practices of desire.[47] Rubin's lust (as an allegory of the free enterprise subject legitimating the free market of no con-straints) is very closely related to another model of excessive subjectivity: what Lyotard (following Kant) theorizes as "the sublime."[48] Rubin's nar-rative of lust, like Lyotard's notion of the "sublime," are strategies of crisis management in late capitalism; thus positing the free subject as an excessive agent erases any connection between the subject and system, desire and history. Rubin argues that "feminism is the theory of gender oppression. To automatically assume that this makes it the theory of sexual oppression is to fail to distinguish between gender, on the one hand, and erotic desire, on the other."[49] Each form of oppression is thus understood as having its own unique, acausal genealogy distinct from all others and requiring its own theory. According to Rubin, "As issues become less those of gender and more those of sexuality, feminist analysis becomes irrelevant and often misleading. . . . Other areas of social life, their forms of power, and their characteristic modes of oppression, need their own conceptual implements."[50]

What we are left with, then, in ludic theories of the social is an ever-increasing localization, fragmentation, and isolation of knowledge of gender and sexual production in which desire is considered both autono-mous and primary, thereby radically suppressing and excluding the prior-ity of needs. But such ludic theories are fundamentally (upper) middle class in terms of the interests they serve, because only those whose basic needs are already comfortably fulfilled (the middle and upper middle classes) can afford to dispense with the necessity of meeting basic needs and focus instead on fulfilling desires.

By restricting their scope to evermore limited localities and conjuc-tures, these theories manage to sever any causal relations and systematic connections among diverse practices in the social. Rubin's demand for the autonomy of lust echoes Mouffe and Laclau's erasure of society into multiplicities of heterogenous "social logics." "Society," Laclau proclaims, "does not 'exist.' "[51] In place of society, we are left with a series of incommensurable differences; these are differences, Rubin argues, that should be considered in their own distinct terms. What exists, to go back to Laclau, exists "in the pragmatic." The affirmation of the "pragmatic" is an affirmation of the actually existing and a withdrawal from the struggle for social change. Such a withdrawal only serves the class interests of the few who are well-off within the actually existing social order.

The ludic erasure of needs is being challenged, however, by historical materialist theorists of gender and sexuality such as Donald Morton, who has adopted the concept of ludic postmodernism to critique queer theory. He raises the basic question for any historical understanding of ludic theories:

Why does the appearance of ludic queer theory coincide historically with the fall of the Berlin Wall? The Berlin Wall symbolized, of course, not simply a particular post–World War II partitioning by Allied powers of a country on the "losing" side. As Ronald Reagan and George Bush's obsession with it indicated, the Berlin Wall symbolized, most importantly, the dividing line between the spheres of influence of two competing visions of the social and allied modes of production, one capitalism, devoted to expansion, reproduction, and commodification of desires (for profit); and another, socialism, concerned with fulfilling needs. Ultimately, ludic queer theory — which belongs with the former and not with the latter — is the kind of Eurocentric theory (it takes its de-historicized notion of "desire" to be desire as such) that sees the fall of the Berlin Wall as what the bourgeois apologist Francis Fukuyama calls "the end of history itself." [52]

Rubin's more recent work continues to influence new sites of antimaterialist, ludic analysis. In "Unthinking Sex: Marx, Engels and the Scene of Writing," for example, Andrew Parker "plays" on Rubin's "increasingly influential essay ... 'Thinking Sex.'" [53] He performs a deconstruction of the production paradigm because, as he says, "Western Marxism's constitutive dependence on the category of production derives in part from an antitheatricalism, an aversion to certain forms of parody that prevents sexuality from attaining the political siginificance that class has long monopolized." [54] He attempts, in other words, to "map the (de)-structuring effects of eroticism ... [and] to explore some ways that sexuality ... thinks Marx." [55] In doing so, he turns the historical materialist theory of production into a parodic "tropology ... where production has been modeled on procreation." [56] But such erotic destructuring of Marx's texts does not provide a new explanation; instead, through parody, it discredits all explanations. Parker, like Rubin, naturalizes the erotic as the excessive practice that moves history but is itself transhistorical. The "always already" world of lust that emerges from this anti-explanation is the one that pragmatically legitimates the interests of capital. In his critique of queer theory, Morton argues that "the understanding of materialism required to account — not just for discrimination or prejudice against but — for the exploitation and oppression of (queer and other) subjectivities is historical — not ludic — materialism. Ludic 'politics' is nothing more than the interminable deferral of that much-needed accounting."[57]

The subject of lust — the allegory of the free entrepreneur — does not account for her/his practices since lust (as the sublime) cannot be accounted for. It is an unexplainable force of "nature." This final return to the natural and the biological shows how, after a relatively long detour (what is usually read as subtlety in the ludic academy), Rubin, Parker, Fuss, and other ludic feminsts and queer theorists arrive at some of the most reactionary and oppressive conclusions: biology (once again) is the grounding truth of feminism. The new subject of biology is, of course, a self-reflexive one that has very little in common with the earlier experiential feminism. But the conclusions of both are the same: it is "nature" (desire/lust) that transhistorically shapes human practices.

What kind of politics do socialist feminists need for these postmodern New Times that are not so new? Can the ludic turn away from Marxism provide an effective "new politics" for patriarchal late capitalism? The best way to answer such a question is to critique-ally engage Donna Haraway's "Cyborg Manifesto," one of the most influential examples of *ludic* postmodern socialist feminism.

In this manifesto, Haraway attempts to map a new "route for reconstructing socialist-feminist politics" (163) by building "an ironic political myth" to deal with the "rearrangements in world-wide social relations tied to science and technology" (161) — what she calls the "informatics of domination." In so doing, she rewrites technology as a sociocultural, if not an outright textual/discursive, entity by reunderstanding it as "coding." As she argues, "Communications sciences and modern biologies are constructed by a common move — *the translation of the world into a problem of coding*" (164). In other words, Haraway is reversing the relation of technology to the mode of production (capitalism) producing it — that is, the relation of superstructure and base — if not severing it altogether. Haraway articulates technology as not only autonomous and self-generating; she represents it as the ground of all other social, cultural, and economic realities. For example, Haraway posits the new economic arrangements, such as the "homework economy" or "the projections for world-wide structural unemployment," as "stemming from the new technologies" (168). Consequently, she erases the very real material conditions of science and technology as *capitalist* science and technology. She occludes the way technology itself is deployed and developed according to the imperatives of profit, and she erases both the exploitation of labor involved in producing the technology and the uses of technology to further increase the expropriation of labor.

Instead, she rewrites material reality as "cyborg semiologies." She argues that "the entire universe of objects that can be known scientifically must be formulated as problems in communications engineering (for the managers) or theories of the text (for those who would resist). Both are cyborg semiologies" (162–63). Thus although Haraway seems, at first, to be quite different from other ludic critics (especially deconstructionists) in her understanding of contemporary social reality, she is in fact subscribing to the same basic logic of the priority of the semiotic and substitutes a semiotic or discursive materialism for historical materialism.

Haraway also critiques "Marxian socialism" in which "labour is the pre-eminently privileged category" (158) without providing any argument concerning why this should not be the case. Why should labor not be privileged? But she is "excused" from making any argument because her position has acquired the status of an "obviousness" in ludic theory. She simply dismisses what she calls Marxism's "essentializing move" as if her own theory of codes is not itself essentializing. She describes Marxist essentialism as "in the ontological structure of labour or of its analogue, women's activity" (158), but it is Haraway, not Marxism, that renders labor "an ontological category" (158). For historical materialism, the extraction of surplus labor is an objective social practice: it is historical not ontological. In class societies, all social differences are produced by the extraction of surplus labor, whether directly or through various mediations (such as ideological practices). The test of the objectivity of surplus labor as the foundation of class societies is simply this: if surplus labor is abolished, then the existing social relations will fundamentally change.[58] Surplus labor is the unsurpassable objective reality of class societies, and on this objective reality (which is not subject to — that is, changeable by — discursive interpretation) depends the oppression of women, workers, people of color, and lesbians and gays, as well as the struggle for emancipation. Labor is indeed the "pre-eminently privileged category" of Marxist socialism because it is the historical basis of exploitation in class societies and there can be no emancipation without changing the labor relations.

Can we at least say that Haraway is describing the new realities for us? Certainly she describes some important changes in the social and cultural relations of contemporary society, but whether these are, as she claims, "fundamental transformations in the structure of the world" (165) is highly debatable. What is at stake is whether these constitute fundamental changes in the structure of capitalism. By subsuming the economic to the technological and then arguing for extensive social changes "stemming from" technology, Haraway misreads diverse social and cultural (i.e., *superstructural*) developments as basic changes in the relations of production and the exploitation of labor: the economic *base*. When we look more closely at economic issues, we find a very different story.

The most important point to be made about the shifting patterns of production and employment — signaled by such terms as New Times, postindustrial, post-Fordism, consumer society — is that they are all grounded on the same basic structural relations of capitalism, that is, *the expropriation and exploitation of "living labor" (surplus labor) for profit.* Moreover, the exploitation of surplus labor is increasing, whether it is goods, services, information, or microelectronics that are being produced in the West or globally. As Callinicos argues:

The fact that manual industrial workers no longer form the majority of wage-labourers does not of itself imply the beginning of the end of the "work-based society." Wage-labour has if anything become a more pervasive feature of social experience in the past half century, with the decline of peasant agriculture and the growing involvement of women in the labour-market. The fact that much of this labour now involves interacting with other people rather than producing goods does not change the social relations involved.[59]

The changes that do occur, then, are changes concerning *how the extraction of surplus labor is taking place, not over whether it is taking place.* As long as there is surplus labor, there are class and other social divisions of labor (according to differences of gender, race, sexuality), because this is the inevitable and fundamental structure of capitalism. Instead of a fundamental change in the structure of capitalism, there is an intensification of its structural processes: the increased productivity of fewer workers, on the one hand, and the rise in low-paid, part-time and temporary jobs, along with the revival of "piece-work" and sweat-shops, on the other hand. Both these things contribute to increasing the rate of expropriation of the surplus labor of workers. This "devaluation of labour power," as one Marxist postmodern critic points out, "has always been the instinctive response of capitalists to falling profits."[60] Central to this process is the regulation and control of labor. This means that, contrary to Haraway's ludic dismissal of labor as essentializing, the social struggles over the division of labor — in short, the class conflicts between labor and capital — are at the very core of the sociocultural and economic changes Haraway calls the "informatics of domination."

This issue of the increasing exploitation of surplus labor is especially important in evaluating one of Haraway's most celebrated theses: "The actual situation of women is their integration/exploitation into a world system of production/reproduction and communication called the informatics of domination" (163). In this "polymorphous" new world, according to Haraway, communications and biological sciences along with microelectronics and biotechnologies mediate "translations of labour into robotics and word processing, sex into genetic engineering and reproductive technology" (165). In Haraway's "informatics of domination," in other words, "production/reproduction" is the province of technology, and labor is replaced by robotics.

But this is a very distorted understanding of labor. Labor has not been translated, transformed, or replaced; it has only been occluded by Haraway's social analytic. The (limited) use of robotics is largely confined to the production of a very few complex consumer durables, and the production of robots and microelectronics, the practices of word processing and genetic engineering, are all based on the expropriation of surplus labor, which is increasingly women's surplus labor. Haraway's logic completely erases the fact that robotics and other automated machinery (the means of production) are, for the most part, *congealed labor.* As the Marxist economist, Ernest Mandel, demonstrates, "The price of machinery consists to a large degree of labor (for example, 40%) and raw materials (for example, 40% also)."[61] But he also shows that, for example, "60% of the cost of raw materials can be reduced to labor. . . . The rest of the cost of raw materials breaks down into the cost of other raw materials — reducible in turn to 60% labor." In other words, "the share of labor in the average cost" not only of machinery, but also of any commodity, is sucessively greater: "the further this breakdown is carried, the more the entire cost tends to be reduced to labor, and to labor alone."[62] In short, all of these new technologies and practices involve the "same old" capitalist relations of labor. The "integration/exploitation" of women "into a world system of production/reproduction" and new communications technology is still an "integration" into capitalist technology, whatever its forms, and thus into the capitalist labor relations of the *exploitation of surplus labor*. What has changed is the increasing degree and extent to which most women globally are now being exploited and even *superexploited* by capitalism.

Haraway, as I have already indicated, has largely displaced capitalism as a mode of production from her new technological realities. This is not to say she does not use the term, because obviously she does. In discussing the "homework economy," for instance, she briefly cites the concept of "capitalist" and addresses issues of "work" and "jobs" (166). But, she treats capitalism largely as an adjective, occluding its relations of production and labor. Her analysis rarely leaves the realm of the superstructure; the "market," the "paid work place," and the "state" all become, in her words, "idealized social locations" in which "there is no 'place' for women . . . only geometrics of difference and contradictions crucial to women's cyborg identities" (170). As a result, her richly detailed descriptions do more to obscure than to explain the existing social and economic realities. For example, the "homework economy" is indeed a "new" way of organizing work (or rather the contemporary revival of piece-work), but it is still structured according to the same old appropriation of surplus labor. These new technological, that is, superstructural, changes have not transformed the fundamental structural relations of the capitalist mode of production; there is no "break" in capitalism. The "homework economy" is an instance of what Alain Lipietz has termed "bloody Taylorization." He uses this concept to describe the " 'bloody' exploitation" occurring in the largely unskilled, "fragmented and repetitive" jobs in the manufacture of exports, especially electronics and textiles.[63]

Haraway's technological and discursive materialism entirely eclipses the struggle against economic exploitation and its necessary connection to cultural politics and ideology critique. Instead, she puts forth a "cyborg politics" that "is the struggle for language and the struggle against perfect communication, against the one code that translates all meaning perfectly, the central dogma of phallogocentrism" (176). But her poststructuralist notion of the "struggle for language" cuts it off from the relations of production and is unable to engage language, "the sign," as "an arena of the class struggle," to cite Voloshinov.[64] Cyborg politics is "freed of the need to ground politics in 'our' privileged position of oppression that incorporates all other dominations" (176); it rejects the efforts of "Feminisms and Marxisms" to "construct a revolutionary subject from the perspective of a hierarchy of oppressions" (176). But such a cyborg politics is indeed a "political myth," as Haraway calls it, because it relies on a discursive sleight of hand (a "recoding") to wipe away the objective historical realities of the fundamental oppression of (most) women and others through the appropriation of their labor. There is indeed an objective, historical hierarchy of oppression: preventing people from meeting their basic human needs by appropriating their labor and denying them equal distribution of social resources is the fundamental oppression. Only those whose basic needs are sufficently fulfilled can afford the luxury of "forgetting" this hierarchy of primary reality. As the African-American Marxist-feminist Angela Davis argued in her address to the National Women's Studies Association in 1987, "The most fundamental prerequisite for empowerment is the ability to earn an adequate living."[65]

Haraway's "cyborg politics" is the practice of semiotic recodings, of writing ("recoding") other stories: "feminist cyborg stories have the task of recoding communication and intelligence to subvert command and control" (175). Haraway's celebrated new "route for reconstructing socialist-feminist politics" (163), then, is to substitute a technological and semiotic matterism for a historical materialism as the ground of feminist theory and practice, and in so doing, occlude production and marginalize labor. The similarities between Haraway's "recoding" as a politics of liberation and Judith Butler's "resignification" as a politics of "self-subversion" and "resistance" raise the question of whether there is any difference at all between Haraway's discursive socialist feminism and poststructuralist textual or "performative" feminism?[66]

The "cyborg perspective" is basically a bourgeois perspective that obscures the class politics of its own privileged condition by suppressing its relation to the extraction of the surplus labor of others, especially women of color. Haraway's "complaint about socialist/Marxian standpoints is their unintended erasure of polyvocal, unassimilable, radical difference made visible in anti-colonial discourse and practice" (159). But what is this "unassimilable, radical difference"? Is it the difference of "women of color," Haraway's representative cyborg, "Sister Outsider"? If so, does this not risk becoming yet another form of colonialization and Eurocentric essentialization of the "racial other" as the "unassimilable"

outsider — this time in the name of the "other"? The "radical, unassimilable difference" in racist, patriarchal capitalism is not the "postmodernist
identity" of women of color but the conditions oppressing them. The
"radical, unassimilable difference" is *poverty*. It is the production of profit
and privilege for the few out of the expropriation of the labor of the many
(the "others"). Poverty cannot be ended; it cannot be assimilated within
bourgeois society, that is, within the existing labor relations of capitalism.
Poverty (i.e., *need*) is the radical, unrepresentable, suppressed "other" to
bourgeois pleasure.

The project of ending poverty, eliminating this "radical difference,"
requires a revolution in the relations of production: a socialist revolution.
But such revolutionary struggle is all but eliminated in Haraway's reconstruction of socialist-feminism as "cyborg semiologies" and "recodings"
that require a "subtle understanding of emerging pleasures, experiences,
and powers with serious potential for changing the rules of the game"
(172–73). The objective in revolutionary social change is not to "change
the rules of the game," which is little more than reformism and, in its
ludic postmodern sense, reduces the social either to "gaming" (Lyotard),
to "hyperreality" and "seduction" (Baudrillard), or to a politics of "dissemination" (Derrida) — for all of whom, changing discursive "rules" is
equated with significant social change. Revolutionary change is concerned
not to change the "rules of the game" but to *overthrow* the "game," that
is, to transform the existing system of racist, patriarchal capitalism.

This shift from revolutionary struggle to a politics of "emerging pleasures" and "recodings" of "rules" is the basis of Haraway's appeal. As
Christina Crosby says,

> The irony of the "Manifesto" is, I believe, the pleasure of the text, the pleasure of
> the unexpected turn. . . . For those readers who have been active in socialist and
> feminist politics, there's the pleasure too, of the politically "incorrect," the break
> with the solemnities of left politics and the reductive dualisms which are all
> too familiar.[67]

What are these "solemnities of left politics and the reductive dualisms"
it is so pleasurable to be freed from? They are, of course, the difficult and
un-pleasurable insistence on the historical reality of exploiter and exploited
and the need to struggle against the exploitation of surplus labor. As the
"struggle for language and against perfect communication," cyborg politics is primarily a discursive politics in which "contests for the meanings
of writing are a major form of contemporary political struggle" (175).

Central to this struggle are the boundary writings, the "other" stories of women of color, of "Sister Outsider," who in Haraway's "political myth . . . is the offshore woman" (174). But what stories does "Sister Outsider" tell us, or rather what stories are cyborg (socialist) feminists willing to *hear?* Haraway tells the stories of Cherrie Moraga, Chela Sandoval, and such science fiction writers as Octavia Butler and Vonda McIntyre, which rewrite the myths of identity and consciousness as nonoriginary, boundary-crossing stories that are "not just literary deconstruction, but liminal transformation" (177).

But the issue is not simply "about access to the power to signify," as Haraway says. It is not simply a matter of "recoding communication and intelligence to subvert command and control," as Haraway proclaims (175), or a matter of "subversive rearticulation" or "resignification" of the symbolic, as Butler calls for.[68] These practices are no more than discursive politics — "cyborg semiologies." Haraway's cyborg politics and Butler's "performatics" are seductive, nonthreatening political fantasies for the already privileged. They will do little to emancipate women — women of color and all oppressed women — from the very real conditions of exploitation. What is missing, what is silenced by cyborg feminism's vigorous suppression of production and labor, are the most urgent and radical, the fundamental root "stories" of "Sister Outsider": the "offshore woman" and the one who lives "onshore" (the one who immigrates and the one who is already here). Her primary story is not a "literary deconstruction" or a "liminal transformation"; it is not simply a "recoding" of pleasurable boundary myths. It is the silenced story of economic exploitation.

It is important to note here that Chela Sandoval's "oppositional consciousness" of "U.S. third world feminism" is not able either to voice the silenced story of "Sister Outsider." Sandoval's "differential consciousness" is itself a ludic identity politics (of the "mobility of identity") that is located entirely in superstructural forms and suppresses the relation of U.S. third world feminists to the mode of production determining them. Sandoval's "differential consciousness" thus cannot tell the silenced story of exploitation.[69] Instead, we need a *historical materialist critique* of economic exploitation, including a critique of bourgeois feminists for their class interestedness and complicity in the expropriation of the surplus labor of others. It is the story, as Margaret Prescod-Roberts says, "about being here for the money — in England and also in the United States."[70] It is the story

about the mammy [in slavery] and about her work, that housework, because it has everything to do with the way capital — meaning big British and American money — was able to accumulate the vast amount of wealth and fortune that it did. It's important to talk about that, and its specially important for us as Black women to talk about that when we say we're here for the money, because what we're saying is that we helped to create that wealth, that we were *pivotal* in creating that wealth. Don't tell us that we have to stay in the West Indies, that we have to work three times as hard to create new wealth for the West Indies. Because we have done three hundred years or more of labour — labour that I have done, my mother, my grandmother and people before me have done. When we look around, when I looked around my village, when I looked around Barbados, the wealth wasn't there. It was some place else. It was in London, it was in New York, from the French-speaking West Indies it was in Paris, from the Dutch-speaking West Indies it was in Amsterdam.[71]

Margaret Prescod-Roberts, an emigre from Barbados and co-founder of Black Women for Wages for Housework, U.S.A., and her fellow "Sister Outsiders" are struggling first over "money" not "meanings." What is needed, what she calls for, is a material struggle over the exploitation of their labor — over all oppressed people's labor — and equal distribution of the wealth produced by their labor. The struggle over meanings, over language, and over cultural practices and politics needs to be fundamentally grounded in the priority of economic struggles and must serve the collective struggle for the emancipation of all peoples from economic inequality. But Haraway and other ludic feminists respond to the call for the priority of "money" over "meaning" by a rereading of Saussure in which linguistic *value* is analogically written into labor *value* — as in Gayatri Spivak's textualization of "surplus value."[72] "Money" and "meaning," in other words, are inscribed into each other as an example of the postmodern hyperreal.

Ludic, cyborgian socialist feminism has become an "ethical" socialism for the bourgeoisie: a displacement of collectivity by intersubjectivity. No matter how much it may describe and decry the condition of women in the "homework economy," the "feminization of poverty," or the growing "structural unemployment" (as Haraway indeed does), unless it directly connects its cultural politics to the revolutionary struggle to fundamentally change the conditions of production, appropriation of surplus labor, and unequal distribution of wealth, it is simply playing with the "bound-aries" of middle-class privilege and pleasures; that is, it expands them here and there to include this or that small segment of the excluded. Haraway's cyborg politics, with its declared purpose of creating "an argument for *pleasure* in the confusion of boundaries and for *responsibility* in their con-struction" (150), has helped justify the current move of many middle-class, professional, and academic socialist feminists and leftists away from revolutionary struggle, which requires that they break with their own class interestedness. Her cyborg myth validates the post-Marxist turn to the more comfortable pleasures of a postclass, ludic politics aimed at semiotic freedom.

However, on the margins of the newly hegemonic ludic politics and cyborgian fantasies, other feminists have continued to work for revolu-tionary knowledges and praxis. I want to especially note one effort from a new generation of feminists struggling to break the silence around the problem of labor and build a collective revolutionary feminism in post-modernism. Jennifer Cotter has written a historical materialist feminist critique of the ludic feminism she is being taught as a graduate student. She argues that

feminism's political effectivity . . . must be determined in relation to this global framework [of capitalism]; feminism must be a project that is concerned not with the personal liberation of a small group of relatively privileged women, but with the economic, social, and political emancipation of *all* oppressed and exploited women on the planet. Hence, the measure of success for feminism must always be determined in relation to its capacity to advance the *material* interests of the most oppressed segments of the female population on the globe.[73]

Socialist feminism cannot afford the luxury of cyborgian political fanta-sies, post-al lust, and ludic discursive materialisms. It needs to return to the necessity of collective struggle against the exploitation of surplus labor in order to "advance the *material* interests of the most oppressed." And in so doing, socialist and materialist feminisms, indeed all feminisms, need to join in the struggle for international socialism. As Angela Davis has told the National Women's Studies Association:

If we are not afraid to adopt a revolutionary stance — if, indeed, we wish to be radical in our quest for change — then we must get to the root of our oppression. . . . Our agenda for women's empowerment must thus be unequivocal in our challenge to monopoly capitalism as a major obstacle to the achievement of equality.

I want to suggest . . . that we link our grassroots organizing, our essential involvement in electoral politics, and our involvement as activists in mass struggles to the long-range goal of fundamentally transforming the socioeconomic condi-tions that generate and persistently nourish the various forms of oppression we suffer. Let us learn from the strategies of our sisters in South Africa and Nicara-gua. As Afro-American women, as women of color in general, as progressive women of all racial backgrounds, let us join our sisters — and brothers — across the globe who are attempting to forge a new socialist order — an order which will reestablish socioeconomic priorities so that the quest for monetary profit will never be permitted to take precedence over the real interests of human beings. This is not to say that our problems will magically dissipate with the advent of socialism. Rather, such a social order should provide us with the real opportunity to further extend our struggles, with the assurance that one day we will be able to redefine the basic elements of our oppression as useless refuse of the past.[74]

It is important to add to Davis's call to action, that we also link our theoretical and cultural work to the "long-range goal of fundamentally transforming the socioeconomic conditions that generate and persistently nourish the various forms of oppression we suffer." Socialist feminist theory, in short, needs to reclaim historical materialism for a transforma-tive politics in postmodernism.

NOTES

1. Michele Barrett, *Women's Oppression Today: The Marxist/Feminist Encounter*, rev. ed. (London: Verso, 1988), xxiv.
2. Ibid., v, xxxiii.
3. Ibid., xxxiv.
4. Linda Nicholson and Nancy Fraser, "Social Criticism without Philosophy: An Encounter between Feminism and Postmodernism," in *Feminism/Postmod-ernism*, ed. Linda Nicholson (New York: Routledge, 1990), 19.
5. Fredric Jameson, *Postmodernism or, The Cultural Logic of Late Capitalism* (Dur-ham, NC: Duke University Press, 1991), 3.
6. Donna Haraway, "A Cyborg Manifesto: Science, Technology, and Socialist-Feminism in the Late Twentieth Century," *Simians, Cyborgs, and Women: The Reinvention of Nature* (New York: Routledge, 1991), 165. Futher references to this work are made parenthetically in the text.
7. Stuart Hall and Jacques Martin, eds., *New Times: The Changing Face of Politics in the 1990s* (London: Verso, 1990), 11–12.
8. Karl Marx, *A Contribution to the Critique of Political Economy* (New York: International Publishers, 1970), 21.
9. In addition to Jameson's *Postmodernism*, see J.-F. Lyotard, *The Postmodern*

Condition (Minneapolis: University of Minnesota Press, 1984); and J. Baudrillard "Consumer Society," in *Jean Baudrillard: Selected Writings*, ed. Mark Poster (Stanford, CA: Stanford University Press, 1988), 29–56. I develop a more sustained critique of ludic postmodernism and the erasure of production in both socialist feminism and postmodernism, including the problematic work of Jameson, in *Ludic Feminism and After* (Ann Arbor: University of Michigan Press, 1995).

10. Jean Baudrillard, *For a Critique of the Political Economy of the Sign*, trans. C. Levin (St. Louis: Telos Press, 1981), 146.

11. See J.-F. Lyotard, *Just Gaming* (Minneapolis: University of Minnesota Press, 1985), and *The Differend: Phrases in Dispute* (Minneapolis: University of Minnesota Press, 1988); M. Foucault, *The History of Sexuality*, vol. 1 (New York: Vintage-Random House, 1980), and *Power/Knowledge: Selected Interviews and Other Writings, 1972–1977*, ed. Colin Gordon (New York: Pantheon Books, 1980); Judith Butler, *Gender Trouble: Feminism and the Subversion of Identity* (New York: Routledge, 1990), and *Bodies that Matter: On the Discursive Limits of "Sex"* (New York: Routledge, 1993); and Haraway's "Cyborg Manifesto."

12. See especially Jacques Derrida, "Differance," in *Margins of Philosophy* (Chicago: University of Chicago Press, 1982), 1–27; and Jacques Lacan, *Ecrits* (New York: Norton, 1977).

13. Foucault, *History of Sexuality*, 92–102.

14. Ernesto Laclau, "Transformations of Advanced Industrial Societies and the Theory of the Subject," in *Rethinking Ideology: A Marxist Debate*, ed. S. Hanninen and L. Paldan (New York: International General/IMMRC; Berlin: Argument-Verlag, 1983), 39. Also see E. Laclau and C. Mouffe, *Hegemony and Socialist Strategy: Towards a Radical Democratic Politics* (London: Verso, 1985).

15. Laclau, "Transformations," 40–41.

16. Judith Butler, "Poststructuralism and Postmarxism," *diacritics* 23, no. 4 (winter 1993): 8.

17. Ibid.

18. Drucilla Cornell, *Beyond Accommodation: Ethical Feminism, Deconstruction and the Law* (New York: Routledge, 1991), 96, 18.

19. My articulation of resistance postmodern draws on the largely marginalized work of other historical materialist feminists and theorists, such as the "German School" of materialist feminists: particularly the earlier work of Maria Mies, *Patriarchy and Accumulation on a World Scale: Women in the International Division of Labour* (London: Zed Books, 1986), and Mies, Veronika Bennholdt-Thomsen, and Claudia von Werlhof, *Women: The Last Colony* (London: Zed Books, 1988); the theoretical tradition of Marxist feminists: notably Clara Zetkin, *Clara Zetkin, Selected Writings*, ed. P. Foner (New York: International Publishers, 1984); Alexandra Kollontai, *Selected Writings of Alexandra Kollontai*, trans. Alix Holt (Westport, CT: Lawrence Hill and Co., 1977); Rosa Luxemburg, *Selected Political Writings of Rosa Luxemburg*, ed. Dick Howard (New York: Monthly Review Press, 1971); Evelyn Reed, *Woman's Evolution* (New York: Pathfinder Press, 1975), and *Problems of Women's Liberation: A*

Marxist Approach (New York: Pathfinder, 1969); and Lise Vogel, *Marxism and the Oppression of Women: Toward a Unitary Theory* (New Brunswick, NJ: Rutgers University Press, 1983); as well as the work of materialist/socialist feminists, such as Michelle Barrett, before their "ludic turn."

However, my work is especially indebted to those materialist/socialist feminists and Marxist critics who have sustained their commitment to Marxist "struggle concepts" and the logic of historical materialism in postmodernism: Lillian Robinson, *Sex, Class and Culture* (New York: Methuen, 1986); Harriet Fraad et al., "For Every Knight in Shining Armor, There's a Castle Waiting to Be Cleaned: A Marxist-Feminist Analysis of the Household," *Rethinking Marxism* 2, no. 4 (winter 1989): 10–106; Angela Davis, *Women, Race and Class* (New York: Vintage Books, 1983), and *Women, Culture and Politics* (New York: Vintage Books, 1990); Lindsey German, *Sex, Class and Socialism* (London: Bookmarks, 1989); Rosemary Hennessy, *Materialist Feminism and the Politics of Discourse* (New York: Routledge, 1993); Ellen Meikins Woods, *The Retreat from Class: A New "True" Socialism* (London: Verso, 1986); Alex Callinicos, *Against Postmodernism: A Marxist Critique* (New York: St. Martin's Press, 1989); Mas'ud Zavarzadeh and Donald Morton, *Theory as Resistance: Politics and Culture after (Post)Structuralism* (New York: Guilford Press, 1994). I also work dialectically in relation to those feminists and critics who occupy a contradictory boundary position between ludic and resistance postmodernism, such as Gayatri Chakravorty Spivak, *Outside in the Teaching Machine* (New York: Routledge, 1993), and the recent work of Christopher Norris, *Uncritical Theory: Postmodernism, Intellectuals and the Gulf War* (Amherst: University of Massachusetts Press, 1992).

20. For a historical materialist retheorization of labor and the relations of production in relation to gender and colonization, see Mies, *Patriarchy and Accumulation*, and her collaboration with Bennholdt-Thomsen and von Werlhof, *Women: the Last Colony*.

21. I engage the ludic notion of "difference-within" and develop a historical materialist theory of difference as "difference-within-a-system-of-exploitation" much more fully in *Ludic Feminism and After* and in my text, "The 'Difference' of Postmodern Feminism," *College English* 53, no. 8 (1991): 886–904.

22. Marx, *Contribution*, 21.

23. Michele Barrett, *The Politics of Truth: From Marx to Foucault* (Stanford, CA: Stanford University Press, 1991), vii.

24. Seyla Benhabib and Drucilla Cornell, eds., *Feminism as Critique: On the Politics of Gender* (Minneapolis: University of Minnesota Press, 1987), 1.

25. Cornell, *Beyond Accommodation*, 79–118.

26. Donna Landry and Gerald MacLean, *Materialist Feminisms* (Cambridge, MA: Blackwell, 1993).

27. E. J. Dionne, Jr., "The Idea of Equality Is Proving Unequal to the Demands of Today," *Washington Post National Weekly Edition* (7 May–13 May 1990): 13.

28. Ibid.

29. David Harvey, *The Condition of Postmodernity* (Oxford: Basil Blackwell, 1989), 179–80; emphasis added.

30. Karl Marx, *The Communist Manifesto*, ed. F. Bender (New York: W. W. Norton, 1988), 75.

31. Nellie Wong, "Socialist Feminism: Our Bridge to Freedom," in *Third World Women and the Politics of Feminism*, ed. Chandra Mohanty et al. (Bloomington: Indiana University Press, 1991), 290.

32. Gayle Rubin, "The Traffic in Women: Notes on the 'Political Economy' of Sex," in *Toward an Anthropology of Women*, ed. Rayna Reiter (New York: Monthly Review Press, 1975), 157–210.

33. Karen Hansen and Ilene Philipson, eds., *Women, Class, and the Feminist Imagination: A Socialist-Feminist Reader* (Philadephia: Temple University Press, 1990).

34. Ibid., 22.

35. Rubin, "Traffic," 203, and Nancy Hartsock, *Money, Sex and Power: Toward a Feminist Historical Materialism* (Boston: Northeastern University Press, 1985), 297.

36. Hartsock, *Money, Sex and Power*, 298.

37. Rubin, "Traffic," 165.

38. Ibid., 166.

39. Andrew Parker, "Unthinking Sex: Marx, Engels and the Scene of Writing," *Social Text* 29 (1991): 28.

40. Lynne Segal, "Whose Left? Socialism, Feminism and the Future," *New Left Review* 185 (Jan.–Feb. 1991): 88.

41. Marx, *Manifesto*, 64.

42. Ibid.

43. Hansen and Philipson, *Women, Class*, 43.

44. Karl Marx and Frederick Engels, *The German Ideology*, 3rd rev. ed. (Moscow: Progress Publishers, 1976), 47.

45. Gayle Rubin, "Thinking Sex: Notes for a Radical Theory of the Politics of Sexuality," in *Pleasure and Danger*, ed. Carole Vance (Boston: Routledge & Kegan Paul, 1984), 307.

46. Ibid., 308.

47. The exemplary of this deregulated subject of desire can be found in the postal celebration of perversity. See Rubin's "The Catacombs: A Temple of the Butthole," in *Leatherfolk: Radical Sex, People, Politics and Practice*, ed. Mark Thompson (Boston: Alyson, 1991), 119–41.

48. On the Lyotardian theory of the sublime, see J.-F. Lyotard, *Lessons on the Analytic of the Sublime* (Palo Alto: Stanford University Press, 1994), and "The Sublime and the Avant-Garde," in *The Lyotard Reader*, ed. Andrew Benjamin (New York: Basil Blackwell, 1989), 196–211.

49. Rubin, "Thinking Sex," 307.

50. Ibid., 309.

51. Ernesto Laclau, "Building a New Left: An Interview with Ernesto Laclau," *Strategies* 1 (fall 1988): 16.

52. Donald Morton, "Practice *Not* Performance: For a Materialist Queer Theory," presented at the Modern Language Association Convention (Toronto, 29 December 1993), 12; also see his "The Politics of Queer Theory in the (Post)Modern Moment," *Genders* 17 (fall 1993): 121–50.
53. Parker, "Unthinking Sex," 28.
54. Ibid.
55. Ibid., 31.
56. Ibid., 41.
57. Morton, "Practice *Not* Performance," 2.
58. Karl Marx, *Capital: A Critique of Political Economy*, vol. 1, trans. B. Fowkes (New York: Vintage, 1977), 240–416.
59. Callinicos, *Against Postmodernism*, 127.
60. Harvey, *Condition of Postmodernity*, 192.
61. Ernest Mandel, *An Introduction to Marxist Economic Theory* (New York: Pathfinder, 1970), 26.
62. Ibid., 25–26.
63. Alain Lipietz, *Mirages and Miracles: The Crises of Global Fordism*, trans. David Macey (London: Verso, 1987), 74–76.
64. V. N. Voloshinov, *Marxism and the Philosophy of Language*, trans. L. Matejka and I. R. Titunik (Cambridge: Harvard University Press, 1973), 23.
65. Davis, *Women, Culture and Politics*, 8.
66. Butler, *Bodies*, 109, 237–42.
67. Crosby, "Commentary: Allies and Enemies," in *Comming to Terms: Feminism, Theory, Politics*, ed. Elizabeth Weed (New York: Routledge, 1989), 206–7.
68. Butler, *Bodies*, 109.
69. Chela Sandoval, "U.S. Third World Feminism: The Theory and Method of Oppositional Consciousness in the Postmodern World," *Genders* 10 (spring 1991): 1–24.
70. Margaret Prescod-Roberts and Norma Steele, *Black Women: Bringing It All Back Home* (Bristol, England: Falling Wall Press, 1980), 13.
71. Ibid., 18.
72. Gayatri Chakravorty Spivak, "Scattered Speculations on the Question of Value," in *In Other Worlds: Essays in Cultural Politics* (New York: Methuen, 1987), 154–75.
73. Jennifer Cotter, "An Open Letter on Feminist Pedagogy," *Minnesota Review*, no. 41–42 (fall 1993–spring 1994).
74. Davis, *Women, Culture and Politics*, 14.

Contributors

ROSARIA CHAMPAGNE is an assistant professor of English at Syracuse University, where she teaches courses in Feminist and Psychoanalytic Critical Theories, Women's Studies, and Nineteenth-century British Literature. This chapter is part of the book in progress, *The Politics of Survivorship: Incest, Women's Literature, and Popular Culture*, under contract with New York University Press.

BARBARA J. COLEMAN is a doctoral candidate in art history at the University of Minnesota. She is presently writing her dissertation on images of adolescent females in the American media of the 1950s.

KATE CUMMINGS is an associate professor of English at the University of Washington, where she teaches on the subject of AIDS, the politics of representation, queer subjectivity, and contemporary American culture. The author of *Telling Tales: The Hysteric's Seduction in Fiction and Theory*, and articles on sexuality, psychoanalysis, and pedagogy, Cummings is at work on a book entitled *Making News of AIDS in the U.S.* She has been a member of various AIDS organizations.

TERESA L. EBERT teaches critical and social theory and feminism at the State University of New York at Albany. She is the author of a number of essays and two books: *Ludic Feminism and After* and *Patriarchal Narratives: Feminist Culture Critique after Post-al Theory* (forthcoming). She is also co-editor of *(Post)modern Discourses on Ideology* (forthcoming), and a co-founder of a new theory journal, *Transformation: Marxist Boundary Work in Theory, Economics, Politics, and Culture*. She is now at work on a Marxist-feminist critique of contemporary postcolonial theory, tentatively titled, *(Post)colonial Pleasures*.

MARINA HEUNG is an assistant professor of English at Baruch College–CUNY, where she teaches courses in film, Asian literature, Asian-American literature, and writing. Her articles on the representation of gender, race, cultural ideologies, and mother-daughter relationships in film and Asian-American literature have appeared in the *Journal of Popular Film and Television, Film Criticism*, the *Michigan Quarterly Review, Cinema Journal*, and *Feminist Studies*. She is currently working on an essay on films and videos by Asian-American/Canadian women for the anthology *Feminism, Multiculturalism and the Media: Global Diversities*.

MINGYAN LAI is a graduate student in Comparative Literature at the University of Wisconsin–Madison. She is working on her dissertation, which examines cultural contestations over notions of the modern and the family in China, Taiwan, and Japan.

JONATHAN C. LANG received his doctorate in Comparative Literature from Princeton University and teaches in the College Writing Program at the University of California, Berkeley. The chapter published here is part of his current project, "The Ends of Travel: Homosexuality and Transgression in the Narratives of E. M. Forster and André Gide."

SALLY ROBINSON is an assistant professor of English at the University of Michigan. She is the author of *Engendering the Subject* and numerous articles on gender and contemporary fiction and culture. She is currently working on a book analyzing the modes of embodiment of white heteromasculinity in contemporary American fiction and literature.

ALBERT ROUZIE is a doctoral candidate and instructor in English at the University of Texas at Austin. He is beginning a dissertation on technoculture and the computer-mediated classroom. He is currently assistant director of the Computer Writing and Research Lab of the Division of Rhetoric and Composition, where he teaches courses in networked computer classrooms and does research. His interests include music, film, food, and breaking down the barriers among literary, cultural, and composition studies.

KAREN SCHNEIDER is an assistant professor of English at Western Kentucky University, where she teaches twentieth-century British Literature, Women's Writing, and Speculative Fiction; she is also active in Women's Studies. Her other academic interests include ethnic-American literature and film. She has recently completed the booklength manuscript *Loving Arms: British Women Writers and World War II.*

CAROL SIEGEL is an associate professor of English at Washington State University, Vancouver. She is the author of *Lawrence among the Women: Wavering Boundaries in Women's Literary Traditions* and *Male Masochism: Modern Revisions of the Story of Love* (forthcoming). She has also published articles on feminist theory, modernist and postmodernist fiction, and film. Her chapter in this issue is part of her current work on late-twentieth-century developments in the representation of sexuality.

MRINALINI SINHA is an assistant professor of History at Boston College. She is currently completing the booklength manuscript *The Politics of Colonial Masculinity: The "Manly Englishman" and the "Effeminate Bengali," 1883–1891.*

Guidelines for Prospective Contributors

Genders welcomes chapters on art, literature, media, photography, film, and social theory. We are especially interested in chapters addressing theoretical issues relating sexuality and gender to social, political, racial, economic, or stylistic concerns.

All chapters considered for publication are sent to board members for review. Your name is not included on the manuscript in this process. A decision is usually reached in about four months. Chapters are grouped for publication only after the manuscript has been accepted.

We require that we have first right to any manuscript we consider and that we have first publication of any manuscript we accept. We will not consider any manuscript already under consideration with another publication or that has already been published.

The recommended length for chapters is twenty-five pages of double-spaced text. They must be printed in letter-quality type. Quotations in languages other than English must be accompanied by translations. Photocopies of illustrations are sufficient for initial review, but authors should be prepared to supply originals upon request.

Place the title of the chapter and your name, address, and telephone number on a separate sheet at the front of the chapter. You are welcome to include relevant information about yourself or the chapter in a letter to the editor, but please be advised that institutional affiliation does not affect editorial policy. Because the majority of manuscripts we receive are photocopies, we do not routinely return submissions. However, if you would like your copy returned, please enclose a self-addressed, stamped envelope.

To submit a chapter for consideration, send *three* legible copies to:

Thomas Foster
Genders
Department of English
Ballantine Hall 442
Indiana University
Bloomington, IN 47405